A System & Plan

ARKANSAS BAPTIST
STATE CONVENTION
1848–1998

C. Fred Williams
S. Ray Granade
Kenneth M. Startup

PROVIDENCE HOUSE PUBLISHERS
Franklin, Tennessee

Copyright 1998 by Arkansas Baptist State Convention

All rights reserved. Written permission must be secured from the publisher to use or reproduce any part of this book, except for brief quotations in critical reviews or articles.

Printed in the United States of America

02   01   00   99   98   1   2   3   4   5

Library of Congress Catalog Card Number: 98-67338

ISBN:1-57736-108-3 hardcover
ISBN:1-57736-109-1 paperback

PROVIDENCE HOUSE PUBLISHERS
238 Seaboard Lane • Franklin, Tennessee 37067
800-321-5692

YOUR ATTITUDE SHOULD BE THE SAME AS that of Christ Jesus: Who, being in very nature God, did not consider equality with God something to be grasped, but made himself nothing, taking the very nature of a servant, being made in human likeness. And being found in appearance as a man, he humbled himself and became obedient to death—even death on a cross!

—Philippians 2:5–8 (NIV)

Contents

Preface

THE STORY OF THE ARKANSAS BAPTIST STATE CONVENTION is one of vision and perseverance. Vision in that there were a few times when the organization could easily have disbanded and given up on the idea of developing some "system or plan" for reaching the state with the Gospel. The first opportunity came within decade after the Convention was organized. With the Sunday School movement faltering, the local associations searched anxiously for something, "some system or plan," that would give them "stability or formness" [*sic*] in their operations. Another occasion for discouragement came with the devastation of the Civil War and the period of reconstruction which followed. By that time the founding fathers and mothers of the Convention were almost all dead and the few survivors who remembered the faith of that generation were sorely preoccupied with recovering from the social and economic displacement caused by almost fifteen years of war and restructuring.

At the turn of the century, the Landmark Movement played havoc with local congregations and caused a major split in the Convention's membership. But the organization again survived.

Perhaps the greatest challenge to the Convention's survival came during the Great Depression of the 1930s. Not only faced with financial bankruptcy, but with its creditability also on the line, another small band of dedicated leaders stayed the course and redeemed the Convention's reputation and finances.

These external events were serious enough, but from time to time the Convention was also challenged by internal strife. Strongly held beliefs and strong personalities sometime became volatile. While not as graphic as, say, the Bible in exposing the contentious human spirit, this narrative has nevertheless provided evidence that members composing the Arkansas Baptist State Convention have not always possessed the "mind of Christ."

The Arkansas Baptist State Convention is also a story about vision and courage of the human spirit. In every generation men and women have had a glimpse of what the Convention could be and refused to be deterred from the guiding principles of the meeting at Mountain Spring campground in Dallas County. They refused to let circumstances or personal differences defeat them. The end product is an organization that is the envy of other religious organizations in the state. With a presence in every county, and most communities, a total membership in excess of 500,000 (about 20 percent of the state's total population) and more than $30 million given each year to mission causes, the Convention is a significant force in the state. But, more than numbers, people have given the ABSC its impact in the state. Leaders in the Convention as well as public officials from governors to city mayors, congressmen to county judges, justices of the state supreme court to district judges, private citizens in the board rooms of the state's largest corporations and law firms, and multiple ordinary citizens have given witness to the purpose and intent of Arkansas's Southern Baptists. Finding some system or plan to perpetuate the work of the local church and association turned from a question to an exclamation point.

C. Fred Williams
April 1998

Acknowledgments

THE AUTHORS WISH TO EXPRESS APPRECIATION TO Wendy Richter, archivist for the Arkansas Baptist Historical Commission, and the staff of the Archives and Special Collections department of Riley-Hickingbotham Library on the Ouachita Baptist University campus. Wendy's superb knowledge of the extensive collections under her supervision was most helpful to each of us.

Ray Granade wishes to thank Kim and Keith Stewart, Julie Abbott, and Melissa Alvey, without whom the work would not have been done on time, if at all; Ronnie, Andrew, Stephen, and Misty Granade for their support, understanding, and encouragement; Sam and Rubilaw Granade and Louise Jodon for their interest, encouragement, and especially their suggestions after reading the first draft; and Ouachita Baptist University (OBU) for a research grant and some time to devote solely to writing.

Ken Startup wishes to thank Dr. Jerol Swaim, president of Williams Baptist College (WBC) for his strong encouragement and support for this sesquicentennial project; Duane Bolin for his careful review of the manuscript; and his wife, Alice, for her constant, indispensable support.

C. Fred Williams thanks Tom Logue, Bob Holley, Don Moore, and Jimmie Sheffield for reading and/or discussing various aspects of the manuscript. Thanks to Jan Kelly for her assistance in the Baptist

Building Library; to Trennis Henderson, Russell Dilday, and Millie Gill Smith at the *Arkansas Baptist Newsmagazine* for providing research assistance; to Jimmy Barrentine and Joy Faucett for providing current statistics and institutional memory; to his wife, Janet, for patience and support; and to grandson Andy Chelf, whose timely visit provided added inspiration to complete this project.

The authors also wish to thank Clarence Allison, chairman, and each member of the Arkansas Baptist State Convention's History Committee who enlisted us for this project, and to Tim Reddin, the near perfect liaison between us, the History Committee, and the Baptist Building Staff. Special thanks, too, to Don Moore, the original inspiration for this history, and to Emil Turner, a historian in his own right who always showed interest and encouraged us in the task.

A System
& Plan

1

Independence, Organization, and Arkansas

FROM THE TIME OF THEIR ORIGINS IN SEVENTEENTH-century England, Baptists have eschewed any earthly power higher than the local body of baptized believers who have made up their churches. James I's famous retort to Presbyterians at the Hampton Court Conference—"No bishop, no king!"—could have as easily been made to Baptists. In an age when religious polity ran to a hierarchy which handed decisions down to powerless local congregations through a chain of command that traced its roots to New Testament times, Baptists fearlessly championed a more democratic approach.

Baptists stoutly maintained that the local church was a group of baptized believers, deriving its authority from the members' soul competency—the priesthood of each believer. As every individual could read and interpret Scripture alone with the Holy Spirit's assistance, so the local church need recognize no higher earthly authority. There was no place in Baptist ecclesiology for bishops, popes, or any other individuals to instruct the local congregation; each congregation enjoyed complete autonomy, absolute self-governance.

As James I foresaw, those who reject religious authority will have little use for political authority, and certainly not for political authority over religion. Just as Baptists have championed democratic church governance, they likewise have championed the separation of church

3

and state. Baptists take legitimate credit for promoting that tenet as part of the fundamental law that governs the United States. Baptists who had been imprisoned for advocating such separation and for resolutely rejecting state support of religious activities were primarily responsible for the doctrine's inclusion in the Bill of Rights.

With such a history behind them, with such a fervent attachment to the autonomy of the local church, it seems strange that Baptists would create any entity larger than the local church. When one adds to that doctrinal affinity for democracy the distinctly American distrust and dislike of central authority, the wonderment grows. Yet Baptists in America have done just that. They have overcome their distrust of larger groupings to come together, with appropriate safeguards, in confederations of churches for specific purposes.

These confederations, which Baptists have called "associations," originated in a desire to spread the Gospel in more efficient and effective ways than a single congregation would accomplish alone, and to provide a bolstering fellowship for those engaged in the work. These associations were voluntary, and exerted no authority over local congregations so affiliated. About a century after the emergence of associations, larger regional groupings likewise emerged, as representatives of churches and associations formed larger confederations, or "conventions."

The area now called Arkansas emerged as a political entity in the midst of this Baptist tendency to congregate. Originally part of the Missouri Territory, Arkansas appeared in 1803, when the Louisiana Purchase provided legal claim to lands west of the Mississippi River for a fledgling nation.

Baptists had grown mightily from their first documented American church in Providence, Rhode Island, in 1639. During the colonial era, the Middle Colonies became the center of Baptist growth and provided the leadership that the developing denomination required. The nation's earliest association, the Philadelphia, originated in 1707 and provided a framework for doctrinal identity, church extension, and fellowship that would be highly important under frontier conditions.

Baptist growth in the Southern colonies, which would plant the work in Arkansas, lagged somewhat behind that further north and developed somewhat differently. Migration rather than organized mission activity spread Baptists westward from the Southern coast, and a greater variety of Baptist groups flourished in the South than in more northward climes. Most importantly, Baptists in the South welcomed opportunities to associate. Less concern that associations would compromise local church independence encouraged a greater degree of denominational identity and cooperation than existed farther north. Different demographic patterns likewise influenced the Southern acceptance of associations; the chance to gather held greater attraction for Southerners who lived on their land in comparative isolation than it did for Northerners with their more urban approach to existence. Perhaps their later development allowed Baptists in the South to observe their Northern kindred's experience with the Philadelphia Association (which had adherents even among Southerners). The strictly Southern experience in associating traced its roots to the Charleston Association's founding in 1751.

Arkansas Baptists inherited a legacy from earlier denominational generations that included adherence to the revivalism of the First Great Awakening of the 1730s and '40s and to the independence and democracy of the American Revolution. Adherence to those two movements bolstered the growth of American Baptists during the post-Revolution era until, by the century's turn, they comprised the largest denomination in the new nation—boasting 979 churches in 1790 with 67,490 members grouped into at least forty-two associations and discussing a national organization.

The first documented Baptist church in the region now called Arkansas barely predated the region's designation as a territory in 1819; the first known sermon was preached less than a decade before. This denomination that began expanding into Arkansas shortly after 1800 simultaneously lengthened its cords and strengthened its stakes. Expansion into Arkansas coincided with growing Baptist strength in an ever-widening area as well as within already familiar surroundings and with growing Baptist organization. Baptists prospered from the Second Great Awakening as they had from the First. Taking place around 1800, the Second was gone by the war, but left its camp-meeting stamp on western religion forever. Between the end of the War of 1812 and Arkansas statehood, American Baptists unified nationally, expanded into new regions, and organized more extensively.

National unity and more extensive organization were sides of the same coin, a coin minted by evangelism. The Second Great Awakening modified Baptists' Calvinistic theological bent to allow more personal responsibility for spreading the Word and responding to it. This prompting of evangelism played out in associations and other, more geographically encompassing organizations.

Associations in Baptist life served a variety of functions and were specifically excluded from others. Church ordinances, discipline, and ordination remained the purview of the local church rather than denominational functions; associations had no control over these. Associations could, as a collective of churches, withdraw fellowship from other churches but not excommunicate individual members, an arrangement which left the local church as sole arbiter of its own membership. These safeguards preserved local church autonomy.

Associations advised, in response to questions from churches, about doctrinal and practical matters—issues like music in worship; divorce and remarriage; discipline; the role of women; whether pastors should be salaried and, if so, at what level; choosing deacons and deciding on duties; infant dedication; alien immersion; and how worship days should be passed when a pastor was absent.

Associations served as personnel clearing houses—"accrediting" or warning against discredited ministers; helping churches which needed pastors and prospective pastors who needed (or needed different) churches; suggesting interim pastors or supplying preachers; and providing outside assistance with matters of church discipline when requested.

Associations promoted benevolent work, primarily education and home missions. Associations provided fellowship, an especially crucial feature in the less populous frontier regions, and provided expository models from which aspiring young preachers might learn.

The example of the Charleston Association was ever before Arkansas Baptists figuratively and literally. That association coalesced around (and thrived by supporting) two major undertakings: ministerial education and home missions. When their turn came to organize into associations, Arkansas Baptists seized upon the latter of these two as their primary impetus. Associational activity among Baptists fixed the concept of mission work through denominational channels, and Arkansas Baptists would follow this path faithfully. Certainly during their formative years, Arkansas Baptists followed the path of home missions pragmatically, seeing the field around them so white unto harvest.

Baptists affiliated themselves in organizations geographically larger than associations, on both the state and the national levels. Each of these organizations represented a further departure from the Baptist tradition that centered on the local church, but each also rested on the strong strain of evangelism that has likewise been part of Baptist tradition.

The germinal idea for state conventions evidently originated in Luther Rice's fertile mind on a trip from Boston to Charleston in early 1814 to drum up support for a general society which would sustain missions efforts. As he later wrote his friend Adoniram Judson, "While passing from Richmond to Petersburg in the stage, an enlarged view of the business opened upon my contemplations. The plan which suggested itself to my mind, [was] that of forming one principal society in each state, bearing the name of the state." Though it had not been successful initially, he noted, "Recently, . . . this same kind of system in substance and effect, but differing in form and modification, begins to come into action. Several state conventions have been formed already, and more will probably be originated."

The first, abortive attempts at statewide organizations centered on missions under Rice's prodding, and in the South became General Meetings of Correspondence. North Carolina in 1811 and Virginia in 1813 were among the first and most successful, but even there, as a Virginia proponent would eventually write, it "failed to produce the enlarged benefits hoped for by its friends" and languished after a decade. Then the idea grasped Baptist imagination with a vengeance, though in an altered form. Beginning with South Carolina in 1821, Southern states would organize state conventions rather than societies, and would broaden their focus. Georgia organized in 1822, Virginia and Alabama the next year, North Carolina in 1830, Tennessee in 1833, Maryland and Mississippi in 1836, and Kentucky the next year. Except for Missouri, organized in 1835, states west of the Mississippi would wait for at least a decade to follow suit—Louisiana and Arkansas would both organize in 1848. In each case, organizers voiced the same reasoning for associating statewide—missions and ministerial education. They sought the economies of scale which would allow greater efforts than those pursued by a few far-flung churches operating through an association.

Just as Baptists organized into associations and on the state level, so they associated into organizations with national reach. Between 1814 and Arkansas statehood, they did so three times. Each time those organizations focused on evangelism.

In 1814 through Luther Rice's prompting, delegates met at Philadelphia's First Baptist Church and formed the General Missionary Convention of the Baptist Denomination in the United States for Foreign Missions. This first national Baptist organization—commonly called the General or Triennial Convention (it met every three years)—would be, Rice hoped, "a general combination of the whole Baptist interest in the United States, for the benefit alike of the denomination here, and the cause of missions abroad" led by a full-time general secretary. Its organization followed the approach most favored by Southerners—an association of churches—and by 1823 sponsored home and foreign missions, education, and publications. So far as Arkansans would be concerned, it ceased to play much of a role after 1826, when it became primarily a society—an association of individuals rather than churches and the approach most favored by Northerners, who more greatly feared the loss of local church autonomy.

The other two organizations with national reach were the Baptist General Tract Society, founded in Washington, D.C., in 1824 and moved to Philadelphia in 1827; and the American Baptist Home Mission Society, formed in New York in 1832 at the instigation of John Mason Peck (missionary to the Missouri Territory and then throughout the West) and Jonathan Going. Both organizations aimed at evangelism. The former sought "to disseminate evangelical truth, and to inculcate sound morals, by the distribution of tracts." The latter planned "to promote the preaching of the gospel in North America."

In organizing as they did, Baptists merely followed national trends. Baptist work in Arkansas was born and spent its infancy in a time characterized by the formation of national societies: the American Education Society (1815), the American Bible Society (1816), the Sunday School Union (1824), the American Tract Society (1825), the American Society for Promoting Temperance (1826), the American Home Missionary Society (1826), and the American Peace Society

(1828). These inter-denominational efforts at national amelioration and conversion held no attraction for Baptists, who always displayed reservations about such groups. Part of "freedom's ferment," though, such efforts did mark the rush of nationalism which followed the War of 1812, that "Second War for Independence"—a rush to which Baptists were not immune.

So Baptists began their work in what is now Arkansas as a denomination with strength of numbers in adherents and churches, and with the habit of joining into associations strongly entrenched. They ventured into these confines of southernmost Missouri at a time when they were organizing at both state and national levels for evangelical efforts. Baptists ventured into Arkansas, in short, at a time when it would be natural for them to think of associations as well as churches, and to think naturally of associating for evangelical purposes, perhaps into groupings even larger than associations.

While Baptist work gained its foothold in Arkansas, between 1814 and statehood, American Baptists prospered and organized and structurally achieved national unity. Between statehood and the inauguration of Arkansas's State Convention, that unity would be lost to Baptist division North from South—a division that would come as much from long standing arguments over societies versus conventions as the organizing principle of Baptist life as from the overt issue of slaveholding by Baptist missionaries. It was a time of flux, of building larger entities while arguing over whether the individual or the church should be the basic denominational building block and the resultant entity a society or a convention, and of coalescing into larger units while dividing over slavery and missions.

2

Baptist Origins in Arkansas to Statehood

NO ONE KNOWS WHO ORGANIZED THE FIRST BAPTIST church in what we now call Arkansas, or where it was. No one knows who preached the first sermon there, or even where it might have been. It could have been among those settlers who came into the northeast corner from Ste. Genevieve, Jackson and their environs. Maybe it was among settlers in the northwest plateau around Fayetteville. It could have been among settlers from the Bastrop Grant in the southeast, or along the Mississippi or Arkansas Rivers, perhaps at Arkansas Post. Individual Baptists spread God's Word across the North American continent without the prodding or blessing of higher authorities, untrammeled and unsupported by any hierarchy. Baptist tenets have meant that while the Word spread and the denomination grew, no one required reports to be dutifully filed for future generations and their edification; no central organization carefully preserved the story.

In the region called Arkansas, between the earliest white settlement and the initiation of United States claim to the land via the Louisiana Purchase in 1803, authorities did not allow Protestant public worship. Under both Spanish and French domination, only Catholicism could be practiced legally. So far as we know, the first Baptist church west of the Mississippi River was established in Missouri in 1805, the first in Louisiana in 1812, the first in Arkansas in 1818, and the first in Texas in

1834, all of which attest to the efficacy of that prohibition on public Protestant worship.

Early attempts to expand Baptist work into Arkansas suffered from a variety of other impediments as well. Movement into, in, or through the region often had to rely upon water, especially where goods were concerned. Fortunately the area was blessed with abundant rivers and streams (generally running northwest to southeast) which offered easy access for shallow-draft vessels.

Overland transportation through the region sometimes relied upon one of the marked trails or traces. The Southwest Trail from St. Louis to Mexico bisected the region from about the state's northeastern to its southwestern corner; the Natchitoches Trace connected that Louisiana town to Hot Springs and then northeast to the Arkansas River at Little Rock; and a postal route connected Monroe, Louisiana, to Arkansas Post before proceeding up the river to the Southwest Trail at Little Rock, then up the trail to the region's first post office at Davidsonville (county seat of Lawrence) and thence to St. Louis. By 1836, three major military roads cut generally east and west across the region: the Fort Towson Road from the Mississippi through Washington and westward; a road from Memphis to Fort Smith (with two branches, one to Batesville and Clinton, the other through Little Rock); and the Carrollton Road, which connected Fort Smith with the Southwest Trail across the northern section.

After 1820, transportation became easier. Steamboats plied the waterways after that date, and after 1826, stage lines increasingly offered coach travel between major destinations—east-west between Hot Springs, Little Rock, Arkansas Post, and Memphis; and north-south between St. Louis, Louisiana, and Texas.

Another impediment to Baptist work lay with the region's sparse Indian population. Unlike Kentucky, to which no Indians laid claim, Arkansas hosted several tribes, three of which divided the region pretty much among themselves and into rough thirds—Osage in the northwest, Quapaw in the east and northeast, and Caddo in the southwest. Not until five years after its acquisition of the land from France would the United States conclude a treaty with the Osage which would begin the process of opening the land legally to white settlement (a process not completed until the year before statehood). Despite these and other impediments, settlers did move into the region. Among those settlers, as settlers and occasionally as missionaries, came Baptists.

Baptists were fortunate in that their movement into what would be Arkansas began in a time when Americans were exhibiting increased interest in church membership. Across the country, one of every fifteen Americans was churched in 1800, one of every eight by 1835, after the Second Great Awakening. Americans were also interested in attending services. During the early decades of the nineteenth century, attendance at a Sabbath service was usually triple the membership. Certainly, in the era between the United States acquisition of what would be Arkansas and the achievement of statehood, national trends were going the right way!

The earliest Baptist witness in what is now Arkansas originated along the present northern and southern borders, and did so at a time when those borders were nonexistent or generally ignored. The scarcity of inhabitants, much less inhabitants who cared about state boundaries, meant a scarcity of any signs depicting political allegiance or differences between the territory of one overlord and that of another. Eastward lay the Mississippi River—an international boundary until 1803 but a formidable obstacle at any time. Eastward beyond the river lay Tennessee and Mississippi, the former a state after 1795 and the latter after 1816. Beyond the river for more than half of Arkansas's length also lay, until the 1830s, Choctaw and Chickasaw lands. Mississippi Baptists, originating near Natchez, had their trans-Mississippi impact westward into Louisiana rather than northwestward into Arkansas. Finally, Baptist witness would of necessity be where people settled; many early Arkansas settlers eschewed the Delta as too flood and disease prone for economic or personal livelihood.

The first five settlements in what is now Arkansas illustrated the importance of water transportation routes in determining where people settled. Arkansas Post (1687), Montgomery's Point (Helena, 1766), Dardanelle (1798), Hopefield (1804), and Crystal Hill (1807) all owe their existence to the Mississippi or the Arkansas. Even Hot Springs (1807) had river connections, though that location's settlement owed more to other factors. By the 1810s, the Southwest Trail had joined the rivers as important to settlement planting. Washington (1812), Davidsonville (1815), Powhatan (1818), and Fulton (1819) are products of the trail, while Cadron (1815), Fort Smith (1817), Pine Bluff (1818),

Little Rock (1819), and Spadra Bayou (1819) owe their existence to the Arkansas and Polk Bayou (Batesville, 1810) to the White River.

By the 1830s, settlement patterns clearly showed this nexus of transportation methods. Arkansas's roughly 30,400 population (about 15 percent slaves) centered at the two ends of the Southwest Trail (Smithville and Lawrence County in the north, Washington and Hempstead County in the south), along the Arkansas River (especially Little Rock and Pulaski County, where the trail crossed the river), and around Van Buren and Crawford County. The most recently developed area of the 1830s was Fayetteville and Washington County, where settlement of land disputes with the Cherokee Treaty of 1828 opened new, good lands to white immigration.

Baptists inhabited the Missouri Territory more than two decades before the Triennial Convention appointed John Mason Peck and James E. Welch "missionaries to the Missouri Territory" in May 1817. When the new appointees arrived at the "rowdy town of 3,000" that was St. Louis that November, they discovered that Baptists had been organizing churches along the Mississippi River from north of town as far south as Cape Girardeau. Indeed, it was in the Cape Girardeau area that the first known Baptists west of the Mississippi River settled in 1796, and there also lay the site of Missouri's first recorded Baptist church.

As part of the Louisiana Territory after 1802 and the Missouri Territory after 1811, Arkansas concerned early Baptists in Missouri. Increasing population south of Cape Girardeau enticed the Missouri legislature to separate a new county off from New Madrid in 1813. They named it Arkansas, drew the northern border from the Mississippi River to the mouth of the Little Red River, and fixed the seat of justice at Arkansas Post. Two years later they acted again, creating Lawrence County between Arkansas and New Madrid Counties.

A year after Lawrence County's creation, Baptists in southern Missouri organized Bethel Association. The very next year, 1817, that association appointed James Phillip Edwards as missionary for that part of the Territory's "destitute regions." Traveling more than a thousand miles visiting widely scattered settlements during his first year, Edwards preached and organized churches wherever possible. According to John Mason Peck, Edwards, Benjamin Clark, and Jesse James in 1818 organized Salem church at Fourche-á-Thomas, the first church of record in both that region and the area that came to be Arkansas.

Even after the political division between Missouri and Arkansas occasioned by the former's statehood and the latter's ascendancy to territorial status, the Bethel Association continued to care for its southern neighbors. In 1822, Bethel supported the organization of two more Lawrence County churches, Union and Little Flock—by Edwards, Clark, and William Street. As was the case with Salem, Union and Little Flock joined the brethren in Bethel Association.

Baptist presence in Louisiana began at about the same time as in Missouri, though it lacked the strength or results exhibited in the latter—in part because of the difference in the comparative size and nature of the settlements. Louisiana's first recorded Baptist church organized in late 1812 in Washington Parish—just across the Pearl River from and sharing its eastern and northern boundaries with Mississippi. The New Orleans First Baptist Church organized in the summer of 1818. However the initial Baptist presence in Louisiana probably came in neither of those areas, but in the Prairie Mer Rouge region, on lands granted to Baron de Bastrop on the condition that he settle not less than five hundred colonists there.

Spanish Governor Carondelet planned this northern Louisiana colony in the Ouachita District to buffer important settlements to the south from the restless Americans. The strong wheat production-based agricultural economy of the proposed colony would insulate it from American pressure and ensure fealty to Spain. Though the original intent had been to people the colony with Europeans, in early 1797, the Baron gathered about a hundred hearty individuals primarily from the extreme western reaches of the United States, including Louisville, Kentucky.

Bastrop planned to exclude any provision from his colony that might hinder hopes of enrolling the requisite five hundred settlers. To that end, before embarking on his recruiting trip in 1796, he requested from the governor agreement that non-Catholics would receive "the liberty of conscience enjoyed by those of Baton Rouge, Natchez, & other districts of the Province"—though no such liberty of conscience existed. Carondelet responded to Bastrop's suggestion by decreeing that "They shall not be molested in matters of religion, but the Apostolic Roman Catholic worship shall alone be publicly permitted." Thus armed on his swing through the western lands, Bastrop enlisted, among others, John Coulter with his family of five, the first known Baptists in what became Louisiana.

Bastrop's "plantings" between the Ouachita River and Bayou Bartholomew were not the only source of Baptist influence in southern Arkansas. When he established himself in Prairie Mer Rouge in 1804, Abraham Morhouse hired William Thomas as surveyor in return for the deed to 1,500 acres. Thomas obviously informed his friends about the newly available land, for in short order he was joined by Prosper King (who acquired 1,600 acres), John Burch (a lay preacher who bought 600), James Bennet Truly, Buckner Darden, Philip B. Harrison, Philip B. Dougherty, and Jacob Free. Soon thereafter came William Bolls, who probably preached the area's first sermon. All of these men came from Jefferson County, Mississippi, from the Salem (or Cole's Creek) church near Natchez—Mississippi's first Baptist church, organized in 1791. Within a decade, Baptist work gained a foothold west of the Ouachita along what became Louisiana's northern border and attracted such ministers as James Brinson, John Impson, and Haywood Alford.

One of the most interesting aspects of Baptist beginnings in Arkansas is the extent to which those beginnings were beholden to missionaries. In much of the South, Baptists spread by transplantings. Groups of individuals, always including family and usually kin and friends as well, moved together from one section to another, customarily in a westering fashion. It was reasonably simple to constitute a Baptist church, since the pastor often moved with the settlers. On occasion, Baptist churches were even constituted without an ordained minister—the Cole's Creek in Mississippi comes immediately to mind as an example. Baptist historians have often cited this feature of Baptist life as the reason Baptists so effectively spread through the South. While there is evidence of that pattern in other states, even neighboring states (as in the "Pilgrim" churches of early Texas, which moved wholesale into the region), it seems less true in Arkansas.

Bethel Association's appointment of James Phillip Edwards to preach and organize churches throughout the lower part of the Missouri Territory proved prophetic in the early establishment of Baptist churches in Arkansas. Edwards's organization of Salem, Arkansas's first known Baptist church; Union; and Little Flock churches and an unnamed one the year after Salem was the norm in early Arkansas Baptist life.

In 1828, thirty-year-old David Orr left Missouri (his home of five years) for Arkansas at the behest of "some two or three pious and cross-bearing old sisters who had never seen my face but had heard that I devoted my time principally to travelling and preaching Christ and him crucified to the destitute of Missouri. . . ." Planning to stay five or six weeks, Orr returned to Missouri to pack up and head south again for the rest of his life. Orr spent his time traveling and preaching in northern Arkansas and, within two years, had organized five churches and led them to form the Spring River Association. Two years after that, Spring River had doubled in size—and Orr had planted all but one of the ten churches.

Like Edwards, Orr owed his allegiance to something larger than the local church. For his first four years in Arkansas, Orr was supported by the Baptist Mission Board of Massachusetts. As soon as it was formed, the American Baptist Home Mission Society assumed responsibility for his support. Between 1833 and 1848, the society sponsored a dozen men: G. W. Baines, Benjamin Clark, John B. Graham, Benjamin Hawkins, W. B. Karr, William Kellett, John McCarthy, Henry McElmurry, Thomas Mercer, David Orr, William W. Settle, and John Woodrome. Most of these the society sponsored for a year or two; Hawkins and McElmurry remained on the field three, McCarthy and Karr four, and Orr was almost six years in the society's employ. Among them, the dozen missionaries reported just over thirty years of service for which they received just over three dollars per month on average—much of it they collected in the field themselves "to the Society's credit."

Occasionally, early church plantings came through the agency of an unlikely missionary. One such example is Silas T. Toncray, who in 1824 took upon himself the responsibility of calling for interested parties to join him in organizing a Baptist church in Little Rock. Like most early Arkansas pastors, the twenty-nine-year-old Toncray was not a full-time pastor; unlike most, he was a tradesman—a silversmith and jeweler who later purchased a drug store. Toncray had been ordained in Kentucky in 1821 and had followed his brother-in-law, Isaac Watkins, to Little Rock three years later. Once there, Toncray advertised in the *Arkansas Gazette* for "Those persons who have been regularly dismissed from regular Baptist churches" to join him at Watkins's house at 11:00 A.M. on the fourth Saturday of that July. With Watkins acting as clerk on that July 24 morning, Toncray organized the church he would serve as pastor until his departure for Memphis five years later.

More than half of Arkansas's earliest churches owed their existence to missionaries, but as statehood neared, the "traditional" pattern of church planting emerged and the role of missionaries respectively diminished. Perhaps that was due to the increased immigration to the state and the resultant larger population; perhaps it was due to the different kind of immigration into the state later in its history. Early Arkansas visitors laid Arkansans' addiction to riotous living to the comparative absence of sufficient women eligible for marriage and of religion's ameliorating influence. Whatever the reason, the experience of P. S. G. Watson, who migrated to Arkansas from Kentucky in 1843 in the company of his father-in-law and ten other Baptists, seems more the norm at that point.

Just as Baptist presence grew in Arkansas when measured by the number of churches, so the churches followed the Baptist tradition of associating for specific purposes. As was true in most of the South, Arkansans displayed few qualms about associating their churches together for common purposes. Perhaps this reflected Arkansas Baptist origins in the northeast, where it was an association's concern that sowed Baptist seed in the fertile north-Arkansas ground.

The state's first association, Little Rock, grew from the efforts of Silas Toncray. The same year in which he gathered the faithful in Little Rock to form a Baptist church during the summer, he also gathered the area's three churches to form an association. On the fourth Friday in November, in the state House, representatives from Little Rock (membership 10), Salem (Clark County, membership 12), and Arkansas (Faulkner County, membership 3) gathered to inaugurate their cooperation.

The second association in Arkansas, Spring River, originated five years later, in 1829. Delegates (calling representatives to meetings "messengers" is a practice that emerged after the Civil War) from four churches founded by David Orr which had joined the Bethel Association immediately after their organization (Richland, Spring River, New Hope, and North Little Fork) assembled with those from

Rehobeth to relinquish their connection with Missouri and initiate one among themselves—in Arkansas.

Spring River Association illustrated an interesting feature of Baptist life on the Arkansas borders, north and south. Until fairly late in the nineteenth century, it was not uncommon to find Arkansas churches in Missouri associations and vice-versa, Arkansas churches in Louisiana associations and vice-versa. Pastors in the border areas moved back and forth with the same regularity. Just as Bethel Association members fellowshipped with the Arkansas churches founded through their efforts, so the Arkansas Association that encompassed Marion, Izard, and Fulton counties included churches from Missouri counties Ozark and Oregon among its flock as late as the 1850s.

Nor did the northern boundary have any monopoly on such cross-border arrangements. Concord Association in northern Louisiana and Bartholomew Association in southern Arkansas found churches changing their membership as travel situations and meeting places prompted such shifts. Four of the nineteen churches in Bartholomew Association in 1854, for example, were Louisiana churches, as were three of the twenty-eight in 1860. One, Mt. Hope, even remained in Bartholomew well into Reconstruction. The same story was true of Liberty Association (west of Bartholomew on the Arkansas-Louisiana border). Five of the twenty-three churches in Liberty in 1849 were from Louisiana, as were six of twenty-two in 1853. Through the late 1870s, Liberty had two Louisiana churches associated with about twenty from Arkansas—both large churches (in the upper 10 percent by membership). Obviously, the churches' commitments were to missions rather than to any particular association or state.

Spring River also illustrated another feature of Baptist life, early or late. Though it grew prodigiously and quickly, in 1840 it dissolved because of internal strife—W. B. Karr, close friend and coworker of David Orr's, had been baptized by Cumberland Presbyterians, and several of the churches refused to acknowledge this "alien immersion." Even early in its existence, Baptist influence in Arkansas was undercut by concerns over personalities and issues which drew the focus away from evangelism.

Between the origins of Baptist work in Arkansas and statehood in 1836, Baptists organized at least one and perhaps two more associations.

The St. Francis (east central) organized in January 1831 at Franklin with Mark W. Izard moderator. Rocky Bayou (northeast) organized in either 1833 or 1840.

Rocky Bayou's origin demonstrates another problem in dealing with early Baptist life. An official 1901 account notes a paucity of sources because so many of the minutes have been lost but asserts that the association organized in 1833 at the Rocky Bayou church in Izard County. David Orr preached the introductory sermon to messengers from Rocky Bayou, Mt. Pisga, Reeds Creek, Rehoboth, Bold Springs (Lawrence County), and two other churches. P. S. G. Watson, who migrated to the state in 1843 and served the Baptist cause diligently throughout his life, contends that the first meeting came in 1840 after the breakup of the Spring River Association, from which it received some adherents. Though logic might support Watson's account and long custom the official version, as is the case with so much of early Arkansas Baptist history, the absence of official record makes true determination impossible.

One other development in pre-statehood Baptist associating presages later developments in the Arkansas Baptist story. The Little Rock Association did not outlast Silas Toncray's residence in the state. When he departed for Memphis after a brother's death in 1830, both the church and the association he had founded died. So the founding of the Spring River Association in 1829 coincided with the demise of the one in Little Rock. Although they lasted until after statehood, Spring River was gone before the State Convention organized; St. Francis lost its animation to anti-missionary sentiment and faltered in 1850. By the coming of the Civil War, none of Arkansas's pre-statehood associations remained.

The fate of churches and associations alike illustrates the tenuous nature of Baptist life in pre-statehood Arkansas. Diminutive congregations relied heavily upon a leadership pool which often proved too shallow. The departure of a key figure for another location could ensure that lethargy would overtake the few remaining communicants. That was especially true when that figure was one of the region's few ministers. In family-oriented churches like those of early Arkansas, a key figure's departure usually meant the departure of a significant number of the congregation as well; the congregation lost numbers as well as leadership. When twenty-five or thirty members constituted a large church, every person counted.

A society which lacked any sense of permanence could not expect permanence in its institutions. A Presbyterian minister noted in 1841 that the population constantly fluctuated because of migrations, and a Baptist colleague in 1852 observed that "Restlessness is a predominant trait in our character—a disposition to be ever going towards the setting sun." The flux which characterized early Arkansas society affected without destroying its religious institutions. A significant characteristic of Baptists lay less in detail than in grand design. Particular individuals, churches, and associations might come and go, but the larger Baptist witness was not dependent upon any one of them. Despite individual changes and the loss of individual components, Baptist witness grew in strength and size throughout the pre-statehood era.

The seventeen years in the Arkansas Territory brought several issues into focus for Arkansas Baptists. For at least three of these, which would be troublesome throughout their history, they found no resolution: political involvement by leadership, and arguments over missions and education between "hardshell" or hyper-Calvinist Primitive Baptists (strongly anti-mission and anti-education) and mainstream Regular Baptists (whose Calvinism had basically disappeared and who championed missions and education and would be the mainstay of organizational Baptist life, including the state convention movement in the post-statehood years).

The nature of church leadership among Baptists in early Arkansas possessed certain characteristics, and those characteristics gave rise to the first issue which would continue to plague Baptists throughout their history—the issue of political involvement by Baptist leaders, especially ministers.

Their emphasis on the laity has meant that Baptist churches have always had strong leadership from local sources other than pastors. Baptist polity has reserved few activities for the ordained ministry alone. Weddings, ceremonies in which the state has a stake, have always been the purview of the ordained ministry by law; funerals, on the other hand, have often been conducted by the laity. In a frontier setting, where pastors were at a premium and conditions often imposed a dearth of ordained personnel for all denominations, lay leadership often performed the funeral service for various communities. The practice was common enough to elicit dialogues in denominational newspapers about the propriety of deacons performing services for the deceased of other denominations. The question of whether deacons should perform the ceremony never arose; the question always centered on the propriety of performing non-Baptist services (most commonly involving some high church liturgy).

The tradition of lay leadership interacted with the milieu in which Baptists prospered in a particular way. Baptist churches in early Arkansas (indeed, until well into the twentieth century in many places) were "quarter-time" churches, meeting monthly rather than weekly with a pastor. What to do on those other three weeks, when the pastor was absent from his flock, also became part of the discussion among Baptists about how the Christian life was to be lived. That discussion also found its way into the denominational newspapers as well as into the meetings of various associations.

Because of this feature of church life, the ordained minister found two facts emerging from his existence. First, he found himself going from church to church, preaching to two, three, or four different flocks in the course of the month. Though each church decided who should preach rather than having the choice imposed upon it, the outcome otherwise resembled the Methodist circuit-rider plan. Second, the preacher in early Arkansas found himself caught up in a time of vocational transition.

Most Baptist ministers in early Arkansas, like their brethren in other parts of the country, found their livelihood outside their calling to preach the Gospel. Though some served as missionaries for an association or missionary society, most earned a living in the fields or as a merchant, just like their communicants. A few taught school, usually in institutions of their own. The Baptist witness in Arkansas was being established just at the time that Baptists were asking themselves whether or not their clergy should be paid, and if so, in what fashion. Should church members take up a love offering for the pastor, or establish some regular method of paying the pastor? At the heart of the discussion was the question of whether a preacher's calling and a pastor's profession were one and the same.

While it seemed the natural order of things for Baptist preachers to engage in the usual pursuits common to their communicants, custom placed certain activities beyond the pale in more settled areas. In a fledgling society, custom had yet to be established. The Arkansas of Baptist beginnings—indeed, the Arkansas of Baptist experience up until statehood—was one in flux, a frontier which needed all the talents of all its inhabitants for it and them to prosper. Here preachers, if they were to partake of life as lived by their communicants, found fewer restraints on their attempts to earn a livelihood. William M. Lea, for example, agreed to undertake missionary work (according to one story) so long as he could continue horse trading (which many considered a less-than-honorable undertaking) and readily acknowledged his activities as a land speculator.

Given the Baptist stand on separation of church and state, the one arena of economic endeavor which would seem closed to Baptist preachers would be the arena of government work of any kind. A denomination which had set its mark on the political scene by principle, rather than by force of numbers, faced a dilemma in its Arkansas setting. Particularly adapted to expansion on the frontier because of its method of constituting new churches and of a church's choosing its own preacher (and ordaining him if necessary), Baptists flourished in the new setting.

Though the question of education would be another issue among Baptists, their ministers were, as a group, more educated than the general population. Those ministers often exhibited leadership capabilities which could be advantageously used by the community. The question, of course, was whether a Baptist minister should use his talents for the community good through the government, or whether such involvement would violate the denominational principle of "a wall of separation" between church and state.

A further question in this complex issue of a Baptist preacher's government involvement was the philosophical division among Baptists between those who saw missions as the only gospel imperative and those who believed in social amelioration as well. Many Baptists averred that spreading the good news was the Christian's only task, and thought that the preacher's sole aim should be proclaiming "Christ and him crucified." They viewed government as an impediment to that task.

Typical of those who shared this view was the comment of a Texas church leader to prominent Baptist minister B. H. Carroll during a heated political campaign over the liquor issue: "Hell will be so full of political preachers that their arms and legs will be sticking out the windows."

Even some of those who conceived of social amelioration as part of the Christian's duty saw government as an impediment rather than an aid in that undertaking. Too many Baptists had personal or family memories of the established churches of colonial days, the last vestige of which had not been disestablished in the South generally until the Revolution (and in Virginia not until 1786)—in short, barely thirty years before the first known Baptist church organized in Arkansas. New York, in which Baptists would locate their Home Missionary Society, had disestablished about the same time as the Southern states; New England did not disestablish congregationalism until Arkansas became a territory—a step not taken in Massachusetts (the last state to disestablish) until 1833, only three years before Arkansas statehood. All in all, a large number of Baptists suspected government as an impediment to religious activities.

When the particularly Baptist concerns about government were wed to the frontier's typical disdain for all forms of regulation and especially government, it would seem highly unlikely that Baptist ministers would be involved in any way with governmental activities. Nothing could be farther from the truth. As Arkansans began to establish a government of their own, in territorial days and those of early statehood, some Baptist ministers sought to serve, and in some cases did serve, as an integral part of that movement. Pragmatism overcame principle.

Silas Toncray, organizer of Little Rock's first Baptist church and two others and of the region's first association, was noted for his political activity as well. He maintained a close relationship with kinsman William Woodruff and the *Arkansas Gazette* and engaged in activities typical of enterprising politicians. Toncray tried unsuccessfully for the Conway County seat on the Legislative Council in 1827 after becoming postmaster at Marion in the same county the year before. His brother-in-law, Isaac Watkins, clerk of the Little Rock Association, likewise undertook political involvement until his untimely demise. "Too good a

Baptist to be a good politician," as Josiah Shinn characterized him, he
lost his bid for the territorial legislature in 1825. Even John Woodrome,
one of the early Baptist missionaries supported by the Home
Missionary Society, joined Toncray as a postal employee.

Perhaps the best example of this Baptist activity in the political
arena could be found in the person of one who served in the territorial
legislature, David Orr. Responsible for organizing some of the region's
earliest churches and its second association, Orr served on the
Legislative Council during its 1831 session and continued to be
involved in electioneering while continuing his preaching career. Even
his involvement in the rancorous "Canvas Ham" scandal of the 1833
election (supporters of a questionable deal involving public lands were
accused of "buying" votes for Kentucky hams and whiskey) seemed not
to affect his preaching opportunities. In 1835, for example, he advertised for all interested Christians to be part of a late spring camp
meeting in Crawford County. His religious activities would continue
until his death in 1847.

The second issue, that of missions efforts, seems a strange one for
Baptists to confront. After all, Baptist witness in Arkansas owed most of
its early organizational success to active mission work by Baptists from
other regions. This issue would take the form of two questions in
Arkansas: should there be missions at all, and if there should, what
agency should be used?

At heart, the missions issue dealt with the agency of conversion. Did
God work directly upon the hearts of the unsaved, convicting them as
He did Saul of Tarsus, seizing them willy nilly from the midst of their
fellows and their sinful ways? Or did God work through human agency,
requiring personal effort on the part of the saved to preach and spread
the good news? To use a scene famous among Baptists, who was right—
William Carey, who spoke of the need for active mission work on the
part of Baptists, or his detractor who replied to Carey's eloquence,
"Young man, sit down: When God pleases to convert the heathen, He
will do it without your aid or mine!"?

Most Baptists seemed most comfortable with Carey's argument,
that activity on the part of the saved was part of God's plan. Though
Primitive Baptists would find a place in early Arkansas, their numbers
would always be few. The exact nature of the effort required by God

was another matter entirely. Precisely how Arkansas Baptists should engage in missions would continue to be an issue throughout their history, an issue exacerbated by pressure from Baptist "reformers."

The year after Arkansas's first known church organized, a Kentucky Baptist preacher named John Taylor published a treatise entitled *Thoughts on Missions*, in which he attacked Rice and Rice's missions program. Simultaneously, an untutored Baptist preacher in Illinois, Daniel Parker, attacked John Mason Peck's efforts in that region and Rice's "new-fangled" mission societies. The next year, 1820, Parker published a book excoriating the new Triennial Convention and its mission efforts. The Convention, he maintained, was not Baptistic because it was not the creature of the churches, nor did they directly control it.

While Taylor and Parker gathered adherents, it was the work of Alexander Campbell which consummated their efforts and quickly came to represent a serious challenge to the collective approach to missions among Baptists. From Pennsylvania, Campbell cast aspersions upon Bible societies, missionary societies, and salaried clergy. In 1823 he began the *Christian Baptist*, a name he changed six years later to the *Millennial Harbinger*. His newspaper and personal revival trips through the west spread his influence rapidly, especially in Kentucky. Given the Kentucky connections with early Arkansas, it is not surprising that the Campbellites (Disciples of Christ, Christian or Reformer [Baptist] Church) displayed such impact in early Arkansas. After his departure for Memphis in 1830, for example, Toncray's leaderless church was enlivened two years later by Benjamin Hall, a Kentucky convert to Campbell's principles. Under his direction, what had been Little Rock's first Baptist church unanimously changed its name and affiliation, leaving the Baptist fold for that of the Christians despite the presence of Toncray's sister in its midst. Even where churches were not converted in name, as happened in Little Rock, congregations often fell under the sway of Campbellite sentiments, which would also rear their heads under other names at later times.

Just as Baptist witness in Arkansas was being founded in the midst of uncertainty over a preacher's role in the church and society and over whether and how missions should be carried out, so uncertainty existed about what if any role Baptists should play in education. This third major issue, that of education, began to be debated almost as soon as numbers warranted discussion of any efforts by local congregations beyond mere survival.

The debate over education was joined in larger Baptist circles in the same manner as that over missions, and for basically the same reasons. Luther Rice, active in establishing mission societies and the Triennial Convention, likewise busied himself with publications and education. His vision was organizational and cooperative, with local congregations accomplishing more together than they could individually. While his theology wed him to the Baptist cause, his thinking along these lines threatened the localism which had long been the hallmark of American Baptists. On these grounds his plans were vulnerable to Campbellite arguments against organizations as well as to those Calvinistic fulminations by Primitives against education as well as mission activity.

The Hardshell argument that God chose individuals for His purposes extended to their preparation. If God wanted an educated man, He would pick one who had prepared beforehand. There was no need for learning in the ministry; God put His words into His messenger's mouth. Beyond that, an education could hinder a minister, unfitting him for his task. Learning could exalt his pride and incline him to self-reliance. It could also distance him from his hearers, especially on the frontier, where a minister of a more high-church denomination characterized the majority as "so ignorant, as to be charmed with sound rather than sense. And to them, the want of knowledge . . . may easily be made up, and overbalanced, by great zeal, an affecting tone of voice, and a perpetual motion of the tongue." Any minister, he concluded, who can "keep his tongue running, in an unremitting manner" and who can quote "a large number of texts from within the covers of the Bible" will find that "it matters not, to many of his hearers, whether he speaks sense or nonsense."

Individual Baptists in Arkansas displayed an active interest in education from the very beginning. Caleb Lindsey, whose son John Young Lindsey became a Baptist preacher in Randolph, Pulaski, and Saline counties, began what was probably the region's first school in 1816 on the Fourche-á-Thomas River. Baptist layman Ezra M. Owen laid out a townsite he called Collegeville about fifteen miles southwest of Little Rock in 1827. Silas Toncray served on the "examination committee" at Jesse Brown's private school in Little Rock in 1824. And even after his departure from Little Rock in 1830, the church Toncray organized continued to allow its building to be used for educational meetings and examinations. An Arkansan even wrote the Baptist Mission Board seeking help in establishing schools for Creek Indians in Arkansas in mid-1833.

Unfortunately, a surer indicator of collective interest would be collective rather than individual actions. In short, the real question was not what individuals might do, but what churches and associations might attempt. Sadly, for the pre-statehood era that information is not available. Nor is the individual activity noted above more than anecdotal and certainly not indicative of denominational intent in any locale. Baptists in Arkansas during the pre-statehood era found themselves too concerned with self-perpetuation to give much energy to a collective activity like education. Certainly the transient nature of individual congregations and associations in this era indicated such a preoccupation.

Some Arkansas Baptists showed a readiness to act, individually and collectively, with other Baptists beyond the bounds of associations—and on occasions even act with other non-Baptist Christians—to advance the Kingdom. Usually this willingness did not extend to activities for social amelioration no matter how "moral" those activities might be. Baptists seemed disinterested in, though not hostile to, the anti-gambling and temperance organizations formed in Arkansas during these formative years. Perhaps it was the presence of Methodist leadership rather than the cause or the cooperative nature of the ventures which left Baptists cold. Efforts which related to spreading the Gospel rather than public morals were another matter.

One extreme example of this cooperative spirit beyond the associations in Kingdom work is the Baptist church organized in Crawford County in the summer of 1825 "on the principles of free communion & fellowship with other denominations." Toncray's presidency of the Little Rock Bible Society, an arm of the American Bible Society, is perhaps a better example. Bible societies gained a foothold in Arkansas in the early 1830s—the Arkansas Bible Society (Little Rock, 1830), the Bible Societies of Hempstead (December 1830), Washington (March 1831) and Crawford and Pope (April 1831) Counties, and the St. Francis Bible

Society (July 1832) included Baptists in their organizations, despite editorial warnings that such organizations were not Baptist in nature or organization and owed their existence to the Methodists.

Baptists in Arkansas stood poised for statehood with other Arkansans at the end of the territorial era. They shared the common propensity for transience, as the story of their churches and associations illustrates. They showed signs of willingness to act cooperatively, a cooperativeness usually limited to other Baptists, in associations and in nondenominational organizations. They faced statehood with some divisions among themselves and with some unresolved issues facing them. But Baptists in the Arkansas Territory faced statehood with one clear certainty: just as the Baptist witness penetrated deepest, darkest Arkansas in search of souls in need of saving, so that impetus to spread the good news would persevere into statehood.

3

From Statehood to Convention 1836–1848

AS THE EIGHTEEN YEARS OF TERRITORIAL STATUS HAD proven insufficient time to resolve the three issues of Arkansas Baptist attitudes toward ministers with political ambitions, toward how missions would be conducted, or toward what part they would play collectively in providing educational opportunities, so the dozen years of early statehood likewise proved insufficient. Those years between statehood and the inauguration of the Arkansas Baptist State Convention did experience a continued dialogue about each of those issues.

A letter-writer to the *Arkansas Gazette* editor in mid-January 1836 feared that the proposed state constitution would prohibit clergy from holding civil offices and protested against such an outrage. The letter indicated that the issue of ministers engaging in political activity would not vanish with statehood's advent.

One reason that the issue did not vanish was that the arrival of statehood did not magically provide a larger pool of individuals with the qualifications and the interest to provide governmental leadership for Arkansas. The 1,062 settlers in the region in 1810 had grown to 14,000 by the time Arkansas became a territory and to 52,000 in the year before statehood, but the change in numbers did not reflect a similar change of composition. The leadership capabilities of ministers were still needed to serve the public good in capacities other than solely those exhibited in spiritual settings.

The *Gazette* letter-writer might easily have referred to Methodist Presiding Elder William W. Stevenson, who maintained the Little Rock mayor's office in his home after his election in 1833 and was elected to serve as commissioner of Public Buildings and on the Board of the Real Estate Bank. The letter might have related to Alfred W. Arrington or F. H. Carr, also Methodists, or to William T. Larremore. Or it could have referred to one of several Baptist ministers.

David Orr, who had earned the nickname "David the High Priest" during his legislative experience because of his height (over six feet), demeanor (serious), appearance (slender, dark-haired and -eyed), vocation (Baptist minister), or "almost unlimited influence" might have been a good candidate. Perhaps the writer was thinking of Mark W. Izard, the best Baptist example of a clergyman holding civil office until after the Civil War.

Mark Izard, only distantly related to Territorial Governor George Izard, came to Arkansas in the mid-1820s and secured the contract to build the Military Road between the St. Francis and White Rivers and settled on a large farm at what would later become Forrest City. While in Arkansas, Izard served both the St. Francis and Mt. Vernon Associations as founding moderator, played an important part in the organization and continuation of the General Association of Eastern Arkansas in 1852, pastored churches from his arrival in 1825 until his departure in 1855, and dabbled in local and state politics. His greatest success was in the state legislature, where he served in the Senate for its first three terms (the second and third as President), then as a House member in the seventh before returning to the Senate for the eighth and ninth assemblies (1850–1854). Izard served as federal marshal in Nebraska before receiving appointment as governor in 1855, a position he occupied for three years before returning to Arkansas.

Izard is certainly not representative of Baptist ministers and their secular political involvement, but he did represent a strong bias among those who would become "organizational men" to improve their world through active social amelioration as well as through preaching the Gospel. The common cry among these like-minded men was the need for "system," or organization. It was no accident that Izard served two associations as moderator.

Just as the era between statehood and the State Convention's founding did not solve the question of ministers' political involvement, so it found the question of how missions should be conducted still alive and well.

As it had in the years before statehood, Arkansas remained the object of Baptist missionary endeavors. American Baptist Home Mission Society support for missionaries continued even after the State Convention's founding, and the new uniquely Southern version of Baptist work, founded in 1845, likewise showed interest in this mission field through its Southern Domestic Missionary Board. Associations gained enough strength in the era to usually field their own witness. Despite objections in some quarters internally and from the Campbellites externally, the Arkansas trend seemed toward cooperative mission endeavors.

The third issue—how important education would be to Arkansas Baptists and if important enough to pursue, how it would be pursued—found a bridge in the person of one of the early missionaries, Henry McElmurry. Serving in Arkansas from 1844 until just before his death at age fifty-five in 1853, McElmurry married while still unlettered. His education paralleled that of President Andrew Johnson, for McElmurry's wife, Nancy, taught him his letters as well as how to read (though not how to write) using the third chapter of Matthew as a primer. Obviously this staunch Baptist missionary found education a personally important concern.

The era between statehood and the Convention's founding, like the one before it, had numerous examples of personal Baptist interest in education and affirmation of its importance. Also like the one before it, this era lacks any surviving record of collective interest in educational activities.

The dozen years between statehood and the founding of the State Convention might not have provided resolution for many of the Baptists' issues, but they denoted one major change. Gone would be much of the organizational instability which marked the pre-statehood era and which owed its existence especially to the paucity of numbers and of leadership. The Baptist witness displayed its growth and strength in the increasing stability of its cooperative endeavors.

Arkansas Baptists entered the era of statehood with fewer than forty churches (sources differ between thirty-one and thirty-six) in two (or three—Spring River and St. Francis for sure, perhaps Rocky Bayou) associations and with about 225 members. The numbers for Baptists in the mid-1830s are questionable at best, coming as they do from a national source with notoriously unreliable reporting systems. No matter how diligent a local reporter, as Baptist clerks would complain until well after the Civil War, communications made accurate statistics a chimera.

The era's start gave little promise of good things ahead. The state was barely a year old when the worst economic panic of American history struck. Measured by impact and duration (seventy-two months—1837–1843), the Panic of 1837 edged out the economic downturn which had followed the War of 1812 (and coincided with the beginnings of Arkansas's territorial status) for this dubious distinction of worst ever. Unlike the panic following the war, this one resulted from a combination of land speculation and poor banking practices (including politicians' use of banks for political advantage, individuals' use for personal gain through land speculation, and the government's failure to protect the public interest in a sound economic system and well-regulated circulating medium).

The *Arkansas Gazette* noted with pride in mid-1837 that "town bustles with activity" despite the economic recession elsewhere. The editor's observation reflected more the state's geographical location than its economic ability. The Panic struck first in the eastern markets and slowly worked its way west, driving the economically displaced before it. Arkansas profited from those seeking their fortune to the west before the Panic's wave hit the state.

Land speculation and questionable banking practices were a way of life in an Arkansas to which private individuals and officials alike tried to attract settlers for public and personal gain. Under its new constitution, Arkansas created two banks—the Real Estate Bank to provide long-term credit to farmers and planters, and the State Bank to provide capital for merchants. Both profited from direct cash subsidies from the state and from the state's pledge of its credit and good faith, as well as from the lack of any meaningful state control. Both would collapse in 1839 and contribute to the arrival of Arkansas's version of the Panic of '37 shortly after 1840.

Evidence of the Panic's delayed arrival can perhaps be seen in the story of the associations between 1836 and the State Convention in

1848. When statehood arrived, Arkansas's first association, Little Rock, was gone and two (or three) remained. The year of statehood, Baptists organized Saline in the center of the state. The next year they organized Washington County (northwest). Four years later, Salem (northwest), White River (northeast central), and probably Rocky Bayou (northeast, if one accepts P. S. G. Watson's 1840 date rather than the official one of 1833) organized. In 1841 Baptists organized Arkansas (north central) and Union; four years later they organized Liberty (south central), then Salem (near Batesville) in another three.

Several things are significant about the eight (or nine) associations organized in the dozen years after statehood, chief among them being their stability. Spring River, founded in 1829, dissolved in 1840 (probably the precursor to Rocky Bayou's organization). The Salems were both short-lived, that near Batesville lasting only a year. Arkansas and Union likewise passed from sight reasonably quickly. But the enduring early associations, names that would grace Convention rolls well into the next century, began here. Saline (which originated the call for a convention in 1847 but was lost in the Landmark Movement split in 1920), Rocky Bayou, White River, and Liberty continued to thrive. Though none of the associations founded prior to statehood flourished after the Civil War, half of those from the dozen years just before the Convention's founding did so, a sure sign of increased denominational vigor.

A second fact attested to by these associations was the continued allegiance of Arkansas Baptists to cooperative endeavors. Arkansas Baptists, as they founded more churches, did not hang back from associating at an ever-increasing rate. The numbers of new associations compared with the number of years illustrates this better than perhaps anything else.

A third feature of the associations' organization is the indication it gives of demographic patterns during these years. The population of 52,240 (9,938 black) in 1835 had grown to 97,574 (20,400 black) in 1840. Settlers in 1840 were reasonably evenly distributed (statistically) throughout the state except for one pocket of high density around Fayetteville (six to eighteen persons per square mile) and pockets of low density (less than two persons per square mile—still frontier) in the north central, northeast, west central, south central, and extreme southwest (from the Red River to the state lines south and west) sections.

By 1850, two years after the Convention's formation, that demographic picture had changed drastically. The population of 209,897 (47,708 black) developed centers (six to eighteen) persons per square mile) in the Fayetteville-Van Buren (and down the Arkansas to about Spadra) region, up and down the White River around Batesville, along the delta from the mouth of the St. Francis to about an equal distance below Helena, and the Washington-Arkadelphia-Tulip-Camden-El Dorado region from the Red to the Ouachita Rivers. Frontier areas (by census definition) would exist only in the upper reaches of the Ouachita River in the Ouachita mountains toward Indian Territory and in the northern half of the Arkansas delta between the St. Francis and Mississippi Rivers.

While Baptists sought to increase their witness, state officials sought to increase Arkansas population by inviting emigrants to come and take up lands which had been forfeited for taxes. Those settling on the lands would have them free of charge and get a deed which "the supreme Court of the state has decided will be valid." The *Little Rock Banner* office issued a volume of seventy-five octavo pages (about 5" by 8") listing all the available lands. Baptists would have to redouble their efforts if schemes like that were at all successful.

The rate of growth during these early statehood years indicated that such land offers encouraged emigration, but offers like that were not the only incentive to cross the Mississippi. Settlers sent back glowing reports to acquaintances in older areas citing good soil and water, healthy climate, and even good society. One Baptist minister, Edward W. Haynes, wrote from south Arkansas that he had traveled Illinois and all the states south of Virginia and the Ohio River as well as those west of the Mississippi, "and I have seen no country where there is less vice than here." Pastor Allen M. Scott wrote, with a similar widely traveled experience, from Mine Creek to friends in Tennessee that "the people with few exceptions are good livers, industrious, moral citizens, just such as form the bone and sinew of a community." Reminding his correspondents that some had represented Arkansas as a "wild, villainous, cut-throat sort of a place," he concluded that the "herd of refugees from justice, that the fear of punishment in the other States once induced to seek temporary homes here, have been mostly ferreted out, or have long since sought a safer retreat in Texas or California." Wealthy south-Arkansas planter and deacon Nat G. Smith summed up those who wrote in like vein when he said that the "delightful region of the country" in which he lived was "healthy, pleasant, productive, water cool and abundant, society the best I ever lived among; we have not a single drunkard, profane swearer or Sabbath-breaker in our neighborhood." Noting their large temperance society, flourishing Sunday School and Bible class and well-attended regular weekly prayer meeting, he concluded "It is the only country I have ever seen I could raise no objection to."

Free land and good society and healthy land were not the only inducements for Baptists to come to Arkansas. Some Arkansans exhibited signs of high anxiety to hear the Gospel. William Montgomery, for example, advertised for a gospel minister to hold services at his house monthly at the White River's mouth in early 1834. While he did not specify a denominational preference, he obviously felt the lack of gospel proclamation keenly.

Baptist ministers often wrote denominational papers in the states from whence they came asking for help from "ministering brethren" there. Allen Scott noted in 1851 that "Most other neighborhoods, in the state, are poorly supplied with ministers. We very much need efficient ministers in Arkansas." These individuals, he said, should be "holy, devoted, self-denying men, who understand our doctrines and are able to defend them." Minister Thomas J. Watts wrote the *Alabama Baptist Advocate* in late 1849 that "Our denomination needs nothing in this country but efficient and zealous ministers of the gospel."

In a plaintive letter from Yell County in April 1850, M. J. Green wrote to the *Tennessee Baptist* that recent emigration into his area over the past year had been "vast," and included many Baptists who are "persuaded to join other denominations, with a conviction on their minds that they ought not to live out of church influences." They do this, he wrote, because of the "deplorable situation of the people in not having the gospel preached to them, in that true and acceptable manner." In his two years in Arkansas, Green added, he had neither heard nor seen a Missionary Baptist minister, "nor is there one to be had, who will come at all, in *one hundred miles square*, from the best I have been informed." "A great many Baptists in this country" wished for a minister among them. "We want one who has a family," he noted, "and who is willing to move and settle among us, and submit to the privation to which all new countries are incident. He can get a good home here with a plenty of land of the very best kind, without money or price, and we would want him to be supported by the different associations there in part for the first year, after which we could keep him afloat." Green concluded, "Surely you can afford to send one good devout minister here under your patronage for a few months." At the year's end, he wrote again along the same lines: "The calls of Christian benevolence are frequent and pressing here, and the magnitude of which should overshadow the petty inducement that a great many young ministers have to remain in the old State, for they would have a larger field here to operate in. . . ."

The problem of insufficient ministers seemed intractable, widespread, and long-term. Writing from Poke Bayou (just north of Batesville) in the fall of 1853, Samuel Halliburton asked *Tennessee Baptist* editor J. R. Graves to say "to the brethren of the older settlements, and where they are generally supplied with ministers; to move and settle here where there is a wide opening to do good." A few weeks later, after a visit to Helena, Graves noted in his report that "Arkansas greatly needs more ministers, but where they are to come from we know not. The field is ripe for them. Churches might soon be planted all over the State, had we the men to labor."

Stories of the land and society and the calls for ministers to come and settle and serve had to be balanced against reports from ministers already on the field and from chance pieces of information calculated to chill the ardor of even the most committed. Hidden among praises for conversions, church plantings, and good services of every kind were revelations of hardship and privation.

The repeated calls for ministers indicated the professional loneliness that prospects could expect. William Hardage reported in late April 1849 that Hot Spring County had only two or three churches and two Baptist ministers—one in his neighborhood on the county's western side and the other in its northeastern corner—and a neighborhood in between "where some of them say they have never heard a baptist [*sic*] preach." Robert Pulley wrote shortly after coming to Arkansas in late 1848 that "I have been informed that there is not a Missionary Baptist preacher in Bradley County except myself." He seemed overjoyed to learn the next spring of another and that though the fellow-laborer had arrived the previous winter "I expect to see him on the first Lord's day in April." Perhaps Baptist layman and deacon Spence Hall best summed up the problem when he wrote to J. R. Graves that being with those of like mind had recently afforded him a pleasure "you in Tennessee can hardly know how to appreciate, surrounded as you are by so many privileges and intelligent brethren and sisters."

Not only would ministers be professionally isolated, the disarray of Christendom on the frontier ensured that their battle would be as difficult against forces within Christendom as against the forces of darkness outside the gates. Letter-writers to the *Tennessee Baptist* noted the "peculiarly disordered state of the church" during the mid-1830s, and noted that "Conflicting and injurious systems of theology disturb, and the oppositions to benevolent effort that prevail are agitating every part of Zion." Writers consistently mentioned the triple threat to Missionary Baptists from Catholics ("Old Rome"—evidence that Baptists shared the general nativist strain in American culture that would see its greatest expression in formation of the American, or "Know-Nothing" party, but interesting in that it took place while Arkansas officials were trying to lure refugees from the Irish Famine to the state after 1847); Methodists (Pedobaptists or "Pedos," who baptized children and who, along with Episcopalians, were Old Rome's "children and grand-children" and characterized variously as "the nurslings of a corrupt or careless hierarchy" or "the usurpers of ecclesiastical hierarchy"); and Campbellites (sometimes called Reformers or even Reform Baptists).

Illness, always a grim reality in an age before modern medicine whether one inhabited a settled or a remote area, cropped up with some regularity in reports from Arkansas. Martha Johnson wrote to her family from Clark County in late 1849 of the "awful calamity" that had come upon her settlement. "We have the Cholera," she starkly observed before (with a shock palpable even through the written word and across the years) dispassionately recounting the timing of seven deaths in the course of the week, mentioning a couple of others, and concluding that "Martha, Howell and Mary are very low, and we do not expect to cure them."

Ministers also reported illnesses that prevented their endeavors on the field. William H. Bayliss found in 1848 that severe illness in his family kept him from following through on a promised undertaking.

His own illness soon after his arrival in Dardanelle in 1851 kept A. B. Couch from even riding to preaching engagements, much less preaching, for two months. Writing about a recently completed preaching engagement at Helena in the early 1850s, a participant voiced the concern felt by others that his "disease of the throat" would force J. R. Graves to cancel his efforts before the meeting had gotten well underway. William Hardage ruefully observed in late March 1849 that illness and weather had prevented his attending a "Macedonian call" from a nearby neighborhood.

References to illness abounded in ministerial communications throughout these early years. Their ubiquitousness, and the mundane intimacy implied thereby, belied the seriousness of those monotonous repetitions. Accepting illness as a fact of existence did not lessen its impact. The cumulative impact of long miles traveled under difficult conditions, often in poor health and even poorer weather, took their toll on Baptist ministers in Arkansas. Sometimes ministerial illness caused a different kind of cancellation from that of meetings. Henry McElmurry's obituary in 1853 revealed that after nine years' service as a missionary in north Arkansas his "disease of the lungs" had progressed to the point of his coughing up blood. Having fought to continue his service as long as possible, McElmurry finally ceased preaching two months before his death.

Even under the best of circumstances, even in good health and weather, hard work characterized the life of Arkansas Baptist layman and preacher alike. M. M. Wallace, Baptist missionary in south Arkansas, estimated that only six ministers devoted all their time to ministry in the state in 1848 among about two thousand Baptists. Robert Pulley noted that around him, "Each one is doing his best to open himself a farm, and it is about as much as they can do to provide the necessaries of life. . . ." He spent his first month in Arkansas in 1849 "working on the running gear of a Cotton Gin for bro. Powell" and that as a consequence "there is not a stick amiss yet on the place that I have settled." As he sadly observed, "They are anxious to hear preaching, but I shall have but a very limited opportunity for some time to come, as I have not yet commenced building my houses, and will not for some time. . . ."

Unless they cleared land and built a residence, these ministers lacked food and shelter, but it seemed impossible to find the time for everything. The rural life of most ministers appeared not to lend itself to ministerial duties amidst the demands of everyday life. More settled surroundings offered nothing better for ministers just beginning their Arkansas service. A. B. Couch, arriving from south Alabama in late 1851, spent his first four and a half months working in a mercantile house in Dardanelle to defray his considerable expenses and purchase a home. Consequently he had not ministered to those in his new surroundings and almost despaired of so doing.

If starting fresh in a new land put difficulties in the minister's way, different ones took their place as time progressed. Except for the winter months, ministers who could do so traveled and preached. In early 1848, an Arkansas minister wrote that in the past seven years he had "visited thirty counties, travelled fifteen thousand miles, and preached about one thousand sermons." A year later, Edward Haynes wrote briefly to *Tennessee Baptist* editor J. R. Graves, confessing in his opening lines that "I have been at home only a few hours, and am obliged to leave in the morning again, on a tour of preaching." M. M. Wallace, in the late summer of 1849, revealed that in the previous six weeks he had traveled three hundred miles, visited eight churches, and assisted in three protracted meetings. The scattered nature and comparatively small size of Arkansas settlements, even after the Civil War, would join with the churches' quarter-time nature to make traveling a regular part of the minister's routine.

Even had the work not involved such physical adjustments, services themselves would have been very different for someone accustomed to more settled conditions. A letter to the Little Rock paper in mid-April 1832 asked people not to take their dogs to church and to not let their children roam about the building during worship. Even as late as 1842, a writer to the *Arkansas Gazette* admonished young ladies to stop whispering and giggling during worship services. Ministers reporting revivals of various lengths usually remarked on the presence of "good order" on the congregation's part as a sign of God's working among His people.

And behind it all, behind the illness and the hard work and the professional loneliness, lurked what was perhaps the most difficult part of the minister's life in Arkansas. Never easy even under the best of circumstances, the choices imposed by the limited time and numerous pressing needs at which Robert Pulley hinted could prove overwhelming.

James P. Kern, a new minister in Arkansas in 1853, spoke of beginning in discouragement but, "Having food and raiment, I commenced preaching." He certainly touched that delicate spot of dilemma when he addressed "my brethren of the ministry in the older States, who are not preaching regularly." Chiding them for remaining where they were instead of coming to Arkansas for the harvest, he continued the agricultural metaphor when he rhetorically spoke about their farms. Reminding them that Judas sold his Lord for money which bought a field, he asked about the cost of their farms in dollars compared to the cost in souls. Picturing the ministers walking their fields with delight while sinners trod "the fiery domain of endless despair," Kern finished with a heart-rending scene: at a child's grave, the "aged parent" laments that "no one was there to point him to God through Christ" and then accuses the errant ministers with "Sirs, had you been at your post, my child would not have died [spiritually]!"

And so they came, convicted by the Holy Spirit or simply part of the great American longing for a better or even just a different place in which to live. They preached monthly to a quarter-time church in their neighborhood or, if possible, to several in surrounding neighborhoods. They usually spent "unengaged" Sundays preaching in whatever homes might welcome them. When they could, they gathered churches of local adherents.

Usually these churches would begin with about a dozen (often fewer, occasionally more) members who were generally related. Spring Hill, at Caledonia, for example, began about 1848 with George Cobb, S. T. Cobb, Ezariah Cobb Sr. and Jr., H. B. Cobb and Harrison Cobb and their wives, A. R. Cobb, and Elijah Cate and J. H. Alford and their wives; Arkadelphia First began in 1851 with two families of Heards, their two married sisters (and one's husband), the pastor's nephew and two Jarmans. Those "reporters" from Arkansas who wrote back to friends in more settled areas, and whose letters found their way into denominational papers, reflect on average about ten as the maximum for founding a church.

Even after founding, Arkansas churches for this era remained small. Extant associational statistics reveal churches averaging about thirty members and ranging from five to the fifties. Church size depended upon location, for those in less densely populated regions would tend toward the low side, while those where settlers tended to cluster more would naturally attract more members.

The result of personal and professional difficulties had different effects on those ministers who came to Arkansas. Some ministers followed the scenario vividly reviled by N. P. Moore in an article entitled "Ministerial Fidelity" in the *Tennessee Baptist* in early 1853. Deriding the appearance of "a spirit different from that of our Saviour's" among some ministers, Moore wrote from Arkansas about how poorly they use the "thirty or fifty minutes" afforded them in the pulpit. They "hesitate and falter to declare the whole counsel of God," and "many much prefer to ride upon the popular breeze, and be wafted gently along by fashion's tide and vitiated taste, than to be heaven's faithful messenger." And why? For fear that they "might wound some good Brother's feelings!" Or perhaps they might "disturb their equanimity!!" Ultimately, Moore wrote, they fear "that if I urge this matter upon my church, and they put it in practice, that it will cause my own salary to be diminished!" Moore's diatribe, of course, only applied to those who actually received a salary from churches, which many, if not most, did not.

For some ministers who moved to Arkansas, the rigors of their new surroundings proved too much and they returned to those fields on which they had wanted to live and about which Kern spoke with such eloquent disdain. A. B. Couch returned to south Alabama after his difficulties in Dardanelle, having stayed there less than a year. The blind minister John Hardeman High, who "became embarrassed" in discharging his ministerial duties in the state in 1845, likewise returned to Alabama.

Those ministers who remained, and remained true to their calling in Arkansas, found themselves spending time trying to "build up Zion" and increase the larger flock as well as their personal ones. Sometimes ministers reported a slow accretion of membership, say, one or two a month over the course of a year. More often they revealed a revival of one sort or another.

The most common revival effort involved a local community. Often the way would be prepared for these efforts by a month of weekly prayer meetings. At the end of that time, what listeners could be would be gathered for a "protracted meeting" of a few days to (more usually) about a week's duration. Daily preaching, often about candle-lighting time, would inspire listeners with details of the second coming, judgment, and the final restitution of all things, or perhaps with stories of "the primitive church's" composition and operation. One minister reported using 2 Corinthians 5:1 as his text; though the sermon was never written (early Arkansas Baptist ministers would certainly have scoffed at such a practice!) it unquestionably emphasized that "house not made with hands, eternal in the heavens." Sometimes ministers preached twice daily, with a morning "Bible study" and an evening evangelistic message. The sermons normally lasted two and one-half to four and one-half hours, longer than regular Sunday offerings.

Both the number and the duration of messages during revivals accounted for the practice of the pastor asking for "ministerial assistance" from several others. Reports of revivals usually mention the presence of two to five additional ministers, though generally the "assistants" rarely spent the entire revival time. Writers usually reported the various arrivals and departures made necessary by prior obligations, illness, or the call of other meetings.

These protracted meetings often occurred in conjunction with a church's founding, led by the convening presbytery in an effort to strengthen the local congregation as much as possible and give it a quick start toward a flourishing condition. Associational meetings often partook of this same flavor, with sermons delivered by the association's best over the course of several days. Sometimes the association's practice of meeting with different churches annually reveals a pattern of gathering at the weaker churches instead of the more robust. In such cases, the intent of bolstering the faithful and adding to their number by the best preaching available in the association seems clear.

The pinnacle of evangelistic endeavor among Arkansas Baptists, even in these early years, was the camp meeting. That practice had been initiated during the Second Great Awakening at the century's beginning. The most famous example occurred in Kentucky in 1801, where thousands spent months at Cane Ridge in the largest gathering the frontier had seen. Arkansas Baptists continued to try and replicate that experience throughout the pre–Civil War years.

Sometimes camp meetings resembled that in Cane Ridge in their makeup. Like their Kentucky predecessor, they would be "union" meetings where ministers from other denominations joined the fray. Those who experienced conversion would join whichever church appealed to them from among the denominations represented. Although they participated in union meetings periodically throughout the pre-war years, Baptists generally preferred solo events. Evidently warnings about the dangers of Rome (and her offspring), Pedos, and Reformers lost their effect when communicants found at least the latter two represented by ministers at the annual camp meeting.

Camp meetings differed little from their simple protracted kindred save in the setting. Tents, wagons, and even huts (constructed on the more established meeting-place grounds) provided dwelling places for participants during the week, or (often) two people would be in residence. Usually one dwelling would be designated the "Preachers' Hut" so that those worthies would not feel the imposition of lodging with participants and could rest from their arduous labors "on the stump" without interruption.

The camp-meeting setting often provided one other significant difference from the protracted meeting: the setting made possible a larger gathering of the faithful, the hopeful, and the willing. One south-Arkansas meeting produced about seventy conversions during the course of two weeks from a total gathering estimated at a thousand. Churches and associations often maintained a campground for such events, and often such gathering places for the various denominations in a given area would be reasonably close to each other. Sometimes a campground would be shared by the denominations, who would occupy it in turn. As the fullness of time approached for a state convention's organization, the camp meeting became an annual event, cherished and anticipated by ministers and campers alike.

In the scene of deceptive physical beauty and bounty that was Arkansas, from which hardships of all kinds crept (sometimes unexpectedly), Arkansas Baptists considered organizing their first State Convention. They did so at the call of an association, and met on a campground to accomplish their ends. To counteract their paucity of ministers and to ameliorate, to whatever extent possible, their situations were two reason for associations and for contemplation of a State Convention. Other possibilities for cooperative endeavors might await a denomination that seemed to have established itself enough in the state to be called mature.

4

The Arkansas Baptist State Convention Begins

SALINE ASSOCIATION, NOT VERY OLD ITSELF, ISSUED THE call for interested parties to meet with a view to beginning a State Convention. The call resulted when a widow, a deacon, and their pastor glimpsed a vision articulated by an East Coast missionary.

George Ann Humphreys Powell Bledsoe was a twice-widowed thirty-one-year-old lady born to wealth and privilege as the daughter of a Tennessee judge. Her husbands had both been lawyers, but both marriages had been short lived (the last less than a year) and childless. After her last husband's death, George Ann moved to live with her mother and an aunt in south Arkansas and found a church that provided solace in her loss.

Brownsville (Dallas County) pastor William H. Bayliss had an education and background that matched Bledsoe's. About ten years her senior, Bayliss had practiced law in western Tennessee, reputedly helped capture the notorious "land pirate" John A. Murrell and fought Indians in 1836 before undergoing conversion and taking up preaching in 1841. In 1846 he had moved to Tulip, opened its first store, and become Brownsville's pastor.

At Brownsville, Bayliss met Nathaniel G. (Nat) Smith, a wealthy owner of land and slaves and deacon and only four years his senior. A North Carolina native, Smith had come to Dallas County about 1830

44

and settled Buena Vista plantation. He served on the board of the Tulip Female Institute and undertook every good work available, allying himself with the Masonic order as well as the church. His daughter Mary married John Seldon Roane, elected Arkansas governor in 1848; Smith remained politically active without seeking office himself.

Bledsoe, Bayliss, and Smith provided the critical mass necessary to convince their association that the time had come to issue the call for a statewide missions organization like that envisioned by Luther Rice. They gave evidence that perseverance, vision, and a plan could begin a great work.

Nat Smith reported the call's origin from a layman's viewpoint in a letter to the *Tennessee Baptist*. The association met with the newly formed Union Church in Jefferson County that fall of 1847. Finding "the brethren encamped on the ground," Smith wrote, the association combined camp meeting and association gathering into one event. Though thirty people experienced conversion, their salvation was not what made it "the most important meeting ever held in the State." Instead, its significance lay in the adoption of "incipient measures for the organization of a Baptist State Convention of Arkansas." "We have recommended," Smith concluded, "the churches to send delegates to the convention, at the Mountain-spring campground, near Brownsville, Dallas county, Ark. on Thursday before the fourth Sunday in September 1848: our association will meet at the same time and place, and we expect to have the *biggest* kind of a camp meeting, and we hope the best kind." A committee had been appointed to invite Louisiana and Texas "to unite and co-operate with us" and enjoin ministers from "abroad" to attend and help "in the wilds of Arkansas," including R. B. C. Howell and J. R. Graves from the *Tennessee Baptist*.

The designated Correspondence Committee, composed of Bayliss, Smith, Edward W. Haynes, Jesse Reaves, J. E. Paxton, and J. B. Pratt, wrote an open letter to "The Baptists of Arkansas, Louisiana, and Texas" to lay out their case. They first denied proposing a novelty. Twenty-two other states ("the great mass of our churches") already had established this "work of tried and proven utility."

Next the letter summarized the objectives of a State Convention or General Association: "to assist feeble churches to procure and support pastors, to maintain domestic missionaries or ministers at large within the State, to encourage the formation of new churches, to circulate the scriptures, tracts, useful books, to promote education generally in the denomination, and ministerial education particularly, and in some cases the cause of Foreign Missions is included among them." These objectives would have awakened no sense of concern among Arkansas Baptist churches in general, though some would find the issue of education a bit alarming.

Thirdly, the committee pointed out the difference between such an entity and local associations: Conventions "usually have some method of raising funds and employing secretaries, agents, and missionaries." "Burying" that probable source of concern on the part of their readers, the committee quickly proceeded to less controversial ground by observing that despite this feature, the "usual character" of such an organization "is that of a domestic missionary society," either independent of or auxiliary to the society headquartered in Marion, Alabama. It would have "no power whatever to interfere with the churches," a prohibition customarily written into its constitution.

The committee's explanation of what supporters of the State Convention idea had in mind ended with an explication of the most prominent features: missionary effort and education. The need of mission efforts they supported by displaying "whole counties without a Baptist church, or a Baptist preacher" in a state having thousands of citizens "who have never heard a Baptist sermon, and even many churches who are in a perishing state for the want of a preacher." Such mission effort was possible in "the congenial soil" of a Republic, where God opens "doors for the reception of his truths." As for education, "those who are educated can appreciate its value, and those who are without education feel sensibly the need" for this "invaluable gem in society" and "useful auxiliary and embellishment in the pulpit." They linked education and missions inextricably, with education necessary to the continuance of a Republic and a Republic's existence a blessing to the Gospel's spread.

The committee closed its letter with the expectation that churches "will be governed by the same rule in sending up their representation as governs them in their local association." Delegates would "meet each other annually, consult, counsel together and put forth their united action in the spreading of the gospel and the building up of the church of Jesus Christ." Delegates should be chosen who had displayed an interest in the objectives for which the Convention was designed and who had the churches' entire confidence. The committee hoped for a "full representation of the churches of Arkansas" and extended an invitation to possible representatives from Louisiana and Texas, which also lacked Conventions of their own. The committee proposed that if, having met and counseled together, the delegates deemed it best to do so, Baptist churches from the three states could organize "a South Western Convention."

The next year, on the appointed "Thursday before the 4th Sabbath in September" at the Mountain Spring campground, forty-four delegates gathered. None came from outside Arkansas that September 21, but one "observer" (George Washington Baines, who had pastored in the state) arrived from Louisiana and one (Obadiah Dodson, who would soon pastor briefly in the state) from Tennessee. Despite promises to the contrary, neither Graves nor Howell came to report the meeting for the *Tennessee Baptist*. Only Saline Association and fourteen churches (all members of Saline Association save Camden [Liberty Association] and Friendship, in Ouachita County) sent delegates. When ministers were invited to take part in the Convention, Baines and Dodson were joined by Franklin Courtney and S. D. Worthington from El Dorado (Liberty Association), J. Y. Lindsey from Saline County (and Association) and William L. Anderson from Clark. Of the six Correspondence Committee members who had broadcast the call, all but J. B. Pratt attended that first meeting.

Bayliss, guiding light behind the Saline Association's call and Correspondence Committee member, chaired the meeting. Delegates chose Brownsville Church member Asbury Daniel as recording secretary and, on the motion of Nat Smith, created thirteen committees involving constitutional, order, finance, nominations, agencies, destitution, foreign missions, education, Sabbath schools, moral and religious condition of the colored population, Bible cause, circulation of books, and rules.

When making committee appointments, Bayliss leaned heavily on members of the original Correspondence Committee. Two (Smith and Haynes) served on the five-member Constitutional Committee, Smith as chair. Five of the other committees—Order, Nominations, the

Colored Population, Bible Cause, and Rules—had committee representatives. Except for constitutional, order, and finance, committees
had three members; in all cases save one, Correspondence Committee
members chaired committees on which they served. Smith chaired the
most important three (constitutional, nominations, and rules); Haynes
and Reaves chaired one each (Bible cause and colored population
respectively), while Bayliss only served on his (order).

Simply gathering, even doing so successfully, would not answer the
Saline Association's call. Institutionalizing an annual meeting in addition to that of the associations might serve no real purpose. The
fledgling Convention's challenge lay in providing avenues of cooperation not available through individual associations and proving that it
would not waste precious resources of personnel and time.

Whether or not the Convention wasted resources depended heavily
upon its committees; any proposed action would be based on their
reports and recommendations. On Friday morning, the Convention's
second day, President Bayliss opened the session at eight with prayer
and proceeded directly to reports. The thirteen committee reports fell
into four general groupings. Besides the "housekeeping" reports on
nominations, rules, business, and constitution, as written they dealt with
three broad areas: finances, education, and missions.

Two "housekeeping" reports, on rules and business, lacked any real
significance beyond indicating the desire to proceed in an orderly
fashion and provide accountability in the new undertaking. Two others,
on nominations and a constitution, revealed characteristics and
concerns about the Convention's makeup and function.

The new entity's constitution called the body a statewide organization of Baptists—the Arkansas Baptist State Convention. It designated
the composition of annual meetings: delegates from associations and
churches, and individual contributors who were members in good
standing of "the Baptist Church." These provisions indicated the
Convention's conception of Baptists in the aggregate. By referring to
"the" rather than "a" church, delegates affirmed their understanding of
individual churches as part of a larger whole—a formulation very much
in sympathy rather than at odds with their cooperative venture.

Second, although the constitution recognized the aggregated
church's importance, delegates carefully retained the churches' roles in

all undertakings. They allotted five delegates to each association but three to each church. Such a ratio ensured that churches would dominate all deliberations and undertakings. The Constitutional Committee also specifically abjured any interest in creating a convention to act as any sort of authority figure. Article four disavowed any "ecclesiastical jurisdiction" or willingness to "even act as an advisory council" or in any other way interfere with "any Church or Association."

Third, the constitution set forth the Convention's two primary objectives as supplying destitute regions and churches with pastors and communities with "such books as may be approved by this body" to communicate the denomination's "distinctive doctrines" and ordinances. Secondarily, the Convention sought ("whenever consistent with the condition of the treasury") to "adopt means for the advancement of education" and the "cause of Foreign Missions."

Finally, the constitution provided the structure for its self-perpetuation—constitutional amendments, annual meetings (the Thursday before the second Sabbath in October), and operational personnel (a president and recording secretary for meetings and an Executive Committee for the interim—president, two vice-presidents, corresponding secretary, treasurer and ten or more managers, with only five required for a quorum).

The Nominating Committee reported after the proposed constitution had been unanimously adopted and the next meeting time set (El Dorado, on Thursday before the third Sunday in October 1849). By unanimously accepting the report, delegates elected a "Board" to provide continuity until the next meeting. Bayliss and Smith became president and treasurer of this Executive Committee, the only representatives of the old Correspondence Committee to be chosen. Their shared membership in the Brownsville Church, largest (and presumably wealthiest) of those represented and bellwether of the Saline Association, probably played a part in that selection.

The vice-presidents, S. D. Worthington from El Dorado and Isaac C. Perkins from Mine Creek (Nashville), represented two important churches. Worthington helped found and pastored Hopewell in Union County, Liberty Association's largest church, before moving to El Dorado. The forty-nine-year-old Perkins had founded one of the first Baptist churches in southwestern Arkansas after moving to Mine Creek in 1835, and in 1848 pastored the second (Mine Creek), sixth, and seventh largest of the nineteen churches in Red River Association.

As Corresponding Secretary for the board, the meeting affirmed G. W. Baines, despite his Louisiana residence. Baines, a North Carolina native and University of Alabama graduate, had pastored around Crooked Creek in Carroll County where he organized three churches and served for just over a year as missionary for the American Baptist Home Mission Board. He left the state in 1844 to pastor at Mt. Lebanon, Louisiana, about seventy miles south of Magnolia. Baines simultaneously provided connections with northern Arkansas and Louisiana. He had also represented Carroll County in Arkansas's fourth General Assembly in 1842–1844, which provided secular as well as religious connections.

The constitution required a minimum of ten "managers," or trustees, along with the five Convention officers to serve as an Executive Committee to provide continuity and conduct business between annual meetings. Convention delegates elected nineteen individuals to that committee, hoping to ensure that the Executive Committee did not vest too much authority in too few people—despite the fact that only five were necessary to constitute a quorum.

Eight of the managers were ministers:

Franklin Courtney, a Virginian with an M.D. degree from the University of Pennsylvania in 1833 at the age of twenty-one who had pastored in El Dorado since 1845;

John T. Craig, an Alabamian who also studied medicine, though only for two years, moved to Arkansas in 1838 at the age of twenty-two and served as Dallas County Coroner (1845–1846) before undertaking a pastorate at Bluff Spring;

Edward W. Haynes, a much revered older southwest-Arkansas pastor (Pleasant Hill) chosen to preach the introductory sermon;

John Young Lindsey, member of a prominent political family who became a preacher in Saline County in 1836 as well as County Treasurer (1836–40) and organized several churches, including Spring Creek (later Benton) and Kentucky (which he named for his home state);

Jesse Reaves, a Benton minister serving churches in Jefferson, Dallas and Saline counties;

Samuel Stevenson, a Philadelphia-born graduate of Georgetown College in 1847 at the age of thirty-two who conducted a school in Arkadelphia and made his mark for Arkansas Baptists as an educator and supporter of missions and Sunday Schools rather than as a pastor until his death in 1878;

M. M. Wallace, a Camden evangelist who later served in southern Arkansas as a missionary for the Convention under appointment by the Southern Baptist Domestic Mission Board; and

William H. Wyatt, a Dallas County pastor (Bethesda) who would be moderator of Saline Association and a Convention Vice-President at his death in August 1853.

The board's eleven non-ministers came from nine different churches pastored by six different ministers (only two not on the board). Radford McCargo and William B. Parker attended Manchester and Asbury Daniel attended Brownsville, both churches pastored by Bayliss. J. P. Alexander and W. L. Estes worshiped at Union (Jefferson County) and Princeton (Dallas County), both pastored by Reaves. D. C. Paxton attended Mt. Zion (Hempstead County), pastored by Haynes, and M. Yeager worshiped at New Harmony (Ouachita County), served by Wyatt. G. W. Whitfield attended Red River (Lafayette County), pastored by J. E. Paxton (Saline Association delegate but not a manager); David Dodd and E. N. Chenault attended Spring Creek and Union respectively (both Saline County; Spring Creek had been organized in Dodd's home), which A. Bolt (association delegate but not a manager) pastored.

The upshot of the choices made by the Nominating Committee, presided over by Smith, was that a small group of interconnected individuals provided the Convention's continuity between its first and second general meetings. All but three committee chairmen (William L. Anderson, books; William C. Randle, finance, and S. D. Worthington, foreign missions) were board members, so those on the board likewise provided the leadership for the first meeting. Nat Smith

52   A SYSTEM AND PLAN

and Samuel Stevenson between them chaired five committees—almost
half those appointed. Only two board members—Yeager and
Chenault—served on no committees and all committees had at least
one board member on them. Since none of the board lived outside
Saline Association, that association obviously furnished the leadership
indicated in its initial call for the meeting.

In the area of finance, the committee's report to the Convention
revealed that the generosity of eleven churches, one individual, and a
general offering garnered $77.55 ($21.30 for domestic missions, $11.55
to defray the cost of printing minutes, and $44.70 for general
Convention purposes). An accounting reported that Brownsville had
contributed the most ($34.50) and Princeton the next highest amount
($15), with others offering from one to five dollars. The Convention
voted to accept the committee recommendation to employ a general
agent—someone who could canvass the state soliciting funds for the
Convention's use. The minutes do not reveal the election of such a one,
but I. C. Perkins, Mine Creek pastor, agreed to serve. When Perkins's
personal affairs deterred him from the faithful execution of his trust,
President Bayliss attempted to take his place.

The matter of education, or as Bayliss called it in his circular letter
on behalf of the Convention the "so great lack of the proper information and instruction," can subsume several reports. The Sunday School
Committee recommended "energetic action and untiring efforts" to
ministers, deacons, and churches to establish schools "in every town and
neighborhood where circumstances will allow" and that ministers
deliver "Sabbath School addresses" to their congregations "as often as
they may deem practicable."

Sunday Schools might enhance the religious education of white
members, but what about religious instruction for the "colored population"? That committee offered three recommendations: that heads of
families, or other qualified persons, instruct "their servants" and require
them, as much as possible, to attend "their family worship"; that
churches provide "some apartment for them to hear the preaching" and
that ministers "preach to them when the opportunity offers"; and that
any church with colored members "have a committee on instruction"
responsible for reading the Scriptures to them once monthly. All this
educational concern pointed to slaves, who were forbidden by law from

learning to read and write; "free persons of color" did not figure in the report at all.

The purpose of education as envisioned by the Convention certainly lay in the ability to read. Baptists, calling themselves "people of the Book," required the facility of reading to live their claim. The concern for reading took two divergent but complementary tacks. Foremost was concern for the ability to read Scripture. To that end, the Convention expressed its concern for the Bible's availability in Arkansas. The committee on "the Bible Cause" stated that members knew of no auxiliary of the Bible society in the state, had no facts to present, and nothing upon which to base a report.

A secondary concern for reading involved materials other than Scripture. The committee on "the Circulation of Books" suffered no such inhibitions as those exhibited by that on the Bible cause. Its task involved books other than the Scriptures which might prove helpful for religious instruction. Its report recommended a dual approach to the scarcity of religious books. First, the committee recommended that the board obtain an agency for books and employ a minister as colporteur who could sell books and preach as he went. Obadiah Dodson, on a trip through Arkansas and Texas, assumed this capacity—self-appointed and self-paid, as J. R. Graves styled it in the *Tennessee Baptist*—though he left before the meeting's end and was not officially retained. Second, the committee recommended that each church establish its own library, presumably for members' use (though the report did not overtly exclude allowing books from such a library to circulate in other hands).

The Convention's interest in education lay not in individual intellectual betterment, but in the Gospel's spread. The Education Committee clarified that point when it noted that theirs was "an age peculiarly distinguished for intellectual and scientific improvement" in which education was "of the utmost importance for the universal spread of the glorious Gospel. . . ." Since hearers would be astute, the Gospel's spread required educated ministers. Agreeing that God "calls and qualifies" ministers, the committee could not believe "that ignorance of His word and works, constitute any part of that qualification." Citing the Apostles' "three years' course of instruction, under the Great Teacher" before being "endowed with wisdom from on high" and "entering fully into the great work," the committee further bolstered its point with allusions to the successes in other states and abroad, especially in Burma, "effected through the instrumentality of an educated ministry." To the end of having educated ministers, the committee recommended "that, as early as practicable, measures be adopted for the promotion of ministerial education in our own State."

Since their conception of education in all its facets aimed at prose-lytizing, education was merely the handmaiden of missions efforts—merely another means to the same end. What kind of mission efforts the Convention might consider reasonable occupied the committees on foreign missions and on destitution.

The Committee on Foreign Missions directed "the attention of the convention, associations, and Churches" to a "consideration of the claims which heathen lands hold upon us. . . ." The committee recommended "that plans may be devised, at as early a day as possible, to come up to the aid of our brethren in the Foreign Missionary enter-prise. . . ." The committee recognized the focus of the Convention's interest in missions when it qualified its recommendation with a request for action as soon as possible. The Convention's eyes might have been on missions, but were on concerns closer to home than "foreign shores."

The Committee on Destitution put forth the most compelling argu-ment for Convention resources, perhaps because it recognized that the Convention's treasure would follow where its heart already lay. M. M. Wallace reported for the committee that five thousand or fewer of the state's 150,000 population were Baptists, "and about one-half of that number opposed to all Missionary operations." Probably no more than fifty ministers stood "ready to co-operate with us" on missions. Saline Association, which issued the call for convention, had ten pastorless churches, and Liberty had several more. Eastward in the state, "where there was once a Baptist Association, there are nine Churches, without one ordained Minister within their bounds." In light of the crying need at home, the committee recommended "the speedy adoption" of measures best calculated to supply ministers for "our own."

Spurred by these reports, the actions of that first Convention indi-cated that attendees had not altogether wasted the time spent together during those two late-September days. Convention-goers dealt with the cooperative nature of their endeavor by stressing communication, without which their far-flung adherents would have found cooperation difficult if not impossible. They recommended to Baptists throughout the state the *Southern Baptist Missionary Journal* (Richmond), the *Southwestern Baptist Chronicle* (New Orleans), and the *Tennessee Baptist* (Nashville) as reasonable ways to maintain contact with Baptist missionary endeavors and with Baptist activities within the state. In addition, they authorized correspondence with Saline and Liberty Associations (to be taken by representatives to the next meetings of those entities) and elected three members (Bayliss, Smith, and Daniel) to attend the next Triennial Convention. Finally, they voted to print a thousand copies of the minutes for distribution, beginning with the *Southern Baptist Missionary Journal*, the *Southwestern Baptist Chronicle*, and the *Tennessee Baptist* and extending to the *Religious Herald* (Richmond) and particular individuals who might "spread the word."

In addition to communication, the delegates exhibited concern for proclamation. Believing that missions begins at home, the Convention ensured that the Word would be proclaimed there first. The group's "elder statesman," Edward Haynes, preached an introductory sermon from 3 John 2, and the delegates voted for President Bayliss to arrange preaching during the session. Accordingly, the Convention was treated to five Sabbath sermons: Obadiah Dodson preached at 9:00 A.M., Bayliss at 11:00 A.M. on missions, and an exhortation by I. C. Perkins followed Franklin Courtney's evening sermon. For the fifth, during the afternoon, G. W. Baines preached an ordination sermon for Samuel Stevenson at the special request of Stevenson's home church, Mt. Bethel (Clark County). As had been the case the previous year when Saline Association coupled its meeting with camp meeting, so the Convention followed suit. In what would become its pattern, its initial meeting coincided with a similar endeavor.

The Convention's attention also focused on finances. At Stevenson's motion on the second day, the delegates subscribed $830 in five annual installments for Convention use. In addition, they gathered an offering of $36.75 cash and $1,685 in subscriptions to be paid over five years for "Missionary purposes." Considering common ministerial comments on the difficulty of convincing Arkansas Baptists to give to worthy causes, this level of support for missions and for the new organization was exceedingly generous.

In keeping with the emphasis on missions displayed in the reports and in their own actions to this point, the delegates ordered Recording Secretary Asbury Daniel to write the Southern Baptist Home Mission Board (HMB) in Marion, Alabama, to "recommend M. M. Wallace to their patronage as a Missionary among us, to be assigned by the President and Secretary of this body." It was the perfect outcome—Wallace, who brought the issue of destitution forcefully to the Convention's attention in his committee report, was the agent of its solution.

The Convention's final official action offered thanks to local citizens for their hospitality. Yet that did not really complete its activity. President Bayliss penned a circular letter setting forth "the designs and objects of a State Convention." The interesting question at this point was how closely the circular letter, designed to answer the questions of Arkansas Baptists about the recently completed convention, matched reality.

Bayliss began his communication on the perfect note. Reminding readers that New Testament and Baptist principles called for independent and distinct churches operating under Christ's direction, Bayliss noted that amidst this diversity there should be "a oneness in sentiment and feeling," like the different strings harmonized on a well-tuned harp. The oneness should come, not from ecclesiastical coercion, but from "fraternal association, mutual instruction, and good example." The Convention should operate as the "common channel" through which the disparate churches could achieve "a concert of action, and a concentration of effort."

What should be the focus of this concerted action? The Convention's "first and leading object" was to supply preaching for the state's destitute regions and churches. Secondarily, as a result of this focus's activity, the Convention must be the agent for forming new churches. A tertiary object focused on circulating God's word, tracts and books, and promoting ministerial education. These activities provided the "proper information and instruction" necessary to combat error. Finally, "though remote" as an object, the Convention might "contribute our mite in sending the Gospel to the benighted nations of the world."

How did the Convention's reality match its originators' dreams? Attendance indicated that Saline Association in general and Brownsville

Church in particular took the call for a Convention seriously, and they wholeheartedly entered into the proposition. If any individuals could be credited with ensuring the Convention's success and that at least one more year would be in the offing, the trinity from Brownsville would qualify. Bayliss, Smith, and Daniel provided the call, a successful meeting and a record thereof, and played key roles on the board to sustain the effort for a year. Mrs. Bledsoe was not part of that effort; an illness, that not even a visit to Tennessee could cure, took her life in August before the Convention's inaugural meeting. Her spirit unquestionably lived on in the meeting and its aftermath; the piano she bequeathed to the Saline Association for missions was transferred to the new Convention, which used the $140 from its sale toward mission efforts.

The Convention's strength and its inaugural weakness coincided. A small group of individuals had, through personal connections, conceived of the need and a way to meet that need. They had used personal connections to gather like-minded individuals and recruit them to the cause. In an era when churches—like secular politics—were family-based, the reach of personal influence was severely limited. This attempt to found a statewide organization relied on similar connections. It drew few adherents from outside the founding association and none from outside the region in which the attempt took place.

Whether or not the newly formed Arkansas Baptist State Convention would be the "link in the great chain of operations, which is to unite us in love, strengthen us in usefulness, and make us efficient as a denomination" as Bayliss proclaimed in his circular letter, remained for the future to determine. Certainly the potential for denominational influence among the people thus spread out across the land of Arkansas seemed questionable. A pitiful few from a severely circumscribed area had answered a statewide call to cooperation. Aside from printing and distributing its minutes and suggesting what they considered good reading fare for Baptists interested in its opinion, the only lasting Convention action had been an appeal to the Home Mission Board for support for a missionary and the dispatch of an agent into the field to raise money.

The Convention's continued existence depended upon its ability to convince adherents that it could perform tasks impossible for any other entity, or at least that it could perform tasks better and truly become the "common channel" for concerted Baptist action envisioned by Bayliss in his circular letter. Were it, as P. S. G. Watson characterized the Union Association meeting of 1856, "entirely harmonious, yet but little attempted beyond the usual stereotyped round of meeting, preaching, noting the increase, declension, &c, of the past year," it would certainly soon cease to exist. What was needed, as the Dardanelle Association observed in 1854, was "some system or plan for the purpose of giving stability or formness to our operations."

5

Through the Civil War
1848–1865

FOR ITS FIRST TEN YEARS, THE ARKANSAS BAPTIST STATE
Convention sought to find itself and its mission, to define what it could
do that could not, or would not, be done by others. It began by discussing
and undertaking everything, an approach that prevailed until 1854. After
six years of what some characterized as futility, the Convention narrowed
its focus following severe questioning by several associations. Then, four
years later, the Convention finally established its identity with a charter
which marked the emergence of corporate as well as legal identity.

Part of the Convention's effort to establish its identity showed in the
pattern of its communications with others of "like faith and order." Until
1854, communication with other conventions continued the importance
indicated at the Convention's inauguration. In 1849, delegates again
exchanged representatives with the North Louisiana Convention. The
next year, delegates added the new White River Arkansas Baptist State
Convention and that of Texas along with Louisiana. In 1851, Arkansans
added the North Alabama and Tennessee General Association to their
conferees, an arrangement that lasted the single year. Louisiana, Texas,
and North Arkansas remained correspondents until, suddenly, in 1854
those correspondences disappeared from the minutes.

Activities other than communications attracted the Convention's
interest. Delegates that second year recommended the *Tennessee*

Baptist and the Southern Baptist Convention's Domestic Mission Board's *Missionary Journal,* asked Jesse Hartwell to write for the *Tennessee Baptist's* new Arkansas Department, and heard reports from ten committees ranging from education to finance.

The Committee on Education called for ministers to receive literary and theological training; that on foreign missions noted the millions of poor heathen and begged the delegates' prayerful consideration and support; that on Sunday Schools observed that their object advanced religion and improved public morals and urged support through public lectures and "other necessary means." The Committee on Bible Cause called for Bible societies in each association and colporteurs to sell Bibles cheaply or give them away if necessary; that on book distribution recommended titles needed "before their places are supplied by the literary trash of the present day." The committee on "the colored population" called for a missionary to be assigned to slaves in southern Arkansas, where owners would give assistance because they would thereby avoid undue influences of "unadvisable collections, or unlawful associations."

The most intransigent issue during that second session, and through the Civil War, involved money. Reporting on the first year of the State Convention's Executive Committee's work, Asbury Daniel highlighted fiscal conservatism when he said that "your Board have endeavored to act with some caution, being desirous not to incur debts, without a certain prospect of the ability to meet them; and thus embarrass" the Convention's future. Noting the need to "take courage and press onward," he stressed the "importance of liberality in the amount of donations, so that the Convention may be enabled to do the next year, at least double the labor of this."

As the Correspondence Committee had remarked in its call for the Convention's initial meeting, the Convention needed some method of raising funds and employing secretaries, agents, and missionaries— people who could give their undivided attention to the Gospel work. The Convention had elected an agent (I. C. Perkins) and an assistant (Samuel Stevenson) to secure money and a missionary (W. B. Knight) to spend it, and the body heard their reports in 1849. Committees on agency, finance, and the treasury recommended ways to raise the necessary money for Convention activities and reported that the treasury had handled $750 and had on hand $11 toward the new year's activities. Their reports boiled down to a recommendation that the Convention secure an agent who would undertake a five-year plan for raising money and that the Convention practice fiscal conservatism. Reports on how to spend what the agent raised were more revealing and daring. An emphasis on use rather than on resources remained a great institutional weakness.

W. H. Bayliss reported that "domestic affairs" had forced Perkins to resign as agent. When no one emerged to take Perkins's place, Bayliss had undertaken the task part-time. The assignment had not been easy: "Owing to the fact that the convention was a new thing to many of the brethren and churches in this State, some were disposed to look upon it with a suspicious eye and a few from old prejudices were openly opposed to it; consequently my main object has been to communicate correct knowledge as to its design and leading objects, do away all opposing and erronius [sic] prejudices, and unite the feelings of all the brethren in favor of the convention as their own domestic institution."

The economic timing of the Convention's founding had appeared fortuitous. The Panic of 1837 and its resultant economic downturn were only a memory. The Mexican War had ended, and Texas offered the opportunity to lure those traveling to the new lands into stopping and casting their lot in Arkansas instead. Baptists in the South in 1845 had broken with those from the North over the issue of allowing slave holders to serve as missionaries. The resulting Southern Baptist Convention would certainly prove more amenable to the needs of a slave state like Arkansas. Perhaps most important, the history of successful experience with an increasing number of associations indicated that Baptist cooperative endeavors found favor with the churches.

Despite the Convention's generous financial start, those who visited the churches as agents found raising money for missions or ministers tremendously difficult prior to the Civil War. Although such undertakings were more remunerative south than north of the Arkansas River, raising money in Arkansas Baptist churches was never easy. Agents and ministers offered four major reasons for the difficulty: people's poverty, thinly spread population, people's parsimony (a reflection of their emphasis on the present and their earthly condition), and the state's economy, which determined what return agents would find on their investment of time on the Convention's behalf.

The state's economy remained largely rural and agrarian. The land-based economy leaned increasingly on slavery and the plantation system. The change in settlement patterns between 1850 and 1860 shows the impact of that plantation system. The greatest rate of population growth appeared in the state's southern section, which the fledgling Convention served, as planters moved into the Ouachita River Valley and the Arkansas's Mississippi Delta. El Dorado formed the focus of the southern development, Pine Bluff and Helena toward the east. Those areas unfitted to farming by slave labor remained the regions of lesser population—the upper reaches of the Ouachita River on the western border, the north-central region, and the upper half of the St. Francis-Mississippi River triangle.

In part because of this population influx, the state's economy boomed as never before during the dozen years of the Convention's youth. That boom centered on railroads (and the speculation that surrounded them) and arable land. Both forms of investment and the growing economy meant that Arkansas would remain a money-scarce economic frontier throughout the pre-war era. In 1830, a Hempstead County minister discontinued his *Pastor's Journal* subscription because he found it "entirely impracticable to obtain Bills of a smaller amount than five dollars" with which to pay the $2 subscription. A Bradley County pastor in 1849 observed to J. R. Graves that "it is difficult to get a bill to send you" to pay for *Tennessee Baptist* subscriptions. Similar examples continued until wartime conditions ended the need to pay subscriptions.

The object of gathering money was to allow ministers to devote their whole attention to the Gospel. A western Tennessee Association in 1835 argued succinctly: If we pray the Lord of the harvest "to supply this destitution" by sending laborers, we must "show the sincerity of our prayers, by enabling those, already sent forth of the Lord, to give themselves wholly to the work. Let us give their wives and children bread, while they are absent, and thus relieve them from the necessity of daily labor at home, when they should be in the field." The struggle between "system men" and "individualists" over the money issue involved the question of ministerial support. Most Arkansas Baptist churches seemed to accept the idea of paying their pastor. Practice was often another matter. Sometimes churches were too poor; sometimes they were too parsimonious. Ministers differed in their assumptions about the matter. Though some adhered to one reason and some to another, in common with other Arkansas ministers, the Baptist brethren agreed that churches generally offered few pecuniary rewards.

Some ministers contended that Arkansans supported their ministers. From near Batesville, H. R. Hotchkiss mentioned his "prosperous church, a good meeting house and a prosperous country" in 1848. M. J. Green wrote from Yell County in 1850 that if they could secure a minister, they could keep him afloat after the first year. From Eutaw Springs, J. C. Wharton opined in 1853 that "if some of our ministering brethren would emigrate here, I believe they would be supported." Besides, he added, "provisions will be abundant and cheap." Writing from Madison County in 1854, C. H. Boatright praised a local congregation's giving the Reverend Lewis Heath $20 for a ten-day protracted meeting. Such liberality, he trumpeted, would free ministers "from a burden that they cannot now throw off." He then proceeded to use that lead-in to urge Tennessee ministers "of a pioneering spirit" to come to Arkansas, where "a fruitful soil will richly pay you for its tillage, and what time you have to labor, you will be abundantly repaid." "It is quite an easy matter in this country," he continued, "for any man that has sense enough to preach the gospel, to make a competent support for himself and his family; nay, to make earthly fortunes by his mechanism, or investing the earnings of a few years' labor in live stock, and turning their increase to advantage, which has been one great cause of so little having been done in North western Arkansas heretofore and too much now." Boatright concluded that "with what the churches will do for you, and the profits of your physical labor, you will not feel in such straightened circumstances."

N. P. Moore, hoping to lure ministers from Tennessee, Mississippi, and Alabama to Arkansas, wrote from Searcy in 1854 that "the people in Arkansas are willing and will sustain you," concluding "I have never found a people more generous and liberal." But only those "willing to suffer, and endure for Christ's sake," should come; "Men who can, 'mid winter's gloomy reign,' swim swollen creeks and bayous—ride under the parching rays of a summer's sun, preach to rough-looking, but honest and willing hearers, in a well ventilated log cabin, or can command the attention and respect of the more refined in our young and growing towns, such are the men Arkansas calls loudly for, and such will be handsomely sustained."

Even those ministers who touted congregational support in Arkansas agreed that Arkansas churches did not support their pastors adequately. The charitable, while admitting the lack of support, attributed it to circumstances. Obadiah Dodson noted from Ouachita County in 1848 that "the country is new and it is too early in the fall to collect much money for any religious purpose." Robert Pulley, writing from Bradley County in 1849, said that in the thinly settled country filled with newcomers, "Each one is doing his best to open himself a farm, and it is about as much as they can do to provide the necessaries of life. . . ." His church had "promised to afford me all the assistance she is able to do," but it was "a small Church numbering only about 10, and all of them . . . in only moderate circumstances." P. S. G. Watson, writing in 1856, noted that the Batesville Baptist Church still labored under the debt incurred when they built their church in 1851: "The debt is not *so large*," he observed, "but the members are *so poor*." In reporting on Cedar Grove during the previous year, Watson remarked that the pastor "received no stipulated salary, but receives such contributions as may from time to time be offered him. Indeed, this is true of the great majority of our churches throughout the State."

Some writers were not so charitable in their assessment of the causes of nonsupport for pastors. M. J. Green laid the lack of money for denominational efforts squarely on a "moral gloom" which permeated the Dardanelle area because citizens "are hard to extricate" from "the engrossing theme of money and general pursuits." And while Robert Pulley allowed that his congregation was doing its best in his support, that "best" was based on their lack of "the light and love of the widow with her two mites in Luke. . . ."

Longtime Arkansas pastor N. P. Moore questioned whether churches really supported their pastors. From Mt. Vernon in 1853, he averred that they did not because "There exists among the present ministry a pucillanimous [*sic*], instinctive dread, of having it thought that they preach for money; and therefore they are exceedingly particular to say nothing in the pulpit, that savors of the Almighty Dollar. In consequence of which they dwindle and starve. A man ought to starve, who, for fear of offending some over-sensitive, squeamish brother, whose heart is so contemptibly small and contracted, that you could not probe an opening sufficient to introduce anything, save a half-dime edge-wise, will disobey God!" Continuing in the same vein, Moore noted that it is the minister's duty to "tell them plainly 'tis her duty to support the Ministry—Foreign Missions, Domestic Missions, the Bible cause, and every institution that has for its object the salvation of death-less spirits, and the extension of the blessed kingdom of our Lord Jesus Christ. Encourage and enforce a spirit of liberality in your churches, my brother, and sir, just in proportion as that spirit is diffused and perme-ates the body of Christ, will their hearts become enlarged, their purse-strings loose and flexible, and the almighty dollar will roll in one continued silver stream into the treasury of the Lord." Any minister who lacks sufficient support lacks because of his "unfaithfulness as a steward of Christ."

The next year, Moore sounded a harsher variation on the same theme. Their "purse proud hearts . . . are so crusted and corroded with the gold and silver of earth, that even should they in an unguarded moment, in the generous magnanimity of their souls, . . . make a desperate struggle to extract a half dollar from their purses, the Eagle would surely be choked to death before it could escape from their deathless grasp!!" They should be a "willing people," for "surely the sustenance of the ministry . . . is a good work." And what about "the almost widow—the minister's wife"?

"An Observer" wrote in February 1855, about the great wrong of deception by churches. In a stinging indictment, the anonymous letter-writer looked at Baptist churches in Arkansas to "see how many of them have sustained a Pastor, though all or most of them promise to do so; yet, perhaps one in ten have done so." Churches concluded that preachers who expressed concern about money were "after the fleece and not the flock." In six years, one church had paid less than a hundred dollars for pastoral support. Pastors were "starved half to death and then finished by slander." To the argument that a "different class of preachers than we have—better educated, and better skilled in science, literature and theology" would be supported, he noted that Bayliss, Courtney, and Clements had left for "some other country where the prospect was better for a support, as they were starved out here. . . ." A number of those who would be useful ministers are "compelled to resort to other professions and employments for a support. Some to the school-room, some to the practice of physic, some to the clerkship, and not a few to the plow, all of whom would be delighted to have their hands loose, in order to prepare for and preach the everlasting Gospel of Christ, but find it impossible to preach regularly and support their families."

P. S. G. Watson, in writing about early Batesville pastors, noted that since the word pastor meant "the same as . . . elsewhere in the State— monthly preaching," two of the church's first four pastors (George W. Kennard and Watson himself) had supported themselves as teachers. T. L. Hay echoed Watson's words in mid-1857, hoping that more Baptist ministers would move to Arkansas: "They will be required to do as their *predecessors* have here and in other States—teach for a few years, and as schools are well sustained, Baptist ministers should be willing to teach for a short time; then, if *efficient men* they will be sustained as *Pastors*, and secure for their schools laymen of the church."

Writing from Clark County in 1857, Miles L. Langley observed that "numbers of ministers who, like the writer, desire to preach . . . are confined to secular pursuits" while destitute churches suffer. "If they would only call and support those ministers who have been driven by stern necessity from the work of the gospel ministry to various other callings," he wistfully remarked. "What an awful thought to be compelled to bury our talents for the want of opportunity to use them," he concluded. Echoing Langley's lament, "A Traveling Preacher" observed in 1858 that most churches had monthly preaching due to "the want of Pastors." Baptists, he concluded, "do not support their Pastors as well as other denominations, this is one cause why we do not have more ministers."

"A. L. H." wrote the *Tennessee Baptist* in 1856 to uphold the other side. Only one minister of his acquaintance, he reported, has surren- dered his call despite "reverses sufficient to divert the stouthearted from their work." That one gave up because "the brethren have failed to support him" though he is "quite an acceptable minister." While minis- ters already in the field may not surrender their call, the effect on young

Christians contemplating their future was another matter: "They see that in the Baptist church in Arkansas the pastors are not supported . . . and know that unless supported, they could not study and thus show themselves workmen that needed not to be ashamed. They know that the labors of the school-room are sufficient of themselves." "The churches in this State could have more than a score of pastors supplying them if supported," the letter averred, "—they do not ask a large support, no more than the Methodist and Presbyterian churches furnish their pastors." Many Baptist ministers do not receive $100 from four churches they serve, despite losing two days weekly from their fields going to and returning from their congregations, "A. L. H." continued, but like N. P. Moore he believed that the situation was the pastor's fault. He personally had found Arkansas Baptists very generous, and "among the wealthy of the State, occupying as high position as any in the State. Do they want office, they can be elected; and in building railroads, school-houses, and other improvements, Baptists of Arkansas are very active." The shameful outcome of it, he decided, was finding Baptist ministers "in schoolrooms, on their farms, or merchandising, while Methodist and Presbyterian pastors are exclusively devoted to their high calling." Baptist churches would support their ministers too, "if the subject is properly brought before them."

If Arkansas Baptists would not support ministers who worked in their midst, how could they be expected to support a distant agency like the State Convention? Some ministers, who counted themselves "system men" and upheld the Convention, proposed solutions to the monetary deficiencies of Arkansas Baptists. In 1852, Thomas H. Compere noted that planters generally cultivated about twenty acres to the slave. Let each planter set apart one acre per slave for religious purposes, "cultivate it just as he does his own, and take special care of the product, and sell it upon the best terms he can for cash, and never use that money for any thing but religion." The yeoman farmer should call himself a hand, and "set apart his acre"; the physician, lawyer, merchant, mechanic, blacksmith, shoemaker, "carpenter, and every one; let his occupation be what it may" should set aside a twentieth of his income. The result would "not impoverish any one, but will enable every one to do great good." "We are careful about being honest with our fellow men, and try to pay our debts," Compere observed; "then let us be honest with God, and pay this first of all debts." Nothing can be done so long as the brethren "wait for spare money." "We must have some system, before we can procure the means," he concluded.

P. S. G. Watson juxtaposed the lack of money with a social evil he decried when he urged the Independence Association in 1856 to adopt his plan to fund missionary work. "Is it religiously right," he queried, "for Baptists to spend more every year for *Tobacco* than for the support of the gospel ministry?" Assuming a negative answer, he proposed a resolution that association members "promise to pay quarterly, to the Treasurer of the Missionary Board, the same amount annually that we spend for *tobacco*." The resolution drew several interesting speeches, Watson remembered: "The delegates professed an ardent love for the cause of Domestic Missions, but when their eyes fell upon the working jaws of their brother delegates, their hearts appeared to fail them, but when they were cast to the floor, at their feet, the sight overcame their missionary ardor. . . ." The resolution garnered a single vote. Watson wondered when the time might come "that Baptists will give to the Lord as much as they puff into the air, or squirt upon the ground?" It was with disgust that he reported to the *Tennessee Baptist* that he found Arkansans able to "masticate from $10 to $40 worth of tobacco every year" and that Phillips County, small though it was, consumed $25,000 worth of tobacco annually—"Enough to pay the salary of the President of the United States!!"

The 1849 Convention's Committee on Destitution summed up the Convention's greatest need, the issue to which Bayliss had given greatest pre-eminence in his circular letter, and which had been cited as the Convention's premier concern in its constitution. The report warned that "many, very many churches, of our order, are not only without a supply, but almost entirely without occasional preaching— some of them able, some not able, to contribute to their own necessities, but all anxious and willing to be taken under the guardian care of the preached word." The issues of destitution and financial resources were sides of the same coin. Arkansas Baptists turned to missionaries to supply the general lack of ministers.

In calling for a Convention, the Correspondence Committee had said that the difference between an association and a Convention lay in the latter's method of raising funds and employing secretaries, agents and missionaries. It would be, the committee promised, a domestic mission society independent of or auxiliary to the Home Mission Board in Marion, Alabama. The circular letter after the Convention's inauguration stressed missions and education. How does the Convention compare with associations on these scores?

Associations remained the focus of Baptist cooperative life during the Convention's struggling early years. They fielded agents to collect money for mission endeavors and missionaries to provide preaching in the midst of destitution, helped define orthodoxy upon request, warned the population of unorthodox or errant ministers, and provided fellowship for the brethren at annual meetings.

Associations consistently fielded missionaries (who doubled as agents) where they could, hiring men to provide preaching within the association's bounds. Those boundaries generally took in large areas. Associations customarily reported fields that measured a hundred by fifty miles and incorporated five or six counties. As population density increased, the number of associations increased and the area of each decreased, but responsibilities remained about the same. Associational missionaries generally reported traveling about five hundred miles, preaching about a hundred sermons, and visiting about seventy-five families in a year. Every single Arkansas Association during these early years employed missionaries.

The Convention's search for identity had to take the nature of associational activity into account, but initially failed to do so. The Executive Board in 1849 reported two missionaries in the field, one above (J. Y. Lindsey) and one (G. W. Grimmett) in the southeastern counties below the Military Road, and a missionary to "the Blacks on Red River" (B. L. Wright). It then remarked on the extent of destitution (assistant agent Samuel Stevenson reported a church of twenty-six members which had been without preaching for two years) before closing by urging churches to seek out and advance the gifts among them, encourage aspiring young ministers to study and undergo "human training," and offer them donations of books to "add to their stock of knowledge."

The Convention's meeting with Mount Bethel church in Clark County in 1850 resembled the previous year's. Delegates again enlisted I. C. Perkins as agent (though extending his range to other states as well) and recommended reading material (this time the *Missionary*

Herald and the *Commission*, both from Richmond, though they ignored the *Tennessee Baptist*) to Arkansans. They planned four collectors—one each in Dallas, Union, Hempstead, and Saline Counties—to augment the agent's efforts at collecting money for Convention efforts. They heard about the Convention's five missionaries, including J. Matchet in the northwestern part of the state. Then they enjoyed reports from the same committees as before, which basically said the same things as before.

Reports concerned with procuring funds were limited to two, on the agency and the treasury. Again they recommended an agent (which the delegates secured) and revealed that Convention finances were precarious—they had taken in $555, paid out $225 for missionaries and minutes, and owed about $70 on the agent's $400 salary. In the course of the year, a hundred individuals had given an average of $5.15 each, though the gifts ranged from $.15 to $60, and two individuals had between them accounted for a fifth of that amount and a third had given $1 or less. The Convention's monetary support appeared broad but thin.

Committee reports on possible activities sometimes merely noted the need or some event without recommending a particular action. The Committee on Destitution reported that some who were forty and lived in southern Arkansas had never heard a Baptist preach; that on foreign missions noted Adoniram Judson's death. The committee concerned with Sunday Schools noted that "Ignorance is no longer regarded as the mother of devotion," for it "engenders infidelity, and leads to every form and degree of vice and immorality." It then ended with the information that the American Sunday School Union had established a book depository at New Orleans, and that Samuel Stevenson had a stock of their books at Arkadelphia which he sold at cost.

Four of the committees recommended particular actions. The Committee on the Colored Population recommended that each church have a committee of three or more to hold services for the slaves; that on the Bible cause recommended Bible societies, in at least each association, auxiliary to the American and Foreign Bible Society. The Committee on the Distribution of Books observed the need to circulate reading material that promulgated the Gospel, especially to "counteract the baneful influence of 'light reading,' which has already flooded our country, and which tends to skepticism, and consequent immorality." The only means of achieving the end, they reported, was a book depository and system of colporteurs.

The issue of education encompassed facets that sometimes overlapped: acquisition of the ability to read, who should be educated, how much education individuals (especially ministers) should acquire, and of what kind it should be. In addition, the issue concerned reading material and what was appropriate. Books or tracts for the unconverted might convert them, but how much more important was "the gift of a few valuable books to a faithful minister of the gospel?" As one Arkansas minister plaintively wrote to the *Tennessee Baptist* the year the Convention formed, "I once had a fine library, but was taken sick on the road to the west, and had to sell my books to pay my way, and never have been able to purchase any more. I would be glad to have Fuller's Works, and some other good books."

Fuller's Works was on the State Convention's "approved list," adopted at the 1849 meeting and published in its minutes, along with Benedict's *History of the Baptists*, Hinton's *History of Baptism*, Howel on Communion and on the deaconship, Carson on baptism, the *Comprehensive Commentary*, the *Psalmist*, the *Companion* "and the other baptist [*sic*] works as circulated by the Southern and Tennessee publication Societies." It was important that books of "right character and of religious influence" be circulated immediately, the Convention agreed, "before their places are supplied by the literary trash of the present day. . . ."

The 1850 committee which recommended the most far-reaching activity was that concerned with ministerial education. Its Committee on Education had recommended to the 1849 Convention meeting that young men entering the ministry "gain information both literary and theological" in preparation for their ministry. This year's committee prepared a more thorough report. It realized that the "peculiar truths of our denomination" had arrayed against them "much of the learning and wisdom of the world" in an unequal contest "between error supported by intelligence, where truth is unaided by education." The committee feared that the world could "propigate [*sic*] error under the cloak of truth" while Baptists were unable to "strip it of its borrowed covering and expose the sophisms upon which it is based." Claiming that "high

intellectual culture and moral discipline" prepared men to proclaim the
Gospel, and expanding on the Sunday Schools Committee's assertion
that "Ignorance is no longer regarded as the mother of devotion" and
that on the contrary it "engenders infidelity, and leads to every form and
degree of vice and immorality," the committee recommended that associations and churches aid those they set apart for the ministry in the
search for education. It further recommended that the Convention
appoint a committee of five to submit a plan at the next session to found
a "Seminary for the education of her Ministry."

In light of the Convention agent's report and that of the Executive
Board, both of which followed the committees, the idea of founding a
seminary seemed unnecessary and grandiose. The agent, who collected
only about $150 more than his salary, blamed a variety of causes for the
poor showing: the extensive area involved and the travel entailed;
protracted winter and spring rains which inhibited travel and agricultural work; the state's "general pecuniary embarrassment;" bad publicity
attendant on the exclusion of several prominent Baptist ministers; "and,
especially, the manner in which missionary funds have, in some cases,
been collected and expended, aside from the operations of the
Convention." The agent plaintively observed that if the Convention
could have even the "small sum of ONE DOLLAR" from each
Missionary Baptist in South Arkansas, it would have over two thousand
dollars. Finally, the report concluded that "Most of our churches are
asking for more ministerial labor, while many of our most acceptable
preachers, find it necessary to labor elsewhere for a support. Not one,
perhaps, within our bounds, obtains a support from churches. . . ."

Baptist schools—or at least schools operated by Baptist ministers—
were already in existence (the prospectus for Samuel Stevenson's
Arkadelphia Institute even appeared appended to the Convention's
minutes, though unmentioned by any committee) and flourished or
languished without Convention intervention. Churches were unable or
unwilling to support pastors. With these conditions and the difficulties
raising money for Convention purposes exhibited in this report, a
Convention committee's recommendation to build a college certainly
seemed beyond reason's realm.

The Executive Board's report darkened rather than lightened the
possibility of enacting the committee's recommendation for a college.

One missionary was ill; the other four had been able to spend only about a third of the year laboring for the cause. Outreach hampered by illness, bad weather, and insufficient funds painted a picture of disarray. The board's recommendation for a contraction of their number, and their selection from the same region because of sparse attendance at meetings, did nothing to counter that impression. The Convention's 1850 meeting did nothing to prompt optimism.

The sense of disarray in Convention efforts grew in part out of the Convention's unfocused approach to discovering its identity. Another part of the scene was the conflict inside and outside the Convention among various Baptist factions. The State Convention's pre-war story would be that of a struggle between "system men," who believed that God's work in Arkansas could best be done by concerted effort under some centralized system, and "individualists," who clung to the Hardshell tradition of each church carrying out its own individual efforts under God's direction without hindrance or help from hierarchy or organization.

That contention might be the result of principle, be economically based, or be some mixture of the two. Cephas Washburn, a Presbyterian minister writing from Bentonville in 1844, noted Hardshell opposition to "all societies" and their willingness to "excommunicate from the church and depose from the ministry" any member who joined any society. In 1846 he again noted their opposition, observing this time that they opposed any religious institution that costs money, or "as they themselves express it, that 'moves on silver wheels.'"

The struggle between "system men" and "individualists" over principle would also involve Campbellites on the outside and the Landmark Movement within. The Campbellites had been active in Arkansas almost as long as the Baptists. Their easy grace (regeneration through immersion) struck denominational opponents as an "insidious course" and certainly one attractive to many Arkansans.

As Campbellites had their trinity of founders (John Taylor the writer, Daniel Parker the preacher, and Alexander Campbell the synthesizer and popularizer), the Landmark Movement had its own. James Madison Pendleton, at the time pastor at Bowling Green, Kentucky, penned "An Old Landmark Reset"; Amos Cooper Dayton served as corresponding secretary of the Southern Baptist Convention Bible Board in Nashville from 1854 to 1858; and James Robinson Graves, through his writing as *Tennessee Baptist* editor and his preaching, became the soul of the Landmark Movement after its incipience at Cotton Grove and then in the Big Hatchie (Tennessee) Association meeting in 1851. Adherents would call them "the Great Triumvirate."

Like Campbell, J. R. Graves adopted the reformer's posture. The thirty-one-year-old editor and preacher clarioned that Baptists had departed from the "old landmarks" of the faith. The first "landmark" recognized the local church as the visible expression of God's Kingdom. The second "landmark" celebrated the "Trail of Blood" by which Baptist churches could trace their lineage to New Testament times. By this, the "Landmarkers" meant historical (organizational) rather than mere doctrinal succession, a stand which to their minds superseded apostolic or episcopal succession. The third "landmark" acclaimed "closed" communion, restricting the ordinance to local church members rather than even adherents of the denomination. The fourth commanded rejection of "pulpit affiliation" (a stand which would allow only Baptists to occupy Baptist pulpits) and "alien immersion" (a stand which recognized only baptisms by Baptist ministers as legitimate). This last was, for Graves and most of his followers, the summation of their stand, the culminating "landmark." Since authority to baptize comes only from a New Testament church, and since only Baptists are New Testament churches, only Baptists have the proper mode (immersion), administrator (representative of a New Testament church), subject (consenting believer), and meaning (symbolic) for the ordinance.

The sense of disarray in the Convention's search for identity during the 1850s came from competition within Regular Baptist ranks as well as from factional disputes and a lack of focus. That competition was geographical in nature and involved first one, then two rival conventions.

In April 1850, J. C. Brickley wrote J. R. Graves from Batesville. Admitting that the few Batesville Baptists were "looked upon as a low ignorant set of people" at least in part for their lack of a meeting house, he advised that they would nonetheless host a convention, "commencing the Friday before the 4th Sabbath" in July. The meeting's object was to organize all Baptist churches north of the Arkansas River that were "friendly to the mission cause" into a unit for a stronger effort to spread "the true Gospel in our destitute land." Then Brickley revealed that organizers viewed this as only an intermediate step to a larger goal: "if we can get the churches in the North to work, it will not be long until we can get the whole State into one general missionary body. . . ."

The organization of the White River Arkansas Baptist Convention (also called variously the Northern Baptist Convention of Arkansas, the Baptist Convention for Northern Arkansas, the Northern Arkansas State Convention, or simply the North Arkansas Convention) reflected a number of realities about the state and Baptist influence therein.

The state's geography fostered division rather than unity. The Arkansas River bisected the state and offered a formidable obstacle to those traversing the Southwest Trail or trying in any other way to move northeast or southwest through it. East-west travelers found mountains north and south of the Arkansas (except at the extreme southern part of the state), and major rivers tended to flow northwest to southeast, into the Mississippi.

Settlement patterns, following geography, likewise tended toward division rather than unity, at least in part because the traditional east-west routes were not followed for Arkansas as they had been east of the Mississippi and as they tended to be beyond the state. The northeast drew settlers from northern regions, the southwest from southern regions. North of the Arkansas, residents tended toward connections with Missouri, especially St. Louis; south of the Arkansas, residents looked toward Louisiana and Texas. Cultural differences showed themselves across the river just as did geographical ones.

With differences in geography and culture came differences in Baptist influences. Northeast Arkansas had ties with Missouri and Kentucky, and back through them to the more northern and north-eastern Baptist influences with their emphasis on society rather than association organization. Campbellites would be stronger north than south of the river; Graves's Landmark Movement would be just the reverse. South of the Arkansas River was more closely tied to the more southern and southeastern Baptist influence.

The results of that difference between north and south of the river were patently manifest. American Baptist Home Mission Society missionaries generally served north of the Arkansas River. Of the twelve appointed prior to the Civil War, only one was assigned to any territory south of the river—John McCarthy's initial field was Pulaski and Saline Counties, which after a year became Pulaski and White. Only one, George W. Baines, eventually wound up on the southern side and only he participated in the Arkansas Baptist State Convention. The society continued its Arkansas efforts even after the Southern Baptist Convention was formed, maintaining John McCarthy and Henry McElmurry until 1849 in endeavors above the river.

Reciprocity of good feelings between those north of the Arkansas River and Northern Baptists also was evident. In December 1851, the White River Arkansas Baptist Convention's Board of Managers noted by resolution "that we feel thankful that our brethren of the Triennial Convention has [sic] recognized us as a missionary society and expressed a willingness to aid us in every good work of the Lord" and also proceeded to "sanction the doings of the Triennial Baptist Convention."

Northern Baptists might have largely confined their efforts to lands north of the river, but the fledgling Southern Baptist Convention considered all of Arkansas home territory. Though Home Mission Board missionaries tended to serve in the south, all parts of the state profited from the Southern Baptist Convention's ministrations. Less than a year after praising the Triennial Convention's efforts through its society, the White River Arkansas Baptist Convention expressed its "tender thanks" to the "Domestic Mission Board in Marion" for its "liberal support." The White River Executive Board consistently notified Marion when selecting their missionaries and always noted their hope that the Marion board would assist their efforts.

Differing Baptist influences were not confined to missionary efforts. Reports to denominational papers eastward from Arkansas show the same kind of division: Kentucky carried mainly news from the state's northern, Alabama from its southern region. Since Arkansas Baptists had no denominational paper until shortly before the Civil War, and only intermittently for some time thereafter, J. R. Graves's *Tennessee Baptist* (under whatever name it appeared at any given time) reported news north and south (as it would for Louisiana and Mississippi and on occasion for Missouri as well), since Graves sought to make his paper the official Baptist organ in the West.

The last and most significant reality about Arkansas Baptists reflected in the White River Arkansas Baptist Convention's organization is that while Arkansas Baptists might agree on the importance of missions and of the need to cooperate in some organizational fashion to promote the missions cause, the numbers, backgrounds, and geographical distribution of Arkansas Baptists made united action a chimera in the pre-war era.

The White River Arkansas Baptist Convention originated two years after the Arkansas Baptist State Convention. Both were missions organizations and both sought statewide influence, though their "friendly rivalry" allowed the two to exchange communications in 1850–1851. The White River's story was short and sad. High waters and extreme cold depressed attendance at the first fall meeting; "God sent a pestilence among the people with great afflication [*sic*] so that the officers of the Board & Members of the Convention are unable to leave their families & go so great a distance" to attend the second. By the third, the White River had suffered a defection.

At the White River's 1852 meeting, Recording Secretary John Bateman of Helena offered a resolution. He noted that the White River's territory "is so exceedingly large and naturally divided by rivers, lakes and bays, as to render it wholly impracticable for the brethren living at the remote boundaries to assemble together, and cooperate effectively in carrying out the great fundamental principles and objects of the convention." "Reliable information and tests of experience" had convinced him that the objects could "be best promoted by two separate and distinct bodies." Thus he proposed to "dissolve our connection with the White River Arkansas Baptist Convention, and organize ourselves into a body, styled, 'The General Association of Eastern Arkansas'. . . ." The new convention's territory lay between the Arkansas River and the Missouri line north and south, and the Mississippi and Black Rivers east and west (drawing the line from Jacksonport on the Black to Little Rock via Searcy). The resolution carried without dissent, and the new convention selected William M. Lea to draft rules of decorum and serve as a vice-president (the other being Mark Izard).

The White River Convention and the new Eastern Arkansas shared much with the Arkansas Baptist State Convention, though they had effectively divided the state among them. All three resulted from the strong missions and organizing impulses among Arkansas Baptists. All three concerned themselves with the state's dearth of presentations of the Baptist brand of God's message (or as each called it, the state's destitution). The Eastern Arkansas even resolved to "send the Macedonian cry to our brethren abroad, 'Come over the Mississippi and help us.'"

That the White River's strength was ebbing away was evident at the board meetings. Some adjourned for want of a quorum; the secretary reported at one that the board was "likely to fall short of means to pay the traveling ministers," and all society members "should consider themselves not only as bound to set an example of liberality, but also to use the whole weight of their influence and everything to procure the necessary funds to carry on an enterprise in which the whole Southwestern Baptist churches have united which is the offspring & under the entire control of a convention in which the whole are represented. . . ."

At its fall 1852 meeting, the heart seems to have gone out of the White River folks. President Henry McElmurry left the November meeting spitting up blood and died soon after the new year. Board meetings lacked quorums through 1853, then the minutes went into hiatus. The last minutes, in November 1856, noted the appointment of seven missionaries for 1857.

The White River's defection, the Eastern Arkansas, never gathered great strength and soon joined it in oblivion. Perhaps the Panic of 1857, a sharp, brief economic downturn that affected industrial more than agricultural and urban more than rural areas, helped doom the White River and its sister convention north of the river. Railroad speculation helped produce and was at the heart of the Panic, and "railroad fever" unquestionably infected the state. Personnel departures certainly played a part in the demise of the conventions north of the Arkansas. Mark W. Izard, one of the Eastern Arkansas's first vice-presidents, left the state in 1855. Perhaps the defection of key individuals to the southern convention was cause, perhaps effect. P. S. G. Watson and George W. Kennard from the White River and William M. Lea from the

Eastern Arkansas first appear on the Arkansas Baptist Convention's rolls in 1856.

Certainly the appearance in 1858 of J. M. Houston and C. H. Boatright from the White River and W. B. Johnson and J. V. Cross (almost certainly the same individuals on the Eastern Arkansas Executive Board) and that of T. S. N. King from the Eastern Arkansas and Spencer Hall from the White River in 1859 signal those conventions' end. The appearance after the war of J. W. Miller, John Hicks, John Q. Taylor, A. Jackson, Lewis Heath, A. S. Brown, Jasper Dunagin, and John Pierce from these two defunct entities (including all but one of the seven missionaries appointed by the White River for 1857) testifies to the new legitimacy of the Arkansas Baptist Convention's claim to statewide status.

The Arkansas Baptist State Convention's 1851 meeting did not change the spirit exhibited at its 1850 meeting or its sense of disarray. The formation of the White River took its toll. Jesse Hartwell's introductory sermon from Luke 19:17 on the faithful servant's reward prompted one hearer to note that "the old preacher stood the earnest advocate of his master's cause" and symbolized the difference between this world and the next. The faithful servant received ten cities; "this poor and aged preacher was deprived of his home, by the cupidity of a *steamboat Captain*."

The 1851 Convention's committees followed their predecessors' footsteps. That on foreign missions called for prayer support for missionaries in Canton and Shanghai, China; that on temperance decried the sale of $250,000 worth of beverage alcohol in Arkansas annually. The Committee on Domestic Missions warned that the Convention should only undertake what could be permanently maintained. That on the Bible Cause urged meeting the needs of southern Arkansas, and the one on the Colored Population recommended circulation of two prize-winning essays. The Sunday School Committee eschewed a lengthy report in favor of a notice that many Arkadelphia Institute students "have been hopefully converted to God. If instead of visiting on God's holy day, professing christians [sic] were engaged as Sunday School teachers such like results might frequently occur."

The Committee on Ministerial Education, so voluble the previous year, satisfied itself with the assertion that words are the weapons of a soldier of the cross, that the "efficient soldier" knows "the powers and uses of the weapons of his warfare," that churches should support the newly called in acquiring knowledge, and that the Arkadelphia Institute and the Mine Creek Seminary offered young ministers free tuition. The minutes revealed nothing of the previous year's interest in founding a college.

Certainly the Convention's descent showed in the report of the Committee on Agents, which recommended not having an agent and relying instead on ministers, deacons, or some other layman where there was no pastor. That of the Executive Board revealed even more. Three years earlier, the board confessed promptness and liberality among donors had prompted expansion of the Convention's interests and activities. Now the Convention was over-extended, over $400 in debt. It faced the "painfully embarrassing condition of our Treasury— the low state of religion in our churches—the great pecuniary embarrassment throughout our State. . . ."

Having accomplished nothing, and having no recommendations for real action before it, the Convention resolved to think about a Baptist paper for Arkansas, commend J. R. Graves and recommend his paper to Arkansans, and request that the Southern Bible Board send missionaries to Arkansas. Delegates then adjourned hoping for a better meeting at Mine Creek the next year.

The Convention's 1852 meeting proved no better. The Committee on the Colored Population urged a monthly meeting for servants, and that on Bible Revision regretted to find opposition among professed Christians and intelligent Baptists to a revision which would translate all the words into plain English and change errors in translation. If we can translate Scripture for the heathen, the committee wondered, why not for ourselves?

Education and money took center stage in 1852, but touted advances came from quarters other than the Convention. The Red River Regular Baptist Education Society made its presence known, provided money for a young minister's pursuit of studies, and heard the Convention agree to include the society's minutes with its own. Convention delegates saw demonstrated what the Convention could and should do but would not.

Why the Convention did not make such progress became clear in Samuel Stevenson's address on domestic missions ("the claims of the

Gospel at home"). Taking as his text Proverbs 1:23, Stevenson reproved his hearers—though he was "preaching to the choir" at the meeting—and, more importantly, his readers (his remarks became part of the minutes). Churches say "shepherd, be ye clothed and be ye fed" to their ministers but do not match actions to sentiments. Instead, "complaints, objections and criticisms come thick and fast, if they are not interested and edefied [*sic*] by monthly sermons prepared at the plow handle, in the school room, or on an ox cart." We should consider our Christian obligations, he thundered. And what of the "legitimate offspring of the Baptist denomination in South Arkansas," that "child of promise" called our "infant Convention"? Should it not too be supported?

Stevenson knew the answer to his rhetorical question. If churches were not supporting their ministers, they certainly would not support the Convention. The Executive Board's report bore out that truism. The Convention had no agent, it admitted, and the board met irregularly (due to high water). But it had adhered rigidly to the "no debt" principle, believing that debt would destroy the Convention. "We regret that we have not been able to affect anything," it lamented, "but as we have no means, it could not be reasonably expected of us." The Convention found itself caught between unacceptable alternatives; it could not accept indebtedness but without debt it could not "affect anything." Unfortunately, even with debt it could not undertake any real action, for the Convention was still in debt despite its care to incur no more.

The 1853 Convention meeting in Camden seemed to mark an upswing in the Convention's fortunes. Delegates memorialized Congress to provide for "security of free toleration in religious worship" in all treaties. The Executive Board reported that the Convention was almost debt-free thanks to the efforts of an agent willing to take a salary of only a dollar a day, and that such a positive move had occurred while two missionaries (A. J. Smith and T. H. Compere) labored in the vineyard. Seeking to take advantage of the Convention's bettering pecuniary situation, the Committee on Foreign Missions recommended that Convention agents also collect for the Southern Baptist Convention's Foreign Mission Board (FMB) to aid missionaries in Burma and China.

The upswing was more apparent than real. The Committee on Domestic Missions reported destitution in Ouachita, Union, Columbia,

Lafayette, Hempstead, and Clark—indeed, in all counties. The Committee on Bible Revision revealed the presence of dissension when its long report repeated previous sentiments but went on to observe that "These and other opinions may prevail, and each may advocate his own sentiments *freely*, and allow his brother the same privilege." Baptists should eschew bitterness and anger, harsh and abusive epithets and ascription of motives "utterly inconsistent with christian [*sic*] integrity," it warned.

It was in the Ministerial Education Committee's report that the depths of the Convention's descent lay revealed. The report abandoned all pretense of fostering a Baptist college in Arkansas. Louisiana Baptists were undertaking such a feat near Arkansas's southern border at Mt. Lebanon. William H. Bayliss moved from Tulip and Franklin Courtney from El Dorado to Mt. Lebanon in 1850, succeeding the departing George W. Baines, all of whom had strong ties to the Arkansas Baptist State Convention. Although they were not the only individuals involved in Mt. Lebanon University's origins, their involvement certainly brought it to their old Convention's attention. Within four years, the new university was conducted by Jesse Hartwell, long-time teacher and pastor who had been a charter teacher at Furman Theological Institution, at Howard College, and most recently at the Camden Female Institute.

In addition to Mt. Lebanon University, the report mentioned a college being built up in Little Rock (St. John's, started and maintained throughout its existence by Arkansas Masons—though the Baptists did not mention the name or affiliation). It was, the committee reported, an endeavor with which Baptists had no wish to interfere. Indeed, the denomination would be proud to be permitted standing as a coworker in this undertaking for which the committee wished every success.

Following this "tip of the hat" to the unnamed college and its unnamed benefactors, the Ministerial Education Committee remarked that Arkansas Baptists needed "a theological institution at some convenient place within our reach, and we respectfully suggest Mount Lebanon as being the place . . ."—between the Arkansas and the Red Rivers on a "contemplated" railroad which would ensure easy access in all seasons. The resolutions the committee offered, and which the Convention accepted, included not only a commitment to cooperate in the new school, but also to invite the university's agent into Arkansas churches to canvass for funds.

While the 1853 Convention indicated the organization's downward spiral, nothing could match the next year's meeting. That gathering marked, as nothing else officially reported ever could, the Convention's pre-war nadir. The Convention seemed to have come full circle, figuratively and literally. When delegates gathered at Tulip for the Convention's seventh anniversary, they gathered on the last Saturday in—indeed, the last day of—September at the place it had all started. Attendance was poor; three associations and five churches sent delegates, eleven individuals joined the mix, and one lone visitor registered with the secretary.

The meeting began on a hopeful note. Samuel Stevenson's introductory sermon, from John 15:7, dwelt on God's promise to those who abide in Him that He would abide in them; the delegates selected Jesse Hartwell and Samuel Stevenson president and secretary respectively, each for the fourth time. The usual organizational assignments took place; ten committees were appointed and the normal manager and officer selection occurred. Then the Convention adjourned until Monday morning at 9:00.

Hartwell, N. P. Moore, and J. V. McCulloch preached the typical three Sunday sermons the next day, though Hartwell's sermon on missions lasted only "two brief hours." To that point, everything seemed normal. When Hartwell called the meeting to order Monday morning, nothing seemed awry. John Aaron opened the session with prayer at the president's request. The Committee on Arrangements reported and the usual progression of reports seemed to have started.

What seemed to have begun halted abruptly. Two of the three associations represented in the meeting offered separate suggestions. The Red River Association suggested that the Convention temporarily suspension operations. The Saline Association, at whose call the Convention had been founded in 1848, suggested that the Convention disband, dissolve in favor of another, new organization.

Delegates spent the day "fully and freely" discussing these suggestions. Organizational and financial problems had plagued the Convention's efforts. Small numbers, especially of ministers; the departure of much needed leaders; questions of focus; competition from two other missionary organizations hoping to become statewide in scope; opposition from within and without; inadequate funding for every effort undertaken—problems had arisen at every turn and seemed to overwhelm the infant Convention. Nothing they had undertaken as an effort seemed to have enjoyed any success. The Convention seemed, in the vernacular of the time, "snake bit," unlucky and doomed to failure.

The associations' proposals seemed to be efforts to salvage whatever could be salvaged from an untenable situation. The Red River approach was more charitable. It merely offered a breather, time to regroup and regain some strength before moving on again. The Saline Association's suggestion was more radical, less forgiving. Rather than throw good money after bad, they seemed to say, Baptists in South Arkansas should just start anew.

Through the morning they discussed and debated. The usual midday recess came and went, ignored as delegates expressed warm devotion for, and grave concerns about, the Convention's past, present, and future. As discussion lengthened, delegates reached consensus on several matters: the Convention's problems lay in its fiscal situation, and even advocates for dissolution expressed attachment to the idea of organization and cooperative ventures. Some delegates left, put off by such a discussion and display of a lack of harmony and unity. The faithful remained, determined to see the crisis through, whatever the outcome.

By mid-afternoon, the few remaining delegates had decided the issue. Secretary Samuel Stevenson summarized the decision with the biblical observation and admonition "If God be for us, who can be against us?" Despite previous reservations, perhaps because of a long discussion that had proceeded, under Hartwell's careful oversight with remarkable equanimity, delegates decided to continue the Convention's work in its present form for at least another year. Whether or not convinced of future success, delegates were convinced that their commitment required more than words. Those present pledged $340, payable in six months, for Convention causes. The secretary carefully noted that former advocates for dissolution were among the most liberal in their subscriptions.

The meeting continued briefly, for delegates adopted the Nominating Committee's report, referred other committee reports to the Executive Board (which they instructed to meet at Princeton in

December and at Tulip in May), made provision for the next annual meeting at Princeton, and adopted several traditional resolutions (including a heartfelt thanks to Hartwell for his "kind, courteous and Christian manner" in presiding) before singing, praying, and adjourning.

Committee reports from the 1854 meeting reveal little of that day's momentous discussion except by indirection. The Committee on Foreign Missions, as usual, mentioned China and translations of Holy Writ for other tongues; that on temperance held out at length before resolving that the Convention would rejoice to see the license law repealed and liquor sold only for "Sacramental, medical and mechanical reasons." These reports were unexceptional and might have appeared any other year. All the rest were different; all the rest indirectly dealt with the heart of the Convention's problems.

Every other committee report dealt with money. The Committee on Domestic Missions compared the previous year's collections (over $3,200) with the low point of 1852 ($90 collected) when the Convention had neither agent nor missionary in the field; the Committee on Duties to Servants tersely noted that limited resources meant that "no satisfactory provision can be made for supplying this much neglected portion of our population." The Committee on Book Distribution recommended establishing a fund as quickly as possible to supply books—and mentioned in passing, though pointedly, that Samuel Stevenson could furnish or order books of every kind and sold Sunday School books at cost. Most importantly, the Committee on Agencies recommended that the Convention make "one united effort" and employ an agent. Let the agent collect for all Baptist endeavors, though especially for the Convention.

The appearance of unity with which the 1854 meeting closed was illusionary. The two associations which raised such serious questions about the Convention failed to return. The lack of minutes for 1855 and the failure of any account in the *Tennessee Baptist* obscures most of that meeting's story. Location and those chosen in 1854 to preside or preach are known quantities, but attendance is another matter. But the minutes that remain for 1856 and 1858–1860 reveal that Red River sent no delegates again until 1859, and Saline did not reappear before the war.

Another certainty about this pivotal 1854 meeting is that the day-long discussion about the Convention and its future served to focus the

thinking of those "system men" who were committed to the Convention
and its future. Competition from those conventions north of the
Arkansas River continued to restrict attendance and, therefore, vision.
Associations competed with Convention activities and seemingly felt
fewer promptings to send their own delegates; only two were represented at the 1856 meeting. But that same 1856 meeting indicated that
the stalwarts who carried the Convention forward had caught a glimpse
of the future.

Meeting with the New Hope Church in Dallas County in 1856, the
Convention assembly decided to continue the pattern set two years
earlier. Under the direction of President Jesse Hartwell, delegates
decided to discuss two items in a committee of the whole: the propriety
of establishing a "Denominational School of high character" and a state
denominational newspaper. After two hours of deliberation, Hartwell's
"indisposition" caused him to surrender the chair to Aaron Yates. Two
and a half hours later, the group had come to some important decisions.

First, they resolved to recommend that the Executive Board hire
three agents to "raise a Ministerial Education Fund" as well as money
to establish a "Denominational Male School of High Character in the
State." Second, they recognized that the associations were already
dealing with home and foreign missions, temperance, the colored population, and book circulation. There was no need to duplicate effort or
engage in any competition in those areas, so they would be dropped
from Convention consideration. Third, the Convention resolved to
"devote all our time and means" to education—though the Executive
Board was to instruct its agents to solicit subscriptions for a denominational newspaper, with the subscriptions payable upon receipt of the
paper's first issue.

The decision to concentrate all their efforts on education through
founding a school and a newspaper was assuredly a good one. The
problem lay in how they would raise the necessary funds. The Executive
Board reported that T. H. Compere had agreed to act as agent for $500,
but only if he could collect that amount. Since there were no funds, the
board had not employed a missionary so as not to incur any debt.
Compere admitted that the difficulties had been many and opposition
great, especially since many associations had chosen to carry out
domestic missions within their boundaries. As a result, he had lacked

almost $137 collecting his own salary. The decision may have been a good one, but the determination required money to carry out. That obstacle seemed insurmountable.

The next year's annual meeting, with the Samaria Church four miles west of Tulip, concerned itself with the specifics of the Convention's commitment to education. Unfavorable weather plagued the meeting, but delegates gathered and discussed at length just what their previous year's decision might mean. W. M. Lea, elected president that year, had confidently predicted, "The work can be done—we have the means." In the previous four years, he noted, Arkansas Baptists had increased about 300 percent.

Perhaps the delegates came already convinced; perhaps Lea's enthusiastic optimism infected their deliberations. Either way, by the meeting's end, delegates had concluded to build a first-class college. Looking toward that goal, they voted to establish an endowment fund of $100,000. As an inducement to give, they decreed that each hundred dollars subscribed would entitle the donor to a vote in selecting the school's location. In addition, delegates agreed that the ministerial education fund, mentioned as part of the previous year's proposed package, would be established. They attached no specific price tag to that endeavor, but did ask that agents gather funds to that end.

The delegates also determined to have a denominational paper. The previous year's decision, exploratory and tentative as it had been, led to more concrete decisions in 1857. Moving on to specifics, they purposed to publish the paper in Camden, for two dollars annual subscription price, with R. M. Thrasher and A. L. Hay in charge. Those two, they agreed, would assume all responsibility once the denomination had purchased a press. No matter how important they thought the newspaper, the delegates were unwilling to saddle the Convention with such a financial obligation—though they did want the Convention to retain as much control of the undertaking as possible.

Just as the Convention's 1854 meeting had proven pivotal—a brush with organizational death avoided and a future course seemingly charted—so that of 1858 proved likewise. It was, in many ways, a second birth for the Convention. Attendance soared in 1858, and significantly the associations returned: Bartholomew, Caddo River, Caroline, Dardanelle, Fayetteville, Judson, and Mt. Vernon all sent delegates.

The list indicated the demise of the conventions north of the river and the Arkansas Baptist State Convention's resulting spread beyond the confines of its origins.

More than just attendance increased. The Convention's decision to concentrate its efforts on education—as embodied in the founding of a male college and of a state denominational newspaper—struck a responsive chord with the denomination. The Executive Board reported that agent W. R. Trawick had collected $21,465 in bonds (ranging from $10 to $1,000) for the college and almost $75 in cash for the Convention's use. Collections taken up at the meeting raised nearly another $5,000 for the college and a few dollars more for missions. Clearly those Baptists visited by the agent supported the new focus.

The promise of funds emboldened the delegates. P. S. G. Watson reported that plans for the newspaper had proceeded apace despite some changes from the previous year, with bids from publishers (the best came from Helena and Little Rock) in hand and decisions on size, format, price ($2.00 annually in advance), and name (the *Arkansas Baptist*) made. T. B. Van Horne, pastor and principal of the Fayetteville Institute, presented the report on the proposed college.

Van Horne proceeded from the proposition that Baptist polity "individualizes" members more than that of any other denomination, making education for lay members as important as that of ministers. All must be prepared for the "conflict between truth and error, now raging fiercely," prepared for "leadership in defence [sic] of Truth." The conflict, Van Horne warned, lay between radical enemies—the Baptists at one extreme and the Roman Catholics at the other. Essentially antagonistic in church polity and principles, these two contested for Arkansas.

Despite the need for an educated laity, ministerial education could not be ignored. The world's learning sustains our denominational positions, the report continued, and ministers "should be able to render this learning available for the maintenance of our principles." Van Horne concluded with the need for training young ministers "at home" in the midst of the people they would serve. This would make them most effective, he believed, and would avoid the loss of young ministers to other fields when they leave the state for their education. A "united effort" by Arkansas Baptists could quickly decide the outcome in the great struggle between truth and error.

Not content with half measures, the Convention also considered the need for educating the membership's females. Part of this united effort lay with the sisters who also had a role in the struggle. The importance, "both politically and religiously," of educating women prompted the delegates to urge Baptists to not neglect their daughters' educations. To that end, by resolution they recommended the "Female Institutes" with Baptist ties in Fayetteville, Camden, and Arkadelphia.

The 1858 meeting demonstrated that the Convention had a mission (education in its broadest sense), a growing body of adherents who could make common cause around that mission, and the wherewithal to pursue the mission. Perhaps most importantly from an organizational perspective, the Convention in 1858 gave thought to its legal existence, its organizational soul. Delegates directed P. S. G. Watson and William M. Lea to secure a charter as soon as possible, named nine trustees who would serve as the Convention's legally responsible parties, and selected Princeton as the Convention's legal residence. After a decade of meetings, of seeking a reason for existence and a mission on which to focus upon which all could agree, the Convention had finally "found itself."

Delegates who gathered in 1859 exhibited a new self-awareness and self-assurance. They heard officially what some of them already knew— that E. H. English had provided the necessary paperwork pro bono and the legislature had issued the charter called for at the previous meeting—it had been approved on February 12. With official standing came certain privileges—or perhaps the Convention's initial meeting in Little Rock merely made certain privileges possible. Peter Hanger, stage agent, provided attendees with half-price fares, for which he received the Convention's official thanks. Delegates also tendered their thanks to "the ladies who have honored, or may honor, this Convention with their presence" and extended an invitation "to the ladies generally to attend." Though this was not the first time ladies had attended— their presence appeared regularly when the names of those contributing to offerings taken at the meetings had been recorded—it was the first time their attendance had been officially recognized.

Another first that reflected the Convention's new sense of self-awareness was its interest in unifying adherents and standardizing theology through music. Though partial hymn lines had appeared in the minutes of earlier years, those for 1859 first record a hymn used in a

meeting—"Am I a Soldier of the Cross"—and recognition of the importance for promoting unity through a common hymnal. Reelected
president for the third time, William Lea appointed a committee of five
to examine hymnals and recommend one for general use at the next
meeting. Reflecting the Convention's broadening base, committee
members came from Little Rock (P. S. G. Watson), Pine Bluff (Lea),
Caroline Association (W. H. Barksdale), and Mount Vernon Association
(John Carroll, T. S. N. King, and B. B. Black) rather than from the traditional southern locus of Convention authority.

The Convention also briefly considered two other issues before
proceeding to the two matters which consumed most of its attention and
time. Delegates discussed building a structure to house Little Rock's
Baptists—testimony to the sad state of affairs in the capital where a
church had been established by Silas Toncray in 1824, only to convert *en
masse* to the Disciples after his departure. They also endorsed L. D.
Pearle as missionary and colporteur "on the self-sustaining plan"—
evidence of their continuing fiscal prudence, if not parsimony.

Fiscal responsibility as a principle certainly appeared in the
Convention's discussions of the denominational newspaper. Delegates
thanked Johnson and Yerkes for publishing the paper for considerably
less than the original contract. While the committee dealing with the
paper noted that a "sanctified press" could be a tool to save thousands
who would not read a book but would read religious papers, its report
prompted considerable discussion. P. S. G. Watson, who had undertaken the paper at the Convention's request, enjoyed the Convention's
approbation of his course of "rejecting all personal articles which in
their nature would tend to strife and contention among the brotherhood." He received delegates' heartfelt thanks and lasting gratitude for
his work. Then came the Convention's fiscal concern. Its final action
concerning the *Arkansas Baptist* was to unanimously resolve to give
Watson the paper "together with all *its assets and its liabilities*." To
ensure that no one missed the point, delegates noted again that after
that day, the Convention "would not be bound for any debt or debts
contracted" on account of the paper. Even on this basis, Watson agreed
to take and continue operating the paper.

Staying true to its decision of 1856 to concentrate on education, the
Convention spent most of its time discussing the issue. That discussion

fell into two categories: educational philosophy and practice on the one hand and fiscal matters on the other.

Discussions of educational philosophy and practice involved familiar territory. Inflammatory words warned of the specter of Catholicism. "The times call loudly for Protestants to educate," the report cautioned delegates, for that would "let science exert her supremacy over traditionary legend." Protestant education, unlike that of the Catholics, would leave the mind free, enriching an intellect "untainted by sectarian prejudice. . . ."

As was to be expected, the delegates found separating the fiscal from the philosophical an impossibility. Commenting on the need for educating "the rising generation" in general and young ministers in particular, and on the need for doing so in the state, delegates agreed that Arkansas Baptists should not send "either our money or our young ministers out of state." Once the fiscal had been raised, it was not to be soon dismissed.

Just as philosophical concerns did not differ from previous years, so the Convention's fiscal interests departed from their past position not a whit. As with the newspaper, so with education the Convention determined not to incur indebtedness. The two Convention agents canvassing the state for educational funds, W. M. Lea and W. R. Trawick, reported $36,550 in bonds. Each covered as much territory as he could, but despite their successes, their inadequacies concerned them. Faced with the agents' report, the Convention responded in kind with praise for their efforts and a recommendation that all ministers take up collections for the college and send the money to the agents.

Most interestingly, the delegates approved a detailed plan to fully fund the college they intended to found and at which they intended to provide an education free of sectarian prejudice. The $100,000 endowment goal, set in 1856, they reaffirmed. They proposed to reach that goal by subscriptions and by scholarships, which would cost $500 each and allow the holder to educate one individual free of further outlay. While they earmarked subscriptions for the endowment, cash offerings or subscriptions of less than $50 would go toward the building, agents' salaries, and similar immediate needs.

Delegates used both carrot and stick in their fund-raising approach. They tried to entice prospective donors by voting that no subscription would come due until the entire $100,000 had been raised or pledged. They sought to encourage large subscriptions by announcing that each $100 subscription entitled the subscriber to a vote on all important matters, and that voting could be done by proxy. Every matter would be decided by a two-thirds vote cast at the Convention, which further weighted large subscriptions. But they also planned to ensure promptness. Those who did not pay their pledge when it came due faced a 10 percent annual penalty.

The 1859 meeting, the Convention's twelfth, was the last held under anything approaching normal conditions for almost a decade. Convention members at the 1860 meeting certainly felt the sectional animosity and tensions that surrounded that year's presidential election. Their October 26–29 meeting at Pine Bluff predated Abraham Lincoln's election and the departure of Southern states from the Union, but no one could escape the political furor and tensions. Sparse representation, no doubt a reflection of those tensions, prompted delegates to append a circular letter to the minutes encouraging attendance at annual meetings.

The minutes reflect the Convention's preoccupation with matters of form and especially of unity. After debate on the second day, delegates adopted five major constitutional changes.

First, the revised constitution reflected changed Convention priorities. The original set forth the Convention's two primary objectives (supplying destitute regions and churches with pastors and communities with books reflecting denominational doctrines) and two secondary ones (education and foreign missions when economically feasible). The revision listed three "primary objects": ministerial education, missionaries, and Baptist literature.

Second, the new constitution provided for income and for accountability in its use. The new definition of membership involved money, for the constitution welcomed individuals or institutions making "adequate contributions." Delegates were apportioned by the same method; the Convention allotted delegates to associations, churches, or individuals on the basis of one delegate for every five dollars paid into the treasury. Any money collected would receive careful supervision; one article provided that funds for the Convention's three primary objectives should be kept separately and punctually appropriated as the contributors had intended.

Third, even while establishing a monetary test for membership and therefore making the Convention more exclusive, the revision broadened the possibilities for active participation in an apparent attempt to encourage involvement. The original provision for a president and recording secretary for meetings and an Executive Committee for the interim—president, two vice-presidents, corresponding secretary, treasurer, and ten or more managers—gave way to a president, three vice-presidents, recording and corresponding secretaries, treasurer and auditor, and twenty others who would collectively constitute a board of managers. This change destroyed the division between "meeting officials" and "continuity officials" and unified direction of Convention affairs by increasing the president's authority. A new article directed the managers to meet at least quarterly—a reflection of dissatisfaction with the Executive Board which had several times reported no meetings for lack of business.

Fourth, after spending almost every meeting adjusting the meeting time in hopes of attracting more participants, the delegates bowed to reality and provided constitutional recognition that meeting times should be set annually. They also established a constitutional provision for board and agent reports at each meeting.

Finally, the new constitution incorporated an interesting twist in an effort to promote cooperation between associations and the Convention, and to give the Convention some say in associational undertakings despite the continued inclusion of an article prohibiting Convention ecclesiastical jurisdiction over, advice to, or interference with any church or association. The last constitutional article provided that funds expended by any association within its own bounds to further any one of the three Convention "primary objects" could be used to secure delegates to Convention meetings. Since all associations maintained missionaries, and since some associations maintained either educational institutions or funds for ministerial education, this provision was a generous gesture. Delegates purchased in that fashion, however, had a high price tag. The article contained a proviso. Delegates could be claimed only if the association met three conditions: the Convention had to confirm any missionaries, the association had to maintain a regular correspondence with the Convention, and the association had to report its funds to the Convention's treasurer at each annual meeting.

Even in the midst of tensions over national divisions, State Convention members in 1860 sought to promote unity among the brethren. Sometimes the efforts mixed positive and negative. The committee's report concerned with these undertakings noted that everyone could work in Sunday Schools, a clear integrating effect of such endeavors, and that Sunday Schools offered children of "the profligate and ungodly" a hope of heaven. More dubiously, it closed by reminding everyone that Sunday Schools can be "powerful engines in promoting Sectarianism"—a damning observation aimed at the duplicity of other denominations while promoting the opportunity to this one.

Most of the efforts presented unalloyed positive views of unifying possibilities. Delegates approvingly agreed when J. S. Murrow and Willis Burns, missionaries to the Creek and Choctaw respectively, reported their churches' interest in joining the Convention at its next meeting in Fort Smith. They undoubtedly hoped that an infusion of new blood at the new meeting place, even if that blood flowed through veins beneath darker skin, would help swell their numbers.

The committee reporting on the possibility of a single hymnal for all Arkansas Baptists presented one of the two greatest possibilities for unity discussed at the 1860 meeting. Relating their familiarity with hymnals in use and the general excellence of those hymnals, the committee maintained that a problem still existed. The lack of a single book that incorporated all the most common and familiar hymns prevented any book's general adoption throughout the state. The committee had contacted the *Southern Psalmist*, published by (J. R.) Graves, Marks & Co. Editors there agreed to add up to fifty hymns of the Convention's choice without additional cost if the Convention would recommend its adoption. Delegates resolved to accept this offer if a committee (P. S. G. Watson, William M. Lea, and J. F. Hooten) could make the selections and arrangements; if not, the committee was to try the same arrangement with the *Psalmody*; failing that, the Convention would then recommend the *Southern Psalmist* anyway. An inferior unifying hymnal was better than doing without.

Ultimately, Convention delegates were convinced that having their own method of education would bind Arkansas Baptists together like no other single effort. This issue absorbed most of the meeting's time. A circular letter prepared for inclusion with the minutes averred that nothing affected human destiny as much as a "thorough, masterly education." Catholics have long known this, the report continued, and they and Protestants educate their youth and through that education inculcate in them the belief that Baptists are "illiterate, bigotted [sic], sectarian." After mentioning what later generations would call the "Trail of Blood," and that Baptists had prospered without the support of "State, money, human learning or popular favor," the report concluded that unity behind an educational endeavor would promote advancement unlike any other enterprise.

The Executive Board reported no meetings—no business requiring a meeting had arisen—but cheered the Convention with the news that agents Trawick and Lea had raised $70,150 toward the proposed Male Institute at which aspiring ministers and other youth would be educated.

The Convention also took up a series of three resolutions about a specific educational venture. The 1859 "Craig Bequest" from the $650,000 estate of Junius W. Craig to Helena had resulted in a proposed school; the Convention proposed to unite that bequest with a fund raised by the Convention, provided that the Convention controlled the resulting institute. To that end, delegates voted for a self-perpetuating committee that would appoint and pay agents and raise the proposed fund and see the project to its successful conclusion—so long as they did not bring the Convention under "any pecuniary liabilities"—and report at the next meeting. W. M. Lea, J. H. Hicks, W. H. Barksdale, T. S. N. King, P. S. G. Watson, W. F. Owen, and Nat G. Smith duly took up the burden assigned them.

Its last attempt to promote unity in the face of the day's tensions involved the *Arkansas Baptist*. Notified that income from the newspaper was insufficient but determined not to entangle the Convention in "pecuniary liabilities," delegates agreed to two actions. First, they recommended the newspaper to Arkansas Baptists; second, they agreed to purchase a press and appurtenances in an attempt to curtail expenses—and raised $580 toward that end in an impromptu offering.

Despite Baptists attempts at unity, the state moved toward war—though it did so haltingly and without universal approbation. The state was not one of those which seceded at the first sign of trouble; leaders awaited an overt act, and left the Union only when no other action seemed possible. W. H. Barksdale, writing to J. R. Graves from Helena shortly after the Convention met, admitted that the cry of disunion had checked the spirit of progress and made money scarce. In a postscript, he appealed to those about to "act precipitately" to wait, have a states' rights convention to define Southern rights, submit that unified definition as the basis for a national referendum, then act upon the results.

While some rushed to war, others headed, literally, for the hills. One Arkansan typical of the latter group figured that it was not his fight, and wrote his sister that he was headed for the hills west of Hot Springs. If they wanted him to fight, he said, they would have to come and find him first.

Baptists were like other Arkansans, divided over their reaction to the war. Baptist churches, like other Arkansas institutions, suffered the ravages of war regardless of their sentiments. When patriotic fervor took young men into military units, churches lost benchwarmers, lay leaders, and ordained ministers. Since they deemed only men eligible for leadership positions, some churches closed their doors due to their lack of males. Some churches relied on lay leadership when pastors volunteered as chaplains, or even as infantrymen.

By the 1861 session in Fort Smith, conditions had changed drastically from those of the previous year. A Confederacy had been formed, and Arkansas had joined it. Political uncertainty had disappeared, but other kinds of uncertainty remained.

In preparation for the Helena meeting of the Southern Baptist Sabbath School Union at the end of November 1861, Corresponding Secretary A. C. Dayton gave a dreary picture of conditions in eastern Arkansas. Through his friend J. R. Graves's paper, Dayton called for postponing the meeting because "the condition of the country is such that it is probable but few would be able to leave their homes," those who could might not because "traveling will be more or less unsafe for some who would meet with us," and the potential gathering would be fewer because many supporters "are in the camps."

Western Arkansas fared no better. Numerous circumstances seemed to conspire against a successful 1861 Convention meeting. Long-time minister among the Indians J. S. Murrow had been "providentially called from his field" during the crucial time that would otherwise have ensured Indian representation. Reports circulated that Fort Smith had suffered a smallpox outbreak, and they circulated early enough to prevent many from attempting the trip. Finally, the general war excitement kept those at a distance from attending. That general excitement was augmented by word that Union Commander John Charles Fremont, the "Pathfinder of the West," was marching rapidly against the black-clad former Texas Ranger, Confederate General Ben McCulloch, with a superior force. "Everyone feared," E. L. Compere remembered, "that Fremont, with his murderous horde, would be among us in a few days."

Despite the obstacles of illness, unsafe travel, and war's alarms, a small delegation gathered for the annual session at the appointed time. They elected seventy-year-old Lee Compere, long-time Baptist minister and missionary and father to E. L. and Thomas H. Compere, as president. The elder Compere had left Mississippi for the Arkansas farm of his eldest son, Thomas, when Mississippi seceded and thus lived reasonably near Fort Smith in Dardanelle. Delegates then selected E. L. Compere as recording secretary.

In a bid for normality, delegates elected an Executive Board as usual (Lee Compere, president, and M. M. McGuire, corresponding secretary) and provided structure for the next year's meeting, though they made no provision for printing minutes. After selecting representatives to the next Sabbath School Union meeting, delegates revised their constitution's fourth and fifth articles. They provided that representation should be afforded Baptists in good standing as individuals or as members of churches or associations, and that in addition to the usual three and five representatives accorded each church and association respectively, an additional representative would be allowed for each $10 expended for Convention objects.

After attenuated sessions and brief business, delegates turned their full attention to the Convention's future. They decided that "hundreds had been providentially prevented from attending this session, who desire to sit with the Convention, where the red man and white can deliberate together," and that since no other town had applied for the next meeting it should be held in Fort Smith again. With a nod to necessity, the delegates authorized the officers to change the place of meeting in case of emergency. They then adjourned and went home.

The next year in Fort Smith proved little if any better. Again the delegation was small; only the threat of smallpox had been removed. Union troops had occupied Helena that summer and Union forces threatened the state's northwest. Delegates chose Willis Burns president and reelected E. L. Compere secretary before conducting a little business. Their thoughts remained on the future's uncertainty, made even more so by the war. Delegates resolved that the next regular meeting would occur in Dardanelle, but provided a change in traditional procedure. Officers elected at Fort Smith in 1862 were to hold office, not for a year, but "till their successors could be elected." President Burns was instructed to call the Convention together at any time after the regular time in 1863 if the exigencies of the situation required delay. Providing continuity and reassembly would, the delegates believed, preserve the Convention's charter whatever eventuated.

Diminutive Confederate General Thomas C. Hindman's preparations to march northward from Van Buren certainly prompted such forethought. His trek through the Boston Mountains toward what would be the battle of Prairie Grove, within forty miles of the meeting, confirmed the need. The delegates' decisions proved prescient, for the second Fort Smith meeting was the war's last.

By time for the next year's meeting, all of Arkansas north of the river had fallen under Union control. Fort Smith fell September 1, 1863, and Little Rock ten days later. Washington became the temporary Confederate capital, only to need defending in mid-1864 when the Red River Campaign brought Union troops southward. Travel, already difficult in the frontier state, became virtually impossible as the war progressed. Union forces outlawed assemblies of disloyal individuals, especially what men remained, in areas under Union control. Even in those areas not under Union control, travel and assembly were problematical at best. Bands of lawless men, often deserters from both armies and generally called "mossbacks" or "graybacks," infested areas in which no one seemed to represent order. Guerrilla bands authorized by the Confederacy were often no better, drawing no real distinction among Union and Confederate sympathizers and those who cared not a whit for either. Arkansas reverted to its status of a half-century before, when travelers commented with great regularity on its lawlessness and one popular joke had a traveling Arkansan calling for his luggage—a knife, a gun, and a deck of cards.

At the end of the Convention's first decade—indeed, until the war's arrival—its presence seems to have made little difference in Arkansas Baptist life. Arkansas Baptists still sent the Macedonian call across the Mississippi River, begging ministers from the older, more settled regions to come to Arkansas. The Convention's feeble efforts to rectify the ministerial shortage had produced no tangible results. Any increase came from the natural westward movement of Americans and the natural increase of local congregations which called from their midst those the Lord had touched.

Training for ministers was left to institutions in other states—Mt. Lebanon in Louisiana, for example. The Convention's inability to raise the money it needed to endow the proposed college and its unwillingness to incur any debt doomed its efforts at education to failure. Educational institutions with Baptist connections during the pre-war era owed everything to individual and nothing to Convention initiative. Mine Creek Male and Female School (February 1851) run by Allen M. Scott and his daughters near Nashville; Arkadelphia Institute and Arkadelphia Female Institute (July 1851) run by Samuel Stevenson and James Milton Gilkey; Camden Female Institute (1851) under Jesse Hartwell's direction; and later T. B. Van Horne's Fayetteville Institute—these received Convention approbation but not its support and certainly not its adoption. Their existence relied on local and personal efforts. The Convention never even deigned to recognize the effort of Arkadelphia Baptists in establishing in late 1858 the Arkansas Institute for the Education of the Blind, which opened in February 1859 with a blind Baptist minister named Haucke as principal and Arkadelphia First Baptist members Harris Flanagin, J. W. Smith, T. A. Heard, and Samuel Stevenson among the nine trustees.

The Convention spent eight years casting about for a mission. Delegates spent the early years looking at every conceivable possibility. Some possible missions had already been appropriated by other entities—"domestic missions," which had originally been the Convention's stated focus, remained the purview of the associations, for example. Some were beyond the Convention's reach because of its intransigent insistence on avoiding "pecuniary liabilities;" the "sanctified press" represented by the *Arkansas Baptist* was perhaps the most outstanding example of this class. Once the Convention focused on education, once it found its mission in a cause around which all its adherents could rally, it seemed destined for success. The Convention's success at raising money for the proposed college endowment, about $75,000 of the $100,000 envisioned, seemed a good foundation for the future.

The war ended the Convention's success. When the war ended, the endowment was gone, a victim of the conflict. The Convention retained its charter, but no one seemed sure how to proceed and others questioned the wisdom of starting up again. The Convention that Red River and Saline Associations had questioned in 1854, which had almost died then, almost died again. What had been a tenuous beginning, an interesting experiment which had avoided death by internal and external conflict, seemed over. With important proponents dead or out of state, chances for resurrection seemed slim.

6

1865–1870s

THE WAR'S END DID NOT BRING AN IMMEDIATE RETURN to normality for Baptist organizations any more than it did for the rest of the state. When hostilities ceased, combatants and displaced persons had to make their way home as best they could. Those who had remained at home faced the task of reconstructing their lives from the ruins and rigors of war's chaos. All faced a new order as sufferers from a new experience for Americans—defeat in war.

Attempts to restore order suffered from a host of plagues resulting from war. The Civil War in Arkansas had involved an internal struggle as well as a struggle against invaders. Citizens were divided against each other just as they had been in other seceded states. That struggle neither began nor ended with the war, though war exacerbated it. The war in Arkansas was truly a "brother's war," and hard feelings north and south of the Arkansas River mirrored those north and south of Mason and Dixon's line. The state's refusal to secede initially, and the divided vote to do so when it finally came, hinted at an ambivalence rooted in vast differences.

Displaced persons took time to return home and some preferred exile to return. Status as clergy or laity made no difference; Arkansas Baptist ministers suffered the same as did their lay fellows. The Compere brothers were a good example. E. L. Compere served Indian

101

spiritual needs through the war, riding with Stand Waite's troops as chaplain. At its end, he sought to recoup his fortunes with a year's stint on his mother-in-law's farm in Mississippi before returning to Arkansas. His eldest brother, Thomas, was one of those Arkansans who chose exile. At the war's end he headed for Texas, winding up in Corsicana with his father and mother, who had moved in with him in Dardanelle at the war's start. Robert M. Thrasher finished the war at Johnson's Island, a Union prison camp in Sandusky Bay of Lake Erie where about three thousand Confederate officers were held at the war's end. According to family lore, an enfeebled Thrasher walked 110 of the roughly thousand miles home from near Richmond, Virginia, to Tulip Creek (Dallas County) after his P.O.W. stint, and covered another 75 miles by canoe.

Many of the men who returned were not of a mind to meekly greet an army of occupation or their neighbors who had fought on the winning side. Many men of an age to enforce order never returned. Arkansas lost about 6,900 of the roughly 60,000 men it supplied the Confederacy during the war, either on the battlefield (about 45 percent) or to illness. Arkansas also supplied about 8,800 white men to Union forces, about 1,700 of whom did not return.

Not only were individuals and their future affected by the war. When the war ended, the Convention's existence, much less its future, certainly was in doubt. Delegates at the last meeting (1862) had done all they could to ensure its continued existence, but that last meeting had taken place in a state unoccupied by enemy forces. The three years between the last meeting and the war's end had seen the capital city seized and the state government operate from exile in a series of towns, even officially being established in Washington, before the Confederacy's capitulation. Now an occupying army controlled the land while political considerations determined what would happen next.

Economic adjustments during Reconstruction were hampered by larger economic readjustments as the nation moved from a land-based economy dominated by agricultural interests to a money-based one dominated by industry and technology. The third and fourth worst panics in the nation's history defined a long-wave depression between them. The Panics of 1873 (66 months) and 1893 (48 months) encompassed an entire generation within the depression that had additional "spikes" from 1882 to 1885 and 1890 to 1891. For an agricultural state like Arkansas, economics had a profound impact on efforts to advance during those years.

For an institution so fiscally conservative as the Convention, seeking to implement worthy undertakings while avoiding encumbrance in debt looked much less feasible than before. The scarcity of money among the populace and the rigors of transition between two differently focused economic systems, one agricultural, one industrial, boded ill for such an outlook. The war's end allowed the interest in railroads, so evident in the late 1850s, to pick up where it had left off; investment in railroads seemed an economic panacea for the post-war era. Money that might have gone to religious activities made its way instead into the coffers of railroad companies.

When the Convention reassembled for its first post-war meeting, at Little Rock on November 8, 1867, the uncertainties of the times were evident. Few delegates attended. The minutes list only eighteen, though the secretary mentioned the presence of a few more he could not remember. They represented five of the sixteen associations (another sent its letter) and two churches; one individual, Samuel Stevenson, tendered his credentials. The Caroline and Pine Bluff Associations were the best-represented; Saline made its first appearance since the momentous 1854 meeting at which its proposal to dissolve the Convention met with disfavor. Red River again sent no delegates.

Associations seemed to recover from the war's effect more quickly than the Convention and even many churches, perhaps because their services were so crucial to rebuilding. Associations offered the community of fellowship and shared resources that everyone needed. In many areas, society faced a new beginning not dissimilar to that original one on the frontier. Just as the churches originally formed associations quickly in Arkansas, so they did again in war's aftermath.

The new president, W. M. Lea, appointed only three committees (Preaching, Business, and Finance) and in a committee of the whole the delegates discussed the future. Samuel Stevenson, for the committee appointed to suggest business, proposed that on account of the small number of delegates, the Convention host at least two missionary mass meetings—at Dardanelle and Camden in March and

June respectively—with an eye to unity and to "restoring the primitive apostolic spirit of missions and rebuilding the desolation in our denomination." The delegates agreed.

From the floor, H. C. Smith of Saline Association submitted a momentous proposal. In light of the loss of the $75,000 raised prior to the war in endowment for a college and of the state's "crippled condition," Smith recommended that the Convention focus on home missions. To meet that objective, he further specified the appointment of an Arkansas Baptist State Mission Board, located in Little Rock and empowered to adopt any means necessary to "supply the destitute." Finally, he nominated twenty ministers to the proposed board.

In adopting Smith's proposal, the Convention took its first step toward systematizing its activities. The newly selected board was the first such Convention entity. Smith sketched an outline of board activities, which included coordination and supplementing the work of associations, but left its brief amazingly vague. Whatever it found to do in pursuing the goal, that it should do. He also designated an annual report to the Convention which would, if possible, combine information on all home mission activities into a single document. That way the Convention would know the degree of destitution and the efforts being made to supply that destitution.

Also for the first time, delegates specified a locus for an ongoing Convention activity. The charter had seated the Convention in Princeton, but delegates prior to the war had never seemed to view that as particularly significant. Though it had a legal residence, the Convention had no real home. Adherents obviously saw it as an annual meeting at which they could fellowship and plan whatever activities the funds they might raise would allow.

Smith's proposal at once created an entity charged with a single duty, provided a geographic focus for Convention activity, and established a model for the kind of bureaucracy which could sustain a year-round and ongoing Baptist presence in the state rather than merely an annual meeting.

The names proffered to the Convention contained a mixture of the old and the new. Six were stalwarts, men long identified with Convention business: W. M. Lea, Samuel Stevenson, E. L. Compere, R. J. Coleman, T. P. Boone, and R. M. Thrasher. They gave continuity to the endeavor, and their presence would do as much as any other variable toward ensuring its success.

The delegates voted for the meetings Stevenson had proposed (as well as selecting preachers for them), recommended Sunday Schools (and selected a representative to the upcoming Southern Baptist Sunday School Union meeting), took up an offering toward the new undertaking, and recommended seven Baptist newspapers and two monthly magazines to Arkansas Baptists before adjourning.

The Convention's first meeting after the war reflected the dislocation of the times, but it also offered promise of a better future. Whether or not the attempted revitalization of united efforts by Arkansas Baptists would continue would be determined, to some extent, by the next year's gathering in Little Rock.

On November 21, 1868, the Convention reassembled in Little Rock. Attendance remained about the same, with twenty delegates representing five associations (plus another by letter) and three churches (Little Rock First, Helena, and Camden). Miles L. Langley, Clark County pastor and frequent Convention delegate, was present but declined the traditional invitation to ministers to join deliberations, perhaps because of his connection with the American Baptist Home Mission Society as missionary to freedmen during 1865 to 1866 or more likely because of his service in the 1868 Constitutional Convention; *Tennessee Baptist* editor J. R. Graves felt no such compunction and gladly accepted.

President W. M. Lea, reelected, appointed seven committees. Four dealt with matters of substance (Sunday Schools, Missions, Publications, and Finance) while three concerned housekeeping (Nominations, Obituaries, and Ministers' Names).

In their reports, the committees dealing with matters of substance struck familiar chords. That on Sunday Schools noted that the majority of converts in Baptist churches came from Sunday Schools, then recommended a Baptist Sunday School missionary (self-supporting, of course) who would promote purely Baptist Sunday Schools using Baptist books. Such a move would enable Baptist churches to retain unadulterated teachings rather than encounter "Pedo-Baptist or union" doctrine. In addition, the report counseled two innovations: organizing an annual Baptist State Sunday School Convention to be held in conjunction with the regular State Convention meetings and linking adult Bible schools with churches' regular Sunday Schools.

The Committee on Publications observed that bad books, like bad company, demoralize society, and that distinctive Baptist principles required defense. In line with that observation, the committee recommended the *Southern Psalmist Hymnal*, the SBC Sunday School Board's paper *Kind Words*, the SBC's *Home and Foreign Journal* and the *Arkansas Baptist* to Arkansas Baptists, with an additional nod for J. R. Graves's paper *The Baptist*. The committee refused, however, to recommend other than placing the Convention's imprimatur on these publications; the Convention still showed no interest in fiscal responsibility, or even assistance, for any publications.

The Committee on Missions began with the remark that "The late revolution and consequent influences have almost swept away the churches." Resultant widespread discouragement and apathy had convinced people that they were poor, with the result that they withheld support from the ministry (no change from pre-war times, some would argue). Churches needed to systematize their contributions, the report concluded. It then offered an example of such a system: let each individual give ten cents weekly for the pastor's support and another cent for missions. Finally, the committee recommended that the Convention reappoint the Missionary Board, appoint a general agent, and advise the board to seek "relief" from outside the state.

The new State Mission Board laid before the Convention proof of outside interest in Arkansas plight. On being informed of the State Board's organization and of the state's need, the American Baptist Home Mission Society was supporting W. M. Lea as a general missionary and had provided a $2,500 loan for a building for Little Rock First.

In the post-war years, Arkansas Baptists received help, as they had in the past, from the American Baptist Home Mission Society. Between 1864 and 1880, the ABHMS appointed nine missionaries to labor in Arkansas. Joanna P. Moore had the distinction of being the first (and only) female appointed to Arkansas when she began her nine-month stint as a teacher for the "Freedman Educational Work" in 1864. All but two of the nine were sent to engage in "colored work" and, except for John B. McKay and Miles L. Langley, served a year or less. Langley and

William M. Lea received statewide appointments in 1865 and 1868 respectively; the others served in the southern part of the state in towns (Lake Village, Helena, and Little Rock) or the southwest or western counties (particularly Sevier, Howard, and Little River). Three of those appointed—Langley, Lea, and W. H. Robert—were associated with the State Convention.

The board concluded its report with the kind of summary for which it had been created. Nine of the sixteen associations reported missionaries active in the field, and although it could not report "a large amount of money passing through the Board," it could report that at least three thousand dollars had been spent by the associations. Delegates left the Convention meeting with a much better idea of the statewide need and the statewide response than had ever been the case before.

In addition to adopting the reports involving missions, the Convention concluded that it should hold another mass missions meeting like the two of the previous year. Success with their mass missions meetings of the previous year encouraged the Convention to change only the number and location; delegates chose Fort Smith for the spring gathering. As had been true the previous year, Convention delegates hoped thereby to attract attention and bolster meeting attendance as well as foster interest in missions.

Despite the Convention's decision the previous year to eschew education as a Convention undertaking, W. D. Mayfield of Helena brought up the most interesting presentation of the whole meeting. Mayfield, who had presented the Missions Committee's report, arose at the Monday afternoon session with a series of seven resolutions. Typical of one who consistently urged the Convention toward "system" in all its activities, Mayfield presented a complete plan of action.

Mayfield proposed that the Convention establish "a female school of high grade" in Helena. A self-perpetuating board (which Mayfield named) would select the president and professors and govern the school's actions. The board would arrange with the Convention's general agent to secure endowment and solicit patronage, though such arrangements would not preclude the board's ability to appoint its own agents. The board should also consult with the Trustees of the Helena Female Institute and see if those trustees might be persuaded to give that institute to the proposed university (including its patronage and property). Mayfield's plan, he promised, would ensure that daughters would be "brought under right influences and receive a liberal education." In a move reminiscent of its 1860 deliberations, the Convention agreed.

The Convention's 1869 Helena meeting demonstrated that loss of the pre-war focus on education had set Convention delegates back in their thinking. The ground so dearly won after almost a decade of discussion and meetings had been another war casualty. W. D. Mayfield's resolutions of the previous year indicated that not everyone agreed with the Convention's discarding the educational focus to return to its initial but subordinated choice of home missions. As if the years between 1848 and 1856 had not existed and the discussions of those years never taken place, the first real piece of business in 1869 was a motion that the Convention meet at night—a previously unheard-of suggestion—in a mass meeting to discuss the question "What is the mission of Baptists in Arkansas?" Subsequent evening meetings would feature a series of sermons by various ministers.

Pursuant to the morning's vote, delegates, interested Helena residents, and visiting parties gathered that Thursday evening. After opening prayer by J. B. Searcy and a choral number by an assembled choir, they heard speeches by J. K. Murphy of Helena, representing New Hope Church, Phillips County; B. F. Thomas of Mt. Dixon, representing Mount Vernon Church; W. M. Lea of Little Rock, representing Pine Bluff Association; J. B. Searcy of Bradley, representing Enon, Friendship, New Hope, and Macedonia churches; J. T. Craig of Edinburg, representing Judson Association; and the inimitable and omnipresent J. R. Graves of Memphis. The "lively" speeches exhibited good feeling and great harmony, according to the secretary. But pitting "newcomers" like Murphy, Thomas, and Searcy against "old-timers" like Lea, Craig, and Graves produced a debate which settled nothing. When Murphy closed the meeting with prayer, the matter had been referred to future Convention consideration. When delegates ultimately decided that it was "the mission of Baptists in Arkansas to let every community in Arkansas know what Baptists believe," they had decided nothing that would benefit the Convention's focus, deliberations, or activities. They had, however, witnessed the struggles of a new generation of leaders to make their impress on Convention business.

When the delegates gathered the next morning at 9 o'clock, President W. D. Mayfield appointed the same committees as the Convention had found necessary the previous year. Hidden amidst the normality of the mundane and customary of the session's organization and operation lay indications that all was not well with the Convention. Claims of harmony and good feeling notwithstanding, delegates resolved to elect officers from that point on by ballot rather than by the customary voice vote. They also resolved to request associations and churches who sent delegates to send money for the minutes and Convention expenses with them. In what could have been a refrain to the song from previous and presumably happier years, delegates learned that the Convention treasury contained only six dollars. Toward the session's end, J. B. Searcy even offered a resolution (which passed) condemning "the immersion of all Pedobaptists and Campbellites" as "unscriptural and therefore null and void." Landmarkism was alive and well in Arkansas.

Committee reports likewise hinted at discontent if not conflict. The Sunday School Committee report elicited lively debate—so lively that the discussion carried over until the next day, when delegates finally adopted it. Much of the debate centered on the committee's gratuitous assertion that a church's first duty was to secure the labor of a faithful pastor and minister to his necessities as the Lord prospered them. Perhaps the committee's assumption that a church's second duty lay in organizing and sustaining a Baptist Sunday School prompted disagreement from those who did not really believe in such an agency's efficacy. Certainly the customary Convention affirmation of Sunday Schools, of *Kind Words*, or of Sunday School Board books would not have provoked lively discussion.

The Missions Committee recommended that the State Mission Board appoint three missionaries for the state. The Publications Committee recognized the *Arkansas Baptist*'s demise only by omitting it from the usual list of recommended literature and proposing instead that Arkansas Baptists adopt J. R. Graves's *The Baptist* as its official state paper (Graves promised a full page for Arkansas Baptist news, edited to the best of his ability, for which the Convention thanked him).

The session's most far-reaching matter came directly from the floor rather than through the usual committee structure. In an unusual move, J. R. Graves suggested an alternative to the kind of literary and theological training envisioned in the pre-war emphasis on establishing a male college. Establish, Graves advised, a Board of Ministerial Education. Authorize the board to raise a $10,000 fund through an agent. Use that fund for a two-pronged educational offensive—to educate young ministers and to conduct a Ministerial Institute.

Elaborating on the fund's use, Graves maintained that some young ministers needed assistance securing a "classical and theological education." They would receive interest-free loans, repayable once they began their ministries. The notes of all who entered "secular business for profit," would bear interest; those of all who became foreign missionaries would be forgiven. "Every living minister in the State," Graves continued, also needed help. Toward that end, the board should hold a Ministerial Institute annually in conjunction with the Convention meeting. That institute should offer six or more courses of lectures on subjects important to ministers—and any other exercises the board should think appropriate—with all expenses borne by the board.

Delegates enthusiastically adopted Graves's resolution and elected a five-person board, creating the Convention's second major agency in three years. In a departure from the earlier approach, delegates located the Board of Ministerial Education with a person rather than in a place: the board's secretary, W. D. Mayfield of Helena. They then followed that precept with the Missions Board, which went to Bradley with secretary J. B. Searcy. Though the trustees remained domiciled at Princeton as the charter provided, the Convention seemed as yet unready to tie activities to a location rather than a person. For the time being, it remained a person- rather than a place-centered entity, more tied to individuals than bureaucracy.

The committee charged with listing the Baptist ministers in the state submitted a list of 163, which they acknowledged was almost certainly incomplete. Perhaps as much as any other evidence from the 1869 meeting, this list embodied the Convention's problems. The delegate list enumerated thirty-eight attendees (representing five associations and twelve churches), three from outside the state. Thirteen of the delegate names also appeared on the list of ministers, which meant that about a third of the delegates were ministers. For a Convention attended by roughly a dozen of the ministers in the state to ask the other 150 to preach an April sermon emphasizing ministerial education seemed a bit presumptuous. To further ask the 150 also to take up a collection for the cause moved the "presumptuous" closer to "preposterous." In most cases those 150 relied for their support upon that same collection process and the generosity of those present for the collection. Requests of this nature certainly violated the ministers' self-interest, especially from a Convention composed of such a small portion of the state's ministers, and one that had commented the year before on the inadequacy of ministerial support.

The Convention's 1870 meeting in Arkadelphia began the new decade poorly in one respect. W. D. Mayfield, selected to preach the Convention sermon, was absent and his alternate, J. B. Searcy, unwell. Meetings which had focused on a plenitude of preaching since their resumption in 1867 began the decade without an opening Convention sermon that Thursday. The lack, presumably, was not so discouraging as it would have been in previous years; the Ministerial Institute, proposed by Graves the previous year and eagerly adopted by delegates, became a reality. Mayfield's arrival and delivery of his assigned sermon the next day was too late to set the Convention's tone.

The 1870 Convention proved memorable for other reasons. Seventy-three delegates representing nine associations and twenty-five churches assembled, and important visitors abounded: G. J. Johnson of St. Louis, district secretary of the American Baptist Bible and Publication Society; John Barry, Sunday School Board missionary for Arkansas; James Nelson from the Mississippi Convention; and J. R. Graves, president of the Southern Baptist Publication Society. It seemed that perhaps in this fourth meeting after the war, the Convention had finally found its feet. It even, for the first time in twenty years, authorized communications with surrounding state conventions.

Each visitor was accorded the privilege of addressing the Convention on matters of their interest. J. R. Graves made the most of his opportunity, providing delegates with "a thrilling speech of considerable length" on Friday morning. Nelson's presentation the next morning eclipsed Graves's effort in substance if not in theatrics.

Offering greetings from Mississippi, Nelson submitted a document for the delegates' consideration that helped the Convention realize the long-cherished goal of collegiate training for its ministers under its own auspices. Nelson began with an offer for Arkansas Baptists, which he also made to those in Louisiana, designed to make Mississippi College a regional Baptist university.

In support of his offer, Nelson observed that like religion, education acknowledges no artificial boundaries such as those separating states from each other. Mississippi College, already in operation instead of merely "on the drawing board," stood easily accessible from all three states—a geographical accessibility enhanced by railroad service. The deserted buildings that had once been Mt. Lebanon University near Louisiana's Arkansas border south of Magnolia offered "crumbling props of the unwise policy of separate State efforts" while "pleading for a wise cooperation." In exchange for "pecuniary contribution and patronage," the Arkansas Convention would have the privilege of appointing trustees proportionally equalling its share of the total number of Baptists in the three states: nine for Mississippi, four for Arkansas, and three for Louisiana Baptists.

After referral to a special committee composed of D. M. Cochran, W. D. Mayfield, and J. B. Searcy, the Mississippi offer returned to the Convention floor with an enthusiastic endorsement. Delegates resolved, in a rare show of unanimity, to adopt Mississippi College as Arkansas's Baptist institution.

Mississippi College's pre-war existence, successful weathering of the recent cataclysmic war, and enthusiastic support by former Mississippians like T. S. N. King (pre-war Mississippi Baptist leader and trustee of the Mississippi Baptist Education Society and now stalwart of the Mount Vernon Association) and the Comperes (with their ties to Mississippi, where E. L. Compere grew up and lived in the immediate post-war years before returning to the Fort Smith area), helped convince Arkansas Baptists that here at last was the answer to their long-standing goal.

For almost a decade, despite maneuvering and uncertainty, the Mississippi College arrangement did provide Arkansas Baptists' answer. Increased support worked its wonders, and in 1872, the trustees reported the college debt-free. Rejoicing at the demise of the debt which crippled the college's usefulness and "imperilled" its existence, they proclaimed it their "first, second, and last duty to stay out of debt." Pursuing that debt-free future, the college sought a permanent endowment. In nine months, the agent solicited $33,400 in interest bearing subscriptions. Then the Panic of 1873 swept the country and began one of the institution's most difficult eras.

An unstable political situation between the war and 1876 hampered economic endeavor; "Redeemers" who then ushered in Democratic rule for the rest of the century brought stability but not economic development. An undependable labor supply only exacerbated the nationwide economic downturn, which depressed cotton prices below the cost of production. A social structure that had depended upon chattel slavery as long as anyone could remember had to adjust to its demise. Finally, the 1870s witnessed severe yellow fever epidemics, the worst in 1878. Social, political, and economic shocks and instability poisoned the atmosphere of progress, and Mississippi College faltered.

It was, as much as anything else, the realization that Mississippi College would be as much of a drain upon Arkansas resources as any other college that caused Arkansas Baptists to rethink their involvement. Their acceptance of the Mississippi Convention's 1870 offer resulted in Arkansans paying half the Mississippi College indebtedness. The 1872 Convention, at which W. D. Mayfield reported the college out of debt, also heard supporters say that only an agent was needed for Arkansas to raise its allotted part of the proposed endowment. In 1879, Arkansas withdrew from the cooperative arrangement. Arkansans continued to patronize the college, and Arkansas Baptists continued to support Arkansas ministers attending the school for several years. Its emphasis had, however, obviously changed.

Part of the Convention's change in emphasis resulted from Arkansas competition with Mississippi College for resources and support. Some Arkansans who promoted Baptist education disliked seeing Arkansans send so much support to another state's institution, especially since Arkansas Baptists only had a quarter of the trustee votes there. Those who preferred a local educational alternative had an option available beginning the same year the Convention adopted Mississippi College.

A native New York minister and Colgate-educated teacher named Matthew R. Forey provided Arkansans with their local alternative. Forey founded a girls school in North Carolina and another in New York before the war. After the war, he moved to Illinois, taught in a private school, then became a financial agent for the University of

Chicago. Concerned with the need for religious education in the South, Forey organized The Baptist College Colony.

The small band reached Arkansas in 1870 determined to establish a denominational school, only to encounter economic difficulties and sectional strife. In less than a year, they found themselves "impoverished and wrecked by land speculators . . . and in the midst of a community recently hostile and in arms." Undaunted, they petitioned the state for a charter; in 1871 the state created Judson University, of which Forey became president. The ambitious Baptists then secured enough credit to buy a 250-acre plantation near Prospect Bluff, which they named Judsonia.

These carpetbaggers from Michigan, Iowa, and Illinois encountered opposition to their presence, their Republican politics and the trappings of culture that adorned their homes. Locals accused the interlopers of nefarious activities; the colonists in their promotional literature carefully observed that they maintained family integrity rather than practicing communal living.

Forey courted St. Louis steamboat owner/operators and the railroad (the Cairo and Fulton came through in 1872) as a way to attract settlers, so that the Colony could pay its mortgage by selling lots. On the other hand, the Colony continued to anger natives: in 1872, the college suspended classes to make the building available for a free school—part of the Republican agenda in the Southern states—and Forey served as chaplain for Arkansas's Republican legislature.

The Arkansas Baptist State Convention first officially recognized Judson's existence in 1873 by recommending it to state Baptists, but Convention approbation could not overcome sectional prejudice and financial insecurity. A severe drought and "unsettled political conditions" scared off would-be settlers. The board erected a new school building on more debt, and in early 1874, described the school's financial status as "embarrassing" with a mortgage due. The trustees sent Forey East to raise money, named Benjamin Thomas of Little Rock to take Forey's place as president, and discussed consolidating with some other institution or forfeiting their property. Thomas, a South Wales native with a Doctor of Divinity degree who had lived in Ohio before coming South, and Forey succeeded: in mid-1875, a nearby newspaper noted that the colony was growing and the debt was paid.

In 1875 and 1876, the *Western Baptist*, published in Searcy, actively promoted the nearby university, calling for statewide Baptist support. The newspaper's campaign set the stage for Thomas's 1876 attempt to have Arkansas Baptists officially adopt Judson. His failure, due in large measure to stiff opposition from the "Mississippi College contingent," doomed any chance of Judson becoming "the Arkansas Baptist College" envisioned by educational proponents.

Speaking and preaching across the state, Thomas raised Baptist interest in the school, but J. B. Searcy remarked that the school's Northern influence tainted it irredeemably. Though Forey and Thomas raised money in their former states, the money proved insufficient to make up for their associations. Thomas's speeches, agents' pleas, and even the dulcet tones of singers sent from Judson across the state failed to secure active Convention support.

To combat the perception that their school owed too much to its Northern roots, the trustees included Southerners in their work. Men like T. B. Espy, Samuel Stevenson, and J. P. Eagle sat on the board almost from the beginning. But the school still lacked the full confidence and support of Arkansas Baptists.

In 1879, the trustees again mortgaged property, then instituted plans to run a tighter financial ship. They began charging the community—including the Judsonia Baptist Church—to use the building and tried more efficient collection methods. Each new economy faced additional expenses. The trustees were reduced to forfeiting land to meet tax levies and creditors were reduced to suing for their money.

In 1880, the board mortgaged additional land to meet another outstanding debt, and Thomas resigned. The trustees replaced Thomas with Michigan native R. S. James. When financial exigencies prompted President James to propose to the trustees in 1881 that Judson ask Arkansas Baptists for an endowment of $50,000, the trustees refused.

In 1882, Eagle, Thomas, and James were Convention president, secretary, and chairman of the Education Committee respectively. Under their guidance, the denomination proposed that the Convention recommend trustees, a move which went nowhere. By the next year, the Convention was making plans for a state denominational college, which would not be Judson; in early 1890, the pastor of the Judsonia Baptist Church pastor wrote the *Arkansas Baptist* a letter which casually mentioned that "The Judson University is dead, and its property sold."

Arkansas's adoption of Mississippi College and dalliance with Judson University did not constitute the Convention's sole efforts at ministerial education. The Ministerial Education Board reported that when William Lea and E. L. Compere had been appointed agents, only Lea had been able to accept; no one had been found to take Compere's place, which left only one agent in the field. Lea and other interested individuals had uncovered opposition throughout the state, and the board related "strong efforts" to destroy the board's "efficiency," if not the board itself. Despite the opposition, Lea had been able to arrange for several churches to support preacher E. H. Owen's theological and literary education, and about twenty others had asked the board's help.

Because of the interest in the board's activities, and in partial response to opposition, the Convention changed the previously adopted plan. Designed to minimize disagreement, the changes discarded the specific amount of $10,000 for the more neutral word "funds"; specified that only licensed ministers recommended by their home churches be considered, and that only after examination by the board; limited aid to "absolute necessities," with a $150 annual maximum; and placed certain personal restrictions on beneficiaries (including a prohibition against their marrying).

The Convention perhaps best demonstrated its interest in ministerial education by their reaction to Nelson's Sunday sermon, preached at 11:00 A.M. in the Arkadelphia First Baptist Church. Using Matthew 3:37 as his text and "Ministerial Calling and Education" as his title, Nelson preached to such effect that listeners contributed about $700 in cash and pledges to the cause.

Committee reports differed more in degree than in substance from those of previous years. The Missions Committee recommended, and delegates voted, that the board appoint six evangelists—two west and south of the Arkansas River, two between the Arkansas and White Rivers, and the last two east and north of the White. The Committee on Sunday Schools noted the concept's advance from religious instruction for poor children to instruction for all children to instruction for all ages and all classes. The next step was the universal application of Sunday Schools to all churches and into the whole year. It then proposed a

Sunday School Convention in each association, a move to provide counsel and instruction—especially in the method of collecting statistics, interesting facts, and incidents. The Publications Committee recommended the usual materials, though it omitted the *Arkansas Hymnal* through design or oversight, and cautioned against all literature that compromised "the great and fundamental principles of our faith which separate us alike from both Catholics and Protestants."

Two additional features of the 1870 meeting marked a departure from the past. For the first time, the Convention proposed to pay an individual for something other than work as an agent or missionary. True, the recording secretary had traditionally been paid a token for producing, printing, and distributing the minutes. Also true, most of the agents and many of the missionaries had been on the "self-supporting" plan in their Convention work. But in 1870, the Convention voted $200 in salary for W. D. Mayfield for his upcoming service as the Convention's corresponding secretary.

Also, the Convention resumed advertisements in the minutes. It voted to advertise "the University (now Mississippi College)," the Bible and Publication Society, and whatever J. R. Graves wished to put on two pages (the latter two advertisements to be paid for with tracts, which the Convention could distribute in the state).

As should be expected, Graves's "advertisement" revealed a different tone of the meeting than did the minutes. True to form, Graves advertised his Southern Baptist Publication Society by attacking whatever might endanger it. No doubt prompted by the presence of G. J. Johnson in the Convention meeting, he focused his attack on Northern Baptists and the society Johnson represented.

Between 1845 and the war, Graves reminded readers, Southern Baptists had cared for the South, Northern Baptists for the North. During and since the war, he continued, Northern Baptist Boards had ("like the Pope") claimed jurisdiction over the whole. They were intent upon "the religious jurisdiction of the entire South" and used the American Baptist Publication Society and Colored School Missions as their instruments, he warned. Having evoked Arkansas Baptist prejudice against Catholics and Yankees, Graves warmed to his subject with another item. Northern Baptists have money, he cautioned—money with which to secure patronage and agents. The results of their plan could be seen in Missouri, where Baptists had been divided and as a result had deserted the SBC.

Catholics, Yankees, and the moneyed class—what more could Graves utilize in calling Arkansas Baptists to stand with him in the Southern Baptist Publication Society and against all opponents? The issue of unity versus dissension became his final argument. He pointed out that "unity of feeling and in action is being destroyed" and dissension engendered "as was manifested in the last Convention. . . ." The Convention's promotion of an approved hymnal (in 1860) had bound Baptists together. Now Northern Baptists were driving it from circulation with "a smaller, inferior, but a little cheaper book, so that now scarce any two churches will use the same hymn book, and when a brother moves, he must purchase a new book." Arkansas Baptists should carefully ponder "whether they will favor the designs of the North in the religious subjugation of the South" or give their patronage to Southern boards and societies.

A careful reading of the 1870 minutes, especially in light of Graves's allegations, could support his contention of dissension among the delegates. The unanimous vote for Mississippi College was the only one listed; for the first time a motion was tabled rather than discussed and voted upon; for the first time a committee report was recommitted; vigorous discussion of several committee reports delayed their adoption, and in two cases that adoption came only after amendment (another first); and finally, for the first time in over a decade, delegates resolved to publish the constitution (for which they chose the original rather than that as amended in 1859) and rules of decorum. Whether these cases merely reflect the usual, which previously went unreported, or whether they reflect a new, less congenial atmosphere lies in the realm of speculation. All the evidence is conjectural, save this one stark warning from an interested rather than a disinterested party. Certainly no one ever accused Graves of mincing his words!

If the decade began with the seeds of dissension, as Graves warned, evidence remained that the seeds sprouted at the 1871 meeting in Magnolia. Despite Moses Green's sermon from Hebrews 13:1 on the theme "Let Brotherly Love Continue," the election of officers as the Convention convened raised a procedural issue. As Secretary J. B. Searcy recorded it, the "question was sprung:" was a plurality or majority vote required for an officer's election? Discussion resulted in a decision for a majority vote, which required reballoting for president. This session, like the previous one, saw committee reports referred back to their origin (this time with the addition of members to the committee in question), report adoptions delayed by vigorous discussion, lack of unanimity in votes, and motions accepted only after amendments. Unlike any previous, minutes of this session likewise recorded credentials examined, the roll called—in short, careful attention to procedure, the kind of attention usually fostered by contending factions. Yet the record also revealed some remarkable steps forward, taken perhaps in spite of disagreements.

Some steps carried the Convention in new directions. Delegates created a standing Committee on Foreign Missions, the first time the Convention had dealt with that issue since 1854. Timing for this addition proved propitious, for a collection netted sixty-five dollars, twenty-five of it designated to "the Rome mission." For the first time, the Convention discussed disaster relief. Delegates invited W. D. Mayfield to speak on behalf of the Helena church, which had had its building "destroyed by wind." From those assembled, he gathered more than one hundred dollars—most of it in cash rather than pledges.

Most steps were continuations, affirmations that previous actions had been correct. Advertisements in the minutes continued—from the same sources (though Central Female College joined the list). W. D. Mayfield's $200 stipend for acting as secretary was continued, though this time for his work as secretary of the Board of Ministerial Education. J. B. Searcy, during discussion of the report on education, revealed that he had pledged on behalf of the Convention to cover half of Mississippi College's $800 debt but had only raised $100. Attendees immediately subscribed the remaining $300, almost a tenth supplied by three women in attendance.

Some continuations could not count as steps forward, but more resembled marching in place. The Domestic Mission Board reported little progress. The board had appealed through the paper for men and money, but received neither. Ministers from other states had indicated interest in the work—but only "if the pay was ample and sure," which the board could not guarantee. Finally some from Arkansas had volunteered on terms the board could meet; they commissioned J. M. Brundage to the

White River country on the self-sustaining plan. Even such a sad report had its moments of progress. It concluded with the news that the Bartholomew Association had agreed to conduct its missionary work in conjunction with the board, and the SBC Domestic Mission Board had consented to match whatever the Arkansas Board paid missionaries they shared.

The board's promise of help from the Southern Convention would only avail the state anything if the state could generate some income. The Missions Committee believed that the fault lay with the ministry, not the members. Estimating that the state had 30,000 Baptists, its report maintained that the ministry's laxity in teaching the churches their duty "inspires them to lethargy."

As the Ministerial Education Board showed in its report, lethargy was relative. In a rare moment, the board admitted that it had enough money to meet all its expenses; it had chosen to work through the ministers rather than through an agent. It supported four ministers at Mississippi College: J. D. Fletcher, Levi W. Coleman, J. D. Jameson, and E. H. Owen. One association was cooperating in the work, and R. A. Venable would soon be joining the other four scholars.

Lethargy did not rear its head during the convention. Representation among the delegates remained at the same high level as the previous year's: seventy-four delegates represented nine associations and thirty churches. G. J. Johnson returned to represent the American Baptist Publication Society and address the Convention on its behalf (though this time W. D. Mayfield followed that address with one asking what the relation should be between Southern and Northern Baptists); A. Dyson and W. T. Everett came from Louisiana and Texas respectively; James Nelson and A. D. Brooks represented Mississippi; and J. R. Graves finally arrived on Sunday to preach and represent the Southern Baptist Publication Society. After Graves appeared and before Johnson's departure, the Convention asked the two men to discuss the shortcomings of literature produced by their respective societies.

Graves and Johnson surely held their own, but the outcome of their evening's talk probably outstripped what they could have imagined. Each wound up admitting weaknesses, with Graves even offering to secure from other sources items which might augment the deficits revealed that night. The report on publications had the last word on the issue, and it certainly must have rankled both men. Speaking for the committee, Aaron Yates observed the difficulty of recommending any literature. He proposed that the convention again adopt *The Baptist* as its organ. He admitted that the committee regarded the *Christian Repository*, the *Home and Foreign Journal* and *Kind Words* as valuable. But when it came to other publications, "we have no Publication Society in which we have unbounded confidence." The committee's final word? "[W]e cannot be too careful in the selection of our religious literature."

Evidence that the Baptists' internal dissension merely reflected the times appeared when William Borum reported the only murder of a Baptist minister in this era. For the Committee on Obituaries, Borum recounted how this pastor of the Fellowship Church in Sebastian County "fell in the work, faithful at his post, by the hand of a fellow creature." Counting Deschamps a martyr to the faith and practices of the Gospel, Borum called his death a calamity for his church and community.

The Convention's 1872 annual meeting in Austin was a first tentative step above the Arkansas River. For the first time the Convention ventured outside its region of origin—though not too far out! Aside from this tentative expansion, the meeting remained remarkably similar to the ones before. Twelve associations and twenty-six churches were represented by ninety-two individuals who, along with five individual members, brought attendance to a record ninety-seven.

By the last (and fifth) day, delegates tried to hurry up the process by limiting debate. An adopted resolution limited speeches to five minutes per individual on any single subject.

The usual committees offered the usual reports. That on foreign missions indirectly revealed one feature of the missions question. Averring that they believed that Arkansas Baptists were "awakening to the importance of mission work, both at home and abroad," the committee revealed its "great pleasure" that receipts for foreign missions ($150, and an additional $56 for Indian missions) had not decreased what had been given for domestic missions. Indeed, the reverse proved true. The committee did not reveal, though it was true, that most of the money collected for Convention causes was taken up at the annual meetings rather than through agents.

The Board of Ministerial Education reported its inability to secure an agent and the resulting necessity of raising funds themselves, mainly through the secretary's work. Nonetheless, it managed to keep in school J. D. Fletcher, R. A. Venable, E. H. Owen, Levi W. Coleman, and J. D. Jameson (though Jameson was supported by his association rather than Convention efforts, the board claimed his support). At least it maintained these scholars at Mississippi College for a time; Coleman, Owen, and Jameson, pleading "feeble health," had returned home "for a season." The committee not only reported its poor luck with an agent, it revealed that Board Secretary W. D. Mayfield had resigned.

The Committee on Education, arguing that the Convention's prime mission was enlightening "the masses" on everything concerning their well being "here and hereafter," urged unanimity and increased activity to enlist the churches in the effort.

The Committee on Documents reported an invitation from the Springfield Association to cooperate in building a high school at Springfield, Conway County, but recommended its referral to the Committee on Education, though with a favorable notice. This committee obviously resulted from increased Baptist interest in documenting all aspects of denominational activity, for it urged the compilation of a comprehensive listing of all ministers (licensed and ordained) and associational moderators and clerks.

The Committee on Domestic Missions reported that the SBC Domestic Mission Board had agreed to assist in the Arkansas work. With that board's help, the committee recommended that the Convention appoint a missionary, who should be paid $100 a month in addition to his expenses.

President M. Y. Moran appointed a special committee, consisting of J. R. G. W. N. "Alphabet" Adams (Dardanelle Association), J. Dunagin (Bentonville Association), T. P. Boone (Caroline Association), W. H. Robert (Mt. Vernon Association) and J. F. Coleman (Austin Church), to consider the issue of Shiloh Institute. The Mississippi College report was tabled until the Shiloh Institute Committee could report, then was amended and adopted. The Shiloh Committee reported that the institute in Washington County was the first denominational school established in the state. Since the school had already been endorsed by the Dardanelle, Fayetteville, and State Corner Associations (as well as the Shoal Creek, Missouri Association), the Committee recommended that the Convention "take hold of this school" and make it a first-class institution. The delegates tabled, but ordered printed, the report.

The Committee on Mississippi College glowingly reported statewide interest and promised that an agent would find the people ready to "do what they can" to endow the school. The college was now out of debt, Mayfield reported, and now had an endowment fund of about thirty thousand dollars. Arkansas Baptists would certainly secure their quota of the endowment goal if only an agent would appear.

The Board of Domestic Missions reported that it had tried to employ G. B. Eager as general missionary agent. To do so, it contacted each of the churches Eager pastored and asked them to release him for the proposed work. All refused, so the board went without. Finally they employed E. H. Owen, who had dropped out of Mississippi College because of poor health. Given the circumstances, they only employed him by the day and received only sixty days of his labor. In late May, they hired J. H. Spann, only to have him resign four months later. Had it not been for arrangements with Bartholomew Association, which employed two missionaries (H. E. Hempstead in the association's northern section and H. Simms in its southern), and Pine Bluff Association, which did also (L. Quinn and T. A. Reid), the Convention would have had no real work in the state. The board reported two important "destitutions" where Baptists had no preaching: Pine Bluff (which had had no regular pastor since the war and was at that point reduced to four male and a few female members) and Tulip (near which the Convention had begun, but which now consisted only of a good building and a few adherents).

The Committee on Publications recommended *The Baptist* as the state paper, *Kind Words* as the Sunday School paper, and the *Home and Foreign Journal*.

The Committee on Sunday Schools reported its inability to properly report the work in the state due to a lack of definite statistics. Brethren in some parts of the state had escaped notice; private letters and public appeals through *The Baptist* and the *Central Baptist* yielded no result. The report revealed that Sunday Schools in Arkansas were isolated, neither influencing nor encouraging each other; that they lacked competent superintendents and teachers; and that what the work really needed was a way to regulate, unify, and invigorate a system of cooperation. Perhaps the way had been found, it added, in the Central Baptist Sunday School Convention, which had just resolved itself into the Arkansas Baptist Sunday School Convention.

With an Executive Committee located at Searcy and headed by B. D. Turner, this state convention had allied with the SBC Sunday School Board and in concert with it had put a Sunday School evangelist (W. H. Robert) into the field. The combination had convinced the Bible and Publication Society (Philadelphia) to reconsider its efforts. Over the previous two and a half years, the society had focused on southern Arkansas and organized over fifty Baptist Sunday Schools (and furnished them with a library, Testaments, hymnals, and other printed materials), three Sunday School Conventions, and several churches. Its missionary had even baptized forty-five converts. Having spent more than three thousand dollars, it proposed to abandon the field to local interests. G. J. Johnson, the society's district secretary from St. Louis, had so informed delegates on Thursday when the meeting opened. The report closed on a somber note: the reported sixty-six schools with 2,718 scholars, which represented probably half of those in the state, had resulted from a quarter-century of hard work. The committee recommended, and the delegates agreed, that the Convention turn over all Sunday School work to the Arkansas Baptist Sunday School Convention, and that the Sunday School Convention work with the SBC, the Bible and Publication Society, or "any other body of regular Baptists in the world" which would offer "*material aid*" to the effort.

The resolutions recommended Shiloh Institute to Arkansas Baptists and allowed the Board of Ministerial Education to examine interested young men in person or by proxy. Also that the Domestic Mission Board secretary be reimbursed for expenses.

The Convention's circular letter, the first since the war, celebrated its silver anniversary. It noted that most of those who led in the Convention's organization were now dead and that some of their most cherished objectives had perished with the war and its results. Assuming a naval metaphor, Secretary Searcy stated that as a new crew in the same old ship with the same old chart and compass, Arkansas Baptists had set out again. The chart and compass pointed to educating young ministers and cultivating the home mission field. Mississippi

College had provided education for four young men who had not graduated, but greatly benefited from their time there. It closed with the observation that students could do most of the required domestic mission work during their vacation, and that "a pittance from the brethren" would satisfy their clothing and incidental expenses at school. The call to put young men to work in the various associations concluded Searcy's missive.

The 1874 meeting at Dardanelle demonstrated a seeming lessening of tensions; the officers were elected by acclamation for the first time since the war. N. H. Parker, the Convention's oldest minister, dismissed the meeting with prayer before a parting hymn closed "a most pleasant and harmonious session." The usual mass meeting for foreign missions ended with a collection for the cause.

The State Mission Board reported its lack of a missionary agent for the year, and that it had only had a missionary (H. E. Hempstead) in the field ("on the self-sustaining plan," of course) for a brief time, and that in the state's southeastern border. The Home Missions Committee recommended dividing the state into halves, with a corresponding secretary for the southern and one for the northern division (J. D. Rasberry and T. P. Boone respectively). Their task would be to foster cooperation among the pastors, associations, and Executive Committee and coordinate reports on all associational undertakings for the Convention. The result envisioned by the Committee would be a statistical account of the denomination in the state.

The Committee on Sunday Schools admitted that the State Sunday School Convention had not met with sufficient success to justify its continuance, and recommended that the Convention "take under its care" general Sunday School work in Arkansas. To accomplish this goal, the committee recommended that the Convention appoint a state Sunday School secretary (and that R. M. Thrasher fill that post). That secretary would be tasked with gathering statistics for the board at Marion, Alabama; serving as liaison between the board and Arkansas; acting as a clearinghouse for information within the state; and reporting statistics to Convention meetings as a way of bolstering the work.

The Committee on Publications, stating that "This is most emphatically an age of reading," strongly recommended the Southern Baptist Publication Society in Memphis, the *New Baptist Psalmist* as a hymnal,

The Little Seraph and *Kind Words* for Sunday Schools, the *Foreign Mission Journal* for those interested in missions, and that state Baptists continue their patronage of *The Baptist*. Almost as an afterthought, the committee also recommended *The Western Baptist* (published at Searcy by Espy and Boone).

Mississippi College reported that enrollment had increased by 25 percent over the past year. On the heels of the trustees' report, the Committee on Ministerial Education gave its own report. They carefully noted that the report did not intend to either disparage "the many uneducated pioneer preachers" who made Baptists in Arkansas what they were or to downplay true piety and God's call to preach. The report continued with the observation that an educated man would be much more useful than an uneducated one. In this respect, the state had been fortunate. Without having raised any endowment, the Convention discovered "a first-class college" offering itself as the Convention's educational institution. By accepting the offer, the Convention found that a third of Mississippi College became "the actual property of Arkansas Baptists." Things had only gotten better. Thanks to the efforts of James Nelson (Mississippi minister who devoted himself to the school and had represented it faithfully in Convention meetings), student board had been reduced from $15 to $10 per month by the erection of Steward's Hall. In light of this good fortune, Arkansas Baptists should bend every effort to ensure that the rising ministry would be able to use "sound speech" against all opponents.

While the committee's report was optimistic, the Ministerial Board's report lacked the committee's enthusiasm. W. D. Mayfield, who had been board secretary, had moved from Helena to Memphis; without a secretary to push the work, the board had virtually nothing. Immediately after the 1873 Convention meeting, four Arkansans had been in school at Mississippi College under board support: R. A. Venable, J. D. Jameson, R. A. Lee, and B. W. Martin. Support had depleted the treasury and the young men had soon been without support. Venable taught school a month; Jameson began pastoring a church (which mainly supported him in school); and J. B. Searcy (who had taken over Mayfield's responsibility after his resignation) managed to raise some support personally.

The Committee on Foreign Missions focused almost exclusively on money. It called for a mass meeting and collection at the Convention's annual meeting. It recommended that each pastor raise a collection for foreign missions before the following April as a way to raise more of the state's pro rata share of the SBC's Foreign Mission Board's needs ($1,000, or three cents per Arkansas Baptist). It recommended that churches use "mite boxes" offered by H. A. Tupper, secretary of the SBC Foreign Mission Board in Richmond, Virginia. Finally, it recommended that the Convention act as Arkansas secretary for Foreign Missions. The State Convention's Foreign Mission Board's report illustrated just how difficult raising the state's portion of the Foreign Mission Board's needs would be—less than $75 had been collected during the previous year.

The Committee on Deceased Ministers reported the deaths of J. V. McCulloch of Hot Springs; F. M. McClendon of Mountain Association; and I. B. Edwards and William Everett of Bartholomew Association.

The minutes for 1874 reported five Convention secretaries devoted to four particular tasks: T. P. Boone of Searcy and J. D. Rasberry of Hamburg for Home Missions above and below the river; T. B. Espy of Searcy for Foreign Missions; J. B. Searcy of Warren for Ministerial Education; and R. M. Thrasher of Malvern for Sunday Schools. The incipient organization was in place for great Convention strides.

The Convention's annual circular letter pointed to the great weakness in attempts at progress by the Convention. It called upon every Baptist to "elevate and sustain the reputation of Arkansas Baptists." Obviously, Convention proponents worried about the denomination's standing in Arkansans' eyes. When Secretary J. B. Searcy called upon all association clerks to forward copies of their minutes so that accurate statistics could be published, he obviously spoke as a good bureaucrat. Implying that there were obviously more than 26,000 Arkansas Baptists, Searcy revealed his assumption that bigger numbers would garner respect from Arkansans in general and sustain the Baptist reputation.

The 1875 meeting in Arkadelphia marked a departure from the custom of meeting times. Since its inception, the Convention's annual meeting had occurred in October or November. In 1874, the Convention had voted to meet in Arkadelphia in late July, which they did.

Minutes of the 1878 Convention meeting in Monticello the second week in August indicate renewed trouble for the Convention. In a special notice, Secretary William F. Mack noted that he had faced the necessity of condensing the minutes to diminish printing costs—but had still found it necessary to advance some of the costs himself. Rainy weather depressed attendance: fifty-one delegates from twenty churches and five associations gathered to hear M. D. Early, from Red River Association, open the Convention meeting with an evangelistic sermon based on Matthew 1:21. Appointment of the usual committees was supplemented by a special one on "colored brethren" and another on constitutional amendments.

Whether from the weather or other causes, the annual meeting lacked the harmony of recently previous gatherings. The election of officers lacked unanimity. Delegates wrangled over credentials and domestic missions. Certain brethren suggested that perhaps some delegates had been admitted contrary to the Convention's constitution and its requirements, necessitating a special committee on credentials—which reported no irregularities. Delegates tabled the Domestic Missions Committee's report to listen to the Executive Committee on Home Missions, which they debated hotly—a debate marked by numerous motions, votes, and appeals from the chair's decisions—before referring both reports to a special committee.

When the special committee reported on home missions, it noted that W. A. Clark had labored valiantly as missionary/agent. Despite Clark's efforts, the report cited thirty-one county seats without Baptist churches; a complete absence of Baptist ministers in Desha, Crittenden, Mississippi, and Lafayette Counties; and languishing churches (some in debt) in Louisville, Camden, Pine Bluff, Hot Springs, Fort Smith, Clarksville, Batesville, and DeWitt. The report ended with a call for special but regular home missions offerings in the churches and for a change in how the Convention appointed its Mission Board. Board members should be chosen with an eye to a more central location rather than scattered over the state; the previous dispersion of members had put the board at a distinct disadvantage.

The report on education likewise engendered lively discussion and debate. The committee likened the comparison of higher to primary education to a comparison of reaping and threshing machines to sickle and frail before arguing that Arkansas Baptists were awakening to the importance of advanced education. Citing E. L. Compere's Buckner College, Shiloh College, Judsonia University, and J. Shackleford's Forrest City High School in the north and "the younger and less pretentious but not less promising" Centennial Institute at Warren (W. E. Paxton, president) and the Arkadelphia High School (B. J. Dunn, president) in the south, the committee lauded efforts so far. It then foreshadowed the special committee due to report on "a central college" which would be "a common institution for the whole State" and provide the capstone to Baptist educational efforts in the state. That committee's report proved anticlimactic. When called upon by the president at the Convention's very end (when the time rule had been suspended to ensure that all the Convention's business could be undertaken), W. A. Forbes admitted that the year-old committee had never met and could therefore not submit a report.

The Foreign Missions report, for the first time, featured a particular mission. Delegates heard a lengthy report on "the Italian Mission," which had originated in 1870 when the missionary accompanied the victorious Victor Emanuel into Rome and thus struck at Popery's heart. The Convention took up two offerings for "the Rome Chapel" but netted only $15.35, far short of the state's allotment of $300 assigned by the SBC. Part of the problem lay revealed in J. B. Searcy's report as secretary of Foreign Missions for the state: Arkansas Baptists had contributed almost $255, but had made all but $93 directly rather than sending it to Searcy.

The Publications Committee promoted the "diffusion of a sound denominational literature" on the grounds that efficient work required that Arkansas Baptists know what had been done, what was proposed, and the means to accomplish the proposals. Observing the need for "a live State paper that is chock full of Arkansas" as a contribution to "the unification of the Baptists of the State," the report recommended *The Western Baptist*, published in Little Rock. Though it showed "the marks of the cruel abandonment," and though Arkansas Baptists could "continue to starve it to death," the committee heartily recommended its support and urged that those who submitted items "write short, spicy articles, and furnish the editors with items of interest." For the first time, the committee had not recommended J. R. Graves's newspaper—which may have been part of the reason for the report's lengthy discussion, featuring (among others) W. A. Forbes, Solomon Gardner, M. D. Early, J. B. Searcy, and J. T. Craig.

The Sunday School Committee renewed its annual call for more involvement, calling on "every brother and sister" to take part in the work and recommending the *International Kind Words* to Arkansas Baptists.

The Committee on the Colored Race urged that Arkansas Baptists help them establish churches and instruct their preachers. "We are too apt to let our prejudice lead us from duty," the committee cautioned, "but we should look to what these people are to be, and not what they have been." They were naturally inclined to be Baptists; their "former owners and now their warmest friends" should give them "every chance to be intelligent Baptists."

The Committee on Constitutional Amendments proposed amendments to provide for the presentation of proper credentials or vouchers by the delegates and their payment of two dollars or more for Convention purposes; for a seat and vote to any Baptist, delegate or not, who paid $2.50 to the treasury; for a mandate to gather denominational statistics; and for a late-November annual meeting date. The delegates adopted them all.

The 1879 Convention meeting at Hope violated the constitutional amendment passed the previous year; delegates gathered at the end of October for the five-day meeting.

R. J. Coleman, appointed in the absence of the previously elected H. M. Bussey, preached from Malachi 3:16–17. Delegates invited the General Association of Southeast Arkansas to correspond before constituting a committee of the whole to consider "the object of its meeting." Following the hymn "All Hail the Power of Jesus' Name," delegates adopted the report based on their deliberations: "The growth of our educational institutions is an index to the real prosperity of our denomination. Therefore it is necessary to our future success that, all things being equal, Arkansas Baptists should patronize home institutions." Support for "Brother Wise" (probably G. G.) at Mississippi College nevertheless was collected; the report concluded that "there should be a college within our bounds, fostered and controlled by this Convention." But until one of the existing institutions achieved "precedence" through work and attendance, Baptists could only urge the development of already existing high schools and "hope that we will soon have a University, around which the Baptists of Arkansas can rally."

The Committee on Education set the stage for the report of the special College Committee. Again, that committee's report was anticlimactic. As it had done the year before, the committee of two reported that it had had no full meetings and was in no position to report. Then it begged to be relieved of any further responsibility. What W. A. Forbes asked, he got; the delegates discharged the committee. Twenty years after the Convention had put education first on its agenda, after efforts interrupted by the war and then resumed, after years of reports stressing the importance of Arkansas having its own college, and three decades after the Convention's founding, Convention loyalists could not even muster a report.

The Committee on Sunday Schools highlighted the Convention's difficulties. The committee admitted growing dissatisfaction among Arkansans with the International Sunday School Lessons. Its report noted that the cause was not in a "very hopeful condition." Churches outside cities and towns seemed to lack interest in Sunday Schools, C. W. Callahan acknowledged. Then, in a futile gesture made before in the same setting, he asked delegates to urge upon pastors "and specially missionaries" the importance of establishing a Sunday School in every church.

Following the hymn "Come Thou Fount of Every Blessing," the Committee on Domestic Missions observed that many associations maintained their own missionaries but attributed advancements in the cause mainly to statewide missionaries sent by the various State Convention Boards. T. B. Espy's report lauded the work of J. F. Shaw (recently resigned missionary) and O. M. Lucas, recommended the continuance of statewide mission endeavors, and urged aid for Camden's suffering congregation. A collection prompted by the report reaped $100 from those assembled, after which they sang the Doxology and adjourned for the day (their daily custom).

The fifth and final day's session opened with Psalm 23 and the hymn "Bless Be the Tie that Binds" preceding parliamentary maneuvering that ended with the delegates amending the constitution. They reversed the previous year's change which had required delegates to pay two dollars before being certified. The new amendment, for the second time in Convention history, deleted any monetary requirement for participation. It also, for the first time, referred to those assembled as messengers. Anyone with proper credentials or satisfactory evidence of appointment would be welcome in the hall. Since the meeting revived the early tradition of inviting any attending minister to participate, the trend was obviously toward inclusion of all interested parties and more individual discretion by attendees.

The Committee on Foreign Missions urged all churches to take up collections for missionary purposes in answer to cries from Africa, China, and Italy (as well as other, unnamed, places). That for Ministerial Education averred that ministers ought to be highly educated where practicable. Then Secretary T. B. Espy admitted that a year in which nothing could be done because there were no means at hand and no time to work up the state had given way to one of more favorable outlook. Brethren Yates and Wise had been helped. M. D. Early of Dardanelle (whose wife had just died) had indicated an interest in attending the Southern Baptist Theological Seminary in Louisville (the first mention in Convention history) and the committee urged the Convention to adopt him as its beneficiary, which was done. Upon R. J. Coleman's resolution, the Convention requested each Association to become its auxiliary and report to it all money expended on missionary work (home or foreign). Delegates also appointed a standing committee on statistics and thanked the officers and managers of the St. Louis, Iron Mountain, and Southern and of the Memphis and Little Rock, and Little Rock and Fort Smith Railways for their assistance to Convention attendees.

In what was certainly an unconscious bit of irony, the Convention adjourned after the hymn "Shall We Gather at the River" to meet the next year in Russellville.

7

The Convention Reconstructed, 1880

"BLESSED IS THE MAN THAT WALKETH NOT IN THE counsel of the ungodly, nor standeth in the way of sinners," the speaker continued, "and he shall be like a tree planted by the rivers of waters that bringeth forth his fruit in due season. . . ." James Philip Eagle, quoted Psalm 1 to the assembled messengers of the Arkansas Baptist State Convention at the annual meeting in Russellville in 1880. The measured cadences of the old hymn, "There is a Fountain," added to the solemnity and meaning of the moment. In the congregation, Eagle could see one of the great Baptist heroes of the era, R. H. Graves, an early Southern Baptist missionary to China. A special guest at the Russellville meeting, Graves represented an emphatic connection to the Southern Baptist Convention and the cause of missions; both the institution and the ideal would figure prominently in the life of James Eagle.

Standing behind the pulpit of the Russellville Church, Eagle, the newly elected president of the State Convention, was beginning a generation of visionary leadership. His election in 1880 was the first of twenty-one such elections; twice he would be chosen president of the Southern Baptist Convention. No individual would do more than James Eagle to shape the life and future of the State Convention.

He was a commanding figure. Full-bearded, with dark penetrating eyes, in black broadcloth suit and white collar, he gave the impression

133

of rugged gentility. His bearing, as his appearance, suggested a man comfortable with authority and command. Eagle had the bearing of a soldier. The commanding and imposing quality of his demeanor was, however, tempered by a certain and apparent kindliness. He readily smiled and when he spoke a certain pliant and deferential note was detectable. Dignified, he lacked any trace of arrogance and so too lacked any need for bombastic or theatrical gestures.

James Philip Eagle's pilgrimage had been an arduous one; his path to the presidency of the Convention had been marked by personal loss, great struggles, privation, striking success, and unusual achievement. Forty-two years old, he had seen and experienced much of the best and worst of the life of his time and region. Like so many of his generation, Eagle's youth—and his subsequent life—reflected his passage through the war. In the war he had learned much about life, about leadership, about victory and defeat. In his rise from private to lieutenant colonel, he certainly learned the limits of human endurance as he learned the difference between heroic posturing and effective leadership. During his nearly five years of military service, Eagle led more than his share of attacks and counter-attacks; on at least two occasions, while a field officer, and with the color bearer dead or wounded, he carried his regiment's flag forward into furious enemy fire. His terrible scars bore unmistakable testimony to his passion for the Confederate cause. No soldier of the South fought with more determination than this tough young Arkansan. In addition to the war's stern lessons on leadership, endurance, and discipline, Eagle learned the vital necessity of adequate supply, careful planning, and reliable communications.

It was during the last year of the war that Eagle professed his faith in Christ. Nothing in his previous life had suggested a special spiritual sensitivity. Indeed, his young years had been largely devoid of religious interests and activity. But under the strain and danger of the war's final cataclysmic months, Eagle listened willingly as two fellow officers pled with him to consider his spiritual peril. Someone gave him a small New Testament; the words of the Gospel message and the witness of faithful friends led Eagle to a profound, dramatic conversion.

Surely he needed his new-found faith as he returned to Arkansas to find his father dead, the family scattered, and their acres neglected and desolate. Though not wealthy, the Eagles had been successful, substantial Prairie County farmers before the war. At least the land was still theirs. Eagle built a small, crude "board cabin" and for the next several years, from daylight to dark, he labored to restore his farm. Each night, in the dim lamplight, he poured over his Bible, turning its pages with calloused, weathered hands, seeking, struggling to grow in his faith. He found encouragement and instruction at the New Hope Church near Lonoke, where, in 1866, he presented himself for baptism and membership.

With the support of his New Hope friends and under the guidance of the church's venerable pastor, Elder Moses Green, Eagle yielded to a ministerial call. Green was surely a formidable influence. By any standard, he stood in the front rank of Arkansas pastors and set a lofty example. For his generation and region Green was rare indeed in his educational attainments. He was a graduate of Tennessee's Union University, one of the South's oldest Baptist institutions. Moreover, Green was a mission-minded, cooperating Baptist. He was a man deeply imbued with the belief that Baptists—as individuals and churches—could do more for the Kingdom in concert than they could do separately. Consequently, Green forcefully supported the Southern Baptist Convention and the struggling Arkansas Baptist State Convention.

Significantly, in 1869, Eagle accompanied Moses Green to the annual meeting of the Southern Baptist Convention in Louisville, Kentucky. William Lea was also present in the small Arkansas delegation to the Louisville meeting. Lea, like Green, was a passionate proponent of cooperation and a determined advocate of the Arkansas Baptist State Convention and its causes; indeed, it was Lea, more than any other individual, who led in the restoration of the State Convention in the immediate aftermath of the war. Attending the Southern Convention in the company of Green and Lea was an invaluable experience for Eagle, an opportunity for intimate interaction with men who believed deeply in the value of Baptist cooperation.

Anxious to prepare himself more fully for his ministerial calling, Eagle, in 1870, enrolled in Mississippi College, the Baptist institution in Clinton, Mississippi. Only modestly prepared for college work, Eagle labored to keep up. The task was made all the more onerous by declining health. The stress of study, his war wounds, the privation and

James P. Eagle served as president of the Arkansas Baptist State Convention for twenty-one years; governor of the State of Arkansas for four years (1889–1893); and president of the Southern Baptist Convention three years (1902–1904).

labor of the preceding decade took their full toil, and Eagle was forced to withdraw from college after only a year. Even so, he had attained a level of education well beyond that possessed by the great majority of contemporary Southerners, including the Baptist clergy. And his year at Mississippi College awakened in Eagle an appetite and appreciation for Baptist higher education which would shape his subsequent life and the life of the State Convention.

When he returned to Arkansas, Eagle labored among small white and black congregations. He especially devoted himself to the "destitute places" in Prairie and the adjacent counties. Like a soldier seeking to reinforce the weak points along the line, Eagle served churches in decline or near collapse. Well before dawn each Sunday, he saddled his mule to begin a long day of preaching and ministering. Heat, dust, cold, and mud, were all taken in their course as Eagle carried his message from one small congregation to another. His careful, straightforward, effective preaching restored the vitality of many small rural churches. Someone nicknamed Eagle's mule, "Gospel," and the preacher-colonel increasingly became known as "Elder Eagle."

By 1880, Eagle was a widely known, respected pastor and evangelist. And over the course of a decade, he became a wealthy planter and also a leader in the state Democratic party. Member of the state Constitutional Convention of 1874, selected as speaker of the Arkansas House of Representatives a few years later—and soon to be a two-term governor—by the early 1880s, Eagle stood in the forefront of Arkansas's political elite. But for all his other pursuits and endeavors, Eagle never lost his zeal for evangelical work and his intense commitment to the Arkansas Baptist State Convention. It was this obvious, profound attachment to his faith and the cooperative ideal, combined with all his other attainments, that made Eagle, perennially, an attractive choice for Convention president.

The Convention that Eagle first presided over in 1880 was scarcely the organization it would be twenty-five years later at the close of his presidential tenure. Indeed, the Arkansas Baptist State Convention of 1880 lacked many of the normative characteristics of denominational organizations in other states at that time. Through some 870 churches and 38 associations, nearly 36,000 white Arkansas Baptists were connected only tenuously to the rather amorphous—equally tenuous—

State Convention. The Convention's relationship with black Arkansas Baptists was, by the time of Eagle's presidency, even more tenuous. Black Baptists were understandably unwilling to accept less than equal respect and standing in the State Convention. Through the 1880s they increasingly developed their own organizations for the promotion of educational and mission initiatives and withdrew from any substantive formal relationship with the State Convention. But, again, there was, in 1880, relatively little that the Convention could offer Baptists, white or black, in the way of consistent financial, educational, or institutional support. At the time, the Convention was less an organization than an ideal. In 1880, the Convention's institutional infrastructure consisted of little more than the published "proceedings" of its annual meetings. Its missionary and educational ministries were rudimentary and erratic.

To be sure, the Convention's committees on missions, education, publications, and the like met with some regularity and, of course, the Convention sponsored an annual meeting of "messengers"—occasionally referred to as "delegates"—drawn from affiliated churches and associations. Moreover, the published Convention "proceedings" suggested a fairly clear vision of missions, schools, publications, new churches, and evangelistic campaigns, but little of that vision had materialized between the war and Eagle's election as Convention president. In 1880, for instance, the Convention collected a paltry $248.00 for foreign missions and $34.00 for home missions—those "domestic" efforts outside Arkansas. The Convention's mission work inside Arkansas consisted primarily of the employment, periodically, of a mission secretary and the rhetorical sponsorship of several "state" missionaries who were largely left to raise their entire financial support under the "self-sustaining plan." As recently as 1874, the Convention failed to appoint any missionaries. Admonitions to associations and churches to support mission work in their own immediate communities made up the balance of the Convention's missionary efforts. Unquestionably, there was much mission work to be done. In 1878, the Convention's Mission Committee reported that thirty-one of Arkansas's county seat towns lacked a Baptist church—this, after nearly thirty years had passed since the Convention's founding.

And in lieu of sponsoring a state Baptist college the Arkansas State Convention, in 1880, only offered a small stipend to students wishing to attend the Mississippi Convention's college. This, despite the fact that the leaders of the State Convention had talked of—dreamed of— founding a Convention college since the 1840s. These leaders of the Convention had realized that without its own college the State Convention, and Baptist work in Arkansas, lacked a reliable force of trained ministers and missionaries. And, unlike most state Baptist conventions of the era, the Arkansas Baptist State Convention lacked not only a convention college, but it even lacked a convention news- paper. The State Convention of 1880 was like an army without a system of training or communication, without even a headquarters establish- ment or a reliable means of material support.

To be sure, Arkansas Baptists had endeavored—across the years— to establish a consolidated Baptist work, including viable educational and publishing entities. However, as of 1880, these tenuous attempts had proved largely disappointing. Not that these disappointments were the result of lassitude or timidity on the part of Convention leaders of the past; to the contrary, much good, heroic work had been accom- plished. But demographic, social, political, and economic forces seemed, time and again, to combine against the Convention and its causes; the war, for instance, had wiped out the Convention's education fund. And the regionalism of Arkansas, mountaineers separated cultur- ally and economically—politically oftentimes—from delta folk, coupled with other diverging social and political patterns, made the consolida- tion of Baptist work in the state all the more difficult. The general poverty of the state, limited educational opportunities, and underdevel- oped transportation and communication resources all mitigated against the development of a stable and energetic state Baptist convention and related institutions and agencies. By the early 1880s, some of the worst of these impediments were lessening, allowing for the possibility, at least, that an influential, stable, consolidated Baptist work could go forward in Arkansas.

With his significant military, business, and political experience to draw upon—and a substantial personal wealth—Eagle became the catalyst for a transformation of the State Convention. Animated by a passionate evangelical zeal, Eagle formulated and pursued plans designed to spread the Gospel through the establishment of Baptist congregations across the state—especially in strategic courthouse towns. He also drove forward the development of Convention communication and educational initiatives. He worked tirelessly to consolidate and coordinate the Convention's fiscal and human resources, to translate the vision of the Convention into reality.

If Eagle emerged as the most visible—and influential—leader of the Convention during the last decades of the century, he was by no means the only significant leader. Indeed, Eagle stood at the center of a cadre of talented and inspired men and women who rivaled his passion for the cause of the Convention and the cause of Christ. Some, surely, even surpassed Eagle, in a single-minded devotion to this or that particular aspect of the Convention's mission. No one, however, surpassed him in the broader denominational perspective. Significantly, Eagle became the symbol and focus of the movement to centralize—or consolidate—the work of the Arkansas Baptist State Convention. In this vision, he, and the many men and women who shared and advanced the cooperationist, consolidating ideal, were actually part of an even larger movement apparent in the Baptist culture of the South during the years between Reconstruction and the turn of the century. Notably, the closing decades of the nineteenth century were marked by aggressive consolidating efforts by the leaders of the Southern Baptist Convention.

The centralizing tendency so evident among Southern Baptists generally in this era coincided with regional and national trends, giving the cooperationist movement in Arkansas additional impetus. The last half of the nineteenth century witnessed an explosion of voluntary scholarly, charitable, political, and civic organizations. Americans seemed to create an organization for every facet of national life. The Indian Aid Society, the United Daughters of the Confederacy, the American Historical Association; these and myriad similar organizations, societies, and conventions were created to advance forcefully the cause or causes cherished by their founders and members. Obviously, this is not to imply that the Arkansas Baptist State Convention was among the newly established organizations and societies of the era, but rather to emphasize the point that many Arkansas Baptists, like their peers across the South, were inspired in the late nineteenth century to see their State Convention play a more forceful role in Arkansas, indeed, a more forceful role in the world. Again, in the minds of many Baptists, a more effective organization, a more structured, better funded Convention, meant a greater capacity for advancing their evangelical ideals and aspirations.

The development of a more effective state Baptist organization was also driven by some measure of state and regional pride. By 1880, the South was largely recovered from the most extreme economic and demographic dislocations caused by the war. And the turbulence of the Reconstruction era had been replaced by what appeared to be a restoration of political stability and a measure of economic prosperity. Simultaneously, many Southerners were animated by a determination to restore fully the prestige and legitimacy of Southern culture even as the Southern economy and political institutions were ostensibly restored. Ultimately, much of this "cultural" resurgence manifested itself in sentimental evocations of the Lost Cause. All across the South, monuments and memorials sprouted, after 1880, as testimony to the mythic heroism and virtue of the Confederacy and its adherents. So too, individual Southern state governments, with a resurgent pride—and also hoping to lure Northern capital for economic development—began in the last decades of the century to advertise aggressively the benefits of their respective states.

As one of state's most prominent and powerful political leaders, Eagle supported enthusiastically the promotion of Arkansas and its human and physical resources. He also fully supported the memorialization of Arkansas's Confederate heritage. Though he rarely spoke of his own service to the Confederate cause, Eagle lent his influence to the creation of a powerful state branch of the United Confederate Veterans; on rare occasions Eagle appeared in public in the "striking," full-dress uniform of a Confederate colonel. This state and regional pride ultimately became entangled—for Eagle and others—with the desire for a more effective Baptist organization. The work of the Arkansas Baptist State Convention should reflect glory first and foremost to God, of course, but the Convention's work should also enhance the image of the state and the South generally.

Never a voice of peaceful cooperation to be sure, but always an influential leader among Baptists in the South, and a venerated figure in Arkansas, John R. Graves had early begun to blend regional, state, and denominational pride as he advocated the use among Southern Baptists of distinctively Southern religious publications. Shortly after the war, Graves chided, "Will the Baptists of the state of Arkansas ponder well these facts, [the need for Baptists of the South to commit themselves to the use of southern denominational publications] and decide whether they will favor the designs of the North in the religious subjugation of the South . . . ?" The language of regional, sectional prerogative and power surely resonated with the men and women who had attempted, only a few years earlier, to create and sustain a separate Southern nation.

At the 1879 annual meeting of the Southern Baptist Convention, Eagle listened as leaders like Isaac Taylor Tichenor and John A. Broadus, revealed their determination to restore the vitality and vision—and prerogatives—of the Southern Baptist Convention. To that end Tichenor proposed a resolution which, though couched in fraternal language, implied a "geographical" delineation of Baptist work; in other words, he intended to claim a special regional domain for the Southern Baptist Convention. Ironically, Tichenor, who had already achieved a reputation as someone willing to confront the "intrusions" of Northern Baptists—notably the American Baptist Missionary Society—into Southern fields was perceived by others as too accomodationist, too timid in moving to secure the South exclusively for the Southern Baptist Convention. Broadus, for one, rejected the Tichenor resolution as potentially tending toward a union with Northern Baptists, which was not Tichenor's intent at all. Tichenor and Broadus both represented the awakening of a movement destined to revive the Southern Baptist Convention and to create a truly cohesive regional organization.

The implications of the Atlanta meeting for Eagle and Arkansas Baptists were profound. At that time, Arkansas had more missionaries and ministers sponsored by the Northern American Baptist Home Missionary Society than by the Southern Baptist Convention. That situation changed completely in a few years. Tichenor, as secretary of the Southern Baptist Convention's Home Mission Board, and James Eagle, president of the Arkansas Baptist State Convention were involved intimately in that transition. Both men were part of a mind set, a perspective, increasingly apparent, to be rid of any lingering inference that Southern virtue and spirituality were inferior forms of the faith or that Southern Baptists needed to be guided by, or dependent upon, Baptists in the North.

The convergence of these powerful cultural and historical perspectives, combined with the emergence of talented, visionary leadership, positioned the Arkansas Baptist State Convention for two decades of remarkable growth and for its movement toward a firm, reciprocal, and exclusive affiliation with the Southern Baptist Convention. Even so, the consolidating efforts of Eagle and his compeers—the vision of a strong, cooperative organization of Arkansas Baptists—faced formidable opposition.

That opposition continued to be grounded in other, venerable Baptist ideals, notably the autonomy of local churches and the soul liberty of individual believers. Ironically, these cherished convictions—when wedded to the same cultural traditions of individualism and localism that helped to build the Arkansas and Southern Baptist Conventions—also mitigated against a placid progression toward a centralized denomination. Then, too, by the turn of the century, powerful personalities and partisan politics emerged to color the debate over centralization and cooperation among Arkansas Baptists. Building the Arkansas Baptist State Convention was not work for the faint of faith or heart.

8

1881–1900

DURING HIS SECOND YEAR AS PRESIDENT OF THE STATE
Convention, Eagle assumed yet another presidency and another responsibility. In 1881, he became the president of the privately owned, newly
created Arkansas Baptist Publishing Company. The primary purpose of
the company was the publication of a state Baptist paper. For Eagle, the
paper was vital. No organization, no political, civic, military, fraternal, or
religious entity could flourish without some means of reliably and regularly communicating with its adherents. Eagle and the other sponsors of
the *Arkansas Evangel* imagined that the paper would serve as a source
of information, a compendium of Convention news. At the same time,
the *Evangel*—as its name suggested—was intended to advance the cause
of Christ as it advanced the cause, or causes, of the Convention. Of
course, in the minds of the *Evangel*'s founders, there was no meaningful
distinction between the Kingdom and the Convention's work.

The first issue, on March 23, 1881, celebrated and promoted the
vision of the men and women who led the Convention. In many
instances the leaders were also—conveniently—the owners of the
Evangel. As previously noted, the paper was produced and distributed
by the privately owned Arkansas Baptist Publishing Company. It was
funded through the sale of stock at twenty-five dollars a share. Along
with Eagle, J. M. King, a pastor and Eagle's former comrade in arms,

144

invested in the *Evangel*, as did Eagle's brother, William.

W. D. Mayfield, another of the original stockholders was a native South Carolinian; he had been active—intermittently—in Arkansas Baptist life since the 1850s; in 1858 he served as president of the State Convention. In 1881, he was serving as a pastor in Little Rock, and periodically, he served as a state missionary—at the expense of his church. Benjamin Thomas, M. M. McGuire, and Dr. O. J. Warren completed the roster of original stockholders in the *Evangel*.

Subscriptions to the *Evangel* were two dollars annually. Advertisers were welcome. The early *Evangel* carried solicitations for Judson College and French Liver Pads; the latter promised to cure virtually everything. The paper featured sermons and Bible commentary. Mission stories and devotional poetry, vignettes from Baptist history, were commonplace in its coverage. The sermons and biblical exposition carried in the paper especially benefited many ministers who lacked formal training for their ministerial vocation.

The *Evangel* operated out of a rented office in the Waite Building in Little Rock. Dr. Fusch, an Illinois physician subscribed half the rent of the office space; the board of the paper paid a fourth of the rent, while the *Evangel* had to supply the balance from subscriptions. Just what prompted the generosity of Dr. Fusch is a mystery—but his largess was typical of the support Arkansas Baptists received from individuals and organizations outside the state.

In their first issue, the *Evangel's* editors, B. R. Womack and J. B. Searcy, asserted that the paper would rival the quality of any denominational paper in the nation. Its size and layout, the editors promised, was second only to Georgia's venerable *Christian Index*. Moreover, the *Evangel* intended to provoke Baptists in Arkansas to ever greater accomplishments for the Kingdom. The emphatic and celebratory passage, Luke 2:14, "Glory to God in the highest," appeared on the paper's masthead, reflecting the enthusiasm and excitement of the *Evangel's* editors and sponsors.

The Reverend R. Lawson of Argenta was also excited about the paper. Lawson, a black pastor, endorsed the paper and its potential benefit to "his people." The *Evangel* responded to this endorsement during the early 1880s by frequently carrying articles praising the piety of black Baptists in Arkansas and saluting especially the work of black pastors. The tone of such articles was paternal, sometimes patronizing, but the editor could also puncture white pretentious with reminders that blacks and whites were both "dust . . . all of Adam" and that "colored brethren" were "joint heirs with Christ." These references advanced no agenda of social equality, but neither did they provide any comfort for those engaging in casual or callous denigration or abuse of African-Americans.

At the end of the first year the paper had 1,100 subscribers. Eagle recommended, and the board agreed, to pass sole ownership of the paper to one of the editors, W. D. Womack. This shift in ownership was not surprising. Eagle and the other stockholders had not apparently expected to make money, but rather had been interested in launching the publication as a valuable adjunct to the mission work and ministry of the Convention. Once established, Eagle and the board were content to let the paper go into another's hands.

With an effective means of communication, a cadre of talented leaders, the Arkansas Baptist State Convention advanced through the 1880s with substantial gains in the number of churches affiliated with the Convention. The decade began with around 880 affiliated churches, by 1890, over 1,100 churches were Convention churches. As before the Civil War, most of the churches continued to be small, rural congregations. Few had regular Sunday Schools, most only met for worship twice a month. Meeting houses were often primitive, hot in summer, cold in winter. Amenities like hymn books and educational literature were at a premium in many of the churches. The ministers who served these congregations were frequently men of great personal piety, but of only modest education. Revivals, "protracted meetings," were the most dramatic events in local church life, occurring once or twice yearly.

The combined membership of these churches reached 55,000 in 1890. These were men and women, generally of the rural countryside and small towns. Like their pastors, they were most often people of limited educational attainments. But—also like their pastors—they were frequently people a great personal piety and devotion. Even so, churches were far from being aggregations of plaster saints. Moral compromises—"backsliding"—often prompted church discipline; use of intoxicating beverages, blasphemy, gambling frequently resulted in expulsion from a local church. Between 1880 and the close of the decade, over 5,000 men and women were "excluded" from Convention churches; only about half that number were recorded as "restorations" during the same decade.

A majority of nineteenth-century Baptist folk made their livings as farmers and the rhythms of church life reflected an agricultural pattern. But the life of the countryside was not a placid—or banal—passage from one season to the next. Indeed, within the living memory of many Arkansas farm folk in the 1880s, the pattern of rural life had been shaped and disrupted by war, economic depression, and the increasing intrusion of mechanized transportation and production. During the 1880s, the rural landscape was alive with dramatic social and political change. These changes ultimately would influence profoundly the course of the State Convention.

By the turn of the century, the State Convention was riven deeply by the politics of organized, agrarian discontent known as Populism. Of course, the political partisanship which marked the life of the Convention also reflected other deep divisions among Baptists affiliated with the Convention. Indeed, the very issue of what it meant to be a Convention Baptist was a point of increasing controversy as the nineteenth century moved toward its close. The consolidating and centralizing tendency of Eagle, Womack, and others, forced Baptists to look closely at the very meaning of "convention" and cooperation.

Much of the tension and soul searching resonated in and through the state's Baptist associations. The oldest form of cooperation among Baptists in Arkansas and elsewhere, the associations, some forty-three in 1890, were important, forceful entities in Arkansas Baptist culture. The associations were vitally, critically important to the State Convention's potential success in missions.

In the last decades of the nineteenth century—with Baptist life still largely de-centralized—associations provided a means for receiving and disseminating information and resources to and from the State Convention. But the relationship of the State Convention to the associations was always ambivalent. Many associational leaders alternatively manifested enthusiasm and suspicion toward the Convention. The sensitivity of the associations to excessive control— or the perception of excessive control—by the Convention, was reflected in the delicacy with which Convention leaders approached the subject, in the early 1880s, of the office, title, and salary for the state mission secretary. This office, deemed essential by some Convention leaders as a means of organizing and expanding the missionary vision of the Convention, provoked suspicion and hostility from other Baptists. B. W. Harmon the erstwhile state missionary warned the Convention in 1881 that Arkansas Baptists would not tolerate an authoritarian mission structure or mission officials. Any successful missions program of the State Convention would have to be accomplished through cooperation with, and deferential treatment of, associations and local churches.

Indeed, to a large extent, in the last quarter of the nineteenth century, the Convention continued to play a subservient—or at least an ancillary—role to the associations. In deference to associational and church anxieties the State Convention equivocated in the 1880s and 1890s over the employment of a state missionary or corresponding secretary. Convention leaders were wary even of giving too imposing a title to the state missionary which might have suggested the attempt to create a hierarchy. Such wariness was prudent. Arkansas Baptists were not likely to tolerate any dominating board or agency. Of course, such domination was unlikely. In 1880, neither the inclination nor infrastructure existed to allow Eagle and other Convention leaders to impose their will on any church or association. At best, the Convention leaders could persuade or plead. As already discussed, the Convention of the 1880s only possessed the barest fiscal and physical existence. The Convention headquarters was little more than a couple of desks in a modest rented office in Little Rock.

While the Arkansas Baptist State Convention may have been tentative in its relations with associations, the Southern Baptist Convention was moving toward the further consolidation of its relationship with various state Baptist conventions. The Southern Convention, like the State Convention, had to move cautiously, ever mindful of the ingrained Baptist suspicion toward centralization and episcopacy. Still, the leaders of the Southern Convention intended to create a more coherent organization in the closing decades of the century.

Among the obstacles, real or perceived, to Southern Convention hegemony was the American Baptist Home Mission Society. With its long history of service in Arkansas and the South, the American Society did not intend to concede the field without a struggle. In fact, much good work had been done for decades by the American Society and its missionaries in Arkansas. As previously mentioned, William Lea, who did much to revive the Arkansas Baptist State Convention after the war, had been sustained as an American Society missionary for several years. As late as 1885, the American Society was funding missionary work in Arkansas. Moreover, the American Society, and its companion organization, the American Baptist Publication Society, provided much Sunday School and other religious literature in Arkansas.

In 1880, the State Convention entered into a formal arrangement with the American Society to channel that organization's funds to the missionary labor among black Arkansans. A similar arrangement had been reached between the General Convention in Texas and the American Society. The Southern Convention disliked these arrangements, and its leaders criticized the American Society for "invading" its territory. With its own growing missionary organizations, Sunday School Board and publishing house, after 1891, the Southern Convention regarded the American Society with some measure of jealousy.

In the immediate aftermath of the Civil War, tensions had flashed white hot between the Southern and the American organizations, when the society announced its intention to return aggressively to its work in the South, especially with the freedmen. Virginia Baptists led the chorus repudiating this "usurpation" and intrusion. The leaders of the American Society seemed genuinely stunned by the rejection, but pressed the matter, and by the late 1860s an uneasy truce prevailed. But the undercurrent of sectional rivalry and sectional perspectives continued to disturb the peace between the regional organizations.

In 1883, at the Jubilee Meeting of the American Baptist Home Mission Society, the absence of formally appointed representatives from the Southern Baptist Convention was duly noted. The few Southerners who did address the Jubilee gathering adamantly praised the American Society while asserting pointedly their Southern allegiance. The Reverend Dr. H. H. Tucker of Georgia asserted, "I stand before you a representative of the South. . . . I am a Southerner by [long] descent . . . born on my grandfather's plantation among the cotton blooms. . . . I sympathize with the Southern people in all their notions . . . [for] which I ask no pardon."

After this pointed assertion of sectional pride, Tucker indicated that the Southern Baptist Convention respected Baptists of the North as fellow laborers with God, but intended to maintain the prerogatives of their "own Southern organization." Tucker concluded by stating to the largely Northern audience, "Stand to your colors, and we shall be sure to stand by ours, but above us all there floats . . . the banner of the Cross. . . ." Surely no one at the Jubilee Convention could have misunderstood; Baptists in the South were moving rapidly to consolidate their denominational resources and to assert their sectional identity.

In 1894, the rivalry between the Southern Baptist Convention and the American Baptist Home Mission Society was confronted explicitly in a joint meeting known as the Fortress Monroe Conference. Representatives from the two organizations met near Baltimore, ostensibly to work out their differences. On the surface the conference produced a recommitment to the tenuous accommodation which had shaped relations between the organizations since Appomattox, but by simply meeting with representatives of the Southern Convention, the American Society conceded the rising influence of the Southern Convention and its claim to speak for Baptists throughout the South.

Significantly, the same year that witnessed the Southern Baptist Convention's assertion of its sectional prerogatives at Fortress Monroe also saw the establishment of the United Daughters of the Confederacy. The UDC rapidly emerged as the most overtly, aggressively sectional organization since 1861. By sponsoring publications, monuments, holidays, and museums, the UDC members hoped to assure a perpetual veneration for the Confederacy. Energetic—even combative—the UDC became a powerful, ubiquitous fixture of late-nineteenth-century Southern culture. Among the early members of the UDC in Arkansas was Mary Eagle, founder and president of the state Woman's Missionary Union (WMU).

During the decade following the Fortress Monroe Conference, the Northern Baptist mission organization and the American Baptist Publication Society lost ground steadily in the South while the status and influence of the Southern Baptist Convention rose dramatically. In Arkansas, the Southern Baptist Convention found willing allies for its consolidationist agenda among the leadership of the State Convention; James Eagle was an unflinching supporter of the Southern Convention, believing in the great good to be accomplished through concerted efforts by Southern Baptists. To be sure, Arkansas Baptists had willingly accepted assistance from the Northern Baptists organizations, even to the point of endorsing formally, on several occasions, the literature of the American Baptist Publication Society for use in Convention churches. However, the relationship with the Northern Baptist organizations was only an accommodation that was quickly abandoned when a distinctly Southern alternative presented itself.

The vitality and prominence of the Southern Baptist Convention, including its resonant call to missions and education, abetted the consolidationist movement in Arkansas. Equally, the Southern Baptist Convention benefitted from the resurgence of the Arkansas Baptist State Convention and other southern state Baptist conventions during the 1880s and 1890s. There was, in fact, a reciprocity and mutuality in the relationship of the state conventions and the Southern Convention. Nowhere was this mutuality more clearly manifested than in growth of the Baptist women's movement Arkansas and the other former states of the Confederacy, a point already alluded to. Moreover, the women's movement within the Arkansas Baptist State Convention also fueled the consolidationist movement among Baptists in the state.

The Reverend M. D. Early, pastor at Morrillton, publicly called for a women's mission organization in 1883. A man long devoted to the cause of missions, in 1883 he was serving as a vice-president of the Home Mission Board of the Southern Baptist Convention. Early had only recently attended the Southern Baptist Convention's annual meeting in Waco, Texas. At the meeting, the leaders of the Convention had called upon all the affiliated state conventions to create women's missionary organizations. Early's appeal for a women's mission organization in Arkansas prompted an immediate response. Of course, Early's call and the response must be set within the context of the time. Two years earlier Womack had used the *Evangel* to make a general plea for women in Arkansas to "rise up" and do their "duty to the praise of God." And Womack's more generalized pronouncement resonated with the spirit of the age, a burgeoning sense that women in the South, and the rest of the nation, were poised for dramatic, expansive political, cultural, and spiritual activity. The suffragette movement was stirring, women were forming and joining societies and organizations in ever greater numbers, and educational opportunities were increasing for women. For Baptist women in Arkansas, the presence of a popular missionary vision and passion—so pronounced in American evangelical life in the late nineteenth century—added to the impetus for a women's mission movement.

In the wake of Early's challenge, a small group of Arkansas Baptist women organized the Women's Central Committee in September 1883. The first president of the organization was Mary Kavanaugh Eagle. A relative newcomer to Arkansas—having only arrived in 1882—Mary Eagle soon became one of the state's most prominent and powerful women. Certainly, the fact that she was the wife of James Eagle contributed to her early prominence, but within a few years she proved herself entirely capable of sustaining and enhancing her influence through her own remarkable abilities. Mary Eagle, as it turned out, was a force to be reckoned with. The daughter of Kentucky blue grass aristocracy, she was well-educated and accustomed to social prominence. Dignified, refined—slightly aloof—in her bearing and demeanor, Mary Eagle was invariably attired in the best fashions. Intelligence, energy, and confidence were also evident aspects of her persona.

For nearly twenty years, she guided the development of the Baptist women's mission movement in Arkansas. As her adjuncts, Eagle could rely on Mrs. M. D. Early, Mrs. M. J. Reaves, and Mrs. M. E. Longley. There was no timidity in these founders; they regarded themselves as soldiers "enrolled for war."

Mary Eagle was an able commander, a talented promoter. She worked in her husband's political campaigns and ultimately gained national attention as chairman of the Committee of Congresses of the Board of Lady Managers of the Columbian Exposition of 1893. In that capacity Mary Eagle coordinated the activities of dozens of equally powerful and influential women from every part of the nation. Responding to critics who suggested that women's activities should be confined to the home, Mary Eagle asserted that the world was the proper consideration and sphere of women. She made no apologies, challenging women to organize, give, and promote, especially when the spread of the Gospel and the elevation of society were the causes.

Certainly, Mary Eagle's aspirations encompassed the world. Speaking in associational meetings, in local churches, at the annual State Convention meetings, Mary attracted attention and admiration. After only a few years, she gained a loyal, devoted following among Arkansas Baptist women and was regarded by many as an ideal representative of Christian womanhood. One young girl, seeing Mary Eagle for the first time at the annual meeting of the Caroline Association, felt herself in the presence of a uniquely distinguished person. Decades later she recalled the elegance of Mary's gray and lavender dress with its fur collar. The future Mrs. W. D. Pye, ultimately to be distinguished in her own right as a superb leader in the State Convention, remembered her encounter with Mary Eagle as a formative—revolutionary—experience, even if her most vivid impression centered on the presence of Mrs. Eagle rather than her message.

Some, however, found Mary Eagle less appealing, less inspiring. She made a very bad impression on Annie Armstrong, who confided her deep dislike of Mary in a letter to an intimate friend. Armstrong found Mary overbearing. Probably, Armstrong had marked a salient, aggressive aspect of Mary Eagle's character. Like many builders of institutions and organizations, Mary was adamant and forceful, impatient with delays and distractions. Annie Armstrong's opinion aside, Mary Eagle was well-respected—actually beloved—by many women in Arkansas and she provided the leadership necessary to launch a cohesive women's mission movement among Arkansas Baptists.

The Women's Central Committee was intended to function as a fulcrum for the organization of missions giving and service among Baptist women. To disseminate its message the Committee had recourse to the pages of the *Evangel.* And there was the constant round of traveling and speaking in attempting to establish local church committees. To make the process easier, the Women's Central Committee provided churches with a sample constitution for women in local congregations to use. Always, the call was insistent and expansive. "Oh, Baptist women of Arkansas! Help us put this powerful engine [a statewide women's mission organization] . . . in motion. . . ." There was never anything small or parochial about the effort to create a viable women's movement in the State Convention.

Coincidental with the emergence of the state WMU was C. E. Smith's departure for Africa in 1884. A native of Massachusetts, Smith had spent much of his youth in Judsonia. He was embraced by the leaders of the Convention as an Arkansan and acclaimed for his heroic missionary commitment. Exceptionally well-known throughout the State Convention, Smith truly was a pioneer, helping to awaken many other Arkansas Baptists to the cause of missions. He was the first of many men and women, with profound ties to Arkansas, who would serve as missionaries on foreign fields.

In 1888, Mary Eagle led a small delegation of women from Arkansas to Richmond, Virginia, and participated in the establishment of the Woman's Missionary Union of the Southern Baptist Convention. One year later the Women's Central Committee of Arkansas reconstituted that organization into the Woman's Missionary Union of Arkansas. As before, under the auspices of the Central Committee, the leaders of the state WMU attempted to cultivate local WMU organizations in Arkansas churches. The process went forward only slowly, but by the end of the century there were forty local church WMUs in Arkansas and a solid tradition of women's mission work had been established in the state.

The center, the ground, of the WMU movement was missions—giving to missions, promoting missions, praying for missions. The missionary efforts of the Southern Baptist Convention and the Arkansas Baptist State Convention were the focus of the Arkansas WMU. In that sense the state WMU became a crucial element in the growth and maturation of the state Baptist Convention. The presence of WMU circles in forty churches across Arkansas meant that the State Convention had an emphatic relationship with those churches—an unprecedented, direct connection from the State Convention to the churches.

Nothing suggests that the male leadership, Eagle, Womack, Early, or that Mary Eagle and her coworkers, consciously, or primarily, aimed at enhancing the status or influence of the Convention when they created the WMU in Arkansas. Their first consideration was missions—and the best means of evangelizing Arkansas, the South, and the world. The Convention was a means to that end. The founding of Ouachita Baptist College in 1886 was also not intended preeminently as a way to create a more cohesive and structured Convention. Nevertheless, the college significantly, profoundly enhanced the ideal of a greater and fully unified State Convention as it too became—with the WMU—a pivotal means for advancing missions and ministry.

That the leaders of the Arkansas Baptist State Convention should have desired the establishment of a state Baptist college is not surprising. As has been mentioned, talk of such an innovation began soon after the Convention was founded. However, by the 1880s, Arkansas remained one of only two Southern Baptist Convention states that lacked a convention-sponsored college. To be sure, there had been Baptist colleges in Arkansas, periodically, for thirty-five years. But these institutions were local, associational endeavors, never very stable and with a limited connection to the State Convention.

There was little in the Convention's history that portended the establishment of a strong Baptist college. Disappointing memories of the pre-war drive to raise $75,000 to endow a college—funds which disappeared in the Civil War—were especially hard to overcome. However, by the 1880s, Eagle and others again talked of a Convention college. Eagle's own experience at Mississippi College had convinced him of the need for an institution in Arkansas to train ministers for work in Arkansas. Indeed, with his vision of new churches in every county seat, Eagle must have wondered where the educated clergy for those churches would be found. Larger issues, including developing a Christian citizenry and the moral elevation of society, also fed the movement for a Convention college. Then, too, there were those Baptists who wanted a denominational college to offer an alternative to what they regarded as the excessively secular education provided at the university in Fayetteville, which had been founded in 1872.

In 1883, the Convention revived the plan for a college by creating a five-member Educational Commission. This body was empowered to actually begin the process of creating a college. The Commission began by soliciting communities and associations for possible sites and even established a board of trustees for the still-to-be founded institution. The first board of trustees was a roster of Arkansas Baptist State Convention leaders. The board's membership crossed the usual geographical frontiers of the state and included politically and economically successful men. Most prominent on the board was James Eagle. The other members were W. R. Womack, A. B. Miller, A. J. Kincaid, J. B. Searcy, J. M. Hart, J. K. Brantly, W. E. Atkinson, V. B. Izard, A. W. Files, A. J. Faucett, J. Dunagin, C. D. Wood, M. F. Locke, and W. A. C. Sayles.

The administrative work of the ABSC could not have been done without the dedication of numerous individuals. Three general secretaries who kept the Convention in touch with local churches and associations were J. B. Searcy (1867–1874), top left; W. E. Atkinson (1899), direct left; and A. J. Barton (1900–1902), top right. Until 1900, the ABSC did not always "employ" a secretary, hence the gaps in years of service.

With Eagle, W. E. Atkinson and C. D. Wood were among state's political elite. Atkinson was Attorney General of Arkansas during Eagle's tenure as governor and Wood served five terms on the state Supreme Court. Still, it is reasonable to argue that the catalyst for the founding of the state Baptist college was James Eagle. He brought the necessary prestige—and resources—to the process.

On January 8, 1886, a special Site Selection Committee met at Second Baptist Church in Little Rock to choose between several communities offering land and stipends to gain the proposed college. The meeting failed to make a final determination on the site, but the committee did determine that the new college would be coeducational. The decision on a site was postponed until April; the committee authorized Eagle, Sayles, and Files to keep looking.

Arkadelphia, refined and restful, won out as the location of the state Baptist college. Having a well-established Baptist high school already in existence, city fathers also offered to cede the facilities of the defunct state Institute for the Blind to the new college. With these inducements the Site Selection Committee decided in favor of Arkadelphia. The site, however important, was no more important than the individual chosen to shoulder the formidable task of actually creating a college. More than daunting, the task was intimidating. Previous Baptist colleges in Arkansas had failed, and the survival rate of private colleges in the South generally could hardly have comforted any new president. Indeed, Southern history, and the Southern landscape, revealed the bleaching remnants of a great many church colleges. The Civil War, had, of course, killed a hundred or more denominational schools; across the decades several hundred more had died for lack of students, lack of funds, lack of determination.

What the Arkadelphia college had in its favor was a cadre of solid supporters, with means, and J. W. Conger. The first president of the fledgling college possessed the courage and commitment to make Ouachita Baptist College a viable institution. Conger's more abstract qualities were matched by a pragmatic, programmatic instinct. He knew that Ouachita would live if he could make the college the Convention's institution. He understood that cooperation among Arkansas Baptists meant life for Ouachita. With passionate determination he stumped the state, lobbied the Baptist leaders, attended the associational annual meetings, plied the messengers to the State Convention's annual meeting, and wrote the letters necessary to wed Ouachita College to the Convention.

Conger was practical enough to look always for the connection, the policy or program, that would lend tradition and stability to the infant college. He was not above asking Governor Eagle for more than money. In 1889, he asked the Governor to authorize a military company at Ouachita, and provide—through a loan from the state—the necessary arms. The request was certainly not unusual; Southern colleges were often home to a military regiment or corps of cadets. Conger was disappointed in this endeavor, however. The governor refused to authorize a military company or provide weapons. "To loan you the arms would put me in a position to be criticized . . . other schools are [also] wanting guns." Eagle expressed his regrets at having to reject Conger's petition and added the admonition, "But such is life—all subject to disappointment." Conger was not the kind to give up on an idea and he eventually got his corps and requisite equipment—after Eagle left the governor's office.

Incidental disappointments and disagreements aside, Eagle and Conger maintained a close relationship. The Colonel was not reluctant to offer paternal—perhaps patronizing—advice. Even after Conger had been president for more than a decade, Eagle instructed Conger—in detail—on the best means of handling donors and collecting their pledges. And Eagle reminded Conger of the obvious, "Be careful to take notes on all amounts subscribed . . . [and] collect it promptly." But again, if Eagle disappointed Conger at times—and too closely advised the intelligent and proud president—he was still the best friend Ouachita, and Conger, had.

Eagle's love for the college derived from his vision of the institution as a center of Arkansas Baptist life—a beacon of Christian idealism and evangelism. Over the early years of the college's life, Eagle and his brother William contributed thousands of dollars to the college in outright gifts or through generous loans. Such contributions were vital, for although Ouachita was the "College of the Convention," support from the Convention consisted largely of expressions of confidence and concern.

Conger recruited an initial class of one hundred students with a faculty of six. Importantly, some of the college's first students were

Founded in 1886, utilizing facilities vacated by the Arkansas Institute for the Blind, Ouachita College not only served as a unifying force for the ABSC but became a primary source for training pastors and workers for the state's churches as well.

Eagles, the nieces, nephews, or grandchildren of James and William. Conger worked assiduously to keep the Eagles at Ouachita, and he adamantly protested and pled when one Eagle niece left Arkadelphia for Tennessee's Belmont College.

Shortly after the turn of the century, yet another Eagle expressed the hope that her son would attend Ouachita instead of "Fayetteville." She noted that the young man had been "carefully and religiously reared" and she was "a little afraid" of sending him to the state university. Mrs. J. B. Eagle hoped her son would go to Ouachita and be "surrounded [*sic*] by good influences."

Certainly Conger's dream for Ouachita was that the college would be a place of good and godly influences. Conger never lost sight of the need for Ouachita to be distinctly Christian in its policies and practices. The college was to inculcate love for God, for church, and for missions. Conger intended for Christian idealism, far more than a symbolic resonance, to be a symbiotic characteristic of the college. In fact, Ouachita soon represented a sort of convergence of the Convention, of missions, and of optimism and pride among many Baptists in the state. Missions pulsated through the culture of the new college. In 1904 the college formalized its relationship with the state WMU by establishing of campus circle of the Young Woman's Auxiliary (YWA), an adjunct of the WMU. The Ouachita Young Woman's Auxiliary was designated—not surprisingly—the "Mary Eagle Band."

As Eagle expressed in an 1893 letter to Conger, the spiritual character of Ouachita brought "glad tidings to the brotherhood of the entire state." Though still a very young institution, the good already done by the college, according to Governor Eagle, could only be "fully known in eternity."

The Convention at last had a college, a rallying point. Other Baptist colleges were established in the next several years; Central Baptist—for women only—in Conway in 1892 and Mountain Home Baptist College in the White River Association a year later. Both institutions were heroic efforts and did valuable work, but neither was destined to survive. And of the two, only Central could truly, fully claim the status of a Convention institution. Hundreds of men and women ultimately carried Central and Mountain Home diplomas into useful lives where

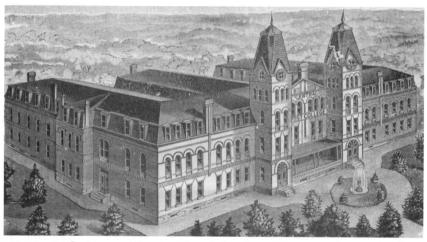

Opening in the Conway Baptist Church October 1892, Central Baptist College was a two-year junior college for women. This three-story "main building" was completed in 1893 at a cost of just over $20,000. Changing enrollment patterns and increased costs forced the institution to close in 1950.

they ministered and labored with dignity, diligence, and faith. Still, these institutions lacked the status and staying power of Ouachita. Central had solid ties to the Convention and even had the benefit of Conger's leadership as president for a time, but as a women's college, Central was fatally disadvantaged in any struggle for equality as a Convention institution. Central did not, after all, produce pastors. On the other hand, Ouachita offered free tuition to all aspiring ministers and so very soon began to fill Arkansas's pulpits with loyal alumni. Scattered across the state, these Ouachitonian pastors, understandably, became an invaluable source of support for their alma mater, a reliable block of votes and voices on Ouachita's behalf.

Mountain Home never challenged Ouachita or Central for prominence in the Convention, since it was only another associational college with no necessary claim upon the State Convention. Moreover, Mountain Home was a two-year college for most of its history; its more prominent graduates often held baccalaureate degrees from other colleges and so had divided loyalties. And, in fact, Mountain Home was—between 1901 and 1923—relegated to academy status under the Ouachita-Central System.

There was another college which received direct support from the State Convention for several years, though it was far from being a Convention college. Arkansas Baptist College, founded in 1883, served the African-American community. Its primary purpose was training ministers. Solicitation by the college's president, the distinguished, visionary A. J. Booker, to the State Convention, usually met with a positive response in the form of small offerings. In 1897, the Convention authorized Benjamin Cox to serve as an adjunct faculty member at the college. Convention minutes of the era were lavish in their praise of Booker and his college. This support of a black college reflected an undercurrent of ambivalence on the part of white Convention Baptists toward African-American Baptists and the larger African-American community. The Convention was publicly, symbolically committed to the idea of higher education for African-Americans. This was an important commitment in light of the fact that many in the South ridiculed the idea of education for African-Americans; but, again, the Convention made no overt plea for civic or social equality.

Certainly, James Eagle was ambivalent in his response to racial issues. Often a guest preacher in African-American churches, an outspoken opponent of lynching, to the point of risking his own life, and a supporter of Arkansas Baptist College, Eagle nevertheless signed the first substantive Jim Crow law in Arkansas, a bill requiring African-Americans to ride in separate railroad coaches. The "separate coach law" was only the first step toward more draconian measures culminating in full-blown segregation and disfranchisement. Yet, Eagle and the Convention leadership apparently perceived themselves as true friends of African-Americans who knew what was best for the African-American community in Arkansas.

Even actions like the coach law were characterized, or rationalized, by Eagle and his peers as progressive measures intended to diffuse racial conflict. Incredibly, some in his own day, enemies and friends, believed that Eagle, and by extension his inner circle and the Convention, possessed a progressive social consciousness.

Undeniably the Arkansas Baptist State Convention evidenced an ideal of social responsibility. Notably, the Convention stood in the very forefront of the temperance movement, agitating, lobbying, preaching, and praying for the prohibition of beverage alcohol. Convention Baptists were clearly convinced that prohibition, voluntary or legislated, would improve dramatically the quality of life in every community in Arkansas.

Then, too, the State Convention in 1894 accepted the challenge of Hannah Hyatt to establish an orphanage in Monticello. It was the first orphanage in the state. Hyatt had not waited for the Convention to act; she had already made her spacious home a refuge for two dozen needy children. She was the first superintendent of the Baptist State Orphanage Home; she was also the matron, Bible teacher, and book-keeper. Committed fully to her vision, Hyatt deeded her house and eighty acres of land to the Convention. Married to S. E. Gardner in 1895, Hannah and her husband continued to serve at the home until 1908. Just as the infant Ouachita had its Conger, the orphanage had, in Hannah Hyatt Gardener, a leader of vision and compassion. The orphanage soon became a cherished ministry of the Convention, bene-fitting from aggressive promotion at the annual meeting, and receiving financial aid from associational and church collections.

From this modest building in Monticello, the "orphan's home," now the *Arkansas Baptist Child Care and Family Ministries,* has grown to a multiple site agency ministering to family needs from infant through adolescence. Much of the agency's success has been due to generous benefactors such as Mr. and Mrs. George W. Bottoms, below, who not only gave to the children's home, but to numerous ABSC programs as well.

For many Convention Baptists, the orphanage represented a melding of social and Christian idealism, an idealism that marked much of the life of Southern Protestantism at the turn of the century. Of course, for most Baptists, the distinction between social and Christian responsibility was lost—irrelevant. If the Bible mandated the care of orphans, then that was enough for many in the State Convention; the fact that the Southern Sociological Congress, or some other progressive advocate or agency, also endorsed the education and care of orphans, or stood for prohibition, was incidental. Service to society was good, service to God much better. And invariably at the heart of every Convention institution or practice was the evangelical ideal—the saving of souls. Ouachita, the orphanage, the WMU, temperance agitation, all were about saving souls—if society was elevated in the process, so much the better.

Blending evangelical zeal and social responsibility certainly marked the Convention's Sunday School endeavors at the turn of the century. In 1897, the Convention established the Sunday School and Colportage Board, an entity to promote the development of Sunday Schools through the distribution of advice and literature. With no stable budget or staff, this board could do little more than the Convention's Committee on Sunday Schools had done in the past, that is, seek assistance—and funds—from the American Baptist Publication Society—or increasingly—from the Southern Baptist Convention's Sunday School or Home Mission Boards. Still, the establishment of a formal board for Sunday School work suggested a consciousness, at least, of what the Convention might do in the future to promote the expansion of Sunday Schools in Arkansas Baptist churches.

More effective than the Sunday School and Colportage Board was the Convention's Mission Board. In 1898, the fiftieth anniversary year of the establishment of the Convention, the Mission Board reported that fifteen field workers established four churches, conducted 174 baptisms, and added a total of 388 members to various congregations. This mission work went forward without the benefit, during that year, of a paid missions secretary.

The Jubilee Year of the Convention was celebrated at the annual meeting in Little Rock in November 1898. The celebration focused largely on the life and accomplishments of R. J. Coleman, who had died less than a year earlier. Born in 1817, Coleman, a native of Virginia, immigrated to Arkansas in the early 1840s. He was the last surviving messenger to the inaugural session of the State Convention in 1848. Eagle, Searcy, and other speakers lauded Coleman as a father in the faith, a Baptist pioneer, and a model preacher. The intense focus on Coleman suggested the somewhat ambivalent, slightly self-conscious sentiments of the Convention's leaders. There was still something unfinished, unsettled about the Convention itself. After fifty years, the Convention leaders still lacked a grounded sense of institutional permanence, hence they evidenced a rather ambiguous sense of institutional history. After all, the Convention still conducted its affairs from a rented office. And its two colleges and the orphanage were still struggling infants. Its organizational structure and missions force changed frequently and suffered from uncertain fiscal support.

The Convention had, in fact, authorized the creation of the post of "historical secretary" in 1890, with B. G. Maynard named to the post. But the position had to be "revived" in 1893 and lapsed again—for decades—after the Jubilee Year. Again, the Convention leaders, for all that had been accomplished since 1848, still evidently lacked, fifty years later, a clear sense of organizational identity, and so too they lacked a clear sense of the Convention's place in history. The Convention remained in 1898 an immature organization.

As the Convention advanced erratically during 1880s and '90s in its structural development and tentative centralization of important mission and educational endeavors, a competitor, a friendly rival, was moving to the end of its existence. In 1899, the General Association of Western Arkansas and Indian Territory voted to disband after a generation of remarkable mission work. Under the leadership of E. L. Compere, the Western Association planted churches and missions and founded a college.

The labors of Western Association missionaries and pastors, including a cadre of talented Native-American evangelists like John Jumper and W. J. Crowder, helped create a thriving Baptist culture in the territory and those adjacent Arkansas counties. Ultimately, inevitably, the efforts of the Western Association—which was really more of a convention—overlapped the work of the Arkansas Baptist State Convention. Both organizations claimed resources from churches and outside entities which the other wanted. Only the goodwill of Compere, Eagle, and other leaders in the two organizations avoided recriminations. As it was, the Western Association—ideally suited for pioneering missions—proved incapable of developing a more comprehensive structure. And, critically, the death of Compere in 1895 deprived the Western Association of its patriarch.

With the disbandment of the association in 1899, and the subsequent faltering of Buckner College, the State Convention surely seemed poised for an era of orderly, unchallenged growth. Moreover, the Convention could now move forward with the consolidation of Baptist work in Arkansas as the indisputable institutional center of Baptist life in the state. But the end of the Western Association did not presage an era of hegemonic stability or placid growth for the State Convention. Indeed, by 1900, the Convention stood on the verge of serious, potentially disastrous disruption and division.

9

1901–1910

PERHAPS AS EAGLE SAT IN THE PARAGOULD CHURCH listening to the angry voices, watching the angrier faces, his mind drifted back across forty years to that terrible, searingly hot July day and to the blood and dust and fury of the battle for Atlanta. In that massive contest Eagle fell, terribly wounded. His survival was little short of miraculous. Now another battle was raging; he was again wounded. But he could bear, however painful, the rhetorical gashes inflicted by his critics. What he could not bear was the thought that the Arkansas Baptist State Convention was about to collapse.

The Arkansas Baptist State Convention in 1901 was riven with political and personal conflicts, involving—among other things—the control of the *Arkansas Baptist*, the appointment of the state secretary for missions, and the whole question of cooperation and centralization. To some degree twenty years of suspicion and antagonism were boiling over—and out—as the messengers in Paragould argued and blustered.

Eagle and his coterie had held sway in the Convention for a generation. They had emphasized cooperation and centralization in the cause of education and missions, and moreover, they had reflected progressive ideas on the role of women and moderation on matters of race. Equally important, Eagle, and others of his Convention inner circle, represented the entrenched power of the old line Democratic party in

Arkansas. This reality, this interrelationship of political power and the Convention leadership, would add tension and trauma to the Paragould meeting.

A rising generation of populist politicians within the Democratic party, notably Jeff Davis, the governor, were anxious to displace Eagle and the old order. Davis, a tentative Baptist at best, with no deep commitment to missions, was elected vice-president of the Convention at the Paragould meeting shortly after the messengers assembled. Evidently his election was mostly a matter of his political popularity in the state, a courtesy extended to a young man of political prominence. Rising on a wave of visceral race-baiting rhetoric and a boisterous condemnation of cities, banks, and insurance companies, he had been elected governor the previous year. His pronouncements were often crude and violent; he celebrated lynching and ridiculed the political aspirations of women.

Davis's election as vice-president of the Convention, in addition to being a deferential acknowledgement of his political status, may also have reflected an undercurrent of opposition to what some messengers considered an excessive amount of cooperation and centralization in state politics and in the Convention. Davis surely represented, in the minds of many Arkansans, and many Baptists, a return to simpler ways—to a more pristine, if not primitive, social and religious order. For all his symbolic significance, however, Davis did not control the anti-Eagle forces at Paragould. That group followed the leadership of W. A. Clark, editor of the *Arkansas Baptist,* and Ben Bogard. And actually, in some measure, Clark was the stalking horse for Bogard, the powerful preacher who had recently moved to Searcy from Kentucky.

As a young pastor in Kentucky, Bogard had been influenced significantly by J. N. Hall, a Baptist evangelist and the editor of the *Baptist Flag*; Hall and his publication also had a considerable following in Arkansas. Bogard regarded Hall as a great man—a standard bearer for Baptist ideals. Significantly, Hall was a landmarker, a leader of that movement which posited an apostolic succession in Baptist history and advocated a strict, even radical, adherence to what the landmarkers perceived as a true, primitive church polity—an intense commitment, for instance, to local church autonomy. Bogard, a landmarker as well, also regarded himself as a serious student of church history and even wrote a book on the subject, *Pillars of Orthodoxy*. That Bogard knew something of Baptist history was indisputable, but his "history" also had a decidedly polemical bent. He clearly tended to invest the past with his own powerful preferences and perspectives.

By 1900, landmarkism was already a deeply rooted, potent force in Arkansas Baptist culture. J. R. Graves, premier Baptist preacher and publisher in the antebellum and post-war South, and a man revered by many Arkansas Baptists, coined the term "landmark" around 1845. For decades Graves championed the cause of landmarkism in the Southern Baptist Convention. But Graves's version of landmarkism was not precisely that of subsequent adherents of the movement, adherents like Bogard and Hall. True, Graves' landmarkism had also been grounded upon the idea of an unbroken line of true Baptist churches back to the apostolic age, but that was essentially the heart of the matter for Graves. This simpler, more circumscribed type of landmarkism was shared by many Arkansas Baptists, including many of the men and women who led the State Convention.

However, in Arkansas as elsewhere in the South, some of Graves's followers had, by the late nineteenth century, expanded landmarkism to include a deep suspicion of, and hostility to, any religious organizations beyond the level of the local church. The fact that this anti-cooperation, anti-organization landmarkism—with its celebration of a chimeric past—converged on many points with the agrarian, populist political ideology of the era, gave this type of landmarkism even more influence at the turn of the century.

Ben Bogard emerged as the leader of anti-Convention landmarkers at the 1901 meeting in Paragould. The fact that Bogard, a newcomer to Arkansas and the State Convention, could play so prominent a role in the disruption of the Convention indicated the depth of landmark feeling already present among Arkansas Baptists at the time. Bogard certainly did not bring landmarkism to Arkansas, but rather, he served effectively as the spokesman and organizer of like-minded Baptists in the state.

Bogard and his supporters characterized the old Eagle order as tending away from what they perceived as the truths—the landmarks— of the faith, especially insofar as church polity was concerned. The Convention under Eagle had become too hierarchical, too centralized, and therefore threatened Baptist ideals of local church autonomy. Indeed, it was impossible to deny the strong centralizing ideal animating many Baptist leaders at both the state and the regional level.

In 1900, the Arkansas Baptist State Convention hosted for the first time the annual meeting of the Southern Baptist Convention in Hot Springs. The leaders of the State Convention were enthusiastic in welcoming this "gathering of Israel's hosts, great in numbers, great in power." The Hot Springs meeting, witnessed by hundreds of Arkansas pastors and laymen, was an impressive celebration of the cooperative, centralizing ideal. The symbolic high point of the meeting was a lavishly sentimental commendation of Isaac Tichenor upon his retirement as head of the Southern Convention's Sunday School Board. Tichenor was the very embodiment of the cooperationist ideal.

The Hot Springs meeting also resulted in the formation of a new Convention entity, the New Century Committee, which was authorized to develop comprehensive mission plans for the Southern Convention. Enthusiasm for the committee was not universal among the messengers in Hot Springs; some questions were raised, forcefully, about the formation of such a committee. A few dissenters averred that the New Century Committee was simply a new Southern Convention board with excessive prerogatives. Despite these objections, the Hot Springs meeting generally resonated with a spirit of optimism and cooperation.

The Hot Springs meeting was a gratifying experience for Eagle, whose reputation as a consolidator and cooperationist was well-known in Arkansas and throughout the South. The following year, in New Orleans, Eagle was elected vice-president of the Southern Baptist Convention. The election was a recognition of his long, staunch support of the Southern Convention. For Arkansas Baptists with landmark leanings—the Hot Springs meeting, like Eagle's vice-presidency of the Southern Convention—only proved again the reality that the leadership of the State Convention was committed to centralized, cooperative, structured denominational work. Of course, no one observing the leadership of Eagle, Atkinson, Barton, Files, and the rest of the leadership cadre—since the 1880s—could have doubted the commitment of these individuals to greater centralization and cooperation in the State Convention.

And as if the record of the Convention leaders since 1880 was insufficient to prove their centralizing tendency, at Paragould the Convention's Committee on Education, chaired by J. W. Conger, proposed and saw passed a plan to consolidate the Baptist colleges and academies of the state into a single system, the Ouachita-Central System, under a single board of trustees intimately connected to the Convention. But the catalyst for the open, drastic division at the Paragould meeting was not this or any other new innovation. Rather, a controversy over the control of the *Arkansas Baptist* and the actions of its voluble editor, W. A. Clark, touched off the firestorm.

Clark had criticized the Convention leaders in the paper for what he perceived as their excesses in centralizing zeal. The editor's motives in criticizing the Convention leadership derived from more than his landmark leanings. His anger with the leadership also grew out of his disappointment at not being named the Convention secretary for missions in 1898, a position that went instead to a passionate cooperationist and Convention supporter, A. J. Barton. Angry at Clark for using the *Arkansas Baptist* to criticize the Convention, the leaders of the Convention censured Clark openly at the Paragould meeting. The Clark controversy rapidly swelled into a larger conflict mixing all the motives and personalities mentioned above. Bogard and the landmarkers certainly saw their opportunity in the Clark debacle to unseat the old leadership. Eagle groped for a compromise, appealed for calm and brotherly love. To mollify Bogard and the landmark faction, Eagle proposed a softening of the Convention's centralization, a toning down of the Convention's commitment to a central state missions office; actually Eagle proposed little more than a change in the title for the state missionary. The compromise language passed overwhelmingly, perhaps because the messengers—even the landmarkers—could not finally, utterly reject the leadership of Elder Eagle as he stood before them to plead for peace and unity. Then too, everyone knew the compromise proposed by Eagle was a chimera; the Convention was hopelessly divided. There was simply no room in the Convention for Ben Bogard—the most ardent landmarkers—and the Eagles, their supporters, and their cooperationist ideal.

The depth of the division between Bogard and the Eagles had actually been demonstrated publicly a month before the Paragould meeting. Returning to their respective homes from the annual session of the Caroline Association in Des Arc, Mary Eagle and Ben Bogard found themselves sharing a railway coach. The two exchanged pointed comments; and a brief, impromptu debate followed. The clash revealed the intensity of Mary Eagle's opposition to Bogard and his ideas. Her feelings were so strong that she had risked transgressing the code of Southern lady-likeness by disputing openly in a public place. Bogard's feelings for Mary Eagle were similarly revealed in the incident.

The extraordinary conjunction of partisan politics, tradition, suspicion, personal and petty conceits, high idealism, and profound convictions had shattered the State Convention. Irony marked the conflict throughout. Notably, the passionate demand for orthodoxy by the landmarkers echoed the State Convention's repeated calls a few years earlier for a doctrinal purification of Southern Seminary in Louisville, Kentucky. The point of contention then was Seminary Professor W. H. Whitsett, specifically his controversial contention that there was no continuous, unbroken line of immersing Baptists back to the apostolic era. Outraged Baptists across the South called for Whitsett's recantation or dismissal. The Arkansas Baptist State Convention formally demanded that the seminary restore orthodoxy—landmark orthodoxy. The crisis passed with Whitsett's resignation, but Convention leaders surely remembered their demands for orthodoxy as the Bogard landmarkers accused these same leaders in 1901 of being unorthodox themselves.

The messengers leaving Paragould went away divided and, in many instances, embittered. One outside observer characterized the division among Arkansas Baptists as "war to the knife between the organizers and disorganizers in Arkansas. . . ." Eagle also characterized the conflict as a war, a violent disruption; enemies, he said, have "come with a sword . . . to tear down" the Convention and its work. Within months, a new Baptist organization had been formed, a landmark organization, the General Association of Arkansas Baptists. Ben Bogard was prominent among its leaders. The Convention moreover abandoned the *Arkansas Baptist* and in January 1902 launched a new, rival Convention publication, the *Baptist Advance*. The motto selected for the new paper succinctly described the mission for the publication and the motivation behind its establishment, "For Christ, the Churches, and Cooperation."

The Convention leaders, in the wake of the split, unabashedly raised the banner of organization and cooperation.

The issues which shattered the Convention in Paragould also soon divided churches and associations. Roughly half of the Convention's forty-seven associations, thousands of honorable and pious Baptist men and women, allied themselves with the new General Association. Others rallied to the Convention and its ideals with renewed determination. County seat and other town churches and pastors tended to support the Convention. Churches like First and Second Baptist in Little Rock, First churches in Pine Bluff, Paragould, Walnut Ridge, and Beech Street in Texarkana were typical of those congregations which remained committed to the Convention. Such loyalty was born in part from a reality that the less rural congregations were more comfortable with the ideas and practices associated with the emergence of a coherent, centralized Convention. Then, too, the county seat churches had always been a special priority for Eagle; nearly fifty had been established with the help of State Convention money during Eagle's era. Indeed, for many of the county seat churches, Eagle was something of a founding father.

In 1902, an attempt was made at reconciliation between the General Association and the Convention. In truth the negotiators of the State Convention gave far more than they got in the negotiations, even tentatively agreeing to sever the "present plan of cooperation . . . [with the] Southern Baptist Convention;" but the incipient arrangement soon collapsed. The division between the General Association and the Convention became irrevocable.

Even while they negotiated with the General Association, the leaders of the State Convention also moved to protect the Convention from future domination by hostile elements. This attempt to preserve and protect the Convention lead to a limitation of the overt power of associations within the Convention. Perceiving that the associations were—in many instances—centers of anti-Convention landmarkism, the constitution of the Convention was amended in 1902. The amendment denied associations the right to send messengers to the annual meetings of the State Convention. Breaking a sixty-year precedent, the leadership of the Convention now seated messengers only from cooperating, local churches. There was, at least superficially, a measure of irony in the Convention's constitutional adjustment; after all, it was the landmarkers who hailed the preeminence and authority of the local church. On the other hand, the Convention leaders had possibly acted shrewdly, accomplishing two purposes simultaneously; they had limited the overt power of the associations in the Convention while reaffirming their commitment to the ideal of local church autonomy and authority. Such real and symbolic adjustments could not, however, keep several hundred local churches from the abandoning the Convention to join the General Association. Still, the constitutional change certainly proved beneficial to the Convention. By placing the issue of cooperation squarely on the local churches, the Convention shifted the potential for conflict away from the Convention's annual meetings and placed the debate within local congregations and associations. Many churches and associations struggled for years with the issues raised at Paragould. The struggle was often bitter. Ben Bogard was a tireless promoter of the anti-Convention Landmark Movement in churches and associations. As late as 1915 one outside observer still characterized the struggle in Arkansas as an ongoing war, though he noted that the "brave and consecrated leadership among Arkansas Baptists" had proven itself equal to the task of sustaining the "Lord and the Kingdom against anti-mission and anti-co-operation" forces. Still, the writer lamented that the conflict continued with the "guerrilla bands of anti-missions . . . firing fusillades" in Arkansas. In the face of the persisting controversy—for fully twenty-five years—some churches and associations divided. New landmark associations and new Convention associations were formed—but the Convention's endeavors and sessions went forward with comparatively little disruption from the continuing conflict.

J. S. Rogers, a young, eloquent pastor apparently welcomed—at least in hindsight—the split in the Convention. Far from being an unrelieved disaster, Rogers believed the division at Paragould liberated the leaders of the State Convention to develop more fully and rapidly a coherent denominational structure and to advance more rapidly the evangelical and missionary causes of the Convention. Though a firm Convention partisan, Roger's estimation must be taken seriously. He knew intimately the history of the Convention during the first half of the twentieth century. At the same time, it is hard to imagine Eagle and

General secretaries: R. G. Bowers (1906–1908), top left; J. F. Love (1903–1906), above center; and J. S. Rogers (1908–1910, 1915–1918, 1922–1929), top right.

his circle as glibly relieved or grateful for the defection from the
Convention of so many pastors and churches. For Eagle the division of
the State Convention was especially tragic given his prominence in the
Southern Baptist Convention and his status as a champion of cooperation. Elected as vice-president of the Southern Convention in 1901, just
months before the split in Paragould, Eagle was elected president of
the Convention the following year at the annual meeting in Asheville,
North Carolina. The front page of the *Arkansas Gazette* carried a
photograph of Eagle and characterized his election as a signal honor for
Arkansas.

As the standard bearer for the Southern Convention, Eagle stood in
a truly ironic position—a symbol of consolidation and cooperation, his
own State Convention had foundered on those very ideals. Moreover,
the division of the Convention came on the eve of the death of his
beloved Mary. Disconsolate, devastated, Eagle never fully recovered;
his own health declined rapidly.

The last large endeavor for Eagle was the publication of a memorial
volume dedicated to Mary's memory. Added to his personal and private
pain, Eagle endured a final political humiliation at the hands of
Governor Jeff Davis, who removed him from the honorific post as a
commissioner of the new state capitol. A great man, Eagle suffered
greatly during his last years.

On December 22, 1904, Eagle was buried in Mount Holly
Cemetery in Little Rock. Only a few weeks before, the Arkansas Baptist
State Convention meeting in Pine Bluff, had elected Eagle president
emeritus for life. He was presented with a gavel made of ivory, gold, and
silver. Among the throng of mourners at Eagle's funeral were many who
soon rose to prominence in the State Convention. The funeral oration
by John T. Christian began with the words, "I have fought the good
fight," from one of Eagle's best loved passages. Christian, pastor at
Second Baptist in Little Rock, hailed Eagle as a patriarch, a singular
leader; with unabashed hyperbole, Christian asserted, "I regard him as
the greatest man Arkansas has ever had."

Even by late Victorian standards the praise accorded Eagle was
lavish. The editor of Kentucky's *Western Recorder* contributed a memorial verse:

"O'er Eagle's tomb, with silent grief oppressed,
Our Southland mourns a hero, now at rest;
But those bright laurels ne'r shall fade with year,
whose leaves watered by the people's tears."

Tributes came from across the South, and the nation. B. H. Carroll, the giant of his generation among Texas Baptists, wrote, "It is a calamity, not alone for Arkansas, but to the whole South. How can your people [of Arkansas] bear up under the deprivation of this so great bereavement? And who that is left can ever wear his mantle. . . ? I do miss him much."

Early in 1905, the *Baptist Advance* devoted an entire issue to Eagle. Articles from old comrades of the war years, pastors, denominational leaders, described Eagle as a man of rare personal discipline, honesty, and kindness. Political allies and former rivals described him as a man untainted by personal corruption. The memorial sent by the African-American congregation of St. John Baptist Church in Pettus, remembered Eagle, "for thirty-four years a faithful worker in the vineyard of Christ . . . a sincere friend and helper to the members of this church . . . a great peacemaker between the races . . . his place among us will be sadly missed."

In June 1905, M. F. Love memorialized Eagle before 12,000 Southern Baptists in Kansas City. Love's paean ran the gamut, from Eagle's youth on the farm, to his heroism in war, his stature in politics, his evangelistic zeal, and of course, his generation-long service to the cause of cooperation among Baptists.

Eagle's death, taken with Mary's the year before, marked a turning point in the life of the State Convention. Younger men and women, fully equal in piety, devotion, and determination to the Eagles, now took up the causes the Eagles had championed for so long. Perhaps the end of the Eagles' era, just as the split in the Convention, represented something of a release for the Convention. Great leaders, Mary and James Eagle were so prominent and influential that they may have impeded—unintentionally—by their mere presence, the elevation of new leaders and new ideas. This is not to suggest that the Eagles' influence declined immediately, abruptly with their deaths. During the decade of transition from the Eagles' generation to a new generation, leadership continued to reside largely in the Eagles' inner circle. After Mary's death the presidency of the state WMU passed into the hands of her protégé, Mrs. M. E. Longley. The daughter of an Indiana minister who migrated to Arkansas just after the war, Longley held the distinction as the first female public school teacher in Arkansas.

Her career as a teacher began under the skeptical scrutiny of her principal who once remarked that women should not, could not, do two things, "teach school and ride astride." Undeterred by such prejudice, Longley ultimately won the praise of the principal, and she proved herself an equally formidable, resourceful leader of the WMU. At her side was an equally capable and determined woman, Mrs. J. L. Hawkins, who served as recording secretary of the state WMU for nearly forty years.

Hawkins was truly one of the Eagles' inner circle. Her father, Captain A. W. Files had served through the war with Eagle, and after the war Files and Eagle were leaders of the state Democratic party, though Files ultimately allied himself with the Populist party. Files was also an active leader in the State Convention, a member of Ouachita's Board of Trustees and treasurer for the college. He had also served on most of the other boards of the Convention. In Hawkins, the state WMU and the State Convention had an individual who represented a remarkable continuity.

But even as Hawkins and Longley represented continuity with the previous generation, new leaders were emerging. The year after Governor Eagle's death, a quite young wife and mother attended, as a messenger, her first annual meeting of the Caroline Association. Mrs. J. G. Jackson (Dixie) was only a few years away from assuming her place as a leader in the WMU and the State Convention. As in the previous two decades, leadership of the state WMU, in the new century, had profound significance for the future of the Convention, given the WMU's proven and intense commitment to the Convention and its causes.

This symbiotic relationship was made more emphatic in 1904 when the State Convention allowed the WMU to distribute literature and correspondence from the Convention's office in Little Rock. In 1909 the Convention authorized a monthly stipend of ten dollars for an assistant to send WMU literature throughout the state. These arrangements were made permanent in 1910 when the women's organization was provided with a small office in Convention headquarters. Clearly, the WMU and the State Convention were solidly unified, much to the benefit of both.

While the WMU went forward in the first decade of the twentieth century, sustained by veteran leaders and enlivened by the participation of young, aspiring leaders, the Convention also benefitted from the admixture of established and new leaders. Prominent among the proven leaders was W. E. Atkinson. Born in Alabama just before the Civil War, educated at Washington and Lee College in the 1870s, by the turn of the century, Atkinson was a prominent leader in the Convention. He often served on several Convention boards simultaneously; in 1890, for example, he served on both the Executive Board and the Sunday School Board. He was a perennial member of Ouachita's Board of Trustees and one of the college's most generous benefactors. Ultimately, Atkinson served three terms as president of the Convention. And like Eagle, Atkinson combined political and public service with his denominational activities. He served two terms as state attorney general.

Energetic and visionary, Atkinson attempted, while president of the Convention in 1908, to launch a Baptist men's movement in Arkansas. Sacrificially investing his time and money in the effort he contacted leaders across the state apprising them of his vision, his desire to awaken men to their obligation to devote "their time, talents, and means to the work of the Lord."

But for all his enthusiasm for large causes and mass meetings, Atkinson also devoted himself to private and personal ministry. As a deacon and Sunday School teacher at Second Baptist Church in Little Rock, he visited the sick, prepared his lessons, counseled the discouraged, and when worried parents needed a letter on behalf of their troubled son, Atkinson could be counted upon to help. And he prayed; those who knew him best found W. E. Atkinson to be a man of prayer, a man devoted to passionate, private prayer. Working with Atkinson were leaders like A. J., L. E., and P. C. Barton. Natives of Jonesboro, college educated, they were stalwart supporters of the Convention's work. A. J. had served as assistant secretary of the Foreign Mission

Board of the Southern Baptist Convention in the 1890s. Together the Barton brothers provided invaluable Convention leadership in the crucial years following the division at Paragould and Eagle's death. A. J. and L. E. were pastors of prominent churches—P. C. was a successful businessman; the brothers guided the early years of the *Baptist Advance*, served on boards, as corresponding secretary, and both L. E. and P. C. served ultimately as Convention president.

Atkinson, the Bartons, Hawkins, and Longley were typical of the men and women who carried the work of the Convention forward into the twentieth century. Together they presided over an expansion of Convention campaigns and causes. Far from being drastic innovators, the immediate post-Eagle leadership cadre, nevertheless, was disinclined to settle simply for the status quo.

The expansion of Convention activities early in the new century, in some instances, built upon innovations already apparent in Arkansas Baptist churches. For example, the first Sunbeam Band in the state had been organized by Mamye Gardner in Monticello in 1891. In 1907, the Convention created the office of state Sunbeam Leader. Only two years earlier the Convention sponsored its first summer assembly. Like the Sunbeam Bands in local churches, the annual assembly was largely intended to inculcate an appreciation and enthusiasm for missions. Based on the popular Chatauqua Movement—and drawing on the old tradition of the camp meeting—the summer assemblies provided entertainment and inspiration for adults and youth.

More than any other individual, H. L. Winburn led the assembly movement in its early years. A graduate of Union University in Tennessee, pastor of the First Church in Arkadelphia, Winburn was a passionate supporter of the State Convention and its causes; he served three terms as Convention president. Winburn organized the first assembly in July 1905. Twenty-eight years old at the time, Winburn suffused the first assembly with his own youthful excitement and energy. He had planned a program to last ten days, a program featuring many of the Convention's most prominent pastors and leaders. Lectures and lessons on history, sociology, science, and the arts were interspersed with sermons and games, music, and "devotionals." Torrential rains forced the assembly to close after only five days, despite Winburn's frantic attempts to secure additional tents for the sodden girls and boys, chaperones, and assorted—drenched—speakers. Undaunted, Winburn pressed forward with an assembly the following year; the movement soon obtained the status of a Convention tradition.

It was in the first decade of the new century that the Convention moved aggressively into the forefront of the temperance movement in Arkansas. For many years the Convention had maintained a temperance committee which regularly advocated the pressuring of the general public and politicians on behalf of the temperance ideal. But shortly after the turn of the century the Convention began to give temperance a prominence nearly equal to its emphasis on missions. The temperance boom in Arkansas was part of a larger, burgeoning national movement driven forward by religious leaders and social scientists.

Along with other temperance advocates in Arkansas and around the nation, leaders of the Convention generally saw alcohol as a scourge which destroyed lives and communities. In 1910, the Convention established a "Temperance Commission," and dispatched E. J. A. McKinney, the new editor of the *Baptist Advance,* to visit Washington, D.C., and lobby for national temperance legislation. In 1913, Arkansas became a dry state. Especially gratifying to the Convention leadership was the fact that the passage of the prohibition bill was superintended by Josiah Hardage, speaker of the state House of Representatives and a Ouachita graduate.

Even if the enthusiasm for temperance rivaled missions, it did not eclipse the essential evangelical ideal of the Convention. In 1909, the Convention inaugurated a small mission outreach to German immigrants in the state. And by the close of the first decade of the new century, the Convention helped to sponsor six associational missionaries and one hundred local pastors. Thirty-eight new churches and over one hundred new Sunday Schools were organized during 1910; Convention mission work resulted in over 3,700 baptisms. Membership in Convention churches stood at just above 100,000; thirty years before, at the beginning of the Eagle era, that number had been only about 37,000. Moreover, the Convention's annual combined home and foreign missions budget for 1910 had risen to nearly $50,000. Only nine years earlier the combined budget had been barely $7,000.

With three affiliated colleges, several academies, an orphanage, an expanding mission vision, growing financial strength, the presence of proven veteran and promising new leaders, the Convention gave every appearance of having reached a historic plateau. From that height, great possibilities and great obstacles loomed in the near distance.

10

1911–1930

THE ANNUAL MEETING OF THE ARKANSAS BAPTIST STATE
Convention convened in Helena in 1911. One of the more memorable
events at the meeting was an address by the Reverend E. C. Morris,
among the South's best known and most eloquent African-American
leaders. Morris served as the president of the National Baptist
Association. That the State Convention had invited Morris and a delegation of National Baptists to meet with them, bespoke something of a
tempering of racial antagonism—even if such gestures failed to represent an explicit and full repudiation of racial divisions. Morris's
appearance at the annual meeting takes on more significance given the
fact that the most powerful political leader in Arkansas, and former
vice-president of the State Convention, Jeff Davis was riding a wave of
political popularity at the time based largely on his vicious and vulgar
racism which included his mockery of education for African-Americans
and his celebration of lynching.

In such a context, Morris's relationship with the leaders of the
Arkansas Baptist State Convention was not, probably, simply a matter of
courteous paternalism. In fact, Morris and several influential
Convention leaders knew and respected each other. Notably, H. L.
Winburn, founder of the Convention's assembly movement and pastor
of First Church, Arkadelphia, served with Morris as a delegate to the

Of his many interests, Hardy Lathan Winburn II was devoted to young people. Founder of the Arkansas Baptist Assembly at Siloam Springs and organizer of the Baptist Young People's Union in the state, his efforts enriched the lives of generations of Arkansas's youth.

Southern Sociological Congress. Conger and Morris also served together as delegates. And over the years Morris had worked with Convention stalwarts like W. E. Atkinson, Benjamin Cox, and Governor Eagle in assisting the struggling Arkansas Baptist College and in the larger cause of black ministerial education.

The tentative assistance from the Convention to Arkansas Baptist College never implied anything approaching adoption of the institution by the Convention. No one on either side of the racial divide ever proposed such a thing. Gifts to Arkansas Baptist College were scarcely more than a token. Still, these modest gifts, just like the invitation to Morris to speak, were a visible sign of the Convention's approbation of African-American higher education.

The paucity of support for Arkansas Baptist College must also be seen in relation to the comparatively modest financial support given by the Convention to its own institutions. The attempt in 1901 to consolidate Convention academies and colleges had not been successful. By 1911, Convention leaders conceded that the Ouachita-Central System was unmanageable. The academies—Magazine, Maynard, Bentonville, Mountain Home—were essentially cut loose to fend for themselves. Ouachita and Central reverted to a more independent status in relation to one another. Several of the academies struggled along for a few years with assistance from the Southern Baptist Convention and local churches and associations.

Abandoning the Ouachita-Central System did not lessen the Convention's emotional and rhetorical enthusiasm for higher education—there had never been very much financial support. But it did recognize structural deficiencies in the plan and the changing cultural and political realities in Arkansas, notably the maturation of the public school system. The development of public education early in the century, largely negated the need for private church-sponsored academies.

The end of the Ouachita-Central System also coincided with substantive changes in the governance structure of the Convention itself. Actually, the organizational structure of the Convention had never been very stable. To a large extent the structural inconsistencies were offset by the presence of committed and skilled leaders. For example, the Eagles provided coherence and direction for a generation, then Atkinson, Conger, Winburn, the Bartons, and their peers carried Convention work forward through the opening decades of the twentieth century. But everyone connected intimately with the Convention knew that a more effective structural framework was needed.

Beginning soon after the Civil War, the nomenclature and structure of the Convention's offices and ministries were regularly altered. The office and title of "corresponding secretary" was changed to "mission secretary," then back to "corresponding secretary;" for a short time there were two mission secretaries, and the position alternated from being salaried for a few years then was relegated to voluntary status, then salaried again. Compounding the inconsistent structure of the Convention was the frequent turnover in personnel—especially in the secretary's position. But then, given the erratic funding and rather ambiguous, but onerous, duties of the position, it was not surprising that few men wished to remain for long in the work.

General secretaries: John T. Christian (1911–1913), top left; R. M. Inlow (1914–1915), top right; E. P. Alldredge (1919), directly above.

The Sunday School and Colportage Board, established in 1897, was consolidated in 1904 with the Convention's Executive Board which became the Mission and Sunday School Board. Even so, everyone continued to refer to this hybrid entity as the Executive Board. In 1900, the Executive Board consisted of thirteen members "at large" and one member from each association. In 1913, the board was expanded to a membership of seventy-five, one member from each association and the rest "at large." Of course, much of the actual work of the Convention during these years was carried out by the traditional committees on education, missions, temperance, and the WMU. These entities provided a solid center of Convention support and service.

The inconsistency in the Convention's organizational structure was the result of varied fiscal and ideological pressures, notably the lingering anxiety about episcopacy and the determination to avoid any appearance of hierarchy. However, beginning in 1912, Convention leaders made a series of significant moves toward greater consolidation of the Convention's organizational structure and toward the creation of a better, more reliable funding system for Convention causes. The Executive Board was recreated at that time and given administrative responsibility for missions, education, Sunday School and Baptist Young People's Union (BYPU) work, the orphanage, and Convention publications. Significantly, the *Baptist Advance* was now formally controlled by the Convention.

This consolidation eliminated separate trustee boards for colleges, the orphanage, and the *Advance,* while creating the new post of general secretary. In its particular details this new organizational framework was not long lived, but the idea it represented, particularly regarding the administrative responsibility of the general secretary, later "executive secretary," and the crucial significance of the Executive Board, as the overarching supervisory structure for the Convention, persisted and matured.

Equally significant, in 1912, was the attempt to create a more coherent and reliable system of funding for Convention causes. To be sure the Convention needed a better system. Although mission giving had been relatively strong since the turn of the century, amounts were unreliable, and the colleges and orphanage were seriously under funded. Ouachita was dangerously in debt by 1913, its tuition and gifts having failed to keep pace with the need for faculty and facilities.

Indeed, part of the motivation for the consolidation of the Convention's boards probably derived from a desire for a more efficient disbursement of limited Convention funds.

In 1912, the Convention implemented, or rather recommended to local churches, a schedule of offerings. January and February collections were to go to education, March and April were mission months, the orphanage was to be sustained through giving in September and December, and ministerial education was to receive emphasis at "convenient times." In 1913, the Convention reiterated its plea for more systematic giving on the part of the churches—though it clarified that the Convention was not attempting to build the endowment of the colleges. That task was left to the institutions. The new emphasis, the "Five Year Plan," resulted in larger gifts overall and the participation of more churches in cooperative giving. Significantly, the plan relieved the colleges and the orphanage, temporarily, of their crushing debt burdens. But for all the significance of these changes, including the development of new funding strategies, the crucial element in the Convention's ministry remained the faithful men and women who served in the institutions, missions, and auxiliaries of the Convention.

Among the best and most devoted of this servant band was Dixie Jackson. A native of Louisiana, daughter of a Confederate veteran, in a sense, Dixie Jackson had two lifetimes, a full life as wife and mother and then a remarkable tenure as a leader of the state WMU. In 1913, recently widowed, Dixie coordinated a ladies round-table discussion in the Caroline Association on "Systematic Giving" for missions; it was an ideal and a theme for which she gave the rest of her life. The following year, Jackson was elected vice-president of the state WMU and, more importantly, she was employed as the full-time corresponding secretary of the organization. The position, as a full-time salaried position, was still new, only two years old. The stipend was modest, but it reflected the dawning realization that some Convention tasks merited vocational status. Jackson succeeded Mrs. W. S. Farmer, who had been the first full-time employee of the WMU, having served for two years.

Quiet, patient, disciplined by the challenges of a large family and personal sorrow, Dixie Jackson, provided nearly a quarter-century of stable leadership for the State Convention through her devoted service to the WMU. Her service carried her to every corner of the state and she became the embodiment of the state WMU—and by extension the State Convention and the cause of missions. Typical of her wide ranging activities, in 1923 she was among the small delegation of Convention leaders who spoke at the dedication of a new dormitory at Central College. More typical were her regular visits to the churches. From Hope to Mountain Home, to Walnut Ridge, to El Dorado, she advocated the Convention and its causes.

Among the most prominent causes of the Convention in the early decades of the new century was the 75 Million Campaign. Perhaps no single innovation since the inception of the WMU so fundamentally strengthened the State Convention as did the inauguration of the 75 Million Campaign in 1919. Though it was a creature of the Southern Baptist Convention, the campaign awakened Arkansas Baptists to a greater, dramatic sense of the potential of cooperative action. Arguably, the campaign stands as one of the most ambitious denominational efforts in the history of American Protestantism. Certainly, it was among the most dramatic religiously inspired movements in Arkansas history. Coming as it did on the heels of restructuring and reassessing the Convention's governance structure, and following fifteen years after the definitive division of the Convention over the cooperative ideal, the 75 Million Campaign took root deeply in the state's Baptist culture.

Indirectly, at least, the path to the 75 Million Campaign led through the Arkansas Baptist State Convention. H. L. Winburn, long-time pastor in Arkadelphia, founder of the Arkansas Baptist Assembly movement, perennial leader in the State Convention, published a book in 1915 which gained the imprimatur of the Southern Baptist Convention and helped perhaps to set the stage for the Southern Convention's massive stewardship campaign of 1919. In his little book, *A Man and His Money*, Winburn mounted a formal, theologically powerful demand for sacrificial giving to God's work. Significantly, the book was published by the Baptist Book Concern—the Southern Convention's publishing arm, an unmistakable endorsement by the larger denomination. And the book's foreword was written by W. O. Carver, among the Southern Convention's most admired Bible scholars and mission advocates.

Though he was living in Kentucky when the book was released, Winburn was an Arkansas Baptist. In fact, his sojourn in Kentucky represented only a brief interlude in his lifetime of service in Arkansas.

Certainly, Winburn expected Arkansas Baptists to rally to his call for sacrificial giving to the Kingdom's work. In a presentation volume to the Central College library Winburn expressed his hope that "Central and her girls [would] add much to the world's sense of stewardship of all good things."

The expectant tone of Winburn's challenge to Central's students mirrored similar calls for greater, more systematic giving by the executive leadership of the State Convention. In the summer of 1918, J. S. Rogers, the general secretary, sent a "four-cornered letter" to Convention pastors. Devoid of the academic tone of Winburn's book, Rogers's letter purported to be about "matters of serious moment that must not be neglected. Surely you will summons [sic] your people to look after them."

What followed, in Rogers's colloquial style, was a pointed solicitation. The secretary especially hoped Baptists in Arkansas would give to support the Southwestern Theological Seminary in Fort Worth, Texas. He assured the pastors that Southwestern was a "soul-winning" institution, "rock-ribbed and unshaken in its old-time Baptist orthodoxy." Rogers also solicited aid for Arkansas's "old, infirm, worn-out preachers."

In mixing more parochial, state concerns with larger Southern Convention needs, Rogers fully anticipated the character of the 75 Million Campaign. Rogers closed his letter with an invitation for pastors to attend a imminent statewide evangelism conference in Little Rock. Significantly, Rogers noted, "Dr. L. R. Scarborough will speak three times." The following year, Scarborough, president of Southwestern Seminary, also assumed the leadership of the 75 Million Campaign. Given the influence of Winburn, Rogers, the WMU, and many others, the Arkansas Baptist State Convention fell into line with the 75 Million Campaign.

Churches, the colleges, associations, the annual meetings of the State Convention, the *Baptist Advance* gained a new sense of unity and urgency from the campaign. The Central "girls" did their part, incidentally, contributing several hundred dollars over the life of the campaign.

In one sense, the campaign struck a chord in Baptist life because the nation was just emerging victorious from the First World War. There was, in Arkansas and the nation, a sense of American involvement in the larger world on an unprecedented scale. The 75 Million Campaign, with its resonating call to worldwide missions and to heroic, sacrificial service, captivated the Convention. Interestingly, the leaders of the Convention offered a "Fourteen Point Plan" to the churches, outlining the goals for the campaign. The idea for these Fourteen Points was unmistakable, borrowed from President Woodrow Wilson's Fourteen Points for world peace released a year before.

Still, the most significant thing about the campaign was its tendency to unite Arkansas Baptist Convention constituencies as few other programs or personalities had done. However, there was irony in the campaign. Although the effort raised an unprecedented amount of money, over two million dollars, the Convention also began—simultaneously—to slide into insolvency. Even a new cooperative giving scheme called the "Cooperative Program" (CP) failed to arrest the decline. Moreover, the Convention established a new office of "Stewardship, Tithing and Systematic Giving" with J. F. Tull as its secretary. These additional innovations notwithstanding, the fiscal circumstances of the Convention declined apace during the mid-and late 1920s.

The financial debility of the Convention was the result of complex circumstances. Foremost among the causes was a decision by Convention leaders—sustained by votes of messengers at annual meetings—to expand Convention ministries. Typical of the expansion was the Convention's move, in 1920, to establish a Baptist hospital in Little Rock. This decision helped to push the Convention into an untenable fiscal position. The hospital project represented a dramatic new draft on Convention resources. Still, the movement to create the Baptist State Hospital could hardly be opposed without giving the appearance of callousness and a lack of faith. Not only did the hospital movement propose to provide inexpensive or free medical care for the poor, but also, peer state conventions were already well ahead of Arkansas in creating hospitals. As if these powerful arguments needed bolstering, the hospital supporters in the Convention arranged in 1921 for George W. Truett to address the annual meeting of the State Convention in Pine Bluff. Truett, possibly the most compelling pulpiteer of his generation—of any denomination—celebrated the high idealism which resonated through the hospital movement.

Davis Hospital, Pine Bluff, Ark.

The ABSC's campaign to raise $75 million, in conjunction with the SBC (1919–1924), allowed the Convention to renovate Davis Hospital (top) and build a new structure, Baptist State Hospital in Little Rock (directly above). Davis had been given to the ABSC by the city of Pine Bluff. However, after World War II, the cost of medical care and increasing governmental regulations forced Convention officials to sell the institution back to Pine Bluff. Baptist Hospital in Little Rock also severed its official ties with the ABSC for much the same reasons in 1966.

Actually, the Convention was suddenly operating two hospitals, the state Baptist Hospital in Little Rock and the Davis Hospital in Pine Bluff, a struggling institution "given" to the Convention early in 1920. J. S. Rogers, peripatetic and forceful, recently general secretary of the Convention, and now, in 1921, superintendent of the Baptist State Hospital, followed Truett's message, reporting that the Pine Bluff and Little Rock hospitals had treated over 2,500 patients during the preceding year. Over eighty of the Little Rock patients were charity cases; nevertheless, Rogers reported that the hospitals both turned modest profits. Missing, of course, from both Truett's and Rogers's glowing promotions, was a clear analysis of the long-term costs associated with the hospitals, including new buildings, staff, and equipment. Early gifts to the hospital effort were encouraging, but perhaps these gifts came at the expense of other Convention causes.

Then, too, adding to the Convention's fiscal instability, and ultimately contributing to the Convention's financial debility, was the lack of strict fiscal accountability on the part of affiliated institutions. The colleges and the orphanage operated as best they could, borrowing oftentimes to make up for their low tuitions, erratic enrollments, urgent capital needs, and uncertain funding from Convention coffers.

An expanded Convention staff also contributed to the financial stress on the organization. From a staff of one in 1901, the number of Convention employees in Little Rock expanded, by 1918, to include a general secretary, assistant general secretary, bookkeeper and clerk, Church Building missionary, five district missionaries, Sunday School and BYPU secretary, editor of the *Baptist Advance*, bookkeeper for the paper and the Baptist Book House, WMU corresponding secretary, and WMU office secretary. The Convention also helped pay the salaries of many pastors and associational missionaries. All these were worthwhile offices and ministries, but together they represented a substantial commitment of Convention resources. Debts added to debts.

Even so, for a short time in the early 1920s, all seemed hopeful for the Convention. The 1922 Convention report revealed more than $320,000 contributed to all causes during the preceding year. But disaster was imminent. Just below the surface, only slightly hidden, was over $130,000 dollars worth of unpaid obligations in 1922. True, that was less than it had been for the past few years, but the fiscal house of the Convention was standing on shifting sand.

Failure of the Convention leaders to gauge the danger was partly due to the mood of the times. The twenties, even in Arkansas, were years of unrealistic expectations and changing attitudes. It was an era in national history, when responsible men and women allowed themselves to believe, for example, that all wars could be forestalled by the simple expediency of treaties. It was the golden age of Hollywood, jazz, and prohibition. Post-World War I American culture cherished, and trusted, its own chimeric superficialities. Part of the chimeric cultural outlook involved the casual reliance on consumer credit based on an assumption of perpetual economic growth.

The men and women who comprised the leadership of the Convention were far from being giddy minions of the Jazz Age, but they were not entirely immune to the power of national culture. And why not carry a debt? The growth of the Convention in numbers and gifts surely presaged a growth in material resources sufficient to cover any long-term debt.

Nor was anyone eager to limit the work of the Convention given the apparent, imminent threat of evolutionary atheism. For several years, beginning in the early twenties, the Convention's churches and leaders were consumed with the struggle against Darwinian theory. And after the Scopes Trial in 1925, the Convention was drawn even more deeply and rapidly into what seemed a struggle for the soul of the nation.

Ironically, the battle regarding evolution was largely over by the time the Scopes Trial seized the public's imagination. In fact, the Scopes Trial was truly more of a culmination than a beginning given the reality that, by the 1920s, evolutionary theory had already gained prominence—if not complete ascendancy—in academe, the press, and middle-class culture. But in Arkansas at the time the struggle seemed desperately urgent. Demands for rigid repudiation of any evolutionary theory embroiled Ouachita and Central in 1924 as the leaders of the Convention demanded a signed statement from all faculty and staff affirming their allegiance to orthodoxy.

The president of Central, former governor and Baptist deacon, Charles Hillman Brough, added to the tension of the time by dissenting from the Convention's demand for a state law against the teaching of evolution in the public schools. Brough found himself locked in a bitter debate with J. S. Compere, editor of the *Baptist Advance* and J. S. Rogers, Convention general secretary. The stormy controversy flashed—and alternatingly smoldered—for several years; in the end, the state law was passed. Even so, Brough, a theistic evolutionist, soon felt compelled to resign his post as Central's president, despite his willingness to sign, under protest, the required anti-evolution pledge.

To be sure, in the minds of Rogers and other Convention leaders, the mid-1920s were no time for retreat, no time for a lessening a commitment to ministry and mission. And there was no retreat; through the era the Convention moved forward on all fronts animated by a dynamic, if somewhat inconsistent, admixture of faith and fear. Further magnifying the fears for many in the Convention was the candidacy of Alfred E. Smith in the presidential contest of 1928. Indeed, an almost rabid tone marked the response of many Convention leaders as they appealed for Arkansas Baptists to reject the Roman Catholic—and antiprohibition—Smith. Long associated with the Democratic party in Arkansas, the State Convention and its leadership was divided; here again Brough and Rogers represented openly contentious factions within the Convention. Some characterized support of Smith as an act of spiritual apostasy. Only intense fear could have prompted some of the exaggerated language and ill-considered attitudes manifested by many Convention leaders regarding the Smith candidacy.

While the Convention veered into spheres of social and political conflict, its financial circumstances deteriorated at a perilous pace. In 1926, the Convention moved to alleviate the situation by subtracting the debts of the hospitals, colleges, and orphanage from the Convention ledgers. This action ostensibly made these institutions solely responsible for their own debts. Actually, this was little more than a technical expedient. The institutions had no substantial resource base outside the Convention, the associations, and the churches. Solicitations by the institutions continued to drain the shallow pool of Convention resources irrespective of attempts at creative and cosmetic bookkeeping. Moreover, and ironically, the Convention's financial debility had derived in large measure from the freelance financial arrangements by the institutions; the 1926 innovation only codified a continuation of that tradition.

By 1928, the Convention's fiscal situation was "grave" despite additional retrenchment efforts that included the suspension of assistance to many pastors and associational missionaries. In the space of three years the Convention reduced, by one third, the number of associational missionaries assisted; only eleven associational missionaries continued to receive assistance. And only twenty-eight pastors were being aided by the Convention in 1928—down from seventy-four in 1925. Moreover, the Convention eliminated its fledgling ministry to college students.

Lenders, unconvinced by these retrenchment efforts, were increasingly reluctant to provide more money for the Convention and its affiliated institutions. Confronted with anxious creditors and many pressing needs, the Convention authorized a massive bond sale, $900,000 worth, to pay off outstanding debts and sustain mission and education causes. The bond sale went well in its immediate phase. It provided desperately needed cash for day-to-day operations. Indeed, hundreds of men, women, and organizations in Arkansas and across the South bought the Baptist bonds, confident that the State Convention was a good investment morally and financially.

But however bright the short-term prospects and results, it was this bonded debt which soon crushed the Convention, bringing it to the point of almost irrecoverable disaster. Blame for the crisis caused by the debt, was variously assigned. Ultimately, Convention leaders of the day, boards of trustees, the Executive Committee, and secretaries of the period, failed to confront honestly, realistically the risks involved in proliferating ministries, staff, and the routinized indebtedness of affiliated institutions beginning around 1915. As previously noted, there were various explanations for this failure, all valid perhaps; but the cause or causes of the disastrous indebtedness were ultimately far less significant than the reality of the crisis with its far reaching implications.

Even so, as the decade of the 1920s closed, the men and women of the Arkansas Baptist State Convention had reason for gratitude. The 75 Million Campaign, which ended in 1924, changed the Convention permanently and positively. At the campaign's conclusion, J. S. Rogers asserted that the effort had awakened a spirit of faithful confidence in the Convention. Moreover, the campaign, according to Rogers, had instructed the members of the Convention in the "fine art of cooperation. . . . An intelligent Baptist who does not cooperate now [1924] by his prayers, efforts, and gifts feels like he is dead spiritually. . . ." Additionally, Rogers added that the Convention had gained nearly two million dollars in "permanent" property as a result of the campaign; the gain was in buildings at the hospitals and colleges. Finally, from Rogers's perspective, the campaign had created an evangelical enthusiasm—paying for more missionaries and missions and helping to support more pastors—which had resulted in 60,000 conversions in five years. The reference to evangelism made an important point. Rogers, and his peers in leadership, like H. L. Winburn, president of the Convention in the late twenties, were not exclusively concerned with evolution and prohibition; both men, with thousands of others in the Convention, shared a profound concern for lost souls, a deeply held commitment to missions and ministry. Truly, at the same time the Convention was sinking financially, and swerving from controversy to controversy, it was reaching a new level of missionary maturity.

It was comparatively easy to ignore the growing debt crisis when H. V. Hamilton, charming and deeply pious, presented his reports on his work as State Sunday School secretary, a position that involved the Convention's "youth work" generally. Beginning in 1922, Hamilton, in fact, transformed that aspect of the Convention's ministry. In his inaugural year he organized the first statewide Sunday School Convention. For the next several years he worked with single-minded devotion to elevate the quality and quantity of Bible teaching programs in the churches of the Convention. Rallies, revivals, letters, sermons, enlistment forms flowed from the energetic Hamilton, reaching into every corner of the state. The success of his labors was widely praised at the time, though the somewhat ambivalent reporting, by local churches, of Sunday School and BYPU enrollments, made statistical assertions hazardous. Still, it seems reasonable to claim that the number of duly constituted Sunday Schools doubled from approximately 180 to nearly 400 between 1921 and 1928.

Less ambiguous was Hamilton's adamant and successful advocacy for the creation of a permanent home for the Baptist Assembly. He was the driving force behind the Convention's decision to locate the Assembly permanently at Siloam Springs in 1926. To the shock of the Convention and especially the thousands of Baptist young people he had met personally, and for whom he cared so deeply, Hamilton died in 1928 at the age of thirty-four. He had made his mark by embodying the ideals of the Convention in the areas of evangelism, education, and cooperation.

To be sure, there was no lack of similarly inspired and idealistic Baptist young men and women who were the compeers of Hamilton. By the close of the 1920s, the state WMU counted nineteen young Arkansans serving with the Southern Baptist Convention's Foreign Mission Board. Most of these men and women had found their way to the mission fields of the world through the direct agency of the State Convention, often through the mission training provided to them as children or youths by the WMU. That was true of Mildred Matthews of Morrillton, who left Arkansas in 1920 to begin an ambitious mission outreach in Cuba; by the mid-twenties she was city missionary in Havana and president of the island's WMU. She was hailed in Arkansas as a "faithful evangelist," devoted to the people of Cuba.

A native of Dallas County, Eva Smith's path to foreign mission service led through the halls of Ouachita and especially the college's YWA and Volunteer Band. Like Mildred Matthews a few years before her, Eva answered a call to service in Cuba. Living in Havana, serving the city's polyglot population as a teacher of elementary-age children, Eva Smith also devoted herself to ministering to the parents and grand-parents of her pupils. She lived in a small room on the second floor of the Baptist Temple in Havana. Vivacious, determined, intelligent she also had an artistic bent and when possible Eva took a few hours to sit with her face toward the sea or the mountains, capturing something of her world on canvas.

Clara and Paul Freeman were not native Arkansans, but their experiences in the state and their association with the Convention were pivotal in their call to foreign service. While still a youth, Paul felt a desire for special service as a pastor or missionary. His education at Union University near his home in Tennessee only deepened his desire to serve God in a vocational context. After an arduous career as a student he accepted the call to a pastorate in Maynard, Arkansas, and to teaching in the struggling Maynard Baptist Academy—a mission field in its own right as part of the Home Mission Board's Mountain School System. The Home Board's loss was to be the Foreign Mission Board's and Argentina's gain. In 1920, at the State Convention's annual assembly, Paul's wife, Clara, listened intently to the persuasive appeal of several mission speakers. Her sense of special call to missions was the confirmation Paul needed, and the couple soon applied for foreign service. Upon completing their educational preparation they devoted themselves to service in Concordia, Argentina.

James McGavock invested his life in Chile. Literally amid earthquakes, political and natural, McGavock planted churches, won converts, taught school, and laid the foundations for the Baptist Theological Seminary in Santiago. Reared in Izard County, McGavock's pilgrimage to Chile led through Union University in Tennessee and Southern Seminary in Kentucky.

Dawson King was a popular young man in Immanuel Church in Little Rock. Destined for an engineering career, he thought, King began his undergraduate career at the university in Fayetteville. His plans were abandoned when he sensed a special call to missions. Transferring to Ouachita, King subsequently earned a masters degree in theology at Southern Seminary. Interested initially in working in Africa, King and his wife yielded to the board's alternative preference for a posting to China.

There had been other, earlier foreign missionaries from Arkansas, for instance, the Winns and the Comperes in Africa briefly at the turn of the century, but Eva Smith, the McGavocks, and Kings were part of a far larger, more self-conscious movement rooted and reared in the missionary idealism of the state WMU and the post-Paragould Convention, a movement which came to maturity around 1920.

The colleges were extremely fertile ground for missionary recruitment and support in this era. The library shelves at Central and Ouachita had been well-stocked, from the beginning, with missions literature. Heavy volumes chronicling various world missions meetings and conferences were supplemented by effusive, evocative biographies and anthologies describing the harrowing but heroic lives of missionaries around the world.

Students at Central, for instance, could not fail to be moved, challenged, by S. G. Pinnock's monograph, *The Romance of Missions in Nigeria*. Published by the Foreign Mission Board in 1917, Pinnock's little book was typical of the missionary literature of the time. In his foreword to Pinnock's book, T. B. Ray complimented the author for disdaining an academic account of missions "where literary nostrils are stifled with dry and dusty lore." Instead Pinnock "lures us . . . out in the open where the freshness of life is." Even more interesting, and emotionally potent perhaps was Belle Brain's, *Love Stories of Great*

Missionaries, dedicated to "the girl who is tempted to say 'no' to her lover, because he is a student volunteer [aspiring missionary]."

Students at Central had their own missionary author, a loyal "daughter" of the college, Una Roberts Lawrence, whose brief, eloquent collection of stories, *The King's Own*, was first published in 1920. The fact that many of the students at Central and Ouachita had met personally—in their churches, at the annual assembly, or on the campus—some of the men and women cited by writers like Lawrence, Pinnock, and Brain could only make this type of book more compelling.

Impressionable, enthusiastic college students were often moved deeply by these accounts of missionary heroism, especially, when they realized that young Arkansans were prominent in the modern missions movement. The young missionaries of the period were, of course, admired not only in college communities, but throughout the State Convention. Recognized and celebrated for their faithfulness, heroism, and intelligence, they too were the very embodiment of the most prized ideals of the Convention. The missionaries represented in their very lives the Convention's causes: evangelism, cooperation, and more often than not they were the product of Baptist education.

The encouragement of this mission movement within the culture of the State Convention was carried forward by many individuals and ancillary organizations. Pastors, Convention committee chairs, the *Baptist Advance*, assembly speakers, local WMU circles, Sunbeam, and Girls Auxiliary (GA) organizations all played a role. Especially prominent among the approving voices were those of Una Roberts Lawrence and Lila Pye. In the space of about fifteen years these two remarkable women, articulate and effective, produced dozens of lectures, articles, pamphlets, chapel talks, and monographs supporting the cause of missions. Deeply committed to the larger effort of the Southern Baptist Convention, these two Arkansans, nevertheless, grounded their perspective in the culture of the State Convention. Both were lifelong workers in the state WMU, both were intimates and adjuncts of Dixie Jackson, both endeavored especially to challenge young Arkansans in the Convention's colleges and churches to open their hearts to the call to missions.

To be sure, foreign missions was not the only mission movement promoted by the Convention. Indeed, in 1926, Lawrence personally

Without God and the WMU it is doubtful the Arkansas Baptist Convention would have survived its first one hundred years. Thousands of women gave countless hours of service to the Convention's programs. Representing the WMU are Mrs. James P. (Mary) Eagle, directly right, the founding president of the state organization; Mrs. J. G. (Dixie) Jackson, top left, whose tireless efforts to present the cause of missions to "all corners of the state" has been memorialized in the annual offering for State Missions being named for her; and Mrs. W. D. (Lila) Pye, top right, whose heroic efforts at fund-raising was a major factor in helping the ABSC overcome its debt problems during the Great Depression.

entered home mission service with the Southern Convention's Home Mission Board, and Pye's largest publication, *Magnifying Missions in Arkansas*, emphasized the importance of state as well as foreign service. Certainly, the State Convention's long tradition of supporting state and home missions persisted and expanded in 1920s.

These stories, these triumphs of the missionary spirit in the Convention profoundly inspired and encouraged the state WMU and the larger Convention. Ironically perhaps, the very success of the missionary movement helped to distract Convention leaders from the impending economic crisis and the necessity of confronting the under-lying fiscal problems of the Convention.

As the dramatic decade of the twenties drew toward its close, the Convention experienced another culmination, another important closure. On January 2, 1929, Dixie Jackson died after a brief illness. Her death sent a shock wave through the Convention. Those who knew her—and her work—described the loss to the Convention as incalcu-lable, devastating. What made the pain so much sharper, more poignant was the suddenness of her death. She had been sick for only a few days; friends who stopped in to see her at home, after church on Sunday night, found her feeling better and talking about getting back to work. Now, so suddenly, she was gone. Many regarded her as a pillar—perhaps the pillar—of the WMU and the State Convention. She had played a direct, intimate role in the expansion of the mission culture of the Convention. For others, her death represented more than the passing of a significant, valued leader; they had lost a mentor and friend. Lila Pye, who had often traveled throughout the state with Jackson, remembered her as kind and genteel, but with stolid resolve. She had a youthfulness which belied her age and had seemed to promise many more years of service. It was a comfort to some of her friends to know that she lived long enough to see a deepening of the missionary and cooperative consciousness among so many Arkansas Baptists. Her friends, of course, could not have known that her sudden death also—in a sense—spared Dixie Jackson. She did not live to see the fiscal collapse of the Convention she loved and served. Perhaps as much as her living presence, her memory would help to inspire the men and women of the Convention as they faced the diffi-cult, dangerous days ahead.

11

The 1930s

A MAN OF COURAGE AND CONVICTION, BEN BRIDGES
publicly challenged the Ku Klux Klan at the height of the organization's
resurgence in the early 1920s. As pastor of First Baptist Church,
Paragould, a prominent county-seat church in northeast Arkansas, his
views were widely known. When Klan activity, and recruitment, spread
rapidly across northern Arkansas in the summer of 1922, Bridges inten-
sified his own opposition campaign. In a revival meeting at Rock Hill in
mid-August, Bridges preached a forceful sermon questioning the
motives and morality of the Klan. He repeated the message at the
Friendship Church a week later. The following week, the pastor's
garage and car burned in a mysterious fire. Unintimidated, Bridges
hastily published and distributed his anti-Klan sermon in pamphlet
form. Ben Bridges was not going to be silenced. Throughout the controversy, Bridges was supported forcefully, openly by the men and women
of his church.

For ten years, Ben Bridges served as pastor in Paragould—ironically
he served the church that had played host to the disastrous annual
meeting of the Convention in 1901. The same church, always passion-
ately loyal to the Convention, helped prepare Bridges for his tenure as
one of the greatest, truly pivotal leaders in Convention history. To be
sure, Bridges sharpened his leadership skills in Paragould, leading the
church in a dramatic building program, resulting in one of the most

impressive sanctuaries in the state. And he led the church in the creation of its first unified budget. The church taught him as well, lessons of loyalty and mature judgement.

A native of Pine Bluff, Benjamin Lafayette Bridges preached his first sermon at seventeen. Subsequently educated at Ouachita and Southern Seminary, he pastored churches in Pine Bluff and Crossett before coming to Paragould in 1919. After a decade of remarkable success there he accepted the call, in 1929, to the First Baptist Church in Little Rock. It was a favored place, a place where Bridges could have ridden out the storms of the Depression years in relative peace and security. But far from seeking or resting in a place of comparative comfort, Bridges accepted, in November 1931, the responsibilities and trials inherent with the position of Convention Executive Secretary. Only the most profound certainty of God's call could have led Ben Bridges to accept the post. By 1931, he knew, everyone knew, that the Arkansas Baptist State Convention was fiscally wrecked.

Since the early 1920s, the Convention's debts had risen steadily; by 1929, the organization was virtually bankrupt. Apart from—and contributing to—its crushing indebtedness, the Convention was also fully awash in the Great Depression. The people of Arkansas were reeling under the national catastrophe, engulfed completely in the economic crisis. In 1932, per capita indebtedness in Arkansas was the worst in the nation.

Like much of the rest of the South, the Arkansas economy had actually been faltering for a full decade before "the crash." Boll weevils and the horrific flood of 1927 contributed to the grinding down of the state's economy. The stock market collapse in 1929 simply deepened the existing economic trials. And, in 1930, the state and region endured a cataclysmic drought. Conditions in many parts of the state went from bad to worse to desperate in the space of a few years. One foreign observer traveling through eastern Arkansas in 1935, asserted, "Never have I seen such an untidy countryside, even in Poland or the Balkans. [Sharecropper shacks are] worse than any rural housing I have ever seen in Europe. . . ."

By the mid-1930s, tens of thousands of Arkansans were fleeing their shacks and shanties, the worn-out fields, and the apparent hopelessness of the state's economy. It was one of the great migrations of the century,

"Arkies" joining "Okies" in a westward current hoping to find work. Most Arkansans were not reduced to such desperate measures, but virtually all Arkansans were touched significantly, painfully by the Depression.

Certainly, Arkansas Baptist folk and their churches, and the Convention, were immersed fully in the economic disaster of the era. The Convention's coffers were empty, indeed $54,000, carefully garnered for the payment of interest on Convention debts, had been lost in the collapse of an insolvent bank. The Convention owed the staggering total of $1,200,000. In February 1931, the Convention defaulted on its scheduled payments to its bondholders. This default came despite a retrenchment program ongoing since the late 1920s that had resulted in the elimination of the Convention's student work and the drastic curtailment of assistance to associational missionaries. In 1930, the Convention was compelled to cease completely all assistance to associational missionaries. As funding dwindled, other Convention ministries and programs faltered as well.

As a member of the Convention's Executive Board, Bridges had attended a February 1931 meeting of the Executive Board and listened to the litany of doom from T. D. Brown, executive secretary since the previous November. All that had been accomplished so far toward the solution of the Convention's fiscal problems was the recent creation of a Bondholders' Protection Committee, an entity comprising a distinct minority of the Convention's bondholders. This committee had made an effort to contact other bondholders—many were unknown to the committee—and had counseled patience and continued confidence in the Convention. The list of bondholders actually numbered well into the hundreds and included the whole range of Southern society, pastors, newspapermen, a professor of Greek at the University of Mississippi, a Federal judge, bankers, attorneys, farmers, doctors, and entrepreneurs. Some easily and gladly forgave the whole debt; for instance, the president of Coca-Cola Bottling in Birmingham, Alabama, surrendered his substantial bond portfolio as a gift to the Convention. Others clung to their Convention bonds, hoping desperately that their bonds would see them through the Depression.

In light of the Convention's complete insolvency, the committee's call for patience and confidence hardly seemed a candid or realistic

In his twenty-six years of service as general secretary of the Arkansas Baptist State Convention, Ben L. Bridges (1931–1957) had many notable achievements. However, his single-minded commitment to paying off the Convention's indebtedness in full may have been his most significant accomplishment.

General secretaries: L. E. Barton (1920–1921), left, and T. D. Brown (1929–1930), right.

recommendation. The Convention's inner circle of leaders certainly knew the desperate seriousness of the crisis as they gathered in February. Indeed, the apparent hopelessness of the situation, the cadence of despair, culminated with T. D. Brown's resignation as executive secretary at the meeting. Despair turned to panic and the Executive Board descended in frustrated, futile debate and argument. Bridges had no solution, but he adamantly insisted that the board should do nothing that would jeopardize nearly a century of Convention work; for his part, Bridges stated he would devote much of his time during the next several weeks to finding a solution to the debt crisis and seeking God's guidance in the matter. He could not have known at the time that he would devote the next decade of his life to the problem of Convention insolvency.

When the Executive Board reconvened in April, Bridges was in the chair. He faced a barrage of questions; no, he still had no solution to the Convention's insolvency, but he was committed to keeping the Convention and its remaining ministries alive. Other board members had had enough; two proposed the dissolution of the Convention. Bridges disregarded parliamentary procedure and refused to recognize the "second" to the dissolution motion. Instead, he spoke for half an hour, summoning all of his eloquence and passion, appealing for calm and for persistence. The board immediately put Bridges's own faith to the test, asking him to take the post of Executive Secretary.

Bridges accepted the challenge. It was the beginning of an heroic pilgrimage, a pilgrimage that began, literally, the following day when he took the train to Nashville, Tennessee, to meet with some of the Convention's creditors. Bridges hoped to buy time for the Convention by arranging a partial payment schedule of Convention debts. Some $900,000 of the Convention's debt was represented by bonds issued by Caldwell and Company of Nashville. These bonds had been sold in the late 1920s to finance the Convention's large debt and continuing operations. If the bond backers would help, especially in identifying the hundreds—perhaps thousands—of bondholders, then a partial payment plan might be arranged.

As the train rocked across the rolling farmland and pastures of West Tennessee, Bridges could only hope that the Caldwell and Company, with its expertise in such matters, would have some useful advice. To Bridges's dismay, he found Caldwell and Company in receivership, a financial ruin. Nevertheless, he secured a fairly complete list of all bondholders.

Back in Little Rock, Bridges immediately wrote each bondholder, clarifying the simple, terrible truth—the Convention had no money. Bridges asked the bondholders to join, or endorse in writing, the Bondholders Protection Committee, as the negotiating representative of all the Convention's creditors. Moreover, he assured the bondholders that a new payment plan would be forthcoming. "Please do not lose faith in us," he appealed. Some bondholders, like James Vance, pastor of Nashville, Tennessee's, First Presbyterian Church, responded by endorsing the committee. Others refused to cede to the committee their private negotiating rights. As months passed without a settlement, or only hints of a settlement, some bondholders, even some of those who had endorsed the committee, became discouraged or angry.

By late 1932, Bridges had to endure letters which sometimes accused the Convention of fraud or other moral malfeasance. One bondholder suspected the whole matter of the Protection Committee was a ruse that involved "withholding the bondholders money so as to depress the market on them [the bonds]," and then redeeming the bonds "at a trifle." The writer added, "I would not have believed there were people in this world that would have resorted to anything of this kind."

The suggestion of corruption by some angry bondholders resonated more forcefully in light of Clinton Carnes's chicanery only a few years earlier. It was revealed, in 1929, that Carnes, treasurer of the Southern Baptist Convention's Home Mission Board, systematically embezzled nearly a million dollars from mission funds over the space of five or six years. Though not related directly to the State Convention, the Carnes's affair certainly, graphically revealed the possibility of corruption in denominational life.

In the face of criticism, suspicion, and frustration, Bridges and the Convention's veteran bookkeeper, Ruth DeWoody, on reduced salaries—with Mrs. Bridges as an unpaid assistant—labored to answer all letters, deflect doomsayers, and critics and compile yet more accurate lists of the Convention's bondholders and creditors. They especially attempted to identify the most needy of the bondholders. Many of the bonds had, in fact, been sold to widows and poor pastors. Some of the bondholders were pastors in other denominations; even the Mission Board of the Cumberland Presbyterian Convention held Arkansas Baptist State Convention bonds. Bridges often sent money, from his own salary, to pay some of the poorest bondholders. But such stop-gap measures were nothing more than that.

Over several months' time, Bridges formulated a long-range plan to repay fully all the Convention's debts. The payment program, recommended by Bridges, was to run from 1932 to 1962. The Bondholder Protection Committee accepted the plan, as did the Convention. However, the Committee could not control all the bondholders and did not speak for several of the largest creditors of the Convention; law suits were filed and the thirty-year plan collapsed. Moreover, giving to the Convention continued to decline, making any payment plan apparently unworkable.

By the mid-1930s, the very life of the Convention was clearly in the balance. The reduced Convention executive staff consisted of only Bridges and a bookkeeper, the WMU corresponding secretary and assistant, and the Sunday School secretary and assistant.

The best legal advice suggested that the Convention seek a release from its creditors by agreeing to an immediate, but discounted, repayment scheme. Bridges disliked the recommendation, but he conceded—for the time being. In 1936, the Convention and bondholders arranged an immediate 35 percent payment plan, sanctioned subsequently by the Federal Court in Little Rock. Of course, the formulation of the plan and the court's approval were only the beginning; the great test was ahead—the Convention must now find the money to pay bondholders the reduced, but still large, settlement.

Ben Bridges was truly an indispensable man for the hour, possessed of the determination and discipline, the courage, to face the mounting crises of the time. But, he was not required to face the towering challenges alone. Otto Whitington was indispensable in his own right. Eloquent, energetic, resilient Whitington, pastor of Immanuel Church in Little Rock, became the great spokesman for the Convention's debt-payment campaign. He traveled thousands of miles throughout Arkansas, pleading, praying with Arkansas Baptists, to increase their giving, to join the campaign to raise the money for the debt-paying plan.

To emphasize the urgency and importance of the campaign, Whitington and Bridges summoned George Truett from Texas. Ironically, fifteen years before, Truett had been brought to Little Rock to boost the idea of a Baptist hospital; now he was invited back to try and save the Convention hospitals, colleges, and the Convention itself. Immanuel Church hosted the rally. On October 8, 1936, Truett spoke for nearly an hour in each of the morning and evening services at Immanuel. Over 3,400 people heard his appeal. The *Arkansas Baptist* (formerly the *Baptist Advance*) reported that Truett had endured an exhausting journey to aid Arkansas Baptists; moreover, he refused any honorarium and paid his own expenses.

The rally was a success in the attention it gained and the momentum it produced, but more than a year of grueling work was ahead. To aid in the campaign, Whitington and the Debt Paying Committee enlisted ten respected preachers to canvas the state in support of the campaign. Virtually all of the associations agreed to host debt-paying rallies. The *Arkansas Baptist*, under the editorial guidance of J. I. Cossey, provided constant coverage of the campaign. In fact, only a few months before the debt-paying program began, Cossey announced the successful completion his own campaign to carry *Arkansas Baptist* circulation past 5,500. To be sure, the larger the circulation of the paper, the better the chances for a successful debt-paying campaign.

Churches, associations, and individuals listened to the appeal of Whitington and "the ten." Whitington especially awakened, revived,

Of the hundreds of dedicated office workers who have served the ABSC over the years, none could match the unselfish devotion of Ruth DeWoody, who for over thirty years served as accountant, bookkeeper, and trust officer through five general secretaries. Historian J. S. Rogers described her as "honest as the multiplication table, almost as eminent as the Golden Rule, marked by fidelity and nobility, as kind as the Bible Ruth. . . ."

While Otto Whitington performed many services—pastor, ABSC president, denominational leader—Arkansas's Southern Baptists perhaps owe their greatest debt of gratitude to him for his unceasing efforts to assist Secretary Bridges in raising money to redeem the Convention's many bond obligations during the Great Depression.

inspired, thousands of Arkansas Baptists to the extent that they gave sacrificially, heroically to save the Convention by paying the required 35 percent on the debt. In hundreds of churches, at dozens of associational meetings, Whitington appealed to Baptist folk to find the fifty cents, the five dollars, the dime to rescue the Convention and its ministries.

If Whitington and Bridges needed more incentive to stay the course, they had only to pore over the voluminous mail which inundated the Convention daily as dozens of bondholders begged, or threatened, the Convention in an effort to recover their money. The letters were occasionally snide; one bondholder wrote, "I was foolish to ever trust anything said by churches." Such letters, questioning the integrity of the Convention, must have stung. How could the Convention witness to a lost world when it did not keep its word? Another angry bondholder accused the Convention's leadership of breaking faith with Christ in failing to keep their promises. How, this correspondent wondered, could the Convention have gotten into such a mess when the Bible clearly warned about indebtedness? Moreover, the letter writer insinuated that the Convention leaders were callous in reducing their commitment to bondholders while enjoying comfortable financial circumstances themselves. Whitington responded to this charge, pointing out that he had lost virtually everything in the Depression.

Most letters were less acerbic, more heartrending than harsh. As news of the devalued bond plan spread, letters reached Whitington and Bridges describing the extreme distress of some bondholders; often in cramped handwriting, widows lamented the Convention's plan to pay only thirty-five cents on the dollar saying that the few bonds they owned were their only source of income. One aged pastor wrote that he and his blind wife had been counting on the bonds to sustain them, that they were only barely eking out an existence with a few cows and chickens which they were both too infirm to tend.

Anyone willing to look could see that behind the Convention's financial woes there was a burgeoning human tragedy made all the worse by the disappointment of many people in the Convention they had trusted. Writing from Monette, Mrs. W. J. Mitchell mentioned her need for money, "I'm badly damaged by the recent flood [of 1937] and I don't know what I am to do. My little home is still under water and I have no idea how or what I'm going to do. . . ." Obviously, telling such people that, at best, the Convention would redeem their bonds at a drastically devalued rate, was a painful, even disgusting responsibility. Some bond-holders asked for other forms of help—in lieu of full payment of their bonds. One bondholder wrote Whitington, "I am sure you are very busy and get awful tired of wants and complaints but I just had to ask for your assistance in helping me get my son into Ouachita College . . . knowing my financial condition as you do." Whitington duly wrote back, and then wrote to Ouachita's president asking that the young man be admitted; in fact, every letter received was answered promptly and personally—thousands of letters.

Some letters were remarkable in their graciousness and generosity of spirit. Men and women who could ill-afford such sacrifice, accepted the devalued bond payments as a part of their service to the Kingdom, as a means of helping the Convention escape its thraldom to debt.

While the Convention leadership attempted to hold the heart of the organization together, the agencies and institutions on the periphery faltered and, in some instances, collapsed and disappeared. Mountain Home College failed in the early thirties. The institution's former pres-ident, H. D. Morton, bitterly criticized the Convention and its leadership for reneging on pledged help to pay the college's debts. The Convention rejected this perspective; in fact, the Convention had grad-ually withdrawn all support from the college during the 1920s. Of course, former President Morton knew the grim truth; without Convention support Mountain Home College was doomed. Since its founding in 1927, Jonesboro Baptist College had never had more than kind words from the Convention; it closed in 1936.

Even those institutions allied directly with the Convention faced desperate trials as the Depression deepened. Central and Ouachita fought to live, bereft of Convention support. The circumstances were harrowing for both institutions. Ouachita borrowed against its small endowment, enrollments declined, tuition was reduced, salaries were cut, and some faculty were dismissed until further notice. The finan-cial straits of the institution contributed, moreover, to the college's loss of accreditation in 1932. By the middle of the decade, under the leadership of J. R. Grant, Ouachita began to recover, but only slowly. Enrollment reached the 500 mark in 1935. With its resources severely limited, the college relied heavily on the pluck—and the husbandry skills—of students. A notice in the 1935 *Arkansas Baptist* captured the make-do character of the times at Ouachita:

> This is hog killing time at Ouachita. In our efforts to decrease expenses the College administration raises hogs from which they obtain meat for the dining hall. The swine are cared for by student labor and fed scraps from the dining hall. . . . Another stock enterprise at the College is the dairy. The cattle are brought here by students who care for them and sell the milk to the College. . . .

Such expedients were adopted at Central College as well, where some 180 students in 1935 depended considerably on the productivity of "seven good cows, six hogs, one horse, [and] one good Chevrolet truck. . . ." J. S. Rogers, president of Central since May 1929, also reported that he lacked $300 paying faculty their full wages, and the roof on the Administration Building was in need of repair at a cost of $500, a sum the college did not have.

Yet, in the very midst of the overwhelming crisis, a gradual, tentative restoration of confidence and commitment slowly emerged. Conspicuous among the leaders rallying the beleaguered Baptists of the state for missions and evangelism was Lila Pye. Her connections with the Convention stretched back across decades. As a young girl, at the turn of the century, Pye attended a large missions meeting in Caroline Association at which her mother offered the devotional. It was an epiphany of sorts. Pye never forgot the intensity in her mother's dark eyes as she "bore testimony for her Lord." Adding to the drama of the experience was the appearance, following her mother's remarks, of Mrs. Eagle. Refined and regal, Mrs. Eagle conferred extraordinary significance on the meeting.

The vividness of this first, formal contact with the WMU, presaged a lifetime of work with and through the organization. Studies at Ouachita and Galloway College and marriage followed in due course. In 1924, Pye was elected president of the state WMU. With the death of Dixie Jackson five years later, she succeeded to the post of corresponding secretary, just as the Convention's fiscal infrastructure began to collapse. Like Bridges, Pye labored to salvage the Convention

financially. As one of the three-member subcommittee of the larger
Debt Paying Committee, Pye was involved intimately in developing
plans and campaigns to settle the Convention's debts. Still, for all her
necessary absorption in the crisis, Pye looked beyond the immediate,
pressing circumstances and confidently endeavored to restore the
vitality and visibility of the state WMU and the larger cause of
missions.

In 1936, Pye edited and published *Magnifying Missions in
Arkansas*. "'Our State for Christ,' our rallying cry; 'Christ for our State,'
does your heart reply? Then lift to heaven on earnest plea That He its
Lord and King shall be." This slightly sentimental verse on the book
frontispiece belied the book's blunt call for renewed commitment to
missions—in spite of the terrible economic conditions.

Among Pye's most emphatic challenges was her appeal for a more
effective mission outreach to black Arkansans. Like other leaders of the
Convention—across the decades—Pye shared a desire to assist, at least
spiritually, Arkansas's large African-American population. The woefully
imperfect performance of that ministry through the years, contrasted
starkly with the truth expressed by Pye in the mid-thirties, a truth that
had been expressed by Convention leaders many times before; "Among
those who believe, on Him," Pye asserted,"'there is no east nor west,' no
color line, no social caste, and in that 'New Jerusalem' we shall all bow
before him. . . ." To reinforce her point and her ideal, Pye praised the
efforts of some white Convention women who were already investing in
the lives of young black Arkansans by leading Vacation Bible Schools for
these children. Pye's attitude toward race relations was rooted first and
foremost in her passionate Christian faith, in a belief that all truly were
one in Christ. Moreover, she was a highly literate, thoughtful individual,
well aware of new social and cultural perspectives. She may well have
been impressed by the work of Edwin Embree, whose 1931 book,
Brown America, eloquently, powerfully outlined both the problems and
bright prospects faced by African-Americans at the time. Pye had a
copy of *Brown America*, a complimentary copy from Julius Rosenwald,
the progressive philanthropist, board member of Tuskeegee Institute,
and founder of the Rosenwald Foundation.

The Convention had, of course, made tentative overtures and
offered tentative support to black Arkansas Baptists for years.

"Fraternal messengers" had been exchanged periodically between the predominant white and black state Baptist organizations since the turn of the century. Modest financial support for the black Arkansas Baptist College had only been terminated by the financial exigencies of the Convention in the late 1920s—not to be renewed until 1938. But even in this interim period, with no practical support to black Baptist institutions, the Convention leadership still openly advocated civil equality for black Arkansans while also condemning lynching and other forms of racially motivated brutality. Still, these expressions of racial reconciliation and racial justice were only modest, tentative steps, hedged with a paternalism that precluded a full interracial fellowship.

In the area of missions work, Lila Pye was certainly not satisfied with the Convention's evangelical outreach to black Arkansans, or the Convention's commitment to missions generally. Pye was doing very nearly all she could do personally to sustain the work of the WMU. Her report to the State Convention for 1935, gave an indication of the efforts of Pye and her lone assistant. The two had "written 4,311 personal letters and cards, prepared and mailed 46,325 mimeographed letters and articles, distributed 89,190 pieces of literature, prepared 13 programs, attended 130 meetings, made 65 talks, and traveled 9,423 miles," all this while Pye served on the Debt Paying Committee and subcommittee. And Pye was working on more than one book during the period.

Somewhat less immersed in the debt-paying process, but no less diligent—or significant—in Convention work, was J. P. "Jake" Edmunds. Completing his ninth year of service in 1936, Edmunds reported dramatic growth in the number of Sunday Schools and Baptist Training Unions—the BYPU had become the BTU in 1935—during his tenure as state secretary. In less than a decade, the 580 Training Unions had grown to 1,554, involving nearly 27,000 young people. Sunday Schools had numbered 643 in 1927, in 1936 there were nearly 800 with a combined enrollment of more than 92,000. With Sunday School enlistment campaigns, Training Union conventions, literature distribution, Edmunds tirelessly promoted the cause of Bible teaching and training in the churches.

Others noticed Edmunds's skill as an organizer and promoter of religious education. He was invited to join the staff of the Southern

Baptist Convention's Sunday School Board in 1936. His replacement, Edgar Williamson, would prove equally capable. Before he left for his new post in Nashville, Edmunds led yet one more statewide Sunday School Conference early in 1937. Regional and statewide leaders were recruited to teach and preach to the hundreds who attended. B. B. McKinney, the winsome songwriter, led the music for the conference— that same year McKinney wrote what was perhaps his most beloved song,"Wherever He Leads I'll Go."

Bridges himself was not exclusively preoccupied with fiscal matters during the mid- and late thirties. With other Convention leaders he organized and promoted state evangelism conferences, missions and associational rallies, while also assisting the work of Edmunds and Pye. All of these efforts were grounded in Bridges's passion for "soul-winning." Appropriating language from the political culture, Bridges called, in 1937, for a "New Deal for Lost Souls," appealing to Arkansas Baptists to win 25,000 to Christ in that year. He worked to enlist associations in preacher training efforts to better equip the ministers and their congregations for effective evangelism. And truly, even as the debt-paying campaign progressed and the Convention struggled to survive, much evangelical work went forward as well—despite the drastically diminished resources of the Convention. In his report on Convention missions efforts for 1937, Bridges cited the work of three Convention sponsored "state evangelists." Together, these three had traveled over 16,000 miles, preached more than 700 sermons, distributed 23,202 tracts, led thirteen revival meetings, and witnessed 357 professions of faith. The state evangelists established three Baptist Training Unions, assisted two churches in creating budgets, and collected $1,722.21 for state missions. The Convention had also been able to again provide some small assistance for nine associational missionaries, whose labors had contributed to more than 200 "additions" to local churches and the organization of one new church, one WMU circle, and one Baptist Training Union. Bridges was not satisfied with these reports. Already he was looking beyond the financial constraints of the day to the employment of six full-time Convention evangelists and the support of twenty-five associational workers. Of course, Bridges assured his readers and listeners again and again that nothing in the future would be done on anything other than a "pay-as-you-go" basis. The gains reported by Bridges in his

1937 report were modest, but again they must be seen in the context of the time. Less than two years earlier, Bridges had delivered a "Frank Statement" to the Convention, "I warn you brethren (and I am not trying to scare you). I cannot keep the doors open this year unless you do better [in your giving]. . . ." Given the dire circumstances of the era, the report of 1937 was, at least, evidence that the Convention was alive, accomplishing some of its goals.

And, in fact, 1937 saw the revitalization of a work destined to be among the premier ministries of the State Convention. Having begun a very limited outreach to college students in the mid-1920s, the Convention—distracted by the Depression and debts—did not substantively advance in this ministry for more than a decade. The first Baptist Student Union (BSU) in Arkansas was probably the Mountain Home campus union of 1924. But the most successful early union endeavor was clearly the pioneer work by E. N. Strother at the university in Fayetteville. This brilliant beginning, however, had been abandoned in 1927, a casualty of the Convention's dwindling financial resources. Now, in 1937, with the worst of the crisis passed, the Convention called for a renewed commitment to the BSU effort. Directly and firmly connected to the Convention through the Sunday School and Church Training (CT) Department, the BSU effort represented a new challenge and a golden new opportunity. Notably, the BSU would soon become an effective recruiting agency for missionaries and pastors, while it would also serve to inspire and prepare thousands of future Baptist laymen and women— men and women often deeply dedicated to the Convention and its highest ideals. By 1939, the BSU—and by extension the Convention— ministered on twelve campuses across the state.

Beyond Ben Bridges's persistent advocacy of the debt-paying program, and his attempts to sustain and advance, however tenuously, the missions and educational efforts of the Convention, Bridges also periodically intruded the name and influence of the Convention in the realm of public policy. More specifically, he occasionally excoriated public officials for failing to curb gambling and other social ills in Arkansas. He also believed legislators could—and should—do more to limit the rising number of divorces in the state.

With the enthusiastic help of Cossey, editor of the *Arkansas Baptist*, Bridges pointedly clarified the position of the Convention on these socially and politically charged issues. Totally unreconciled to the end of prohibition, he pressed consistently for state "dry" laws. Nor did he confine his criticism to state and local officials. Long after the matter was closed at the federal level, he continued to attack Franklin Roosevelt's administration for its successful efforts to repeal prohibition. Bridges did, however, temper his severe criticism of Roosevelt with the acknowledgment that he personally admired the president.

Still, for all of their attention to public issues and missionary efforts, Bridges and the Convention leadership were centered—during the better part of the decade—on the debt-paying campaign which went forward relentlessly through the end of 1937. And even after the "victory" in the debt-paying campaign was announced on April 8, 1937, Bridges faced the exhausting process of distributing the 35 percent settlement. In fact, the actual payment of creditors, through a court-appointed agency, involved almost as much time and effort as the fund-raising had required. Occasionally Bridges's tone became tense, sometimes peevish, as the tedious payment process began. Only six weeks after the "victory" announcement Bridges wrote in the *Arkansas Baptist*:

> Is it necessary to keep saying . . . over and over again that we are making progress in the matter of settling our debts. It requires as much thought, wise planning, careful negotiating, and patience [sic], prayerful, persistent work . . . so we say again, "be patient, brethren, and trust your leadership." The funds are all in trusteeship and not one dime has been disbursed. There is infinitely more worry in trying to complete the settlement than there was in raising the funds. Our nerves are taxed to the limit. Please do not add to our worries by trying to goad us on.

Part of Bridges's testiness surely resulted from the cumulative strain of several years, and also Bridges was not truly happy with the settlement plan—he did not believe that thirty-five cents on the dollar was a fair settlement, however legal it may have been. Then, too, Bridges had sustained a series of personal losses in the campaign year, losses which took an inordinate emotional toll. E. J. A. McKinney died in July 1936, and H. L. Winburn died on March 18, 1937. Convention stalwarts in every way, and Bridges's personal friends, these men had also been mentors to Bridges and his generation of Convention leaders. They had remained steady during the crisis of the thirties.

More devastating, however, and totally unexpected, was the death of Arden Blaylock. Pastor of First Church, Little Rock, Blaylock was known throughout the state, and across the South, as a truly great preacher. During his tenure of five and a half years at First Church, the Sunday School grew from 549 to 936. Thousands professed faith during his regular services and in the numerous revivals he led. He seemed almost desperate in his desire to get the Gospel message to everyone. Not long before his death, he began an outreach ministry in the state's schools for the blind and the deaf. Blaylock was often characterized as a "tireless" worker for God, willing to lend his energy and enthusiasm to any cause calculated to advance the Kingdom. Some more mature ministers, had worried—and warned—that the young Blaylock would destroy his health in his zealous, selfless labors.

Suddenly ill after his Sunday evening service, he underwent emergency surgery the following day. For three days his congregation gathered for special prayer meetings on their pastor's behalf. Bridges was at a prayer vigil at First Church when the news came, at midnight, that Blaylock had died. Ironically, the congregation had just been singing the old hymn, "Go on your way in peace to heaven, and wear a crown with Jesus." The mourning for the thirty-nine-year-old Blaylock gripped the whole city—crossing denominational lines. For Bridges, the pain was truly poignant. Blaylock had been devoted to the debt-paying campaign, adding the promotion of the campaign to his already crushing schedule. Indeed, among his last words was an admonition to press forward with the campaign. In Blaylock's passing, Arkansas Baptists lost a preacher of remarkable passion and power; the Convention lost a champion, and Bridges lost one of his dearest friends.

The announcement of the success of the debt-paying campaign followed only two weeks after Blaylock's funeral, on January 6, 1938. All bondholders and creditors were to receive their settlements within a week or so. The final payment had been delayed an agonizing additional few weeks while four large churches collected and forwarded their last commitments. These four were among hundreds of churches, mostly small congregations, that had participated in the debt-paying campaign with special offerings. And it was only on Christmas Eve, 1937, that the Convention received a large payment from the Baptist Hospital in Little Rock. The terms of the settlement plan had required the hospital to reimburse the Convention for more than $150,000.

The worst part of the ordeal was finally over. The Convention leadership could now seriously look forward. Yet, before they went forward, Convention leaders paused collectively to reflect on the past. In April, the state WMU observed its Golden Anniversary. Several hundred women gathered in Little Rock at Immanuel Church for two days of celebration and recommitment. Sermons and addresses highlighted the history and ideals of the organization.

Lila Pye's singular contribution to the anniversary was her monograph history of the state WMU, *The Harvest of the Golden Years*. Intimately familiar with the organization's past, Pye offered, in her small book, well-drawn vignettes and narrative tracing of the development of the WMU. The high point of the anniversary proceedings was a nighttime candlelighting ceremony honoring the memory of those women who founded the organization. At ninety-two years of age, Sue Denton Perry, was the lone eyewitness to the state WMU's inaugural session at Russellville's First Church in 1888. But Mrs. Perry was not the only venerable person present. Indeed, the place of highest honor went to Mrs. J. L. Hawkins. Her name had first appeared in the proceedings of the state WMU in 1889; she first held state office in 1891. And now, in 1938, she was continuing her unbroken tenure as recording secretary stretching back to 1909. Within two months of the WMU Golden Anniversary Celebration, Mrs. Hawkins died, truly loved and admired.

The WMU's anniversary celebration duly emphasized the contributions of a worthy, past generation of faithful men and women who had persistently and sacrificially advanced the cause of missions in Arkansas and around the world. What many at the anniversary celebration did not fully grasp was that they too were part of an heroic generation that was writing its own story of courage and devotion.

In the terrible testing time of the 1930s, these faithful individuals, like Lila Pye, Ben Bridges, Arden Blaylock, Whitington, Winburn, Cossey, Rogers, Hawkins, Edmunds, and so many others, had truly fought the good fight. Their conduct had not been perfect, their faith wavered at times, and anger and frustration flashed intermittently from some of the best of these men and women. Yet, in the face of truly desperate days, they had remained true to the ideals which had animated and inspired the leaders and supporters of the Convention for nine decades.

Unquestionably, these men and women had earned their place beside the Convention's finest leaders from the past. Bridges had sensed, at least partially, this larger historical, and spiritual, significance of the Convention's trials during the period. Early in 1938 he wrote, "We consider now that we are passing through a great crisis, spiritually. . . . We must practice the principles of Christian love toward each other. . . . We must have faith enough to undertake great things for God, and at the same time possess the wisdom enough to locate the line of demarcation between faith and presumption." The ordeals of the Depression years, Bridges indicated, should serve as lessons of the power of faith and love, of the need for wisdom and godly discretion, and as a foundation for greater service to the Kingdom. Matured spiritually by the time of testing, by its own failures, and the power of faith, Bridges believed that the time had come for the Convention to press forward.

12

The 1940s

A SENSE OF IRONY FOLLOWED THE ARKANSAS BAPTIST State Convention as it entered its tenth decade. Two weeks after Ben L. Bridges announced the settlement with the debt problem, and as the state Woman's Missionary Union began to celebrate its Golden Anniversary, President Franklin D. Roosevelt warned the nation about "storm signals from across the sea." Before the year was out that warning had turned to reality as Germany moved aggressively against its neighbors and plunged the world into another war.

The irony of the situation, however, was that while state and national leaders were drawn more and more into the dark, depressing cloud of total war, Convention leaders began to see a silver lining in what had previously been clouds of darkness. Not only had the burden of debt been eased, but a new sense of unity seem to prevail among members as the Convention prepared for its centennial decade.

The devastating impact of the national depression, coupled with the heroic efforts of Bridges, Otto Whitington, Lila Pye, and others in traveling the state to promote the debt payment plan, drew Convention Baptists together. The dissension and frustrations of the preceding decade evaporated and a new spirit of togetherness began to prevail.

This new spirit was evident as early as 1937, when Convention members voted at Fort Smith to adopt a Three-Year Plan promoting evangelism and church growth. Perhaps it was the opportunity to be "for something," or to think about growth rather than the debilitating effects of economic hard times that shaped the new atmosphere. In any event, messengers enthusiastically endorsed a broad based program to increase the number of district missionaries from three to five; double the number of salary supplements paid to associational missionaries from ten to twenty; conduct campaigns on evangelism an stewardship each year of the plan; baptize 50,000 new believers; enlist 40,000 tithers, and increase the budget of state missions to $25,000.

The Three-Year Plan was highly successful. When Bridges gave the Executive Board's report at the 1940 Convention, he called it "an epochal year for Arkansas Baptists." Discounting the number of tithers, which everyone admitted was difficult to determine, the Convention had realized all its goals except the number of baptisms and mission dollars.

But even in the areas where the goals were not realized, there were reasons for encouragement. Members had contributed over $20,000 to the mission effort and over 30,000 new converts had been baptized. The peak year came in 1939, when churches reported 11,854 baptisms—a record that stood until 1948, when 13,147 were immersed. The 1940 annual meeting at First Church, Monticello, was a time of thanksgiving and rejoicing.

The success of the Three-Year Plan encouraged the board to develop a Four-Year Program. The new campaign was to began immediately and concluded with the 1944 Convention. That date was chosen in part because it ushered in the Southern Baptist Convention's centennial meeting in the spring of 1945.

The new plan featured a ten-point program that challenged Arkansas Baptist to view their cooperative efforts with a broader, world view than they had yet envisioned. Conceptually, the program organized into four broad categories. The first group related to the ominous war clouds spreading over Europe and Asia. The United States was not directly involved in the war and national public sentiment was strongly against getting involved. Most Arkansans also favored a policy of neutrality.

A second group of objectives in the new Four-Year Program dealt with mission activities. This focus had a two-pronged approach. On the one hand, the ABSC pledged to raise more money by organizing four mission campaigns each year (associational, state, home, and foreign) and establishing funding goals for each. A second mission emphasis encouraged more participation in mission projects by ABSC members. The board also made a "call to our colored brethren" to enlarge their missions program "among their brethren."

The enlargement campaign called for more attention be given to the "seasonal [migrant workers] problem" in the state. Finally, the board pledged to increase the number of missionaries as rapidly as "funds will allow." To that end, Convention messengers voted to raise at least $40,000, for missions by the end of the campaign.

As with all Convention Baptist campaigns, the new program also called for a renewed emphasis on evangelism. In addition to continuing the statewide evangelistic efforts each year, ABSC leaders also pledged to conduct at least one revival "in each needy place" in the state and baptize at least 60,000 believers in the four-year period.

A final area for emphasis on the ten-point program concerned education and training. Using the Sunday School and Training Union departments ABSC leaders hoped to increase membership through a series of "enlargement campaigns"—although they failed to establish any enrollment goals. Coinciding with education and training, the new program challenged the membership to do more in stewardship and budgeting and to continue the District Bible Conferences.

There were also other signs of revived strength in the ABSC. For the first time since 1931, the Executive Board was in a position to resume operation of the *Arkansas Baptist*. As previously mentioned, the paper was operated under a lease agreement throughout the 1930s. But the Convention's financial health had improved enough in 1940 to allow the board to hire Dr. L. A. Myers as editor and resume its oversight of the publication. Dr. Myers served until September 1943 when he resigned to enter the chaplaincy service. The board then employed C. E. Bryant who had been serving the magazine as the associate editor.

The "Minister's Retirement Plan" was another cause for celebration in 1940. Even though the plan had been adopted two years earlier, lack of funds prevented it from becoming a reality. The program required ministers to contribute 3 percent of their salaries; the host church matched that, and the State Convention contributed 2 percent. These funds were then put into an annuity program. Secretary Bridges, while saying the program had "added perhaps forty percent" to the work load at the "headquarters office," said that he was pleased that Arkansas had "been able to make the best showing of all the Southern states" in providing for its senior members.

Messengers left the eighty-second annual meeting with enthusiasm and a plan to do even greater work in the coming year. Few could have anticipated how difficult 1941 was going to be. The war in Europe continued to go badly for America's friends. Germany continued an aggressive pace, overrunning France and tightening the pressure on England by dropping tons of bombs on the island nation. While Americans became increasingly uneasy about the escalation, few wanted to get involved. Yet, the nation was involved. Increasing military expenditures continued to stimulate the economy and drove memories of the Depression further into the background.

Programs under the Executive Board's direction had only limited success in implementing the first phase of the Four-Year Program. Financial contributions increased, but "spiritual" results in several areas failed to keep pace with the preceding year. By the time the Convention gathered in Jonesboro for its eighty-third meeting, the record showed that baptisms, Sunday School, and Training Union enrollments all declined.

Secretary Bridges called 1941, "one of the most serious . . . that we have experienced" and offered three reasons why he thought so. First, he noted, "international hatred . . . has bubbled over into the hearts of Christian people." He also thought that the return of "material prosperity" had made it "difficult to get lost people to hear and heed the Word . . ." and he wondered if his own staff may not have "worked less diligently than . . . when material benefits are reduced."

But, as difficult as 1941 appeared to be, it paled in comparison to the next four years when war in Europe extended its influence. In less than a month after the Convention adjourned, Japan bombed Pearl Harbor and the United States entered the war—making the conflict truly worldwide in scope.

To many Arkansas Baptist, World War II was more depressing than the hard times of the 1930s. More than 200,000 young Arkansans were called into military service, and there was hardly a family in the state that did not have at least one of its members in the war. The anxiety over physical safety and the pain of extended separation sorely tested the faith of most Baptists.

Military conflict was not the only problem that Arkansas Baptists faced. The rapid mobilization that the United States went through immediately following the Japanese attack had a profound impact on most Arkansas communities. Miliary bases at Fort Chaffee near Fort Smith and Camp Robinson near North Little Rock brought thousands of new settlers into the state. Defense plants at Jacksonville, Pine Bluff, Camden, Hope, and Marche, as well as bauxite mining near Benton, Arkadelphia, and Magnet Cove offered thousands of good-paying jobs to many Arkansans who had been chronically un- or under-employed for more than a decade.

Each of the above communities saw a dramatic increase in population. For example, Hope doubled between 1940 and 1942 (7,475 to 14,475); Little Rock increased by some 12,000 people in 1940, and the surrounding Pulaski County grew by more than 25,000. Fort Smith increased by 5,100 between October 1940 and October 1941.

This rapid influx of people created a severe housing shortage but also greatly increased the prospects for church membership. In some communities mission churches were established to meet this need, while in others, existing congregations absorbed the increase. For example, Calvary in Little Rock was started as a mission of Pulaski Heights on the edge of Cammack Village, a planned community built especially to house personnel associated with Camp Robinson. To some extent, all established churches in the defense industry towns showed an increase in attendance and contributions between 1940 and 1945.

While individual churches and associations were dramatically effected by the wartime changes, the ABSC had to deal with the dynamics of a shifting population. Small rural churches had been the hallmark of the Convention since its founding and even in 1940, 78 percent of the state's population was still rural. That figure changed rapidly, more than 10 percent per decade (rural to urban) after 1940, and Convention leaders were forced to reevaluate many programs. The challenge was how to meet the continuing needs of rural churches and associations, many of which were decimated by the population shift, and at the same time respond to the new circumstances in urban areas.

The war not only served as a catalyst for human migration but, as has been mentioned, it brought a return to material prosperity as well. In many respects, as Secretary Bridges pointed out, materialism was more difficult for ABSC leaders to deal with than urbanization. The all-out effort to support the war sapped the energies, emotions, and perhaps most of all, the time of Arkansans. Local churches and the State Convention had to take what was left over.

The board's first response to the growing war presence was to give more attention "to the needs at Camp Robinson." In 1940, Camp Robinson was the state's only active military base, and personnel assigned to the base grew steadily through 1940 and 1941. With the United States's entry into the war, Robinson became a training facility. Young men from all over the nation were brought to the camp, isolated in a confined area and given several weeks of intensive physical training. Homesick, scared, often disoriented, these young men had special needs that soon challenged the resources and faith of the ABSC.

In response to the military's special needs, the board called the Reverend P. A. Stockton as "missionary to the soldiers" in early 1941. He began weekly visits at the camp. In August, the Executive Board rented a building at 116 East Sixth Street in Little Rock and established the "Baptist Center for Soldiers."

The new center included a reception area and rooms for reading, writing, and recreation, as well as a chapel and a prayer room. The Reverend Stockton served as chaplin, and Mrs. J. L. Fisk was enlisted to serve as "house mother." The site became a popular gathering place for the enlisted men. The Reverend Stockton conducted worship services at the center each Sunday afternoon at four o'clock (he encouraged the young soldiers to attend area Baptist churches on Sunday morning and evening). In its first year of operation he was able to report seventy conversions, numerous rededications, and a revived interest in church attendance.

This type of mission work was new to Arkansas Baptist. However, it quickly became "one of the most fruitful. . . ." In 1943, the board was authorized by Convention messengers to open a "Soldiers' Center" at Ninth and Rogers Streets in Fort Smith. The Reverend Don Hook was enlisted as chaplin and Mrs. B. D. Paterson hired as the hostess. The Reverend Hook returned to the pastorate in 1944; the board enlisted the Reverend Ford Gant to continue the work. The Fort Smith Center also proved popular with soldiers. By the time the centers were closed at war's end they could report over 400 conversion decisions and hundreds of rededications. ABSC influence with these young soldiers was carried around the world.

An even more novel mission opportunity came in September 1942. Following the bombing of Pearl Harbor, some 120,000 Japanese-Americans, most of them citizens, had their civil rights severely restricted through special action by President Roosevelt and the U.S. Congress. Viewed as security risks, federal officials wasted little time in rounding Japanese-Americans up and assigning them to ten selected locations through out the United States. Two of those camps and some 15,000 Japanese-Americans were detained at the small communities of Rohwer and Jerome in the southeastern portion of the state.

Ministering to these new arrivals posed a significant challenge to the ABSC. After much discussion, Convention leaders decided to seek help from the Foreign Mission Board and get a missionary from that staff stationed there. Before the year was out, the FMB had enlisted Kensalineo Igaraslei for the Jerome camp and Masazi Kakichara and K. Harper Sakaue for the Rhower site. The results of their efforts among the detainees did not get recorded in the ABSC's book of reports. However, Kgaraslei, Kakichara, and Sakaue were welcomed and recognized at the annual meeting in 1943.

The Second World War was a serious disruption to the new Four-Year Plan. From 1942 through most of 1945 the ABSC leadership, churches, and associations concentrated on the war effort through prayers, family support, and specialized services to meet war-time needs.

When Secretary Bridges addressed the annual meeting at Little Rock's Second Church in 1944—the original target date for the Four-Year Plan, he reported that the Convention was making "steady progress." However, the growth was uneven. The number of baptisms, Sunday School, and Training Union enrollments remained flat or declined slightly through the war years. But financial contributions, to all causes, increased greatly during the same time.

This dynamic was due in large part to what Bridges called a "problem . . . in our rural work." Rural churches had a higher percentage of their members in attendance, but the number of rural congregations was declining. Beginning in 1943, Convention leaders began to give increased attention to churches in the rural areas of the state. Outgoing President J. S. Rogers, used "Revitalize Our Rural Churches and Reemphasize Our Distinctive Baptist Doctrine" as the title for his keynote address at the annual meeting that year.

Focusing attention on the rural churches began to pay dividends by the end of the decade. Ben Bridges reported that the number of "full-time churches" doubled and some 150 churches were at least "half-time." In reality, the rural to urban changes in Arkansas were going on all over the South and the Southern Baptist Convention also began paying attention to the problem—particularly in the last half of the decade.

By the time the ABSC's ninety-second annual meeting convened with Little Rock's First Church in November 20, 1945, the war in both the European and Pacific theaters was over. A spirit of relief and thanksgiving filled the meeting—also a feeling of anticipation. A number of people making reports spoke of a "new era" in Baptist work. That attitude was not only due to the war being over, but also because the Southern Baptist Convention had launched its second century of operation with a new theme of "Centennial Crusade: A Program for World Redemption." This three "E" campaign, "Evangelism, Education, and Enlistment," along with "Stewardship, Missions, and Benevolence," promised a plan for "rebuilding war's wreckage" and "relieving humanity's hurt." Arkansas Baptists wanted to be a part of this new beginning.

Excitement over the war's ending was high, but no one could have imagined how difficult the new era would be. The twin traumas of a decade-long economic depression, followed by almost five years of total war, was disruptive beyond all belief. Moreover, as frustrating as the short term problems of runaway inflation, jobs for returning veterans, adequate housing, and myriad other problems were, the long-term problems were even more challenging:

Of all the changes caused by the war, few were as dramatic as the shift in population. This change had a profound impact on Arkansas Baptists. A rural people since Colonial days, Baptist gained much of their distinctiveness and numerical influence in the frontier regions of the nation. Arkansas had been a particularly favorable environment to the denomination. But three centuries of religious development was transformed in less than twenty-five years after World War II. This change was so dramatic, and came with such rapidity, that it fit almost everyone's definition of "revolution"

In time, more complete statistical data told of even more complex and pervasive changes. But in 1945, enough was known to ABSC leaders to realize that they their work was caught up in new developments of epochal proportions.

To be sure, Arkansas was still statistically rural in 1945, and remained so until after 1960. But it was not the same ruralness as before the war. Tractors, self-propelled combines, and more complex machinery in general not only brought a fundamental shift in farmers' relationship to each other, but to the land as well. Sharecropping and tenant farming rapidly disappeared. The need for day laborers declined dramatically as more efficient machines replaced "field hands." Between 1945 and 1960, sixty-nine of the state's seventy-five counties lost population. The state as a whole lost almost 10 percent of its residents during the same time. But, every county-seat town gained population, as did the state's major regional cities.

ABSC leaders first responded to the new circumstances by reviewing their traditional approaches to planning the Convention's work in the state. First on their agenda was revisiting the last "Four-Year Plan" which, given the war-time activities, had not been fully developed. That plan was now reworked into a new Five-Point Program, similar in concept but different in design to the previous emphasis.

The new plan focused attention on five state missionaries who were given broad responsibilities for assisting the associations. In addition to supplying for churches without pastors (or part-time pastors), these individuals led stewardship campaigns, conducted revivals, and promoted church growth on a statewide basis. Formerly, these individuals had been assigned to specific associations and limited their activities to that district. The Convention also continued to supplement salaries of associational missionaries—the number had grown to thirty-eight by the end of the war and provided financial support to churches with special needs.

Other aspects of the Five-Point Plan included a loan and technical assistance program for small churches that aided them in remodeling and constructing new buildings and a new initiative for supporting a Baptist Student Program at the University of Arkansas.

A significant new emphasis in the post-war era came in the area of church music. Interest in hymns that were more Baptist distinctive had been growing since the turn of the century. Responding to this, the Southern Baptist Convention published the *Broadman Hymnal* in 1940 and promoted its usage among member churches. A common hymn book was also the basis for encouraging churches to formally organize programs and begin systematic training in music.

The focus on music also led church musicians to organize a statewide "Church Music Conference and Festival." This meeting, at First Baptist Little Rock, September 2, 1941, resulted in the group organizing the "Arkansas Baptist Church Musicians Association,"—the first of its kind in the Southern Baptist Convention. The musicians also elected Mrs. B. W. (Ruth) Nininger, music director at the host church, to be president of the group.

At the 1941 annual meeting Mrs. Nininger reported to the messengers that "it is with great joy and pardonable pride that we introduce to you today, our new baby, the Arkansas Baptist Church Musicians. Born in answer to prayer and dedicated to the service of Christ in his church, this child solicits the warm hearted and sympathetic understanding of pastors and people alike and the chance to prepare and present an adequate program of training in church music . . . if Baptist churches are to render the best in worship and praise to Almighty God." The ABSC messengers ratified the new group and elected Mrs. Nininger as "State Music Director." Her duties included conducting church music institutes to teach both young and old about the intricacies of music; holding hymn-sings that focused primarily on singing and directing; assisting churches with music for revival; and working the summer assembly at Siloam Springs. As the program became more developed, Mrs. Nininger expanded her efforts to doing radio programs on church music, providing music for the "Baptist Hour," and doing general promotional work to improve music in the state's churches.

The new emphasis on music was well received by Arkansas Baptist. Mrs. Nininger worked tirelessly in promoting the program—traveling more than 6,000 miles around the state in her first year in office—all

Arkansas became the first state in the Southern Baptist Convention to have a Department of Church Music—thanks in large part to Mrs. B. W. (Ruth) Nininger who served the ABSC for fifteen years as director of Church Music.

without a salary. In recognition of her efforts, the Executive Board recommended in 1944 that she be made "Church Music Secretary for Arkansas." Although still an unpaid position, the board did allow her to receive honorariums and expenses from the churches she served.

Interest in church music continued to grow in Arkansas after the war. From Sunday morning worship services, music soon spread throughout the church. Parents in particular wanted music training for their children and looked to the State Convention for assistance. In partial response to that interest, Ouachita College began hosting an annual Youth Choir Festival on its campus beginning in 1947. This event attracted young people from throughout the state and allowed them an opportunity to work with some of the most talented musicians in the state and the Southern Baptist Convention. The meetings were not only popular, but also led to rapid improvement in church music.

The emphasis on music also brought a new atmosphere to the Sunday morning worship. Church choirs led in calls to worship, prayer responses, and doxologies. Music directors balanced worship hymns and anthems with gospel songs so popular in the pre-war era. Pastors and musicians also began to pay greater attention to detail and the amount of time scheduled for worship. By the end of the decade a printed order of service was becoming common place in urban churches.

The growing emphasis on music was yet another indication that World War II had a profound, even transforming, impact on Sunday church services. The emphasis on war production schedules and deadlines made a generation of workers, previously guided by sun time, increasingly clock conscious. These feelings carried over to Sunday. Rather than seeing Sunday as a "Holy Day," a day of worship, rest, and fellowship, that day of the week came to be a time of reprieve from the rigors of the production line. The war-time experience also made many Arkansas Baptists aware of new technologies—particularly of amplified sound with microphones and speaker systems. Awareness, coupled with war-time prosperity led an increasing number of churches to install public address systems to aid in worship services.

The war's influence on technology was also instrumental stimulating some ABSC members to become interested in a radio ministry. That radio was a pervasive influence in the state's culture, hardly any doubted. However, the policy matters as to whether the ABSC should get involved, and if it did to what extent and in what way, were not easy questions to resolve. The matter was first brought up at the annual meeting in 1944 and a three-member committee chaired by J. F. Queen, and including Harvey Elledge and Bruce Price, was appointed to consider the matter.

The committee quickly determined that the central questions revolved around the method of broadcasting. They saw three options. One was for the ABSC to have a Baptist network with one central operating station capable of reaching all sections of the state. Existing technology made this both difficult to do and expensive. Only six radio stations in the state had that capability in 1944. A second method utilized a less powerful station and had copies of the broadcast made for distribution to sections of the state not covered by the anchor station. A third possibility was for the ABSC to avoid broadcasting directly and instead, record material that could be copied and distributed through existing stations.

The ad hoc committee was not prepared to approve one method over the other. In their report to the 1945 Convention, they recommended that messengers approve a permanent "radio commission" and let that body make the decisions on how best to utilize radio as a spiritual resource. The Convention accepted that report, and President W. J. Hinsley appointed a fellow Hot Springs resident, B. H. Duncan, to chair the "Committee on Radio." O. L. Gibson, L. H. Roseman, C. E. Lawrence, and Oscar Ellis were also appointed as members to the new committee.

Accepting its charge to select "the best method available for broadcasting the Baptist message" and armed with $12,000 budget, the Committee began its work. They had no easy task. The national radio networks already controlled most of the "best listener time." And, air time not under contract to one of the networks, was controlled by either the Catholic Church of America or the Federal Council of Churches. There was little room for a new group wanting to get into broadcasting. Even the Southern Baptist Convention's Radio Commission, which had launched its "Baptist Hour" before the war, could offer little help for the Arkansas market.

Not to be discouraged, Duncan and his colleagues adopted the third option reported by the original committee—to broadcast over existing stations. Relying heavily upon their own talent and volunteers, the group produced a thirteen-part series and contracted with the six strongest stations in the state to air programs. The first program aired on April 28, 1946, and continued on a weekly basis. The committee soon realized that the work involved was more than a group of volunteers could do. For a second series, they hired Little Rock radio talent Bob Buice to be program announcer and *Arkansas Baptist* editor C. E. Bryant to produce the program. Buice was already one of the best known radio voices in the state and he remained so for almost four decades. Bryant, through his work at the news magazine had a wide range of contacts with ministers and musicians in Baptist work. The radio broadcast was a small, tentative, yet creative effort to meet the changing needs of Arkansas Baptist.

Changes in church music, the worship service, and a growing interest in radio were primarily urban issues. However, Bridges and other ABSC leaders realized that over 70 percent of the state was still rural and wanted different assistance. As has been mentioned, this need was recognized early in the decade, but preoccupation with the dislocations caused by the war delayed plans for addressing the issue. The Southern Baptist Convention also made rural churches a priority in the post-war years through its Home Mission Board. Stimulated by a study guide, authored by John D. Freeman, a former Home Missionary to the Arkansas Ozarks, and published by the HMB's as *The Country Church: Its Problems and Their Solutions*, Arkansas Baptist prepared to enter into partnership with the HMB for this new work.

In January 1945, Otto Whitington was employed by the HMB as the superintendent of Rural Missions for Arkansas. Whitington had a long involvement with Baptist work throughout the state and chaired the State Missions Committee. At the 1945 annual meeting, he led his committee to recommend a $12,000 appropriation to help rural churches build "meeting houses." Messengers adopted the report, and in the coming year Whitington was able to put the money to good use. By the next annual meeting, messengers were ready to assume an even greater responsibility for the work and accepted the Committee's recommendation to create a Department of Rural Missions under the direction of the Executive Board.

Adoption of the State Missions report required the Executive Committee to do some fast homework. Creating a new office not only had personnel ramifications, but integrating that work into the existing organization was a bit delicate. However, the recommendation was not unexpected and in the closing session of the Convention the committee presented a new "Executive Board's Plan of State Mission Work."

When messengers adopted the plan they served notice that the ABSC intended to fundamentally change the way they had been doing state mission work for over twenty years. First, the existing missions structure was discontinued as of 1946. A new missions policy was then implemented to "promote the work of Rural Missions [through] a department" headed by a "Superintendent." In addition to the department head the new office was staffed with "three general field workers, three pioneer missionaries, a department stenographer." With eight staff members and an annual budget of $47,500, the new department was positioned to promote the Convention's message in rural Arkansas.

C. W. Caldwell, pastor of First Church Fordyce, was enlisted as the first superintendent of Rural Missions. Whitington continued his work with the Home Mission Board. Caldwell began work in February 1947 and over the next three years he and his staff did an amazing amount of work.

Following a policy of only going where they were invited, Caldwell and his team of rural workers promoted ABSC work on a broad front. Enlisting pastors and assisting them in working full-time with congregations; building or remodeling church buildings; and using every opportunity to promote ABSC work and the SBC's Cooperative Program paid quick, and large, dividends. By the end of the decade Secretary Bridges reported 50,000 new members in churches affiliated with the ABSC. A large number of these were the results of the rural initiative.

The rural evangelism program paid more dividends than just new members. Perhaps from a long-range viewpoint, its greater importance lay in its work of identifying needs, educating pastors and key church leaders about the ABSC's mission and methods, and building buildings. A growing number of communities had a local congregation's "testimony" as to its identity and commitment by the presence of a new or remodeled "church house." In his last report for the decade, Secretary Bridges noted that, since the end of the war, the number of full-time pastors had increased by 223, the number of part-time pastors had decreased by 169, and fewer than one hundred churches had quarter-time pastors.

Associations and associational missionaries were also direct beneficiaries of the rural initiative. With combined assistance from the ABSC and the Home Mission Board to supplement salaries and provide promotional assistance, these hallmarks of Convention work in Arkansas began to show new vitality. Their strength and importance became even more developed in the 1950s.

The excitement and enthusiasm generated by the ABSC's Centennial Celebration also stimulated church growth. Part of the celebration included publishing a history of the Convention's first century and holding a commemorative service on "anniversary day," September 21, at Tulip. But, ironically, the Centennial Committee reported that the property where those first pioneers met to organize "was in the possession of [the Presbyterians] and [they] are unwilling to dispose of it." Undeterred, approximately "2,000 Baptist" gathered near the site in "the open air" for a one-day session.

The time of remembrance occasioned by the ABSC's centennial was also a time to plan for the future. Messengers used the annual meeting to establish the Arkansas Baptist Foundation (ABF), a concept that had been under discussion by Executive Board members since the Minister's Retirement Fund was created in 1943. The foundation's expressed purpose was to "obtain and handle contributions for and in the interest of the various agencies and institutions of the Convention." Despite its modest beginnings, this new program became one of the most memorable in its long-term impact on Arkansas Baptist.

Leaders of the Arkansas Baptist Convention were justifiably proud of the way the membership responded to new ideas. However, as they closed out the first century of work and prepared for the end of another decade, many took time to reflect on the past. The innovations had been exciting and successful, but Bridges and his associates in the Baptist Building knew that success came from careful and consistent planning. It was the traditional departments in the building that carried out the Executive Board's assignments on a day-by-day basis that made the difference.

Throughout the decade of the 1940s, personnel and programs in the building remained surprisingly stable given all the war-time pressures.

And, except for the new initiatives, the organizational structure, consisting of departments for Religious Education, the Woman's Missionary Union, and the *Arkansas Baptist*, remained largely unchanged. The WMU continued its special relationship with the Convention, functionally a part of the state program but organizationally tied to its national headquarters in Birmingham, Alabama. Programs outside the Baptist Building but still under the jurisdiction of the Executive Board included State Missions, Benevolence, and Christian Education.

The *Arkansas Baptist*, surpassed only by the secretary to the Executive Board's office in tenure at headquarters, had the most changes during the decade. As previously mentioned, the board resumed administrative control over the paper in 1940 when it employed Dr. L. A. Myers as editor. At that time the circulation was about 7,000, and income was just under $11,000.

In 1943, Myers received board approval to hire the Reverend C. E. Bryant as assistant editor. Bryant had a great deal of experience with publications and public relations. He became editor of the paper when Myers resigned in June to become a chaplain. Despite problems with war-time shortages, circulation steadily increased and the paper became a vital element in promoting other departments and programs in the ABSC.

In 1947, Bryant resigned as editor to accept a position with the Executive Board of the Southern Baptist Convention. The board chose Hot Springs minister B. H. Duncan as the new editor. Duncan remained as editor through the balance of the decade. At that time circulation exceeded 35,000. Between 1940 and 1949, individual subscriptions increased from $1.00 to $2.00 per year but increased advertising revenue and an annual supplement from the Cooperative Program budget more than paid for the cost of publication.

The Religious Education Department, initially called the Sunday School, Training Union, and Student Union Department, became the largest office in the building by the end of the decade. Headed by Edgar Williamson throughout the period, the unit also included the Summer Assembly Program at Siloam Springs and after 1943, the Church Music Program.

Williamson was initially assisted by Miss Blanche Mayes, who served as assistant secretary and worked primarily with the "young people's training programs." In 1944, Miss Mayes accepted a position with the Sunday School Board in Nashville and was replaced by Miss Rosalea Webster. In 1944, Secretary Williamson was able to add the Reverend Ralph Davis to head the Training Union Program and the entire office was reorganized into the Department of Religious Education. After Davis joined the staff, Williamson assumed full responsibilities for Sunday School work; Miss Webster was made secretary for the Student Union work, and, as has been mentioned, Mrs. B. W. Nininger was secretary for the Church Music unit.

In 1945 the department went through more restructuring. The student work was renamed the Baptist Student Union (BSU), and in 1947, R. O. Baker joined the staff as secretary of the Sunday School. Edgar Williamson then devoted his full time to the administrative details of the department.

For most of the decade the Sunday School work focused on training programs for Sunday and Vacation Bible School workers. In addition to an annual statewide conference, a number of the districts also offered training opportunities for their local associations. Training Union work began to shift away from being primarily "a young people's program" and increasing attention was devoted to adults. The department began the decade with two professional staff members and a program budget of $5,200 provided by the ABSC and a $3,600 supplement from the Baptist Sunday School Board. It ended the decade with five professional staff and a budget of $30,000 from the ABSC and $12,000 from the Sunday School Board.

The priority for the Student Union Program, as directed by the Executive Board in 1937, was to have a Student Council at work on each campus in the state. By 1940 councils were in place at all the state's four-year institutions as well as the Baptist Hospital in Little Rock. Training for these councils was conducted at the annual State Student Union Convention and at an annual Spring Retreat. Members of Student Councils, working in conjunction with the Training Union Program, also did summer field work by promoting the Training Union in rural areas of the state. World War II interrupted this work momentarily in 1943, but it was resumed in 1946 and continued through the decade.

Following the war, surging, post-secondary enrollments stretched Student Union work to the limit. Limited funding made it difficult to

build buildings fast enough to keep up with the growing college popu-
lation. Rapid expansion in proprietary professional and technical
schools added to the challenge. Responding to that need, T. D.
McCullock, who replaced Miss Webster May 1, 1946, began to enlist
local churches to help with the work. For example, First Church
Russellville and First Church Monticello each employed a Student
Union worker with the local college campuses in their respective areas.
First Church Russellville also built a student center adjacent to the
Arkansas Tech campus and made space available to offer a Bible study
course as an elective in the college curriculum. The Arkansas Baptist
Assembly at Siloam Springs became an increasingly important part of
the work after 1940. Committed to being an "All Baptist Program for all
Baptist," the assembly offered one week of training each summer for lay
church workers. Until 1947, leaders tried to provide assistance to both
Sunday School and Training Union volunteers. But, growing specializa-
tion among the churches' professional staff convinced the ABSC staff
that two weeks of training were necessary—one for Sunday School, one
for Training Union.

The Woman's Missionary Union continued to serve as the "glue" to
cement the ABSC's work in the state. An anchor of faith in the depths
of the depression, Baptist women were called upon in exceptional ways
to provide support for the war effort. Some of the work was traditional
such as prayer support and fund-raising for all aspects of the Missions
Program. But as the dark days of World War II began to take its toll on
families, women of the WMU gave extra attention to children and
young people by conducting special conferences and training programs.

A note of sadness came into the program in 1945 when Mrs. W. D.
Pye resigned as treasurer and program editor. She had served the
WMU for twenty-six years, but the thousands of miles of travel and
countless meetings to promote missions had taken a toll on her physical
strength and she was forced to retire. The board chose Mrs. C. H. Ray,
the program secretary, to assume Mrs. Pye's duties.

The two programs "outside headquarters" but still under ABSC
supervision, Benevolence and Christian Education, showed mixed
results in the 1940s. The Convention's work in benevolence included
the Bottoms Orphans' Home at Monticello, Davis Hospital in Pine
Bluff, and Baptist Hospital in Little Rock. Of the three, Baptist

Hospital recovered almost miraculously from the debt embarrassment of the 1930s. In 1940 the institution had 4,473 patients and a $261,186 budget—of which, $41,513 was carried as charity.

After 1938, the state Baptist Hospital was financially independent and no longer accepted direct financial aid from the ABSC. World War II, depleted the staff of physicians, pharmacists, and nurses for a short time, and many of the nonprofessional staff left for better-paying jobs in defense-related industries. But, the increase in financial support from military contracts more than offset the inconvenience of personnel shortages.

Of more consequence than financial issues was the administrative relationship between the hospital and the ABSC Executive Board. At the 1943 annual meeting, messengers adopted a board recommendation that the hospital contribute $30,000 toward the Convention's debt retirement carried over from the previous decade. The hospital's directors objected to the request for a transfer of funds on legal grounds and the matter was tied up in court for most of 1944. The Executive Board won in the lower court, the directors won at the appellate level, and the state Supreme Court reversed the decision and ruled in favor of the board. Leaders with both institutions tried to mend the breech, but full fellowship was never really reestablished.

A similar "breech in fellowship" developed with Baptist Memorial Hospital in Memphis, Tennessee. Arkansas had originally joined with Tennessee and Mississippi Baptist Conventions to open the hospital. But, as with the Little Rock institution, Memphis Memorial had become financially independent of Convention support. The problems developed when the institution's board of directors voted to open an orphanage in Memphis. The ABSC Executive Board objected to the hospital's unilateral decision and got messengers to approve a resolution objecting to the action. Hospital officials withdrew their plans for the orphanage, but, as with state Baptist Hospital, the two groups were never again in full fellowship.

The ABSC relationship with Davis Hospital in Pine Bluff ended rather abruptly in 1942. The hospital had fallen in disrepair and Secretary Bridges, along with other Executive Board leaders, was reluctant to assume new indebtedness so soon after the debacle of the 1930s. Moreover, Pine Bluff city officials had indicated a willingness to assume

responsibility for the institution. With that information, messengers to
the annual meeting in Jonesboro accepted the board's recommendation
that Davis Hospital be turned over to the city of Pine Bluff, with no
further liability accruing to the Convention.

The Bottoms Orphanage also recovered nicely from its financial
difficulties of the 1930s. The population ranged between sixty and
eighty students throughout the decade. War-time prosperity allowed a
steady increase in designated contributions, and the ABSC was also able
to resume its support. By the end of the decade, Convention funds were
approximately one-fourth of the institutions total budget. One discor-
dant note in an otherwise optimistic picture came in 1946 with the
retirement of Mr. and Mrs. C. R. Pugh, the orphanage's caretakers. The
Pughs had been with the orphanage for over twenty-six years and had
developed a large support network throughout the state.

The ABSC's involvement in Christian education followed a pattern
similar to its benevolence program. In 1940, the Executive Board still
had supervisory responsibilities for Ouachita College in Arkadelphia and
Central Junior College in Conway. Central was an all-girls school with a
limited enrollment. As the only "girls school" in the state, school officials
emphasized its "quality instruction," in a "Liberal Arts Education."

Beginning the decade with just over one hundred students, Central
anticipated a new period of growth and financial support as the depression waned. Unfortunately, circumstances did not develop as planned.
To begin with, J. S. Rogers, who had been president of the institution
for twenty years, retired in June 1940. His active role in the ABSC and
extensive personal network among pastors in the state had been a major
asset for the school.

New President O. J. Wade, tried to build on Rogers's foundation
and used Central's Fiftieth-Anniversary Celebration in 1942 to appeal
for more support from the Convention. However, the influence of
World War II worked against his plans. The two areas in which the institution drew its strength, (a two-year girls school with liberal arts
emphasis) limited its ability in getting training contracts from the
federal government. And, as happened to so many other institutions,
job opportunities in defense-related industries drew students away.

Problems continued to plague Central throughout the decade.
Enrollment slipped below one hundred in 1943, and the campus

suffered major damage when first a tornado and then a fire destroyed major buildings. With deficits mounting and enrollment patterns working counter to the school's mission, messengers to the 1948 annual meeting approved the board's recommendation to relocate the institution in Little Rock and sell the Conway property. For two years Central used space on Camp Robinson, became coeducational, and appealed to veterans using "the GI Bill" to return to school. However, these changes came too late to revive the institution, and it closed permanently in 1950.

Ouachita's experience for most of the decade was quite different from Central's. The war did drain away students and enrollment slipped below 400 in 1943. But financial assistance from the federal government more than made up for the loss in tuition. With a four-year, coeducational program, Ouachita was well positioned to receive contracts from the federal government for training related to the war effort. The first contract, coming in 1943 to train 250 aviation cadets, was followed with an agreement to establish an Army Reserve Officer Training Program. Each contract included budget for building or remodeling the space necessary to operate the programs.

For two years after the war, federal support through the GI Bill continued to aid the institution. School officials estimated that approximately 40 percent of the budget came from federal sources between 1942 and 1948. The college got much needed support from a $1 million fundraising campaign as part of the ABSC's Centennial Celebration in 1948.

Unfortunately, funds from the centennial campaign did not accumulate fast enough to offset the loss of students whose GI Bill funding began to phase out after 1948. Moreover, an accreditation team from the North Central Association, identified problems in several areas—particularly with library holdings and low faculty salaries. The team's preliminary report noted that the institution's academic standing would be seriously impaired if those deficiencies were not corrected.

Ouachita ended the decade in a more difficult circumstances than when it began. A dip in enrollment, a severe loss of income, a threat to its academic reputation, severely tested the faith of the college's faithful supporters. As if to add to the test, J. R. Grant resigned as president after the 1949 commencement ceremonies. He had served for sixteen years. During the night, following his announcement, fire destroyed a major portion of the central administration building.

The ABSC's centennial decade was not without problems. However, few people wished to trade it for the preceding decade of depression and debt. The telltale signs of trouble included the relationship with the hospitals and the growing state and federal influence in the area of education.

In many respects, the 1940s served as foundational years to regroup and reground the associations and churches in the work of Convention Baptist. In 1946, messengers approved a new set of by-laws that strengthened the Executive Board's ability to set policy between annual meetings, and war-time prosperity gave the Convention's headquarters staff more ability to meet needs throughout the state. In some respects this decade served as a "lull before the storm" triggered by the post-war "baby boom" and the nation's greater role in world affairs.

13

The 1950s

ORGANIZATION HAD ALWAYS BEEN THE STRONG SUIT OF the Arkansas Baptist State Convention and nowhere was that better demonstrated than in the 1950s. As previously mentioned, Arkansas began losing population at an alarming rate during World War II and continued to do so for more than a decade after the conflict was over. Between 1940 and 1960 national population increased by more than 15 percent but Arkansas saw an 8.4 percent decline. Initially, state business and political leaders thought the out-migration was being caused by the wartime economy and would correct itself when the war was over.

The out-migration did not get better, in fact it got worse as the 1950s progressed. The issue became a matter of serious concern. Worse yet, the age cohorts showing the largest losses were in the nineteen to thirty-five-year-old age groups. If left unchecked, the state stood to lose its most productive work force and reproductive citizens. For the short-term, membership in churches affiliated with the Southern Baptist Convention grew despite the state's population loss. But, ABSC leaders realized that it was only a matter of time before the state's problems became a problem for the Convention as well.

Solving the demographic problem was no easy matter. As disappointing as the out-migration might be, a matter equally challenging was the internal shifting in population from rural to urban areas.

Between 1940 and 1960, sixty-nine of the state's seventy-five counties lost population—some lost over 40 percent But, the county-seat towns in every county continued to show an increase. For the ABSC, which had joined the "rural initiative" with the Southern Baptist Convention in 1946, the problem was twofold. Allocating money and staff time to a declining population, while laudatory in its own right, might limit the ABSC's ability to reach the growing number of people living in towns.

To respond to this changing need, Executive Secretary Ben L. Bridges and Superintendent of Rural Missions C. W. Caldwell began work on a plan to respond to the changing circumstances. Guided by the principles which had been the hallmark for Sunday School work for a quarter of a century, the two leaders focused on creating new units and training leaders to staff those units.

A key factor in staffing included paying bivocational workers a salary that allowed them to spend more time on the mission field. With Executive Board endorsement, the plan was implemented in 1951. The office was also expanded to became a Department of Missions that included a superintendent of City Missions and a major initiative to reach new areas of need. L. B. Golden joined the staff to work with city mission projects.

Strategy for the new era moved on a broad front, an inclusive approach, rather than focus a few major needs. The wisdom of such planning was seen almost immediately as the ABSC began to see unprecedented growth in its membership.

The Superintendent of City Missions began work in Little Rock and soon extended activities to Pine Bluff, Fort Smith, and other towns through the state. Among the activities this new department performed were recruiting and paying workers to translate sermons into sign language for the deaf. First Baptist in Little Rock began such a ministry in the 1930s, and by the end of the 1950s services for the deaf were being conducted in selected churches throughout the state.

A ministry for migrant workers also grew out of this new strategic plan. Due to a shortage of agricultural workers during World War II, federal officials in Washington, D.C., entered into a labor agreement with Mexico, the so-called "Bracero Program" to recruit workers for American farms. This informal agreement was formalized by treaty in

1946 and continued until 1964. Terms of the treaty focused on "migrant workers" who followed the harvest seasons for various crops.

In Arkansas, most of the migrants entered the state at Texarkana and federal officials built a supervised "labor camp" just outside the Hempstead County town of Hope. These new workers were first used in the cotton harvest, but gradually extended to include tomatoes, and other fruits and berries. Most of these new workers were poor, had limited education, and arrived with minimal skills in the English language. For the ABSC, the challenge was to obtain suitable literature and enlist workers sensitive to migrant needs. The primary purpose was evangelism but most "missionaries" also relied heavily on ministry concerns, including supplies for personal hygiene, day care for preschool children, and tutoring for school-age children.

Another area for the ABSC's urban mission thrust focused on work among African-Americans. Before World War II, an overwhelmingly majority the state's black population lived in rural areas. But, as has been mentioned, opportunities created by World War II, led to a major movement into towns, and by 1950 all the towns in the Delta, the Arkansas River Valley, and the Southwest had a significant number of African-American residents.

To meet the growing opportunity to work in black communities, Bridges and the Executive Board shifted the assignment of Gwendoline Luster, whose salary had been paid by the WMU Department, to the Missions Department. Mrs. Luster was primarily responsible for working with women and youth in churches having predominately black memberships, but she also served as a liaison between the various black churches and the ABSC. To assist with training additional workers for ministries among the African-Americans, the ABSC continued to carry line items in the annual budget for Arkansas Baptist College, a historically black institution in Little Rock, and Morris-Booker College in Dermont.

The Convention also conducted a series of training conferences for African-American leaders and encouraged local churches to have special offering days to support work in black communities. All these efforts were carried out under the "separate but equal" rubric and no attention was given to promoting racial integration among the various churches. Given the diversity of congregations between the "hill country" and the Delta, the ABSC allowed race relations to be a matter for local churches to decide.

In the 1950s ABSC members also began to give more attention to institutional chaplains. J. F. Queen, long-time chaplain at Arkansas Baptist Hospital, was joined in 1948 by Charles Finch, who accepted an appointment as chaplain at the Tuberculosis Sanatorium at Booneville. In 1952, E. A. Richmond was appointed chaplain to the Boys' Training School at Pine Bluff. Arlis Sims was also appointed chaplain at the Sanatorium for Negroes at Pine Bluff.

The ABSC leadership's faith in launching bold initiatives in the face of threatening circumstances was richly rewarded. But these men and women were not content to rest after a few successes. Before the decade of the 1950s was over, the State Convention had broaden its efforts to include organizational support for local associations and key institutions in Baptist work as well.

One of those "key institutions," Ouachita College, remained in the forefront of Baptist work throughout the decade. For a few years in the early 1950s the college struggled. The disastrous fire to the Administration Building not only took away critical space, but also led to more debt. This setback made it all but impossible to meet the recommendations from the North Central Association's accreditation team, at least within the time frame given. That problem was compounded by a transition to new administrative leadership.

After J. R. Grant resigned, the board appointed Dr. S. William Eubanks, a member of the Religion Department since 1946, to be president. His tenure was noted for frequent conflicts with the faculty, and when the school was not reaccredited in 1951, he resigned.

The board then appointed Harold A. Haswell, the dean of the faculty, first as acting, then as permanent president. Haswell restored harmony with the faculty and guided the college back into the good graces of the North Central Association. Ouachita was accredited again in 1953. Haswell resigned at the end of the school year to take a job in Texas. After a quick search, the board then appointed Ralph A. Phelps as president—the school's fourth chief executive in as many years.

Phelps brought an "alert, aggressive, administrative style" and was both an active recruiter and fund-raiser. Ouachita had just under

500 students when he became president, and by the end of the decade that number had more than doubled. In the 1959–1960 academic year, enrollment topped 1,000 students for the first time.

A new educational institution, Southern Baptist College, began receiving ABSC support in the 1950s. Organized at Pocahontas in 1946 by Dr. H. E. Williams, the two-year, coeducational school appealed to students in the Northeastern regions of the state. In 1947 President Williams moved the school to an abandoned air cadet training base in Walnut Ridge. In 1949, messengers approved the Executive Board's recommendation to include SBC in the budget. In return, the school awarded the ABSC nine, nonvoting positions on its board of trustees.

The ABSC's relationship with Arkansas Baptist Hospital continued to cool during the 1950s. With Convention dollars decreasing as a share of its overall budget, the Hospital Board became increasingly independent. In 1950 the institution took an even greater step toward financial independence by investing in a "Doctors' Office Building" in West Little Rock. In 1954, the institution expanded its space by more than one-fourth and added 125 new beds. The Little Rock Chamber of Commerce contributed over $600,000 toward the expansion.

Work at the Bottoms Baptist Orphanage remained largely unchanged during the 1950s. Mr. and Mrs. C. R. Pugh had established the home's reputation during the desperate years of the Depression and World War II and the institution continued to build on the foundation they had established. The Pughs retired in 1947 and were replace for a year by L. B. Snider. In 1948, H. C. Seefeldt replaced Snider and stayed on as superintendent throughout the decade.

Central to the ABSC's outreach was the support it received from the regional associations. The shifting population patterns presented special problems for these groups. In some communities the out-migration was so great that formerly thriving congregations had scarcely enough members to hold services. Church buildings fell into disrepair, and the congregation could ill afford to pay for the repairs or the salary of a full-time pastor. Other communities were overcrowded with great needs to enlarge existing buildings and starting new congregations. The state leadership addressed these needs by

creating new line items in the budget to supplement salaries of associational missionaries and providing a loan program to assist with
building renovations and construction.

Supplemental funding from the ABSC was essential and some
churches would not have survived without it. But, the long-term benefit
lay more in the partnership arrangement between local associations and
the state office. To a generation familiar with the "team effort"
employed in winning World War II, cooperation was an essential ingre-
dient in society. The enthusiasm with which that group of leaders
embraced the concept, and the good will engendered by the efforts, was
evident in the results they obtained.

The team concept was also evident in 1952, when the board reorganized the Religious Education Department. Each of the program
areas—Sunday School, Training Union, Baptist Student Union, and
Church Music, was made into a separate department.

Another example of the ABSC's reorganization also came in 1952,
when the Department of Evangelism was created—to be effective
January 1, 1953. The concept of a staff evangelist was not new but the
application of the ministry was, and in the immediate post-war years
ABSC leaders were determined to make it a full-time undertaking.
After formally considering the matter in 1949, the Executive Board
moved to create the new department. I. L. Yearby was selected as the
first secretary and for six years utilized citywide or areawide revivals, as
well as youth revivals, all in conjunction with local associations and
churches. However, while acknowledging the importance of "soul
winning" the ABSC's membership was slow to respond to this initiative.
Ironically, churches in the rural areas proved to be the most responsive
but never in numbers large enough to support the office. When
Secretary Yearby retired in 1958, the board voted to reassign the duties
to the Department of Missions.

Restructuring the Department of Evangelism out of existence
should not be interpreted as negative move. Indeed, the ABSC leadership believed that soul winning was an integral part of every one of its
departments and programs and an emphasis on witnessing did not
necessarily need a separate department to be effective. That evangelism
could be effective in any number of organizational settings may best be
illustrated in the growing interest in summer camps. Again, the concept

of using camps for outreach was not new—Siloam Springs having been inaugurated following World War I. But the decade of the 1950s brought together a number of related currents that provided a unique opportunity for witnessing. For one thing, the "baby boom" which followed World War II was making its presence felt. Admittedly, Arkansas lagged behind the national birth rate but an even casual look at local church attendance showed a growing number of children and youth. The continuing prosperity which followed the war, made "camp" feasible for many families and an increasing amount of leisure time made it possible. Armed with the knowledge that most conversions came in the preteen years and "surrender to Christian service" often came during adolescence, Convention leaders sought to make evangelism and missions a special focus of the camp experience. The same year the Evangelism Department was phased out, Convention messengers adopted a recommendation to place Siloam Springs Assembly under the direct supervision of the board.

The WMU and the Brotherhood Departments also worked hard to complement the focus on children and youth in the 1950s. The WMU's work had long been established among young women and needed only to restructure its literature and worker training activities to respond to the need. Under the leadership of Nancy Cooper, who replaced Mrs. C. H. Ray in 1949, the WMU extended its work of mission education to boys by creating the Royal Ambassador (RA) Program. The newly organized Brotherhood, under the direction of Nelson Tull, found the going a bit more difficult. Conceived as a men's mission organization, the Brotherhood often felt the constraint of time and had struggled since 1946 to find a focus. Some in the organization thought the Royal Ambassador Program had the potential to provide direction and in the early 1950s the SBC's Brotherhood Commission moved to take over sponsorship for the RA Program. Beginning a three-year apprenticeship as a joint-sponsor with the WMU, the Brotherhood assumed full responsibility for RAs in 1956. J. D. Wagnon was employed in 1953 to work with Director Tull and had specific responsibilities for the Royal Ambassador Program.

In many respects the ABSC achieved its outstanding success in the 1950s because of a rising tide of affluence. Post-war prosperity allowed the Convention to pay off its Depression-era debts in 1952. Secretary

Ben Bridges had never been satisfied with the partial settlement made in 1937. Even though the Convention had met its legal obligations, Bridges insisted the ABSC was "honor bound" to pay 100 percent of the original debt. He kept that issue before the messengers at every annual meeting. In 1943, Convention representatives voted to accept Bridges's exhortation and pay off the balance. To that end, the ABSC formed the Honor Club made up of individuals who agreed to contribute $1.00 each month until the debt was paid. Ten years after the commitment was made, Bridges was able to realize his dream.

Contributions from the churches remained strong throughout the decade. Even though the national economy went through two periods of recession during that period, support for Convention remained strong. To be sure, there was an unevenness to both economic growth and contributions to the ABSC, but overall giving was up and the board concerned itself more with priorities for the budget rather than lack of income.

Church buildings became one evidence of the new prosperity in the fifties. Not only did overall value increase multifold but the design and use of the buildings changed dramatically also. Early in the decade the ABSC staff concentrated on providing loans to assist with renovations and smaller construction projects. However, as the decade wore on, building projects became more expensive—exceeding the Convention's lending capabilities. Staff assistance then turned to technical assistance, in layout, design, and program needs.

The ABSC joined this family of new construction in 1952 by acquiring more property for its executive offices. In 1947, the board voted to rent the top floor of a two-story building located at 401 West Capitol. However, in five years the headquarters staff had outgrown that space and the board agreed to purchase the entire building. According to Secretary Bridges, "This building is located in one of the most desirable business areas of the city, and has practically doubled in value since we purchased it."

For all its success in the eleventh decade of its existence, there were signs of trouble for the ABSC. The percentage of Sunday School enrollments, compared to overall memberships, among the churches began to decline after 1954. After an all-time record of 16,600 in 1950, the number of baptisms was irregular before beginning a steady decline after 1955. Brotherhood enrollments, even WMU participation, began to decline by the end of the decade, and the surging youth movement began to recede. Although it was not immediately apparent, the transition from a rural to an urban society began to have an impact.

Signs of a new era in Baptist history showed first in the youth movement. In the early 1950s, teenagers took an increasingly active role in church affairs particularly in the area of music. Youth music began to influence Sunday morning worship. New types of songs and new instruments, at least the guitar, began to be used in many churches on a regular basis.

Mrs. B. W. Nininger, the founding secretary of the office, was often called upon to provide support services for churches who employed full-time "ministers of music" and developed graded choir programs. In many respects the decade of the 1950s became the foundational period for a new direction in church music, particularly in the urban areas. With ABSC assistance, churches moved to offer handbell choirs, a limited orchestra, special ensembles, and robed choir members to lead in worship services. The decade between Mrs. Nininger's appointment and her retirement was an epochal period in Arkansas church music. She was followed by LeRoy McClard, who assumed duties in August 1955.

McClard established a "standard of excellence" as a goal and guide to help churches in their musical growth. Choirs began wearing robes, and performance ensembles became an increasing part of the worship service.

Ironically, as the ABSC moved to assist churches in "modernizing" their programs, secular society also offered many competing influences. Television (the first TV station in Arkansas went on air in 1953) and other forms of leisure activity began to seriously erode attendance and various Convention, association, and church events. Responding to this problem, leaders in the Sunday School and Training Departments redoubled their efforts to train church leaders in using the literature designed especially for young people.

As a direct result of this new planning Ralph Davis led the Training Union Department to host its first statewide workshop for nursery, beginners, and primary children's workers—a sign of the "baby boom."

He also hosted the first, statewide youth rally in April 1958. The concept for both programs was well received, and Davis agreed to make the workshop and rally annual events. To broaden the perspective a bit, Davis and his staff also introduced a "sword drill" for preteen children. Robert Dowdy joined the Training Union staff in 1954 as assistant secretary.

Edgar Williamson used campaigns from the SBC's Sunday School Board to promote his own work in the state. The "Million More in '54" Sunday School enlargement emphasis became a prime motivator for associational and church workers to enroll more people in Sunday School. Arkansas's quota of the 1 million was 36,000.

The Baptist Student Union Department also made a strong effort to complement the work in the Sunday School, Training Union, and Music departments. Dale Cowling replaced Fred J. Vogel in 1950 as secretary and served until 1952, when he resigned to accept the call to pastor Little Rock's Second Baptist Church. The department was without a director for a year before Riley Munday became director in 1954, but he too left the department within the year.

Despite the turnover in leadership, establishing "student centers" on each campus became a program priority during the 1950s. Both Williamson and Bridges shared this vision, and by mid-decade buildings had been acquired at the University of Arkansas, Fayetteville; Arkansas Technical College, Russellville; Arkansas State College, Jonesboro; Southern State College, Magnolia; and Arkansas A&M College, Monticello. Typically, a BSU's first "center" was a house near campus. However, by late in the decade efforts were underway to construct new buildings specifically designed for BSU program activities.

In 1955, the department finally found stability with its leadership when Tom Logue, a Texan, became director. Under his guidance the BSU launched a program to broaden the BSU's ministry offerings and add more physical space for prospective students. Enrollment in the state's colleges and universities was still limited, but the planning that began in the 1950s allowed the program to be in position to handle the huge increases in college students in the 1960s.

Working with the First Baptist Church in Conway, Logue acquired a site in 1956 to add a student center at Arkansas State Teachers

College. Under this cooperative arrangement, the ABSC provided half the cost for the building and the remainder, plus some limited furnishings, were raised by the host church. James Smalley, minister of Education at First Church Conway, was employed to serve half-time at the center while continuing half-time at the church. After a year in this cooperative arrangement, Smalley became the full-time director for the BSU center.

Logue also soon had plans underway to enlist more workers for the growing student enrollment. By the end of the decade full-time directors were actively involved at each of the state's four-year colleges. In addition to Smalley at ASTC, the other directors and their assignments were: Jamie Jones, UA; Neil Jackson, ATC; Juanita Straubie, Baptist Hospital; Carol Burns, ASC; Maurice Fennell, A&M; and Mrs. Joe Simmons, who served both Ouachita and Henderson State on a part-time basis.

In addition to these site directors, Logue also employed Jim Boyd to serve as a "citywide director" for Little Rock. He was assigned to work with students at Little Rock University as well as the medical, nursing, and pharmacy students at the University of Arkansas Medical Center in Little Rock.

Of great importance to the development of the student programs was the opening of a "chair of Bible study" at Arkansas Tech State College and the University of Arkansas in 1958. Working with officials at those institutions, students were given the opportunity of taking Bible courses in the BSU Center on those respective campuses. Ouachita agreed to grant college credit to students taking those courses. This new offering was particularly significant in that the state colleges enrolled 80 percent of the students identifying themselves as a member of a local Baptist church.

Camp and assembly programs represented still another strategy used by the ABSC in the 1950s to reach young people. As has been mentioned, the ABSC originally considered the two programs separately and each operated under its own board. However, by the end of the decade, a number of pastors and youth leaders were calling for the programs to be more integrated and operated all year. The Executive Board responded to these inquiries by recommending that the programs be placed directly under the board's supervision. The boards of trustees for both camps passed unanimous resolutions approving the change.

Calling the camp and assembly programs "one of the greatest needs in our denominational life" the board moved to build support. This included a plan to operate the facilities on a year-round basis. To move to this format required an outlay of almost a quarter of a million dollars to "winterize" the buildings. However, ABSC leaders urged the Convention to take such a step because "our camp and assembly programs are with us to stay and they can render a ministry that cannot be approached through any other method."

In 1957 the ABSC lost the services of its "trusted and tried leader" Ben L. Bridges. Having begun serving Arkansas Baptist in 1920, he had witnessed some of the most difficult years in the Convention's history. Committed and dedicated; however, he guided the work in a model of consistency through the desperate times of the Great Depression, the embarrassing experience of debt default, and the trying times of World War II. He "stayed the course," and when he left the board on August 1, the Convention was on sound financial footing "with all departments of the Executive Board actively engaged in the Convention's work." After resigning from the board, Dr. Bridges accepted employment as secretary of the Baptist Foundation, a work which he believed in deeply but would not be as physically and emotionally demanding as the larger work with the ABSC.

The board chose S. A. Whitlow, pastor of the First Baptist Church of Arkadelphia, to "fill the important and strategic position as Executive Secretary and Treasurer." Dr. Whitlow began his duties in time to prepare for the upcoming annual meeting.

Other significant changes in the state office in 1957, included a new editor for the *Arkansas Baptist*. Dr. B. H. Duncan, who had served as editor for ten years, died on March 19. He was succeeded by the Reverend Erwin L. McDonald. There was also a change in the Music Department. LeRoy McClard was appointed the new director of that department.

Changes in key staff areas caused the Executive Committee to reevaluate the organizational structure of the office staff and the various agencies. The matter was discussed at successive meetings in late 1957 and early 1958. In the latter meeting the committee voted "to appoint a joint committee composing of two members from the Executive Board, and two members from the Central Office staff, with the Executive Secretary and the Associate as ex-officio members." The committee was charged to "study the organizations in the Baptist Building with the view of coordination" and "study the work of our departments with the view of working out a cooperative program of work and coordinate the state, district, and associational meetings of the various departments."

The committee spent several months carefully reviewing various options. In a report to the board late in the year, they recommended a reorganization of the staff in the Baptist Building and a possible restructuring of the Executive Board. The committee also recommended that the Woman's Missionary Union "consolidate their bookkeeping with the accounting department of the Executive Board. The WMU had previously expressed an interest in making such a change in order to better utilize its limited staff.

The Executive Committee accepted the report and moved almost immediately to implement the recommendations. The board was restructured into six committees—Operating, Program, Finance, Nominating, Executive, and Advisory. Likewise, the staff in the Baptist Building was reorganized. Not only was the WMU's bookkeeping transferred to the general accounting department, but also, a central workroom was set up to handle printing and mass mailing for all the departments in the building. Additional changes included adding the office of "business manager," and for the first time since the central staff had been assembled, a salary schedule was adopted to reflect both merit and tenure in office for the employees. And, the board also adopted a plan to provide fringe benefits—including sickness and accident coverage and a graduated vacation policy—for Baptist Building employees. Related to that, the board also prepared job descriptions for each staff position. The newly constituted Operating Committee (OC) of the board was assigned the responsibility of reviewing job performance and recommending salary.

Melvin Thrash, with an undergraduate degree from Ouachita and a Master's of Business Administration from the University of Arkansas, was selected to fill the business manager's position. Other key personnel changes included a new director for the Sunday School

Department when Lawson Hatfield was named to replace the retiring Edgar Williamson. Dr. Williamson served twenty-two years as superintendent, but the rigors of time and travel had taken its toll, and he decided to relinquish the duties to a younger person. He continued to serve as an associate in the department for the next several years. The Reverend Hatfield, a native Arkansan and graduate of both Ouachita and Southwestern Seminary, was employed by the Baptist Sunday School Board in Nashville, Tennessee, prior to assuming his new duties.

The State Sunday School Department had long been an integral part of church growth. As has been mentioned, the number of baptism among the churches began to decline after 1954. To respond to that, Secretary Williamson and his staff did a careful review of work among the associations and various individual churches. Beginning with the 1954–1955 church year, the department adopted a five-point strategy designed to reach more people. That program included: (1) every association fully organized for Sunday School work, (2) every association Sunday School officer trained for his task, (3) every association used the Associational Standard of Excellence as a program of work, (4) every association each year conducted group or simultaneous training schools, and (5) every association held a simultaneous enlargement campaign.

Assistant Secretary Ernest Adams was assigned to promote the new program among the associations, and for the next four years churches and associations responded to the challenge with enthusiasm. At the time the program was implemented, only 39 percent of the associations were organized along the model being proposed. However, by 1957–1958, almost 95 percent of the associations were organized, and there was a corresponding growth in attendance and training. But, as the decade came to an end, enthusiasm for the Five-Point Program began to wane. The number of "organized" associations dropped to 90 percent, and it became necessary to develop new approaches to reaching people.

Another defining moment in the 1950s came in the area of race relations. As has been mentioned, the ABSC had shown a sensitivity to this issue since before World War II. However, the autonomous nature of each church, the organizational structure of the State Convention, and the diversity of membership among churches associated with the

Two individuals have served as President of both the Arkansas Baptist State Convention and the Southern Baptist Convention. James P. Eagle and Brooks Hayes (above). Hayes, also a member of the U.S. Congress, was President of the SBC during the Little Rock School Crisis of 1957.

ABSC had kept the matter of segregated churches from being a priority item. But, national circumstances early in the decade focused attention on the matter of race, and before it was over Arkansas had been the object of international interest.

Much has been written about the U.S. Supreme Court's decision of *Brown v. Topeka*, its impact on racial integration of public schools, and the organized resistance to such integration in Little Rock. The "Central High Crisis" became front-page news around the world, and as the heated emotions of the moment began to cool, analysts and commentators began to raise questions about why more churches were not involved. Given the high profile that Southern Baptist churches had in the state, many individuals, within and outside the state, began to ask why individual churches and the State Convention were not more proactive in supporting the "law of the land" and, indeed, why some actively opposed integration. In later years the ABSC was criticized for failing to even acknowledge the school situation at its annual meeting which came just weeks following the forced desegregation.

Messengers to the 1957 annual meeting did not address the Little Rock school integration issue either by resolution or formal report. Their meeting was held at Little Rock's Immanuel Baptist Church, just blocks away from where the "Central High Crisis" had occurred just two months before. It goes without saying that most if not all those representing their respective churches and associations knew about the crisis and at least the general outline of the issues.

Why did Arkansas's Southern Baptist and the ABSC leadership not formally speak out on the school integration issue? In many respects they did. For example, they elected Brooks Hayes president of the State Convention in 1957 and again in 1958. He was also elected president of the Southern Baptist Convention in 1958. Hayes was a politician with a career that spanned two decades of Arkansas political wars. Admittedly, he was not the "typical" Arkansas Southern Baptist. But his views on race relations were well-known. In 1949, seven years and three elections into his congressional career, he made a speech on the floor of the U.S. House of Representatives that left no doubt about his position on civil rights issues. He outlined what he called his "Arkansas Plan" to extend "full civil rights to minority groups." Many newspaper editors pointed to that speech as a "historic utterance for a

Southern politician." His work on civil rights legislation led to his appointment to the Platform Committee of the Democratic party in 1952 and 1956. He had signed the well reported "I'll Take My Stand" document critical of the *Brown* decision, not out of personal conviction but on the basis that integration should be initiated at the local level, over a specified period of time, as the Little Rock School Board had planned to do. In short, he was elected to be the symbolic head of the state's largest Baptist organization.

Students in the Baptist Student Union also took a strong stand for improved race relations. Those attending the BSU's annual fall conference in 1957—just weeks after the Little Rock Crisis, adopted a resolution outlining what they believed to be the "Christian position on race relations." That position stated in part "Upholding the teaching and example of Jesus regarding the equal worth of all individuals regardless of race, color, or station in life." President Dwight Eisenhower sent a telegram to state BSU President Dale Jones commending the students on their action.

B. H. Duncan, editor of the *Arkansas Baptist*, urged his readers to support a resolution adopted by the Southern Baptist Convention calling the *Brown* decision "Christian and constitutional." Duncan said the SBC's position was "a fair and conservative statement." Ouachita president, Ralph A. Phelps Jr., encouraged Arkansas Baptists to support the decision and end segregation in the ABSC's churches and institutions.

Other individuals also spoke out. Dale Cowling, pastor at Little Rock's Second Baptist Church, urged that congregation to support the *Brown* decision and from the pulpit called upon Governor Orval Faubus to do so as well. O. L. Bayless, pastor of First Baptist Hot Springs, chairman of the State Mission Committee, and member of the SBC's Home Mission Board, called upon Arkansas Baptists to "help not hinder the progress of brotherly love; that we may exercise patience and good will in the discussions that must take place, and give a good testimony to the meaning of Christian faith and discipleship." Cowling, W. O. Vaught, pastor of Little Rock's Immanuel Baptist, and Harold Hicks, pastor of Pulaski Heights Baptist in Little Rock, three of the cities largest Southern Baptist churches, signed a statement protesting the position of Governor Faubus. The Pulaski County Association also adopted a resolution in its 1958 annual meeting calling on its members "to pray earnestly and sincerely, both in private and in public assembly for God's will to be done in the public school crisis now affecting the lives of so many of our people in this area."

The latter resolution came in the year that Little Rock's high schools were closed and students were using extraordinary means to attend school outside the city. Many, more black students than white students, did not attend at all. Responding to the school closing, Ouachita joined with Second Baptist Church in Little Rock to open a "Baptist Academy" in 1958–1959 for white students with preference to Baptist but without restriction on "religious affiliation."

In short, only one pastor of a Southern Baptist church in Little Rock spoke out in opposition to racial integration of the schools and he later left the Convention. By contrast, the ABSC began as early as 1954 to respond to the court's decision which was handed down in May. At the November annual meeting, the ABSC voted to employ Clyde Hart, pastor of a Central Baptist Church in North Little Rock, as a member of the Missions Department. In making his first annual report to the 1955 Convention, Hart noted that his department had focused on "promoting college and seminary extensions schools; conducting Bible institutes, stewardship conferences, and revivals; organizing Baptist Student Union work at Arkansas Baptist College, Philander Smith College in Little Rock, and Arkansas AM&N in Pine Bluff; conducting Vacation Bible Schools and summer field work; and encouraging associational and church leaders to invite black leaders and workers to white Vacation Bible School clinics and other training conferences. The Missions Department also employed Gwendoline Luster, a well-known female leader, to conduct youth camps for black young people and to work with women's organizations in black churches.

In 1957, messengers voted to create a new department in the Baptist Building on race relations, and Hart was chosen to serve as director. For the next several years he organized a summer camp for black young people, first renting Aldersgate, a Methodist camp near Little Rock and by the end of the decade the ABSC had established "Hart of the Hills" a new camp near Ferndale for black youth. This approach was in the vein of "separate but equal" and reflected the prevailing sentiment of the day. A poll taken in 1956 reported 80 percent of white Southerners opposed school integration. Southern Baptist in Arkansas reflected this attitude even though a growing number admitted that the "Bible did not support racial segregation." While the ABSC had taken a public position on certain issues, such as beverage alcohol, it typically did not address social or political issues. Its response to school desegregation and race relations in general was in keeping with that tradition. In the next decade the ABSC made considerable social progress in these areas, but unfortunately, internal problems began to arise to trouble the fellowship.

14

The 1960s

THE PARADOX BETWEEN THE ARKANSAS BAPTIST STATE Convention's growth pattern and the state of Arkansas continued in the 1960s. For the state, the decade finally saw a reversal in out-migration and the beginning of a new cycle of prosperity. For the ABSC, growth rates began to flatten out and became sluggish. For Arkansas and the nation, the 1960s were times for change and troubled relationships. The Vietnam War became a deeply divisive issue. Mounting inflation stimulated by national social programs of the Great Society and military spending for the war added to the discomfort of thousands of citizens in the state and nation. The social and political policies shaped by national legislation, including civil rights, open housing, and voter registration contributed to the divisiveness in the nation's society. President Lyndon Johnson described the "state of the union" as a "ship on a troubled sea."

For the ABSC it was a time of adjustment. Unlike the 1950s, which saw a high degree of consensus among the churches and associations, the new decade became increasingly fractious. Much of the divergence was attributed to a widening gap between rural and urban churches in the state. By the end of the decade a majority of the state's citizens were classified as "urban" and the state's social mores began to reflect this new society.

The rural-urban dichotomy was heightened by improved technology and an expanding multimedia industry. Television, still a novelty for most Arkansas Baptists in the 1950s, became an essential item in a majority of homes by the end of the 1960s. This medium, coupled with changing themes among motion-picture producers, transported traditional urban issues involving sex, gambling, violent crimes, juvenile delinquency, drug and alcohol addiction into all parts of the state.

These social issues were made more complex by a growing "generation gap" as the "baby boomers" become older adolescents. Exposed to an increasingly "permissive" national culture and lacking the defining experiences of depression and total war, young people became more and more alienated from the older, adult society. This alienation was especially defined in debates involving the role of the federal government in society.

For the ABSC the changes came so rapidly that it was often difficulty to respond. Given the autonomous nature of their constituency, it became increasingly difficult for Convention leaders to develop a consensus on major issues. But this did not keep them from trying. Indeed, the ABSC became involved in more social problems than at anytime in its history. In his 1963 annual report on behalf of the Executive Board, Secretary Whitlow noted that "we must ever be engaged in an effort to devise new and better ways of making known 'The Old, Old Story.'"

But with the variety of activities came increasing financial responsibilities. The headquarters staff worked hard on efficiency and accountability. But more was needed. Responding to that in 1963, President C. Z. Holland and the board took steps to implement a "management by objective" administrative structure. The next year, the board under the leadership of new President Walter L. Yeldell, introduced a "budget formula" for allocating resources. Even so, by mid-decade it was evident that an increasing number of contributions came in designated for specific programs rather than general offerings to the Cooperative Program.

The third step in the master plan for reorganization, the Division of Services, became operative in 1965. This new unit was designed to assist each program area to "project its program before the Baptist of

Arkansas." In addition to that, the division was responsible for the general maintenance on the camps, assembly grounds, and the Baptist Building.

Taking a proactive position on complex, sometimes controversial issues made it mandatory that the ABSC stay in close contact with the associations and churches. To that end, the board designated May as "Denominational Month" and directed Secretary Whitlow to organize teams from the various departments in the central office to work with churches in specific associations. The board was also mindful about the amount of time required for a promotional event and encouraged the various departments to consolidate their program activities whenever possible.

In a similar vein, the board asked the associations to hold their annual district meetings during the second week of October so that "denominational personnel" could be prepared to attend. By so doing, churches were assured of receiving the most up-to-date information about SBC/ABSC work from "those primarily charged this responsibility."

To position itself for the new decade, the ABSC finalized the plans for reorganization that had begun in 1958. The first step had been to reorganize the Executive Board. Aided by extensive research from the Southern Baptist Convention, the state office was restructured to reflect the SBC model and the staffing arrangements being put in place by the larger churches. The new plan established Divisions of Religious Education, Missions, Business Management, and the *Arkansas Baptist*.

Also, the ABSC's new look provided for a "promotional man" to be assigned to one of the associational districts. This was a "pilot plan" for promoting all ABSC/SBC programs with special emphasis on those units in the Division of Religious Education.

After careful review of the ABSC's eight districts, Secretary Whitlow recommend that District Four in Western Arkansas be selected for the pilot project and that Ernest R. Adams, an associate in the Sunday School Department, be appointed as director. Adams began work in 1962 under the supervision of the J. T. Elliff, director of Religious Education. The program had slow going due in part to the lack of clarity about its intended purpose—particularly as it related to the associational director

Executive secretaries: S. A. Whitlow (1958–1969), left; and Charles Ashcraft (1969–1979), right.

of Missions. In 1964 Adams retired and was replaced Charles Gwaltney, minister of Music and Education from Central Church Jonesboro.

Also as part of the restructuring, messengers at the 1960 annual meeting approved changes in the ABSC constitution to give the Executive Board more administrative control over the various agencies. Specifically, the concern related to the role of agency trustees in fund-raising and accountability. Speaking on behalf of the board, ABSC President Bernes Selph noted the problems that arose when an individual trustee or agency sought unilateral support and failed to recognize the common needs of the Convention as a whole. It was the board's recommendation, and the messengers agreed, that all such activity be coordinated through the executive secretary's office and approved at the board level before being undertaken.

In 1962, the ABSC followed the SBC's lead in broadening the traditional definition for "ministers of the gospel." Messengers at the SBC's annual meeting in 1961 voted to recognize "ministers of religious education, ministers of sacred music, and ministers of religious

organizations . . . as commissioned ministers of the Gospel." The ABSC
messengers agreed with that action.

This "statement on status" reflected the growing diversity in Baptist
work but it was not without controversy. In many respects it was an indication of the urban-rural divergence within the state. Incoming
President C. Z. Holland, 1962–1963, assigned the issue to the board's
Operating Committee and asked that group to identify those eligible to
be commissioned.

In the 1960s the Executive Board also became increasingly
involved in the SBC's Cooperative Program. Associate Executive
Secretary Ralph Douglas was placed in charge of this area, and he
energetically promoted financial support. As the decade began, ABSC
churches gave 11.78 percent of their total budget to the Cooperative
Program, which allowed Arkansas to rank fourth among SBC states.
However, Douglas also pointed out that church members only gave 3
1/2 percent of their income to a local congregation. A couple of years
later Douglas commented, "There is a note of sadness because we see
a trend that is not good. The church members have more income than
ever before but are giving a smaller percentage of that income through
their churches."

The new divisions in the headquarters building also prepared for
the new decade by reevaluating their traditional programs. One of the
first visible changes came in a new name for the *Arkansas Baptist*, when
"Newsmagazine" was added to the masthead beginning in 1960. Editor
Erwin McDonald pointed out that the publication's mail was frequently
sent to the Baptist Hospital and that perhaps the new name would help
eliminate some of that confusion.

New features were added beginning in 1962 with a weekly index, a
page devoted to women's issues, a page on youth concerns, and a weekly
column by Herschel Hobbs on "What Baptists Believe." For a brief
time in the mid-1960s the paper featured a sports column "Outdoors
with Doc," written by Ouachita president, Dr. Ralph Phelps. The "Life
and Work Sunday Commentary" began appearing in the paper in 1966.

The Arkansas Baptist Foundation got a new executive director, Ed
F. McDonald Jr., who joined the foundation in July 1962 as its fourth
director in twelve years. The organization got an outstanding break in

The "official voice" of the ABSC has traveled by different names. Chartered as the Baptist Advance *in 1902, the newspaper's name was changed to the* Arkansas Baptist, *and then in 1960 became the* Arkansas Baptist Newsmagazine.

1966, when it received a $60,000 bequest from the M. M. Blakely estate. This was the largest gift the foundation had received up to that time and increased its assets to more than $200,000.

The Baptist Student Union program continued its focus on adding full-time directors and improving the student centers at the various college campuses. Ouachita and Henderson State College shared a director until 1962, when full-time directors were appointed at each institution. Changes among the directors came throughout the decade. Walter Smiley replaced Jim Boyd as citywide director for Little Rock, and Darrell Coleman replaced Maurice Fennell at Arkansas A&M. In 1966 Doyle "Windy" Burke replaced Linda Allen, who had previously replaced Walter Smiley, as city director. Burke also assisted Dr. Logue in the central office on a limited basis. Gerald Cound replaced Darrell Coleman at Arkansas A&M in 1967, and Danny McCauley was appointed to work with those colleges who had no director.

New student centers were opened in Little Rock at the University of Arkansas Medical Center (1960) and at Arkansas State College, Jonesboro (1962). In 1964, Pulaski Association gave the BSU a "small house adjacent to Little Rock University," and "a Baptist friend" did a similar thing at College of the Ozarks in Clarksville. After the Baptist Medical Center severed its ties with the Convention in 1966, the Executive Board authorized funds previously budgeted for the hospital to pay off the indebtedness on the center at Henderson State College, Arkadelphia.

New programming introduced in the decade included a statewide BSU Convention and work with international students. In 1960, there were fewer than 200 international students identified on the various college campuses. Most of those were in Fayetteville at the University of Arkansas. However, by the end of the decade enrollment had grown to over 1,000, and they were distributed throughout the state. Director Logue had a particular concern for international students and kept the need before his colleagues in the Baptist Building and the Executive Board.

The Division of Religious Education, the second unit in the reorganized central office, became a reality in 1961. The board chose the Reverend J. T. Elliff as director of the new division. The Brotherhood,

Church Music, Sunday School, and Training Union Departments, and after 1962 the Camps and Assemblies Programs, were all part of the new divisional alignment. Having these programs in one administrative unit allowed the secretaries of each to be better informed and to coordinate their respective programs. Staff members in the new division also made a major effort to communicate with the local associations and churches. In 1962, Director Elliff began publishing the *Religious Education News* to give a more complete picture of the division's work, and in 1963 the staff from the various departments organized into "Teams" and traveled throughout the state to present "Denominational Night" to area churches.

Beginning in 1964, the Executive Board directed the division to implement a "management by objective" program for its work. This concept required the staff to know what local churches identified as their "felt needs," establish "measurable goals" to meet those needs, and make budget allocations accordingly. This approach which Director Elliff called "programming," meant "how we plan to get where we are going." To achieve "programming" the division followed a three-step process known as: ATE (Analyze, Test, and Evaluate); PDA (Program Design and Adaptation) and Field Service. The latter meant enlisting and training associational and church workers. About 60 percent of the Division's budget for Sunday School and Training Union was spent on Field Service.

The Brotherhood Office, under the continued guidance of Nelson Tull and Associate C. H. Seaton, perhaps experienced the biggest changes in the decade. Beginning in 1960, the office was reorganized to reflect four priority areas—the Royal Ambassador Program, evangelism, stewardship, and world missions. The state network was also reduced from fifteen districts to the eight associational districts utilized by the other offices in central administration. In 1961, the department began hosting a annual Brotherhood Convention during RA week at youth camp.

In 1965 the program was given an even sharper focus when the Southern Baptist Convention charged it with providing "mission education and mission activities, involving men and boys." Two years later the structure was revised again. Along with a new definition—"all the male membership of the church nine years of age and up" the program was organized into three divisions: Baptist Men (ages 25 and up), Baptist Young Men (ages 18–24), and Royal Ambassadors (ages 9 to 17). Nelson Tull retired in 1967 and the board named C. E. Seaton to replace him.

Seaton was responsible for the RA Program. In 1961, the National office reorganized this program into three groupings including: Crusaders (ages 9–11), Pioneers (ages 12–14), and Ambassadors (ages 15–17).

In another new focus, the Brotherhood also became actively involved in a "camping program" for both men and boys. Camping became an integral part of both the Royal Ambassador Program and the Mission Friends organization of the Woman's Missionary Union. Early in the decade, Executive Secretary S. A. Whitlow presented the board with a plan to acquire property and build camping facilities for the work in these areas.

Following favorable action by this body, a committee selected a 266-acre property site in Saline County and construction on the new camp began in 1962. Called Camp Paron, to identify its location near the small community by that name, the new facility was ready for campers in 1964. By that time, camping had become such an integral part of all ABSC work that the camp was operated on a year-round basis for all age groups and programs.

Summer camps, along with the annual Assembly Program at Siloam Springs, became a major part of evangelism strategy. A key factor in this outreach lay in "modernizing" the facilities. Secretary Whitlow was frequently made aware of the "camping comforts" annual attendees expected at Siloam, and he kept that issue before the board throughout the decade.

The Siloam Assembly also began to add new features to its traditional format. In 1964 the Division of Religious Education added a separate "Youth Assembly" and began offering training for "District Age Group workers" for Sunday School and Church Training.

The Brotherhood Program became increasingly involved in "pioneer mission" projects during the summer months. Using volunteers from local churches, who paid their own expenses, Tull coordinated teams of men who went to areas in Ohio, Colorado, Nebraska to do mission work. These men most frequently were involved in construction projects, but some also conducted revivals, distributed literature, and conducted Bible studies.

For the Church Music Department, the decade of the 1960s brought an emphasis on "revelance." Folk music influenced musicals such as *Good News, Natural High, Tell It Like It Is,* and *Celebrate Life.* LeRoy McClard continued as director until 1963 when he was replaced by Hoyt A. Mulkey. One matter not resolved from the 1950s was a definition for "Music Ministry." After more than a decade of evolving, various models had come into existence in the several states. The secretaries of these state music programs decided to clarify the issue at their 1961 semiannual meeting. By consensus they defined a church music ministry to be in place when a local church (1) elected someone to direct music, (2) organized at least one music group that met on a regular basis, and (3) used music to strengthen the church's worship, education, and evangelism efforts. A common definition was such a basic concept, but it proved invaluable in promoting the music program in the associations and churches.

As in previous years "hymn sings" were the most popular outreach programs. However, strong attendance at summer music camps, workshops, and festivals, continued to strengthen the children and youth music programs and, ultimately, the adult choirs. The number of full-time "ministers of music" increased steadily through the decade and also had a most positive effect on church music. Related to that, Director McClard also expressed gratitude that Ouachita was instituting a new graduate program in music in 1962. Having opportunity for more training helped musicians at all levels.

The Sunday School program began the decade with the theme of "Reach, Teach, Win and Develop." Lawson Hatfield continued to serve as director and made evangelism a top priority. He noted that "one out of three people who are saved" and "eight out of ten baptisms" come from individuals enrolled in Sunday School.

New areas of emphasis included the "First Annual Sunday School Week" at Siloam Springs, and a "10 for 10" program in conjunction with the SBC's campaign for adding 10,000 new churches and 20,000 new mission sites. Ten for 10 meant starting a "10 percent increase in new Missions and Sunday Schools in a 10 week period."

Mary Emma Humphrey joined the department in 1961 as an associate director for elementary work. In addition to having responsibility for all preschool and children's work, she also assisted in keeping records for training awards, Vacation Bible School, and standard Sunday Schools. Jerry Don Abernathy joined the team in 1964 as an associate for youth work. Pat Ratton replaced Abernathy in 1967. Don Cooper was added to the staff in 1968 to work with associational promotion and Vacation Bible School activities.

But even with a larger staff and promotional support from SBC headquarters, the Sunday School program could not match the growth it had experienced in the 1950s. Enrollment continued to increase. However, the number of churches meeting the minimum requirements to be considered a "standard" Sunday School (i.e. age-grouped classes, regular planning meetings, and an outreach program) dropped to 78 percent—compared to over 90 percent through much of the previous decade.

The rapid social changes in the 1960s presented a challenge to the Church Training Department. With more than a decade of experience, Director Ralph Davis had seen many movements come and go. However, he recognized special needs accompanying the latest developments. True to its roots, Church Training continued to devote a considerable amount of its resources to young people. Youth night, youth week, speakers tournaments, and leadership schools were all designed to prepare young people to be future leaders in their churches and communities. But a new emphasis focused on a "total church" training program with particular reference to the needs of new church members.

Building on the "Honor Program" instituted in 1959, Davis, Associate R. V. Haygood, replaced by James A. Griffin in 1962, and Field Worker Ruth Tolleson promoted six areas of training. These included an annual youth week, speaker tournaments and Bible drills, annual study course units, quarterly reports filed with the Church Training Office, standard study course and training units, and an increase in enrollment. Those churches who participated in these six areas by training their workers and offering opportunities to their members were awarded a "diploma" that recognized them as having an "Honor Church Program" in Training Union.

In 1968 the department's name was changed to "Church Training" and it was given three additional work assignments. The first, church administration, emphasized training in long-range planning, office administration, and recognition of individual achievement. The second area was concerned with family ministry and focused on church-home cooperation, education for marriage and family living, and personalized care for family members.

The third new assignment had to do with vocational guidance. This program required a twenty-hour training program to prepare individuals to be counselors at state and associational assemblies, summer camps and adult conferences. Robert Holley, newly appointed associate in the department, was assigned to work with the vocational program.

The problem of having "too many meetings" became common to all the departments in the Baptist Building, particularly as the decade progressed. Changing life styles made it more and more difficult to get volunteers to come to a meeting. But at the same time, added program responsibilities stretched staff members for the central office to the limit. As part of the management by objectives style, Secretary Whitlow agreed to a proposal to limit associational meetings "promoted by the Baptist Building" to twelve a year. Those meeting were allocated four to Sunday School, four to Church Training, and four to the Church Music Department and Brotherhood. The Missions, Evangelism, and Stewardship Departments agreed to "piggy back" on one of those meetings rather than conducting separate meetings of their own.

The combined Mission-Evangelism Program spent the early years of the decade adjusting to its new status. In addition to Superintendent C. W. Caldwell, the office started the decade with the structure adopted in 1958. This included two staff evangelists and two chaplains. M. E. Wiles and Jesse Reed continued their assignments as evangelists; Charles Finch and E. A. Richmond continued their work as chaplains. Lee Dance replaced L. B. Golden and continued the special ministry of City Missions in Pulaski County. In 1966, Dale Barnett joined the department as a Rural Mission worker for North Central Arkansas.

By 1968 the missions side of the office had taken on a number of new ministries. The state's shifting population focused more and more attention on the cities and their attendant problems. Broken homes and single parenting became increasingly evident and some associated that information with the rising juvenile problems. Crime statistics rose dramatically as did the number of individuals incarcerated in the state prison system and county jails. A growing number of Arkansans used their vacation and leisure time to escape the problems of the city and enjoy the state's many resort areas.

The Missions Program responded to each of the above areas. Typically, the office arranged a partnership with a local association or church to employ an individual for a "Special Ministries" project. For example, Johnny Biggs, as a liaison between the families of problem children and the courts, was employed for a ministry in "Juvenile Rehabilitation" in Pulaski County. Bill Bramlett accepted a position, in conjunction with Little Rock's Second Church, to work at Hope House—a halfway program for adult prisoners. Harry Woodall, working with the Central Association and the Home Mission Board, began a resort ministry at Hot Springs National Park. Dr. J. Everett Sneed was employed in 1969 as director of Special Ministries. In addition to juvenile and adult rehabilitation, he also had responsibility for migrant and literacy programs.

By mid-decade, the chaplaincy had developed its own identity as a program area. Richard McNeil became a part-time member of the team in 1965 when he accepted appointment as chaplain for the Girls' Training School at Alexander. He was replaced the next year by Leroy Patterson, pastor of the Alexander Baptist Church—still on a part-time basis. W. W. Heard replaced Boyd Baker as chaplain at the state sanatorium.

In 1968 the Chaplaincy Program was officially organized as a department in the Missions Office. R. H. Dorris was employed as Director of Chaplaincies and began coordinating work at the Girls' and Boys' training schools and at the tuberculosis sanatorium in Booneville. He also began working toward setting up an industrial chaplaincy program.

After 1961, the Executive Board began to place increased emphasis on evangelism. Jesse Reed was appointed associate director of the department in charge of evangelism. This was followed in 1966 with an important new work called the "Student Preaching Program." The idea was to use ministerial students in "financially weak areas to maintain a Baptist witness." Paying these students $25 per week, and 5 cents mileage, the Missions Department was able to continue its outreach in the remote sections of the Ozark region of the state.

Early in the decade, the Missions-Evangelism Program focused on establishing new mission sites and organizing new churches. Superintendent Caldwell committed the department to working closely with the Southern Baptist Convention's campaign to add 10,000 new churches and 20,000 new missions to the SBC family by the end of the decade.

Unfortunately, this area of the work progressed slowly. At the end of the first year Caldwell reported only fifteen new churches organized and "about a like number in missions stations." To assist in this area, the Executive Board created a new office, that of "Church Survey and Development Ministry," in 1962; M. E. Wiles was named director and began a thorough investigation of local church needs.

Part of what Wiles discovered was that volunteer workers among the churches tended to be either extremely long-term or short-term. The former typically developed a tradition or method they were reluctant to change, and the latter did not stay involved long enough to become familiar with ABSC/SBC publications and practices. Wiles retired in 1963 and was replaced by R. A. Hill, a former associate in the Sunday School Office.

Another area in the Missions-Evangelism Program, that of working with Mexican laborers, began to decline sharply after 1962. This was due almost exclusively to the expiration of the U.S.–Mexican Labor Relations Agreement, originally signed in 1948. Superintendent Caldwell noted in his November 1962 report that the work was "considerably decreased this year because so few [Mexicans] are coming as compared to former years."

While work among Mexican migrant workers declined, new opportunities developed elsewhere. A strong "summer mission program," assisted by the Home Mission Board, kept workers "in strategic places,"—particularly the Ozark Mountain region of the state. New work was also begun with deaf people. In 1964 the department joined with First Church Little Rock to employ Joe Johnson for this ministry. In addition to in Little Rock, services for deaf people were also conducted at Mena, Fort Smith, Lake City, Corning, and Fayetteville.

In 1969, evangelism was again separated from the Missions Program and made a new department. Jesse Reed was named director. Clarence Shell Jr. joined the new department as the state rural evangelist.

The Office of Race Relations, created in 1958 following the Little Rock School Crisis. Under the direction of Clyde Hart, the primary purpose of this new office was "to help the Negro Baptist of Arkansas help themselves in developing better churches." In addition to the Reverend Hart, staffing included two missionaries, a chaplain and secretarial support. S. M. Taylor and M. W. Williams were employed as missionaries, Arlis Sims as chaplain, and Lou Alice Watson as office secretary.

The office became operational in 1959, and focused on in-service training for ministers, workshops and clinics for church workers, and a summer camp for children and youth. Missionaries Taylor and Williams assisted Director Hart in conducting the training activities while Chaplain Sims devoted his time to the "Negro Tuberculosis Hospital" at McRae. Beginning in 1961, funding from the Home Mission Board made it possible for the office to employ summer interns to assist with neighborhood Vacation Bible Schools.

Early in the decade Hart and his colleagues focused on four areas for building the work. The first addressed the need for leadership training for both men and women among the older population. Next they turned to the children and youth and organized summer camps— the only camps for black young people in the state. Then Hart enlisted "summer mission volunteers" sent out by the Home Mission Board to conduct community Vacation Bible Schools.

As a final program emphasis, Hart worked to build the Baptist Student Union work at Arkansas AM&N College. This included building a new student center and hiring the Reverend Lacy Solomon as program director. The utility of the center was improved considerably in 1968, with a $15,000 gift from A. O. Smith a layman from Stamps. The money was used to add a chapel to the building.

The department got a major boost in program assistance in 1964, when it received its own space to hold summer camps. The area in question was the site near Ferndale in Western Pulaski County previously used by the Royal Ambassadors and Girls Auxiliary before those groups moved to the newly constructed Camp Paron. Renamed "Hart of the Hills," it was the first of its kind in the state.

Admittedly, the Ferndale camp was a "left-over," and camping was still being done on segregated basis, but at least the Reverend Hart did not have to rent space from the Methodist's camp at Aldersgate as in years past. The Executive Board also allocated $10,000 to improve the facilities before the next camping season. Volunteers from BSU programs throughout the state worked on the renovation under the supervision of Arkansas Tech Director Neil Jackson.

The Office of Race Relations came in for increasing attention during the 1960s. While the 1950s had focused on education, the new decade placed more emphasis on civil rights and voter registration. Federal initiatives in these areas became increasing controversial throughout the South and eventually brought stress into church families and the ABSC.

As has been mentioned, Convention leaders had been sensitive to the race issue since the late 1930s and included a line in the annual budget for Arkansas Baptist College. Periodically, the Convention also did fund raising and sponsored training programs for black church leaders and ministerial students. However, there was mounting concern in some circles that the ABSC should be doing more.

The Woman's Missionary Union under the continued leadership of Nancy Cooper held continuing planning sessions to prepare for "the rapidly changing status of woman [*sic*]." In 1965, WMU joined with the Sunday School Department to host an "Elementary Workshop" to train workers about issues in early childhood education and missions.

In 1961, Director Cooper noted "a regrettable decline in the Lottie Moon Offering for Foreign Missions." Noting that "in every community there are groups of people who will never be reached for the Lord without special attention," she and associates increased their efforts to promote missions. But, as with all areas of church work, it became increasingly difficult to raise enough money to meet program goals. In 1966 Moore commented again that the "WMU shares concern of other church organizations in the slow down in growth."

At Baptist Hospital John A. Gilbreath continued to serve as administrator. Admissions passed the 20,000 mark early in the decade and the demand for space and services continued to increase. The need for

"HART OF THE HILLS" BAPTIST CAMP

FISHING LAKE

SWIMMING POOL AFTER FILLING

INSTRUCTIONS

1. The Camp will be held at new Camp site, near Ferndale on 12th Street Pike.
2. The Registration Fee is $1.00 per person. Registration Fee will be deducted from the total Camp cost. Registrations are accepted and Reservations are made on a First Come, First Served basis. Send Registration Fee to: Rev. M. W. Williams, 1022 West 23rd Street, Little Rock, Arkansas, or Dr. Clyde Hart, Rm. 205, 401 West Capitol Ave., Little Rock, Arkansas.
3. Cost of the Camp to each person will be $12.00. The $1.00 Registration Fee, paid in advance, will be deducted from this amount. This cost includes Room and Board, Insurance, use of Mission Study Book, and material for one Handcraft Project. The total camp fee may be paid at time of Registration. (Special offer — $3.50 on first 80 Campers from each age group.)
4. Each Camper should bring a sheet, pillow, bathing suit, soap, towels, wash cloths, toothbrush and toothpaste, notebook and pencil, and Bible. You may also bring a camera, athletic equipment (especially ball glove), and musical instrument. **Do not bring blanket.**
5. The Camp will open at 12:00 noon on Monday and close at 1:00 P.M. on Friday.
6. All Campers are expected to stay through the ENTIRE CAMP PERIOD, and are not permitted to leave Camp except in case of emergency.
7. There is a TELEPHONE AT CAMP for use in an emergency. If a Camper needs to be contacted, call the CAMP DIRECTOR. He will get in touch with the child. DO NOT CALL THEM.
8. Excellent food, in a well-balanced diet, is served three times daily in the dining room.
9. The Camp Program is built around activities which they love, and which help them toward better manhood and womanhood. The program is well balanced and includes the following basic areas of activity: Worship, Devotion and Inspiration, Singing, Study, Individual Projects, Fun, Play, Guided Recreation, Swimming, Hiking, Exploring, Handcraft, Campcraft, and Group Projects.
10. A Life Guard will be on duty at all Swimming Periods. No Camper will be permitted in the swimming pool area except at regular swim periods when the Life Guard and assistant are on duty.

CONCRETE BOTTOM OF SWIMMING POOL

WORSHIP SERVICE

Following the Little Rock School Crisis in 1957, the ABSC became much more involved in matters related to race relations. One such effort was "Hart of the Hills" Baptist Camp for children and youth in the African-American community.

REV. N. H. McGILL
Counsellor and Teacher

DR. CLYDE HART
Sponsor, Race Relations Dept.

REV. M. W. WILLIAMS
Camp Director and Pastor

BAPTIST YOUTH LEADERSHIP CAMP

JUNIOR BOYS (AGES 8 - 12)   JUNE 28 — JULY 2, 1965
JUNIOR GIRLS (AGES 8 - 12)   JULY 5 — JULY 9, 1965
TEENAGE BOYS (AGES 13 - 17)   JULY 12 — JULY 16, 1965
TEENAGE GIRLS (AGES 13 - 17)   JULY 19 — JULY 23, 1965

Make an Investment in Christian Training of Youth By Sending a Boy or Girl to Camp

ALL CAMPERS NEEDING TRANSPORTATION FROM LITTLE ROCK TO CAMP SITE REPORT TO ARKANSAS BAPTIST COLLEGE, 1600 HIGH STREET, LITTLE ROCK BETWEEN 10:00 A.M. AND 12:00 NOON ON MONDAY, THE BEGINNING DATE OF EACH CAMP.

CAMP GROUNDS

A double-page advertisement for "Hart of the Hills" camp from the Arkansas Baptist *is shown here on facing pages, calling for an investment in training and Christian youth.*

"highly developed tests carried out . . . in modern laboratories" added to patient costs and influenced care. Responding to the rising patent load, the Hospital Board voted in 1962, to acquire Memorial Hospital in North Little Rock. This facility added 118 beds to the system's operation. The board also received approval from the ABSC to borrow $1.2 million for expansion in the Little Rock that same year.

A key to the expansion was a plan to build a mental health unit on site. Offering a wider range of services also made it desirable to broaden the name from Arkansas Baptist Hospital to Arkansas Baptist Medical Center. As the board planned its future activities it became increasingly apparent that changing societal needs and the growing number of regulations from state and federal government made it necessary for the hospital to change its corporate structure. To that end, the board voted in 1964 to organize a separate corporation to construct and operate the mental health unit.

Child care services at Bottoms Baptist Orphanage experienced considerable change during the 1960s. Fifteen-year veteran H. C. Seefeldt retired as superintendent in 1962 and was replaced by J. R. Price. That same year the institution's name was changed to the "Arkansas Baptist Home for Children." This move was taken to be more in line with the name identity of the thirty-two other homes operated by churches in the Southern Baptist Convention.

Price wanted to take the home in a new direction from its traditional, "institutional care" model and convinced the board of the need for change. The new approach focused on a "multiple service approach" that included an adoption program, foster home service, and a mother's aid program. He also took steps to have the home licensed by the Arkansas Department of Public Welfare and to invite the Child Welfare League of America to visit the site and recommend improvements.

The facility's enrollment stayed relatively stable through the decade—ranging between 150 and 200 children. Seefeldt noted that "the number of children needing care [is] double the number [we care] for in any given year," but facilities and budget prevented further expansion.

Another sign of the changing times was reflected in the ABSC's participation in the "Christian Civic Foundation of Arkansas, Inc."

(CCFA). This ecumenical organization among evangelical churches began operation in 1959. Throughout its history, the Convention had been concerned about alcohol, gambling, and similar corrupting influences. Traditionally, Baptist had followed their own course in these areas. However, by the 1960s the enormity of the problem had convinced the ABSC leadership of the need for a new strategy in confronting these issues. President Bernes Selph joined with Secretary Whitlow to encourage ABSC participation in the organization and promoted it among the churches.

The CCFA was organized under the leadership of William E. Brown and focused its early attention on three areas—education, legislation, and gambling. Lee Dance, in addition to his duties with City Missions in Pulaski County, worked closely with Brown in the area of legislation.

For Ouachita College the decade of the 1960s presented twin challenges. On the one hand enrollment continued on a record pace. But this rapid increase made it almost impossible to provide adequate funding and add sufficient space for the new students. President Ralph Phelps made note of this dilemma in his 1960 report to the annual meeting. He pointed out that while enrollment had increased about 110 percent since 1953, "Ouachita's allocation from the Convention has increased only 28.4 percent."

Not only was the total dollar allocation significantly behind enrollment trends but the percentage of Convention funds had also shrunk about 3 percent (18.66 percent to 15.57 percent). Phelps was concerned that Ouachita could not keep pace with competing public institutions and might also be forced to reduce standards if the funding problem was not solved. Messengers responded to this need by approving a board recommendation at the 1962 annual meeting to begin a $2 million endowment campaign. But even though this was a major, even extraordinary, effort on the part of the ABSC, the funding gap continued to widen between Ouachita and neighboring state colleges.

Adding to the funding problem was a growing realization by both Phelps and H. E. Williams at Southern Baptist College that each was competing for the same, limited resources. While neither president wanted to approach that issue directly, each tried in subtle ways to make a case for his institution's special needs before messengers at ABSC's annual meetings.

In his 1963 report Phleps noted that "While other states have fragmented their efforts [and] the quality of their several schools continues to grow poorer, Arkansas Baptists have [united] their efforts in building a first-rate college." President Williams in his report the next year reminded messengers that there were two and a quarter million people within one hundred miles of his institution but that the school was "experiencing developing competition . . . from the Church of Christ." He noted that that group had started a junior college at

Southern Baptist College was chartered in the immediate post-World War II period in partial response to surging college enrollments and the absence of a "Baptist institution" in Northeast Arkansas. Founding President H. E. Williams led efforts to acquire a decommissioned World War II Airbase and used the facilities to open a two-year college. In the 1980s the curriculum was expanded to a four-year program. The institution's name was also changed to Williams Baptist College in honor of its founder.

Paragould, only thirty miles from Southern Baptist College. He concluded, "Arkansas Baptists will not do wisely if they continue to be indifferent to the opportunity Southern Baptist College offers to . . . northeast Arkansas."

Funding was adequate to allow Ouachita to continue to add degree programs and keep them properly maintained. In 1962 all master's degree programs were accredited by the North Central Association and the teacher education program was approved by the National Commission for Accreditation of Teacher Education.

When Broadman Press published Ralph Elliott's commentary "The Message of Genesis" in 1962, President Phelps went to great lengths to reassure messengers to the annual convention that Ouachita was "unashamedly conservative theologically and makes no apology for believing that the Bible is the inspired Word of God." He went on to say that "Christian truth is not served at Ouachita as if it was dispensed through a short-order stand across the street from the school." Rather, it was "part . . . of everything that happens at the school."

Southern Baptist College faced problems similar to Ouachita but not as acute. In the early years of the decade President H. E. Williams concentrated on leading the school to be accredited by the North Central Association. That objective realized in 1963 he then moved to improve the physical facilities and build the endowment.

In 1965, Convention President Walter Yeldell appointed a committee to "study the inclusion of [the college] in the family of Arkansas Baptist institutions." The committee was directed to make a recommendation to the Convention no later than the annual meeting in 1967. However, when that time arrived, Committee Chairman Mason Craig reported that the group still had not been able to reach a decision. The following year the committee did recommend that SBC "be included in the family of Arkansas Baptist institutions." However, the committee touched off a controversy with an additional recommendation that both Southern and Ouachita be brought under the same board of Christian Education. After some debate, messengers voted to reject the second recommendation.

The mounting tensions between the Ouachita-Southern factions in the Convention were symptomatic of larger problems. In a very real sense "culture" had encroached on Baptist life in the 1960s and messengers at the annual meetings were not immune from the influence. It was a turbulent decade, and national public opinion was as divided as it has ever been. And, that division was seen on the floor of every Convention after 1965.

Actually, the first hint of trouble surfaced in February 1964 over a free-speech issue. A member of the Bulgarian Communist party was denied the opportunity to speak at the University of Arkansas in late January. The Reverend James Loudermilk, director of the Methodist Student Center, invited him to give the speech at his center—which he did. Dr. Erwin McDonald defended the Reverend Loudermilk's action in an article in the *Arkansas Baptist Newsmagazine*. Upon reading the editor's comments, twenty-one members of the Concord Association in Western Arkansas passed a resolution condemning McDonald for his statement and demanding that he be fired. The Executive Board received the resolution but voted 45 to 5 to retain Editor McDonald.

The following summer another controversy arose over federal aid to education. In 1963 the U.S. Congress passed the Higher Education Facilities Act which allowed private institutions access to public monies to construct buildings. Ouachita President Ralph Phelps wanted to apply for these funds and gained the support of the college's trustees to do so. But, Phleps got a cool reception to the idea when he presented it to a group of church leaders meeting in Little Rock in August 1965. While admitting Ouachita's need for more classroom space, many in the ABSC were more concerned about accepting "federal aid" being in violation of the denomination's traditional position on "separation of church and state."

At its regular meeting in September, the Executive Board devoted a lengthy discussion to the possibility of using federal funds for construction purposes. *Newsmagazine* editor Erwin McDonald supported Phelps position and suggested the matter be left for the college's trustees to decide. But no consensus had developed on the question when the Convention gathered in November for its annual meeting. Phelps restated his position in his report to the messengers but did not persuade a majority. Rather than endorse the idea, messengers asked President Walter Yeldell to appoint a committee to study the matter. They also voted to allocate an additional $67,500 for higher education and designated over $50,000 of that amount for Ouachita.

Debate on the federal aid issue sparked what a reporter describe as "the most controversial issue in years." Two weeks after the Convention adjourned, an unnamed foundation withdrew a $900,000 gift it had planned for Ouachita, citing the ABSC's refusal to seek federal dollars which could be used as matching funds. President Phelps reported that the foundation's decision, coupled with similar action by individuals, had cost the college over $1.25 million. He also pointed out that other church-sponsored schools, notably Harding University and Hendrix College, were taking advantage of federal funds to improve their facilities and recruit more students. But a majority of ABSC members continued to believe that the liabilities of federal funding outweighed its merits.

In many respects the federal aid issue was caught up in the culture conflict then engaging the state and nation. The long-standing suspicion towards central government and its involvement in private and local matters was reawakened by the Little Rock School Crisis in 1957. It continued to grow with the focus on civil rights and the "Great Society" programs of President Lyndon Johnson. The burgeoning enrollments in higher education, and the "student activism" on social issues that embroiled many college campuses, also became a matter of concern for many of Arkansas's Southern Baptist. The federal funding brought these two concerns together.

This division of thought was best expressed at the ABSC's annual meeting in 1967. Convention President Don Hook, in his address to the messengers, attributed much of the controversy in the larger society to "situational ethics" and said, "A large segment of contemporary society confuses personal freedom with anarchy." While President Hook did not mention college students, Dr. Ralph Phelps understood the remarks to be directed primarily to that audience. In his report for Ouachita, President Phelps responded that "Unless there is a serious attempt on the part of adults to understand the influences that are at work on their own children, . . . the chances of losing [them] permanently from Baptist life is going to increase."

Another matter that divided ABSC members concerned Baptist Hospital. Although the Convention had granted the hospital title to

The ABSC acquired its first central office in 1912 when it rented space on the fourth floor of the Federal Bank and Trust Building, Seventh and Main Streets in Little Rock (opposite page, top). Outgrowing that space, the ABSC office then moved to the 400 block of West Capital Street in Little Rock and rented space on the second floor of this two-story building (opposite page, bottom). In the 1950s the Convention acquired the first floor as well before relocating to its present building (above) at 525 West Capital in 1969. The small building in the foreground was acquired in the 1970s.

the property in 1937, it continued to make annual contributions to the hospital budget. But, as previously mentioned, the complexity of health care—including federal funding—began to change the relationship between the ABSC and the hospital early in the decade. Given these new circumstances, the Hospital Board petitioned the ASBC's Executive Board for approval to sever official ties with the Convention and form a nonprofit corporation. The Executive Board agreed and prepared a resolution to that effect for the 1966 annual meeting.

However, the Executive Board's recommendation to support the hospital's request met with opposition on the Convention floor. A series of motions attempted to block the action. Opponents were concerned that the hospital's new status would allow it to receive federal funds for several programs and violate the Convention's traditional stance on church-state relations. All motions opposing the board's action failed and the recommendation was approved by more than a 60 percent margin.

Following the Convention's action, opponents filed a lawsuit in Pulaski County Chancery Court. The suit asked that the state set aside the Convention's action because the vote had violated the organization's constitution. Chancellor Kay L. Matthews did not agree and ruled in favor of the Executive Board.

Opponents appealed the decision to the state Supreme Court, and while awaiting that court's decision, brought the matter back to the floor in the 1968 Convention. After failing to get the messengers to "strike the word Baptist" from the hospital's official name, the group then moved to amend the ABSC constitution in order to make the previous votes "legal." That effort failed too. Following a ruling also favorable to the Executive Board from the state Supreme Court, the hospital issue was finally put to rest—but not without fueling strong feelings among ABSC members.

A dispute over doctrine became the decade's most troublesome issue for the ABSC. It began in 1965 when the First Baptist Church of Russellville, after "much study" accepted members who had been baptized by another denomination and allowed individuals not members of First Church to a take communion. The church's position was challenged by the local association and messengers to that body voted to "withdraw fellowship" from the Russellville church.

Undeterred by the local action, Russellville FBC elected messengers to the ABSC's Convention meeting later that same year. However, when the Credentials Committee recommended that all messengers, including the two from FBC Russellville, be seated, the Convention as a whole refused. Citing a resolution adopted earlier which placed the ABSC on record "as objecting to the reception of alien immersion and the practice of open communion," messengers rejected the credentials from the Russellville delegation. They also elected Don Hook, author of the resolution on alien immersion and open communion, to be president for the coming year.

The matter of local church practice on baptism and communion stayed before the Convention for the next three years. Before harmony was finally restored on the issue, three more churches (First Baptist, Malvern; University Baptist, Little Rock; and Lake Village Baptist) were dropped from "fellowship" by the ABSC. These churches were ultimately "restored to fellowship" in the Convention. However, the debate not only divided ABSC members, but also, much of it had been carried out in the secular press to the detriment of the Convention's overall work.

But as has happened so often in the history of the ABSC, there were silver linings just when the clouds seemed darkest. Despite the controversies, the Convention did some of its best work during this time. In the area of race relations, the ABSC joined with the Southern Baptist Convention in adopting a "Statement on Equality" that rejected racism and called on all Southern Baptist "to engage in Christian ventures in human relationships, and to take courageous actions for justice and peace." This effort to restore harmony among the races, generations, and regions served as a spring board for the "Crusade of the Americas," a conventionwide evangelistic campaign to take the "gospel message" to every region in America. Refocusing attention the denomination's historic role on missions and evangelism did much to dissipate the doctrinal disputes.

In the last year of a the decade the ABSC also occupied a new headquarters building in Little Rock. The property, a three-story building at 525 West Capital Street and four vacant lots at Sixth and Arch Streets in Little Rock had been purchased in 1967. A former site for the Coca-Cola Bottling Company, remodeling on the building began almost immediately and the new offices were ready June 3, 1969.

Executive Secretary S. A. Whitlow used the transfer from the old Baptist Building to the new as a time to announce his retirement. He returned to the pastorate on a part-time basis. The Executive Board selected Charles H. Ashcraft as the new secretary.

Secretary Whitlow's retirement and the Executive Board staff moving into a new headquarters building was in some ways a parody on Arkansas's Southern Baptists in the 1960s. On the one hand the Convention continued to be steeped in its historical tradition as reflected in its conservative approach to church polity and doctrine. But on the other hand the decade was a time of change, exchanging the old for the new, symbolized by the new Baptist Building and a new administrative team.

15

The 1970s

DESPITE ITS NEW BUILDING AND NEW EXECUTIVE director, the Arkansas Baptist State Convention began the 1970s on a down note. The "Committee of Twenty-Five," created by the messengers to the 1969 annual meeting to resolve the church ordinance dispute, symbolized the trouble in the ABSC fellowship. Appointed by incoming ABSC President Tal Bonham (1969–1970), the new committee met throughout the summer in an effort to reach a consensus. But the group was unable to find common ground and was forced to ask the 1970 Convention for another year to study the matter.

The committee met several times in 1971 and gradually reached consensus on a report to present to the annual meeting. West Helena pastor Wilson C. Deese, chairman of the committee, said the group recommended that "all duly elected messengers from regular Baptist churches" be seated as messengers. Regular Baptists were defined as "those Baptist churches which in doctrine and in practice adhere to the principles and the spirit of The *Baptist Faith and Message*" adopted by the Southern Baptist Convention in 1963. The committee also recommended that the ABSC Constitution be amended to reflect this definition of "regular Baptist" and to accept the *Baptist Faith and Message* as "the doctrinal guideline for this Convention."

The troubled emotions of the preceding decade had also taken a toll and contributions to the Cooperative Program began to slip. In one of his first major decisions Executive Secretary Charles Ashcraft recommended to the Executive Board in December 1969 that funding for most program areas be reduced by 1 percent in the coming year. While total receipts were still greater than the preceding year, the increase was not enough to meet the budget formula adopted in 1964.

To counter this decline in giving, Secretary Ashcraft also recommended that the board plan a promotional emphasis among the churches to increase giving. Under President Dr. W. O. Vaught Jr.'s leadership, the board developed a three-year campaign to call attention to needs among ABSC programs and encourage churches to help. Messengers to the 1970 Convention approved the board's recommendation.

The first year of the campaign, beginning in 1971, focused on increasing support for the Southern Baptist Convention's Cooperative Program. The plan called for each church affiliated with the ABSC to give a minimum of 10 percent of its undesignated contributions to the Cooperative Program. The second and third years of the campaign were to be devoted to raising $3 million for Christian education. The funds were proportionally shared by Ouachita Baptist University and Southern Baptist College. OBU was highlighted in 1972, and SBC received the promotional attention in 1973.

The Ouachita-Southern fund-raising campaign proved to be a transforming experience for the ABSC. In addition to both schools working together in a mutually beneficial way, their direct appeal to the churches gave many local congregations an opportunity to hear first hand about events on the campuses and within the ABSC as well. Being asked to be a part of a statewide campaign was well received by most churches, and they responded enthusiastically to call. W. O. Vaught, who served as chairman, announced in early 1974 that the campaign had reached its goal.

Meanwhile, promotional efforts for the Cooperative Program continued. After the special emphasis year in 1971, newly elected Associative Executive Secretary, Roy Lewis, a pastor from Lilburn, Georgia, was assigned to continue promotional efforts for the CP.

Lewis replaced Ralph Douglas, who retired at the end of 1970 after seventeen years of service to the ABSC.

Lewis's joining the Baptist Building team was the primary reason for an Executive Board decision to rename the Stewardship Department the Stewardship-Cooperative Program Department.

In an effort to be more responsive to needs created by the state's shifting demographics, messengers to the 1970 Convention asked the Executive Board to "study the existing district boundaries." Board President Vaught, pastor of Little Rock's Immanuel Church, assigned that project to the Operating Committee, chaired by E. E. Boone. The OC spent most of the year reviewing various options and realignments among the ABSC's eight districts.

While there were pros and cons for more districts, as well as fewer districts, the committee came to see that there were two overriding points to consider. One was committee members' belief that "the initiative to change boundaries should come from the churches or associations" not mandated from Little Rock. A second point was based on the fact that the program areas in the Baptist Building were organized to promote the work of the ABSC and the SBC through the districts. In view of these factors, the committee recommended that no changes be made in the district boundaries.

The "districts study" also gave the Executive Board an opportunity to reexamine its relationship with the local associations. As has been mentioned, associations played a critical role in organizing and perpetuating the ABSC's work. However, after the 1950s that relationship began to undergo some changes. As the associations became more financially secure, the role of the "state missionary" also began to change. Gradually, funding for this position was phased out at the state level and the work was taken over at the local level by a "Secretary of Missions." Initially this position was primarily to coordinate work among the local churches, However, with the many programmatic changes coming from the SBC in Nashville and the ABSC in Little Rock, that office too began to change.

By the 1970s the secretary of Missions' responsibilities had evolved into the office of director of Missions (DOM). Part administrator, part pastor, sometimes evangelists, and counselor, the DOM became a vital link between the state office and the local church. Modernization in communication and transportation made it possible for a director to be in almost instant contact with Little Rock or his home churches. Being the "bridge" between the program strategies of Baptist Building and the application of those strategies in the local churches gave the DOMs tremendous influence and responsibility.

Rising administrative expenses in the early 1970s forced the Executive Board to further reevaluate its structure. Both Ouachita and Southern continued to be burdened with high inflationary costs as did the Family and Child Care Services agency. In partial response to those needs, Secretary Ashcraft asked the board to authorize a statewide, Ouachita-Southern fund-raising campaign beginning in 1972. He also asked the board to reconsider the budget formula used for funding ABSC programs that had been adopted in 1964.

The board adopted both of Secretary Ashcraft's recommendations. Under the new budget formula, effective August 1972, "Christian education" (i.e. Ouachita and Southern), the Arkansas Baptist Family and Child Care Services, and the Arkansas Baptist Foundation each received a significant percentage increase for new money contributed above base funding. The new formula and special funds raised in the Ouachita-Southern Higher Education Campaign gave temporary relief to a near crisis in funding for the educational institutions.

The 1970s also saw a new reorganization among staff in the Baptist Building in 1973. At Secretary Ashcraft's recommendation, and under the leadership of Executive Board President Dillard S. Miller, the board reevaluated the office alignment of the central staff. The new structure relieved the executive secretary of some administrative detail and increased the responsibilities of the assistant to the secretary. In a related matter, the board also approved an Office of Information Services to assist church staff workers in finding positions of service. This new office became operational in January 1974.

Changes in family lifestyles and demographic patterns led to additional ministries by the ABSC. The national energy crisis in the early 1970s accelerated a trend of retirees moving into the state from Northern states and the Midwest. This trend began in the 1960s and grew rapidly in the 1970s. By the end of the decade Arkansas ranked second in the nation in the percentage of population over age sixty-five. Responding to this, the Executive Board authorized an extensive study on possible "ministries to the aging." Based on that study the board recommended in 1979 that the Convention employ a "Director of Development for Ministry to the Aging." That person was to assist in establishing an "Arkansas Baptist Retirement Village" and to work with churches and associations in establishing local ministries to the aging.

The board also approved an "employee annual evaluation," and established a grade and salary scale for personnel in the Baptist Building, beginning in 1975, and agreed to pay board and ABSC committee members 15 cents per mile for official Convention business. The ABSC's first computer was installed for the accounting services section in 1976, and in 1977 the board approved Secretary Ashcraft's request to purchase five cars on a "two-year trial basis" for use by those employees "who traveled the most." Just who those employees were, was left for the secretary to decide.

As the decade of the 1970s progressed, ABSC member churches became increasingly aware of social attitudes on a number of issues. Sometimes joining with the SBC in Southwide programs, other times acting alone, the messengers to the annual meetings asked the Executive Board to become involved in more and more social causes.

Beginning in 1974, the board joined with the SBC to promote an annual Race Relations Day. The next year Arkansas joined with other Southern Baptist to call attention to world hunger and take special offerings on World Hunger Sunday.

In 1976 the ABSC joined with the SBC to celebrate the nation's Bicentennial with a "Life and Liberty" campaign. Each department in the Baptist Building developed individual goals relating to this central theme. These departmental goals culminated in a statewide Life and Liberty evangelistic rally at War Memorial Stadium in Little Rock. Special guests for the rally were Paul Harvey, Anita Bryant, and National Baptist Minister Manuel Scott.

The rally sparked a great deal of enthusiasm among Arkansas's Southern Baptist. Contributions, which had been increasing significantly since 1973, surged ahead, and the Executive Board was able to fill a large number of "wish list" needs beginning in 1977. New positions were added in the Missions, Church Music, and Stewardship Departments.

Evaluating the list of needs that had accumulated over the years caused Secretary Ashcraft to conclude that the central staff needed more restructuring. With board approval, a new Office of Business Services was created to coordinate the internal affairs of the Baptist Building. Roy Lewis, already serving as an assistant to Secretary Ashcraft, was made associate executive secretary and placed in charge of the new department.

The Arkansas Baptist Foundation became one of the bright spots for the Convention in the 1970s. After struggling for more than two decades to establish identity among the state churches, the patient efforts of Secretary Ed McDonald Jr. to keep the foundation's mission before the churches and associations began to pay off. The ABF also received considerable assistance from Secretary Ashcraft, who had worked with a similar foundation in New Mexico. Ashcraft knew the value of such a program and encouraged McDonald in his work.

Foundation assistance was an important contribution to the Ouachita-Southern fund-raising campaign in 1972, particularly in the area of deferred giving. By the 1970s Secretary McDonald had developed quite an expertise in discussing the advantages of "Estate Planning" and gave frequent seminars on that topic among the churches. The cumulative effect of his encouraging members to designate ABSC programs in their wills began to have an impact by the end of the decade.

The *Arkansas Baptist Newsmagazine* broadened its coverage in the 1970s. Traditionally given high marks by its peers in the publication business, editor Erwin McDonald moved to enhance the *Newsmagazine's* reputation and improve the quality and quantity of its reporting. In addition the regular mission of "helping its readers to keep informed on what is going on in the denomination and the world around us," the *Newsmagazine* also tried to stay in touch with Baptist opinions and attitudes. A new section "The People Speak" gave readers an opportunity to "express their own views and take issues with views contrary to their own."

McDonald's retirement in 1972, after fifteen years of service, brought J. Everett Sneed to the editor's chair. Sneed, formerly director of Special Ministries for the ABSC, was particularly interested in "increasing the coverage of local news from the churches." He asked each association to elect a reporter and promised more space in the paper for individual and church news.

Addition of new staff members Betty Kennedy, managing editor, and Millie Gill, staff writer, helped the *Newsmagazine* to broaden its coverage. Kennedy soon established herself as an award winner by receiving state and national recognition for excellence in layout and design. Gill's writing and photography skills and the addition of Danna Sample as a second staff writer in 1979 allowed the paper to cover local church news in greater detail and provided a more personal feel at the paper for ABSC members.

In the mid-1970s inflationary pressures began driving up the costs of paper and postage. For example mailing costs increased from $14,000 in 1972 to more than $60,000 in 1979, and newsprint increased almost $7,000 a year during the same time period. Editor Sneed work to counter these new expenses by adding subscribers and increasing advertising revenue. However, the increase in cost was to great to be borne by the existing rates, and he was forced to raise subscription prices. In 1904, when the original "church family plan" was adopted, the price per subscription had been approximately $2.00 per year. It remained essentially unchanged until 1975, when Sneed began to increase the price in small increments. By 1980 the price for the church plan had risen to $3.12, still minimal by most standards but an unusual change for the *Newsmagazine* in a few short years.

In a major reorganization step in 1979, the ABSC Executive Board recommended that the *Newsmagazine* be allowed to operate under a separate board beginning in 1980. The recommendation was for a three-year trial period to determine if the paper would function better as a separate entity. During that time a special committee was appointed to monitor the paper's performance and make a recommendation to the 1983 annual convention as to whether the arrangement should be made permanent.

Director Tom Logue worked hard to keep the Baptist Student Union program and mission relevant to the changing moods of college students. The enrollment boom of the 1960s began to subside in the 1970s and the "issue oriented" student body began to become introspective. Nevertheless, some traditions continued—including the annual "spring-break week" which saw thousands of student from all over the nation travel to the beaches of Florida. Arkansas's BSU students traveled there too, but as missionaries to witness and hand out evangelistic literature.

Other students not involved with the Florida project, used the week of spring break to do work projects in Home Mission sites and with their local communities. Added emphasis was also given to campus evangelism as Arliss Dickerson, new director at Henderson State, coordinated a pilot program in this area for the 1971–1972 school year. The emphasis featured special Bible study groups and WIN (Witness Involvement Now) Week at each of the twenty-one college campuses where BSU had a presence.

The "spring break missionaries" received international attention in 1972 when CBS Television and the Associated Press Newsservice did a story on thirty-two BSU students from Arkansas doing mission work in a ghetto area of Baltimore, Maryland. The military publication *Stars and Stripes* also carried the story in its overseas editions. Contrasting the self-indulgence of students on Florida beaches, the story noted the influence of Christianity in these students' lives and their commitment to service to others.

In the mid-1970s the BSU began an new ministry to international students. Since joining the ABSC in 1955, Director Logue had a concern for students from other countries on Arkansas's college campuses. But, their limited number and other more pressing needs forced him to delay plans for implementing a special program for internationals.

By 1974 foreign student enrollment exceeded 1,000, and while still small, the students' social needs and the evangelism opportunity, caused Logue to begin phasing in this ministry. The first step created a host family program which paired an international student with a family active in a local ABSC church. Janet Williams coordinated the assignments in Little Rock area, Maureen Thompson continued a similar effort in Conway, and Mrs. Gary Gray extended the work to Fayetteville. The host family, coupled with an annual International Student Conference, which began in the fall of 1974, represented unique efforts on the part of Arkansas's Southern Baptist to reach students from other countries.

The BSU's participation in the nation's bicentennial celebration was called "Project '76"—a strategy to "present the Gospel and share the Word" with students at each residential campus in the state. By the time messengers met for the 1976 annual meeting, Director Logue could report that the campaign had been highly successful. Not only had BSU students reached their contemporaries, but they had also extended their witnessing into the communities as well.

Messengers to the 1976 Convention also approved BSU's request to be selected for a special fund-raising effort. Called the "Third Century Campaign" it was the only statewide funding appeal for BSU in the ABSC's history. The strategy called for a three-year campaign to raise $1 million for a BSU endowment. Interest income from the fund was designated for a wide range of special projects on an annual basis. Jamie Jones took temporarily leave from his position at the University of Arkansas to serve as director of the campaign.

Changes in state government in the 1970s to allow and encourage the growth of community colleges led to a need for more campus BSU directors. During the 1970s it also became necessary to remodel and rebuild student centers—particularly those built in the 1950s. New buildings were erected at Arkansas Tech (1970), Arkansas State at Beebe (1971), and the University of Arkansas at Little Rock; and major remodeling was done at Arkansas A&M (1970) and at the University of Central Arkansas (1976). As in previous years, Director Logue continued to work with local churches and area associational committees for funding, voluntary labor, and technical expertise. For example, the ASU-Beebe center was built under the direction of Director Don Norrington using only volunteer labor—the first building to be so constructed.

The Brotherhood Department in the 1970s emphasized its role in missions education. The Royal Ambassador Program increased in enrollment and participation through most of the decade, but a declining number of adult workers began to limit activities as the 1970s neared an end. Associate Director C. H. Seaton, named director in 1973, placed emphasis on worker-training and held regular statewide training opportunities for leaders working with both men and boys.

As the Brotherhood work became more established, leaders of the various local units became increasingly interested in mission work projects and disaster relief. In 1976 a major earthquake in Guatemala gave opportunity to combine both of these activities. The state office organized a team of sixteen volunteers and made travel arrangements to allow them to work for a week at the site. The enthusiasm from this group served as the basis for creating a "disaster team" specifically trained to deal with physical emergencies.

Secretary Seaton also followed the national office's lead in putting emphasis on men and the family. Using the Camp Paron facilities, the state office sponsored a series of conferences beginning in 1976 on "Family Life and the Role of the Father in the Home."

Camp Paron played a vital role in Brotherhood work. Not only did the camp serve as the basis for the RA Summer Program, but also it became the center for weekend retreats and special workshops for leaders in men's work. In fact, demands for the camp's services reached the point in 1971 to merit special attention. Seaton, in addition to his Brotherhood work was named manager for Paron and coordinated activities for other ABSC agencies wishing to use the camp. By 1973 Paron was running a full schedule from June through August. The Royal Ambassadors used June for their summer camp programs, the Girls Auxiliary had July, and the month of August was, as well as all weekends, reserved for special needs from other groups.

Increased use meant a greater need for facilities. Throughout the decade, a number of Brotherhood and older RA chapters donated their time to add and remodel buildings at Paron. An infirmary building, a snack shack, and a camp store were all completed in 1974.

The Church Music Department began the decade with a new director. Ural C. Clayton left his position as minister of music at Little Rock's Immanuel Church to become the fourth secretary for the department in August 1970. He resigned in June 1972 to return to a church staff, this time as Minister of Music at First Church Little Rock. Clayton was replaced by Ervin Keathley who joined the program in 1973.

Secretary Keathley, while leaving the department's mission, remained largely unchanged, did place a major emphasis on outreach and meeting a variety of needs. The program continued to focus on teaching music; training people to lead and play music; providing music in the church and community; and providing and interpreting information regarding the church and denomination. The training function received a major boost in January 1972 when the Sunday School Board launched a new program for preparing volunteers to work with the methods and materials of church music. Using concepts learned in an intensive two-day training program in Nashville this group of specialists then conducted workshops in each of the state's eight districts to train other specialists in all aspects of the Church Music Program workshop.

In addition to these special workshops, the department carried out its mission by using the traditional workshops, festivals and summer music camps for children, youths, and adults. A special emphasis on training leaders for preschool and children's choirs began after 1971, as was a new program for volunteer and part-time directors, instituted in 1973.

Under this consistent format, church music programs became increasingly complex as the number of people trained began to a accumulate. While new music forms began to make an appearance, for example cantatas were widely popular among the larger churches, variety was still the adjective to describe church music in the 1970s.

In 1975 PraiSinging premiered a new edition of the *Baptist Hymnal*. Handbell ringing also saw increased emphasis as the decade progressed. The training and variety in music also contributed to a greater interest. In 1974, ABSC churches led the Southern Baptist Convention in the percentage of growth in music enrollment. The SBC averaged a 6.8 percent increase while Arkansas had a 13 percent gain. Much of this growth was attributed to the multiple outreach efforts led by Secretary Keathley.

Growth in the number of programs among the churches created a need for more staff support in the central office. In 1978 the board approved an associate position for the department and Secretary Keathley recruited Glen Ennes for the job. Ennes, a former public school band instructor, was assigned to work with instrumental groups and with small churches.

In the mid-1970s the Church Music Program became increasingly involved in evangelistic efforts. Beginning in 1974 a twenty-seven member team traveled to Alaska to provide music leadership for a week-long series of revivals. This team also conducted workshops on church music in the host churches prior to revival services.

For Ralph Davis, who began his twenty-fifth year as director of the Church Training Department, the work became an even greater challenge. With Robert Holley, his only full-time associate, the two tried to meet an ambitious mission. The last restructuring in the 1960s added "church recreation" and the "church library" to the department's training areas. A new emphasis on "vocational guidance" and "family ministry" coming out of the national office in Nashville brought still further change to the department. The traditional work in "training union" and "church administration" was forced to compete for attention.

Undeterred, Davis, Holley, and a staff of trained volunteers worked closely with churches and associations to provide training throughout the state. The task was to assist local churches to do a better job in reaching their respective communities. No two congregations were alike, but the Church Training Department offered programs to orient new Christians about the functions of the church, prepare leaders for the specific duties of their respective church office, and assist members to better understand the theology, ethics, history, and polity of Southern Baptist organization and development.

Working with pastors and deacons also became an important part of the Church Training Program. Using special retreats for "deacons only," "pastors only," as well as joint meetings of both groups, a team of consultants went throughout the state to meet with these groups and train them in their unique roles in church leadership.

As the summer camp programs became more developed at both state and associational levels, the need for vocational guidance increased. The department trained counselors to assist "those who felt God calling them to a church vocation," as well as those making decisions about salvation.

Training in using recreation as a church program also became an integral part of the department's work. This program, initially coordinated by volunteer consultant Jim Maloch at Little Rock's Second Church, became increasingly important as Arkansans turned more and more to leisure time activities, as the decade progressed. Using the state youth convention, special workshops, and local church consultation, the department assisted churches in planning a program in recreation to reach specific audiences.

The new program in Family Ministry, assigned to the department in 1970, had a slow beginning. Needs in this area were complex, required special training, and had not previously been a part of ABSC work. But, with generous support from the national office in Nashville, the Church Training staff prepared for what proved to be a growing need among the churches. Initial training focused on three areas: church-home cooperation, education for marriage, and family living and care.

Ralph Davis stepped down as director following the 1973 annual meeting and the board named Robert Holley as the new director. Davis continued to serve in the department until his retirement in May 1974. When he began in 1945 churches reported almost 46,000 enrolled in Training Unions in the state. At Convention time in 1973 there were 84,009 enrolled. But while Davis had seen significant growth on his watch, the long-term trends on enrollment were not good. Beginning in 1962, the number of people enrolled in Training Union programs declined every year except one until 1974.

Mindful of these numbers, Bob Holley made a determined effort to reverse the decline. Joining with the SBC in his first year as director, Holley and new Associate Gerald Jackson, pushed "Church: the Sunday Night Place for Experiencing Discipleship," as a way to generate new interest. But, the new emphasis had only limited success. Attendance bounced back for two years but then returned to their decade long decline.

Faced with an erosion in the traditional program, the Church Training team turned to more innovative approaches to reach people. One new approach came in the area of family ministry. Although that program had been added to the unit's mission in 1970, it was a complex program to implement and had been largely neglected. However, beginning in 1975 with a Marriage Enrichment Retreat, the department placed more emphasis on this area of meeting needs. Additional conferences were conducted on "Family Enrichment," "Engaged Couples," and "Single Adults."

The expanded areas of training and mounting problems among the state's youth, demonstrated a need for another staff member. Secretary

Ashcraft included the department's request in his 1978 recommendations to the Executive Board. The board approved that request and Bill
Faulkner was invited to joined the department as an associate for youth
work. Faulkner's responsibilities included youth ministry, church recreation, and vocational guidance.

Having a wide range of training programs, and additional staff,
helped the department to stabilize the decline in enrollments. Holley
and his staff were far from satisfied with the numbers, but even so, the
department ended the decade ranked second in the SBC in the
percentage of churches reporting Training Union programs.

Other efforts to assist churches achieve their mission included a
New Member Training Program.

As the decade began, Evangelism Secretary Jesse Reed noted that
"Everyone is in favor of evangelism and talks in favor of it, but when it
comes right down to doing it we find it hard work." Indeed that work
got harder as the decade wore on. Reed, and Associate Clarence Shell,
stressed that "evangelism is the function of the whole church" and
worked to equip pastors and church leaders with the skills needed for
evangelism.

Evangelism training programs used a variety of methods. Beginning
in 1971, the department cooperated with the Southern Baptist
Convention in promoting the WIN (Witness Involvement Now)
Program for presenting "the Good News." Secretary Reed, who became
director of Evangelism in 1971, emphasized that "enthusiasm" was "an
essential factor" in carrying out the work. The WIN Program was
complemented by a WOW (Win Our World) emphasis targeted
primarily for youth and college students. Those programs were in turn
supported by a PREP (Presenting Revival and Evangelism Preparation)
team and a TELL (Train Evangelistic Lay Leaders) Program. Also by
the end of the decade, Secretary Reed had also purchased a "revival
tent" to use in "Area Crusades" as an appeal to people uncomfortable
attending church.

To set an example in evangelism, Secretary Ashcraft designated
Thursday afternoon of each week as a time for "personal witnessing"
and allowed any member of Baptist Building staff to take time away
from the building to do personal visitation. The department also
encouraged churches to observe the annual "Soul-Winning

Commitment Day" scheduled in January, and continued to host the annual State Evangelism Conference—typically held in January too. These statewide promotions were supplemented with "Area Evangelism Conferences" that targeted specific associations.

In 1974, the board appointed Dick King as precollege associate in the department. This new position recognized the growing importance of evangelism among young people. As one of his first activities, King organized the ABSC's first statewide Youth Evangelism Conference. Held in Little Rock, the conference not only provided the young people with an outstanding slate of evangelistic speakers, but also, youth leaders were trained in a variety of methods for presenting the message of salvation.

King only stayed with the department for one year before joining the staff at University Baptist in Fayetteville. He was replaced by Neal Guthrie who continued the strong youth outreach with a WOW (Win Our World) Program for training youth and their leaders in personal evangelism. Guthrie was replaced by West Kent when the latter moved to the Brotherhood Department in 1979.

Adopting a "lifestyle evangelism" strategy the Missions Office worked hard in the ABSC's "Life and Liberty" campaign during the year-long celebration of the nation's bicentennial. A central part of this campaign was a series of simultaneous revivals among the churches. Over a five-week period, 596 ABSC churches participated in the revivals and reported 3,100 professions of faith.

The bicentennial rally was a good motivator for the SBC's "Bold Mission Thrust" campaign scheduled to begin in 1978. The excitement in seeing over three thousand people saved convinced many of Arkansas's Southern Baptist that the national goal of allowing every person in the United States to hear and respond to the Gospel was a real possibility.

For J. T. Elliff and his staff in the Missions Department, the 1970s expanded areas of opportunity in new types of work. As has been mentioned, the growing interest in leisure activities by Arkansans and the American public had a significant impact on all phases of church work. In the missions area a new program in "Resort Missions" offered great potential. This "need" also provided an opportunity the department to cooperate with other agencies in the Baptist Building—particularly the

BSU program. Assisted by the Home Missions Department of the SBC, the ABSC Missions Program was able to employ BSU summer missionaries and other volunteers to work the numerous resort areas throughout the state. To reach people in this new "mission field," Directors Elliff and Logue designed a pilot program for one of the state's largest resort areas at Lake Ouachita. Placing a "camper" at the lake, the directors then selected two students to live "on site" and provide special weekday recreational activities for children and youth followed by a flexible worship service on selected evenings and Sunday.

Success at the Lake Ouachita location led to the program being extended to other sites in the state—including Fairfield Bay and Bella Vista. Associations and churches located near resort areas also became involved in this ministry. By the middle of the decade the Missions Department found it necessary to host an annual "resort ministry" conference to assist churches in this work.

Secretary Elliff resigned from the department just before the annual Convention in 1971, and moved to Oklahoma. He had devoted many years of service to the ABSC. The board appointed R. H. Dorris, director of Chaplaincies, as the new secretary of Missions. He began his work in November 1971.

The Chaplain Ministry also experience significant growth in the 1970s. From a staff of one in the 1940s at single institution, the program had grown to sixteen members by 1970 and had chaplains serving not only in hospitals but also in state institutions, military bases, and private industry. As with the resort ministry, this program too reflected changing cultural patterns in the state and nation.

Military chaplaincy saw the greatest program increase. The build-up in Vietnam in the mid-1960s that continued for almost a decade, and the attendant problems which lingered much longer, placed a premium on chaplaincy skills. By 1970 the Missions Department had two chaplains placed at Little Rock Air Force Base and sixteen "Baptist pastors" specifically trained to work with military reserve units in the state. This need continued through 1975 when the military withdrawal from Vietnam began to ease the demand somewhat.

Ironically, as the military need began to subside, a new area of need developed in private industry. Oak Lawn Farms, Inc., a private company at Pine Bluff, had become the first industry in the state to employ a resident chaplain when company officials hired Henry Jacobs, a pastor in Osceola in 1970. This business-industry area continued to expand through the decade as small community industries, nursing homes, motels, and hospitals began to recognize the value of having access to a chaplain. Typically, these institutions used pastors at local Baptist churches to serve as the "staff chaplain." But it also gave the ABSC an opportunity to expand its ministry and meet new needs in a changing society.

Other chaplains joining the department in 1970 included Dewie E. Williams, a Tennessean who became the chaplain at Cummins Prison, and Marion O. Reneau, a Texan, assumed chaplain duties at the Girls' Training School in Pine Bluff. Larry P. Henderson was appointed in 1975 to fill a vacancy at the Boys' Training School at Pine Bluff when E. A. Richmond died. W. H. Heard, after ten years of service, took early retirement from the sanatorium at Booneville in 1976. Chris Copeland was elected to replace Chaplain Heard.

With the increase need in the chaplaincy area, the Baptist Medical Center began offering a six-weeks "in residence" course to provide training for new chaplains. In addition to cosponsoring the Medical Center's program, the Missions Department also began conducting "Clinical Pastoral Education Seminars" for chaplains at eight designated sites in the state and hosting an annual Conference for Chaplains at Camp Paron.

After Clyde Hart retired from the Cooperative Ministries Department, the program was reorganized and placed under the administrative responsibilities of the Missions Department. Director Elliff recruited Robert U. Ferguson from a pastorate in Mobile, Alabama, in May 1970 to head the new office. Work with the National Baptist Convention continued much as it had in the 1960s. Significant attention was devoted to the BSU program at Arkansas AM&N in Pine Bluff, and summer camps at Hart of the Hills continued to be held for children and youth. But attendance began to decline, and in 1973 the camping season was reduced to just a two-week program.

Extension classes for in-service training continued to attract pastors and church leaders at Augusta, Camden, El Dorado Fordyce, Helena, Hot Springs, Lewsville, Malvern, Little Rock, and West

Memphis. Also, a new program implemented by Director Ferguson created a "joint committee" made up from National and Southern Baptist leaders at the associational level to advise him on local needs in various areas. Joint Committees were organized at Camden, Helena, Pine Bluff, West Memphis, and Little Rock. From churches in theses communities, the joint-committee concept extended to associational level. Committees were formed in the Arkansas Valley, Bartholomew, Calvary, Central, Harmony, North Pulaski, Pulaski, and Tri-County Associations.

In 1974, the National Baptist work was reorganized and again made an independent program called the Department of Cooperative Ministries with National Baptist. Robert Ferguson was named director and reported directly to the executive secretary.

Work with deaf people also grew in the 1970s. Led by C. F. Landon, the Missions Department assisted twelve churches and sixteen Sunday schools in meeting the need of deaf members. In addition to conducting weddings, funerals, and interpreting for court cases, the program also provided a retreat for deaf students and conducted classes to train interpreters.

Robert Parrish assumed responsibility for the Deaf Ministries Program in 1973 and three years later was assigned additional responsibilities as director of Language Ministries. This new Office of Language Missions was a joint project between the Home Mission Board and the ABSC's Missions Department. In addition to existing ministries to the deaf, the Spanish, and the Vietnamese, Parrish was asked to formulate plans to extend service to other language groups as needed. Parrish resigned in 1978 and was replaced by Pete Petty, former director of missions in Washington-Madison Association.

Early in the decade, changes in federal policy provided an opportunity to reopen the Migrant Missions Center in Hope. When the Migratory Labor Agreement was not renewed in 1964, seasonal workers in the state all but ceased to exist. However, new legislation in 1968 led to a growing number of new immigrants from Mexico and in May 1972 the board authorized the Missions Department to reopen the center. More than 30,000 "migrants" stopped at the center during the first six months of its operation and provided the ABSC with another fertile field for evangelism.

Work among migrant workers led to a Spanish-speaking mission being organized in Little Rock, the first ethnic, church-sponsored mission in the state. Sponsored by the Lakeshore Drive church, the Pulaski Association, the ABSC's Missions Department, and the Home Mission Board, the new mission began work in 1975 under the leadership of Pastor Donosco Escobar. By 1978 the state's Hispanic population had increased enough for the Bartholomew Association, using ministerial students from Ouachita, to open a Bible study/worship center at Warren.

Federal officials' decision to relocate 50,000 refugees from the war in Vietnam gave the department another missions opportunity. The initial strategy was to develop a host-family program by using ABSC churches to place Vietnamese individuals and/or families with Christian families throughout the state. By the end of the decade, Laotian and Cambodian families had been added to this ministry and Grand Avenue Church in Fort Smith provided worship services with Vietnamese and Laotian interpreters.

As mentioned elsewhere in this text, changing settlement patterns in the state caused all the ABSC programs to make adjustments in strategies for outreach. For the Missions Program an important area lay in acquiring sites for new work. Suburbs became a factor around the state's largest cities, and the retirement boom, which continued through the 1970s, brought new communities into existence. Secretary Dorris and the Missions Program team spent a great deal of time analyzing where the new "bedroom communities" would develop and preparing space there to establish a new church.

A significant boost in new property acquisition came as part of the Missions Department's response to the Life and Liberty campaign. Director Dorris set a goal of adding fifty new churches to the ABSC during the two years the campaign was going on. Calling the strategy "50 FOR THE FUTURE," he reported eighteen new churches in 1975 and twenty-five in 1976. While the forty-three fell short of the goal, the 21.5 average far exceeded the ten-year average (1963–1973) of 7.3. However, a troubling note emerged when the full results of the campaign were tabulated. A combination of population shifts, mergers, and realignments, caused the net gain over the two-year period to only be fifteen new churches. When the same criteria were applied to the preceding decade, the ABSC's net averaged was only one new church per year.

The drive to establish new churches continued under the Bold Mission Thrust Program of the Southern Baptist Convention. The ABSC Missions Department set a goal of adding twenty new churches per year through 1982 when the first phase of Bold Mission was completed. Also a part of the Bold Mission strategy was a plan to match state conventions in traditional Southern Baptist territory with pioneer work outside the South. The ABSC agreed to cooperate with the Indiana Baptist Convention beginning in 1978. This cooperation took the form of simultaneous revivals throughout Indiana. Over one hundred pastors and church staff members from Arkansas participated in the crusades.

By mid-decade the Missions Program also became involved in a "continuing education" program. The various seminaries sponsored by the SBC developed an extension program to provide seminary training for place bound students. An extension center opened in Little Rock in 1974, named the Boyce Bible Institute, under the coordination of Dr. W. T. Holland. While initial enrollment was slow, interest began to increase after 1976 and remained stable through the decade.

Secretary Dorris resigned in 1979 and was replaced by Conway Sawyers.

To stimulate lagging contributions to the Cooperative Program, Annuity Secretary T. K. Rucker organized a statewide workshop at Camp Paron and five "Area-Wide" workshops to encourage giving. He also publicized the names of those churches who gave the highest percentage of their budget for CP causes. This was a good start toward reversing a troublesome trend at the state level. However, most church leaders recognized the Cooperative Program was in need of major revision and the Stewardship Commission at SBC headquarters in Nashville took steps to do this.

Hosting its first ever "National Stewardship Seminar" in April 1971, the Stewardship Commission made an all-out effort to revive support for Cooperative Program giving. The various state conventions followed this lead and adopted changes at the state level. As has been mentioned, for Arkansas this meant restructuring the office, extending its duties, and adding personnel. The new office became the Stewardship-Cooperative Program, and Roy Lewis was recruited from Georgia to become the new secretary.

Lewis had been deeply involved in the Stewardship Commission's new strategy and wasted little time in implementing a similar plan in Arkansas. In essence his approach was to use personal contact, space in the *Newsmagazine*, and a variety of printed materials to inform ABSC churches about needs in the program. These tried and proven techniques had been utilized by the SBC since the Cooperative Program was established in 1925, and they began to payoff again. In July, Lewis reported that a new record had been set in giving to the Cooperative Program and a "new spirit of optimism seems to prevail among Arkansas Baptist."

Building on the renewed momentum, Lewis led the ABSC churches to participate in Operation One, a SBC-wide, three-year emphasis on Cooperative Program giving. Beginning in 1973 and culminating in 1975 with the fiftieth anniversary of the CP, Lewis used every effort to get churches involved in the campaign. In the first year contributions increased by just over 10 percent; they rose by some 17 percent in 1974 and 13 percent in the year of celebration.

Lewis also tried some innovative program ideas in an effort to draw attention to stewardship and the Cooperative Program. One such program he called a "Stewardship-Camp In." Working in conjunction with the Missions and BSU Departments, he conducted a special Bible study on "stewardship of the land," and "stewardship of time," as part of the Resort Missions outreach. A small group of those attending the Bible study organized the Arkansas Baptist Campers and continued the event on an annual basis.

Each week of the Siloam Springs Assembly, Lewis arranged to have a group present a skit to promote aspects of the Cooperative Program. He also established a "missionary-in-residence" program in 1974. This activity featured a foreign missionary, in the state on furlough, serving full-time in the department to promote Cooperative Program causes.

In January 1977 Lewis assumed full-time responsibilities as Associate Executive Secretary and relinquished his administrative role with the Stewardship-Cooperative Program Office. Lewis was replaced by James Walker, a pastor in Warren, and the unit was renamed to the Stewardship Department. The revamped department was designed to assist the ABSC do its part in the SBC's "Bold Mission Thrust," that intended "to plant a Baptist witness in more than 600 countries and double the number of foreign missionaries by 2000 A.D." To meet that challenge SBC officials needed to double Cooperative Program gifts by 1982, and it was crucial that every member Convention be involved.

Director Lawson Hatfield took major steps to make the Sunday School program more visible and relevant in the 1970s. He was assisted by four associate secretaries. Don Cooper, who served as youth consultant, had promotional responsibility for Vacation Bible School and was the department's liaison to the associations. Mary Emma Humphrey was the children's consultant, with responsibility for promoting Weekday Bible Study programs, and was departmental representative for programs and activities involving the mentally retarded. Pat Ratton, consultant for preschool and kindergarten, also edited the *Sunday School News*, a departmental newsletter sent to the churches and associations to promote department activities.

Of the four major programs assigned to the office, Sunday School, Vacation Bible School, Weekday Bible Study, and Church Administration, the weekday program saw the most change in the 1970s. The growing practice of two-income families and policy changes in public education stimulated a mounting demand for weekday programs for preschool and kindergarten children. Responding to this, the department began to offer annual workshops to train preschool and children's leaders in Sunday School work.

Beginning in 1974 as part of the SBC's national campaign to "Share the Word Now" campaign, the department launched a "People-to-People NOW" Program to emphasize evangelism through the Sunday School. This year-long effort was designed to raise consciousness among the associations and churches by using a multi-faceted approach to reach people. The campaign also paid big dividends as Arkansas led the SBC in enrollment gain for the 1973–1974 Sunday School year.

In conjunction with the SBC's "Life and Liberty" campaign, Secretary Hatfield and the Sunday School staff adopted a new outreach program called ACTION. The focus of this new activity was to encourage church members to enroll their family, friends, and neighbors in Sunday School. The strategy was a five-step action program that included "house to house" visitation, "telephone" enlistment, a special appeal to "youth," a "bus ministry" for children, and a "pastor's Sunday

School class," for newcomers. Those churches who adopted the full program were awarded a "Standard of Excellence" presented by the state Sunday School Office. Seven churches were selected to participate in a pilot program in 1975 and had an average growth of 233 new members. The restructuring of the 1960s brought the Arkansas Baptist State Assembly at Siloam Springs under the administrative control of the Sunday School. In 1971, Lawson Hatfield, in addition to his duties as Sunday School secretary, was made director of the Siloam Springs Assembly grounds.

The reorganization did not change the assembly's mission but other factors did influence the program. Originally conceived as a "youth camp" with a limited schedule during the summer, the 1970s brought a growing number of children to the assembly, and changing program needs caused the Assembly to be extended. A fourth week was added to the schedule in 1972, a fifth week came in 1974, and by the end of the decade the assembly was running six weeks with an occasional seventh week added for youth emphasis.

Composition of the weekly campers also began to change. The increasing number of children brought more families to the assembly grounds, and while youth continued to dominate, it became necessary to add family housing. A twelve-unit "family building" was completed in time for the 1973 assembly.

The assembly's changing composition also caused the Executive Board to reevaluate the camp's mission. After more than a year of study, the board voted to shift the focus from "youth oriented activities" and provide a "full assembly concept" that included programs for children, youth, and the adult sponsors who accompanied these groups. In addition to more balanced summer program, the board also encouraged the headquarters staff to promote more year-round use of the facilities.

The new plan went into effect in 1976 with dramatic results. Attendance increased more than two and one-half times and placed a severe strain on the existing facilities. With income generated from the larger attendance, Hatfield led a team of volunteers to build or replace most of the existing facilities with new concrete block structures and build a series of hard surface roads in the campgrounds.

Responding to changing cultural patterns Secretary Hatfield and his team of volunteer consultants regularly added new training opportunities to the assembly schedule. An "On-To-College" class and contemporary, "folk-type musicals" were among the new offerings. Changing needs among the churches also led to the Sunday School staff restructuring work assignments after 1973. The new model was built around four consultants trained in all phases of Sunday School, each working with eleven associations. The former plan was for each member of the professional staff in the Baptist Building to work with all forty-four associations—an almost impossible task.

New staff members in the office included Harold Vernon, who accepted appointment as children's consultant, and Freddie Pike as youth consultant. Both men came in 1974. Pike resigned in 1978 to return to the pastorate and was replaced by Martin Babb.

The Woman's Missionary Union experienced the culture changes of the 1970s perhaps more than any other program in the Baptist Building. Two-income families increasingly found it difficult to devote time to any type of volunteer activity—including church. Executive Secretary Nancy Cooper made reference to this problem in her report to the 1970 Convention. She commented "increasing numbers of women are employed outside the home and are thus lost to organizations meeting in the day, both as members of the adult organization and as leaders of youth organizations."

WMU leaders also redoubled efforts to bring attention to the program. Emphasizing that the union was "a people" from adults through preschool, with a "purpose—Missions," Secretary Cooper reminded churches that the program's historic role had not changed and was in even greater need of support. In 1973 the department introduced project "Giant Step," a two-year effort to increase the number of WMU organizations in the state and to encourage greater use of literature in missions education.

The WMU also joined with Stewardship's Operation One campaign to promote Cooperative Program giving. Emphasizing "Weeks of Prayer" for foreign and home missions and a "Season of Prayer" for state missions, Director Cooper called attention to mission needs around the world. Churches responded by giving in record amounts each year of the campaign.

New staff members joining the WMU included Nan Owens, who became director of the Adult Division in 1970, and Julia Ketner, who became director of the Children and Pre-School Division the same year. In December 1974 Nancy Cooper retired after twenty-six years of service to the WMU and the ABSC. The WMU Board chose Julia Ketner to be the new director.

As the decade drew to a close, the Executive Committee anticipated a growing need in Arkansas society by creating the new Christian Life Council. Since World War II the ABSC had worked with the Anti-Saloon League and other inter-faith groups to oppose alcohol abuse and other moral issues including gambling and pornography. By 1979, however, circumstances had caused the board to feel a need to create a separate agency with a distinctive Baptist stamp.

The primary focus of this new work was to emphasize the "qualities of Christian citizenship in an applied way." The board was particularly concerned with conflict in family life and a general decline in personal ethics. Robert A. Parker was recruited from Florida to direct the new office. In one of his first activities, Parker contacted members of the Arkansas Congressional delegation in Washington, D.C., and member of the state General Assembly to inform them about the office and concerns the ABSC had about moral issues. He also enlisted BSU students to assist him in disseminating information that highlighted the ABSC's traditional position on a wide range of social issues.

The decade ended as it began with a change in the Executive Secretary's office. Dr. Ashcraft informed the Executive Board before the 1979 annual meeting of his desire to take early retirement. He said he wanted to become involved the SBC's Bold Mission Thrust and was particularly interested in returning to the western states to help with the mission effort.

Under Ashcraft's leadership the divisiveness which had character-ized the ABSC in the last year of the 1960s subsided. The 1970s saw Southern Baptist work in the state continue to grow, although perhaps not as rapidly as it had in the 1950s and early 1960s. In those years the state was losing population but ABSC numbers increased. In the 1970s the state's Southern Baptist did not keep pace with overall population growth.

The decade of the 1970s was also a difficult time for religious work of all kinds. Organizational changes, including changing the names for several agencies, were a part of the National Convention's attempts to prepare SBC churches for contemporary culture. The continuing trouble from the Vietnam War, the crisis in the U.S. presidency caused by the Watergate scandal, the excessive inflationary spiral caused by the oil embargo, and the Iranian hostage crisis took its toll on both the nation and church work. But even with the national issues, most of Arkansas's Southern Baptist looked forward to the next decade with its Bold Mission Thrust and optimistic outlook of reaching the world for Christ before the end of the century.

16

The 1980s

SOUTHERN BAPTISTS FROM ARKANSAS BEGAN THEIR fourteenth decade together with a call to "Grant unto Thy servants, that with all boldness they may speak Thy word" (Acts 4:29). That request was perhaps prophetic given the revolution in communications that broke on the scene in the 1980s. The Cable News Network (CNN) went on air in June 1980, promising around-the-clock, around-the-world news coverage. Music Television (MTV), targeting the eighteen-to thirty-four-year-old audience followed the next year, and the revolution was on. Before the decade was out, numerous other "cable channels" made their appearance and "the information age" had taken hold of American society.

This outpouring of words presented a serious problem to the Arkansas Baptist State Convention. To thousands of Arkansans, who could remember when the state's first television station went on air in 1953, this deluge of sound—enhanced with visual effects in "living color" and calculated to reach a targeted audience, was all but overwhelming. For ABSC leaders, the challenge came in developing a strategy that allowed "Thy word" to be heard above the din.

To complicate plans for developing that strategy, the Convention began the decade without an executive secretary. Following Dr. Charles Ashcraft's resignation, the Executive Board appointed R. H. Dorris, a former director of the Department of Missions and then assistant pastor at North Little Rock's Baring Cross Church, as "interim executive secretary-treasurer." The search for Dr. Ashcraft's replacement was of short duration. In May 1980 the board named Dr. Huber L. Drumwright Jr. as the Convention's new executive. A native of Walters, Oklahoma, Drumwright was dean of the School of Theology at Southwestern Baptist Theological Seminary at the time of his appointment. Prior to becoming dean, he served as professor of New Testament and Greek at Southwestern. He assumed his new duties on September 1.

By 1980, the ABSC had grown to 1,241 churches representing 428,348 members, with an annual budget of almost $8 million and properties valued at more than $291 million. But while those figures would have been unimaginable less than fifty years earlier, the growth was not sufficient to meet the 1978 goal of sending as much money to the Cooperative Program as was spent on statewide causes. After messengers to the 1978 Convention adopted the Cooperative giving plan, the Executive Board appointed a "50/50 by 1985 Committee" and charged it with developing a plan for reaching the goal of sending 50 percent of all contributions received at the Baptist Building on to the Cooperative Program.

The continued "stagflation" in the national economy kept contributions to ABSC causes flat and jeopardized an increase in giving to the Cooperative Program. Facing that reality in 1980, the committee prepared two plans for the board. That body, chaired by Joe Atchinson, pastor of South Side Church in Pine Bluff, in turn placed the proposals before Convention messengers. One plan called for a drastic reduction, more than 50 percent, in the percentages of future budgets reserved for Christian Education and Family and Child Care Services, and the Arkansas Baptist Foundation. An alternative plan recommended that the percentage of "un-designated funds" be increased to 2.6 percent each year through 1985.

The 1980 Convention met with Little Rock's Immanuel Church, Dr. W. O. Vaught host pastor. President John Finn called the meeting to order. As director of Missions for North Arkansas Association, Finn had had an active year. In addition to his work with the ABSC, he also served as co-chairman of the "dry-forces" opposing the sale of alcoholic beverages in Boone County. He was not only successful in leading his group to defeat the "wet forces" in a local option election, but he conducted such a positive campaign "that he was able to sit down and witness to the leader of the opposition."

In one of their first items of business, messengers took up the two board proposals for giving to the Cooperative Program. After much discussion, they voted to delay action on either proposal and continue the budget formula previously adopted.

On a different front, messengers to the 1980 Convention also made an effort to define "alien immersion" and "open communion." These doctrines had been divisive issues among the churches for almost a decade. By majority vote, messengers defined alien immersion as "immersion for baptism administered by a group which does not follow New Testament teachings on salvation and the church." Open communion was defined by the same vote as "corporate observance of the Lord's supper," in which individuals who have not received New Testament Baptism are invited to participate.

Huber Drumwright's leadership of the ABSC sparked a spirit of enthusiasm and optimism among the membership. Arriving in the state just weeks prior to the annual Convention, he had little opportunity to shape the budget. However his presence was a powerful force, and *Newsmagazine* editor Everett Sneed said the 1980 meeting was "the best over-all convention that we have ever attended." He attributed that in part to "the respect for the leadership that is being given by Executive Secretary Huber Drumwright."

Before adjourning the 1980 Convention, messengers reelected John Finn to be president for 1980–1981. Joe Atchinson was also reelected chairman of the Executive Board.

Over the next twelve months Drumwright traveled throughout the state preaching a central theme, "unity in diversity" among Arkansas's Southern Baptist. To help ABSC members take their minds off internal differences, he pushed hard to complete the partnership arrangements begun in 1978 with the state of Indiana. Other than a series of "simultaneous revivals," little had been done to promote the work in that pioneer area. The new secretary urged churches to support the effort and the Executive Committee readily agreed. After meeting with his counterpart in the Indiana Baptist State Convention, Arkansan R. V. Haygood, Drumwright organized a plan to provide both money and volunteers to establish new churches and mission sites in the Hoosier state. This program proved highly popular and successful for both states.

The new executive secretary also worked to establish a satellite link-up with the seminaries. With this program, Arkansas's Southern Baptist were in contact with the SBC's most dynamic educators and able to offer a wider selection of faculty and course offerings. It complemented the work being done by the Boyce Bible Institute and was also cost effective if considered in light the expense involved with professors traveling to Little Rock from any of the cooperating seminaries. As an aspect of cost, Drumwright also moved to restructure the ABSC budget in an effort to meet the SBC's Bold Mission Thrust campaign.

No one could have anticipated that the ABSC's new leader would die just two weeks before the 1981 Convention. He died from a heart attack shortly after returning to Little Rock from a Sunday speaking engagement at First Church El Dorado. That day he preached on Barnabus the Encourager—a role that many thought ideally suited Drumwright.

In one of his first actions after joining the ABSC, Drumwright hired Dr. L. L. Collins, a former colleague at Southwestern, to be the associate executive secretary of the ABSC. The Executive Committee asked Collins to be the interim executive secretary until a replacement for Drumwright could be found. Collins assumed his new duties just days before the 1981 Convention met at First Church, Fayetteville with Jere Mitchell host pastor.

President Finn called messengers to the annual meeting to order and noted that he shared the sense of shock over the turn of events in the past few weeks., However, he urged those present to continue the "spirit of unity" so emphasized by Drumwright in his brief tenure. He then called upon L. L. Collins, as Drumwright's long-time, close friend, to express a brief memorial to the former executive secretary. Collins told the assembled messengers that Drumwright was "not to be mourned but rather remembered for the unifying projects he had begun in his year as Arkansas's leader."

All messengers were seated without challenge and turned quickly to the business at hand. The new budget formula that Secretary Drumwright and the Executive Board developed over the summer was one of the high priority items. That formula called for an annual reduction in funding to state programs by three-fourths of 1 percent until the 50/50 ABSC/CP ratio was reached. Also, the formula called for establishing a "Cooperative Program Reserve Fund," to absorb contributions that exceeded the program needs of the various ABSC offices. Messengers approved the new budget formula to go into effect in 1983. Also a part of the proposed budget for 1982, the Convention approved a $10,000 allocation to support the seminary satellite project.

In other action, messengers approved new wording in the constitution that required future changes in the document to be read at "two successive annual meetings." The term "southwide" was also deleted from the constitution because as its sponsor Freeman McMenis said "Southern Baptists are not confined to the Southern portion of the United States." Church representatives also approved resolutions opposing beverage alcohol, gambling, illegal drugs, and pornography. And, they called upon the Arkansas General Assembly to pass a "Comprehensive Obscenity Statute." The latter was in response to a federal judge's decision overturning the state's existing obscenity laws.

Before closing the 1981 Convention, messengers elected Dillard Miller, pastor of First Church Mena for more than twenty-five years and past president of the Executive Board, to be president for 1981–1982. Ken Lilly, a physician from Fort Smith, was elected president of the Executive Board. Dr. Lilly had served as chairman of the Program Committee the previous year.

Early in 1982, the Convention acquired additional space for some of its agency staff. Property at 601 West Capital Avenue, across the street from the Baptist Building, came up for sale. ABSC President Miller, in concurrence with Executive Board President Ken Lilly, agreed to call the ABSC into special session to consider purchasing the site. As has been mentioned, space became a pressing problem for the headquarters staff in the late 1970s. For example, the Baptist Foundation was forced to rent a suite of offices in a nearby building and several other departments worked in crowded conditions. However, the cost of building new space was more than messengers wanted to pay and the matter was unresolved. Acquiring an existing building appeared to be a good compromise, and the board recommended that such be done. More than 700 messengers gathered in Little Rock in late January and unanimously approved that recommendation. The *Arkansas Baptist*

Executive secretaries: Huber L. Drumwright Jr. (1980–1981), left; and Don Moore (1982–1986), right. The title was changed from "executive secretary" to "executive director" in 1984.

Newsmagazine and the Family and Child Care Ministry (FCCM) agency moved into the remodeled building in 1983.

In other action, Presidents Miller and Lilly and the board spent much of 1982 searching for a new executive secretary. By October the group had reached a consensus and elected Don Moore, then pastor of Grand Avenue Church in Fort Smith. As a former president of the ABSC (1974–75), president of the Pastor's Conference (1972), vice-chairman of the OBU Board of Trustees, and cochairman of the statewide Evangelistic Campaign (1976), Moore was thoroughly familiar with ABSC work. His reputation as a "dynamic," "evangelistic" preacher, and his strong interpersonal skills were also factors in his being chosen as the secretary.

As with Drumwright and Collins, Moore assumed his position within days of the annual Convention. However, unlike his predecessors who were new to the state, Moore was on a first name basis with most of the pastors and did not have to undergo the "orientation" of a new work.

Ironically, while Drumwright and Collins were able to move into their posts during a time of Convention unity, Moore assumed his new duties amidst controversy. Two issues, one external one internal, had bothered a number of churches most of the year. The outside matter concerned the teaching of Dr. Dale Moody, professor of theology at Southern Seminary in Louisville, Kentucky. Moody had attracted attention throughout the SBC by his statement on "falling from grace." At its August meeting, the ABSC Executive Board adopted a resolution saying this "stance was in conflict with the Baptist Faith and Message [*sic*]" and requested a response from Moody.

Dr. John Wright, pastor of First Church Little Rock and president of the 1981–1982 Pastor's Conference, arranged to have Moody address that group on the eve of the 1982 Convention, which met with the Park Hill Church in North Little Rock, Cary Heard host pastor. The seminary professor was received politely but his message that "people who think they can believe and be baptized and live like the devil are going to get a surprise at judgement" apparently was unconvincing to his audience.

President Miller called the 1982 Convention to order amidst the concern about Moody in particular and Southern Seminary in general. In addressing the messengers, Miller indirectly responded to Moody by asking rhetorically, "Why should God's servants keep on doing what they do?" He responded by saying, "the promise of reward in heaven, the love of Jesus for each individual, the role model of Jesus, God-given vision, and the threat of personal judgement in heaven." He also stressed that Christians should be "encouragers" of each other.

Messengers may have understood Miller's comments, but there was still strong sentiment in some circles that Moody be "fired" immediately. A group prepared a resolution to that effect to present to the messengers. However, Dr. Clyde Glazener, pastor of Calvary, Little Rock and chairman of the Resolutions Committee, wished to avoid conflict with Southern Seminary on that matter. He pointed out that Moody was sixty-eight years old and facing mandatory retirement at age seventy. This was effectively his last year of appointment at the seminary. Moreover, by the time Southern's trustees could act, there would only be two weeks left in the academic year. Any resolution on immediate termination would only be viewed as punitive and not instructive.

Rather than taking a hard line, the committee recommend a resolution that reaffirmed the ABSC's traditional adherence to the "doctrine of security of the believer."

But, on the Convention floor, some messengers insisted that a more strongly worded document be prepared. They amended the committee's resolution and called "for Southern Seminar trustees to consider terminating Moody and any other teacher who 'advocates' apostasy as a true doctrine." The amended resolution passed even though many voters admitted they did not think their action would change Dr. Moody's status.

The other issue grew out of notification by officials at Southern Baptist College of their plans to expand to a four-year degree granting institution. The Executive Board appointed its own "study committee" to review the matter, and that group gave a favorable recommendation to the proposal at the board's August meeting. Support for the baccalaureate degree was included in the list of recommendations the board submitted to the Convention.

To the surprise of many, the recommendation on Southern's four-year status attracted strong opposition. Some speakers raised questions on the added expense to the Convention, particularly in light of the increased contributions to the Cooperative Program. Others pointed out that college enrollment was declining in the state and were concerned that another baccalaureate institution would take both students and money from Ouachita. Still others were bothered by Southern's accepting federal funds in order to expand the program. After extended debate, in which the time limit was twice extended, the messengers finally voted to table the proposal.

Despite the strong feelings and divided thoughts at the 1982 Convention, messengers reelected Dillard Miller unanimously to a second term as ABSC president. Ken Lilly was also reelected president of the Executive Board for 1982–1983.

In his first full year as executive secretary, Don Moore traveled extensively among the churches and also promoted the theme of unity. He told his listeners that "our preoccupation with things that divide us is costing us." He continued to emphasize unity when messengers came together for the 1983 convention in Pine Bluff. In his address to the group Moore said, "Arkansas Baptists have reached an all-time low in respect for each other and an all-time high in disregard for the commands of God concerning our obligations to each other."

Moore went on to say "we have twiddled our thumbs and fussed around while the population of Arkansas jumped 18 percent in 10 years." During that time (decade of the 1970s), he pointed out "the number of Arkansas Baptist churches increased only four percent." By contrast "Methodist churches increased by 12.6 percent, Presbyterian (USA), 52.9 percent, and church of God, 76.5 percent." He asked rhetorically "Could strife be the cause of our spiritual ineffectiveness? If so, the Bible knows no cure but repentance."

His address may have had an effect. When the four-year status for Southern was reintroduced, Paul Sanders, pastor of Little Rock's Geyer Springs Church and the church where Executive Secretary Moore held membership, moved to cut off debate and vote immediately on the issue. Sanders noted that "everyone has already prayed about this" and more debate might only be divisive. Messengers agreed with those sentiments and not only approved Sanders motion, but also voted to support SBC's baccalaureate program.

The cooperative mood continued as messengers also voted to make the *Newsmagazine's* three-year trial in agency status permanent and agreed to change the "executive secretary" title to "executive director." They also approved the board's budget recommendations, which included an additional $102,000, over two years, to support Southern Baptist College's new status and another $200,000 to the Annuity Board to meet new federal regulations on retirement funds.

Moore praised the messengers for their show of unity and noted that the coming years would require full cooperation from everyone. Not only would the ABSC incur added expenses to support Southern Baptist College's expansion, and the Annuity Board, but also at least five departments in the Baptist Building were requesting additional personnel to meet the growing requests from the churches. And, he said, "no budgetary or program provision has been made for these."

Newly elected President (1983–1984) Jon Stubblefield agreed with Moore's assessment. In his acceptance speech, Stubblefield urged the messengers to promote giving in their home churches. "To do all we are committing to do," he said, "we must increase giving." At thirty-eight years of age, Stubblefield was one of the youngest presidents in ABSC

history. However, he had a long list of denominational accomplishments—serving as cochairman of the BSU Third Century Campaign,
president of the Pastor's Conference, and immediate vice-president of
the ABSC. Jerry Wilson, pastor of West Side Church, El Dorado was
elected president of the Executive Board.

In a post-Convention interview, Stubblefield said, "I think one of
the major roles of the President this year is to bring is to bring Arkansas
Baptist together. We need healing and reconciliation." The new president's message, coupled with the work Director Moore had previously
been doing to build unity, paid large dividends.

When Stubblefield called the 1984 Convention to order, the results
of that work were evident. The Convention met with Grand Avenue
Church in Fort Smith and the host pastor, James Bryant. An indication
how much harmony among ABSC members had improved came early
when messengers voted to seat "all properly elected" representatives
and that included those from First Church Russellville. That church's
messengers had been refused seating since 1965. The move was both
substantively and symbolically important. New pastor, Steven Davis,
apologized to the Convention for "past actions" and the matter was
settled.

In addressing the messengers on "significant churches" Moore
talked about the importance of being involved in the community. He
noted that "the greatest indictment that could fall on this generation of
churches would be that nobody noticed what we do." Being noticed
required a balanced approach to action involving both evangelism and
discipleship. As he pointed out, "the most obtuse phenomenon of our
age is the church which does nothing but evangelize. . . . Evangelism
must be balanced by discipleship training."

In his presidential address Stubblefield, told the messengers that
"Christian living is marked by right living as well as right belief." He also
said, "All that Jesus began to do and teach is now the responsibility of
the church. Since the church is the continuing incarnation of Christ in
the world, his work depends on his people. Will we fail him?"

To assist messengers in answering that question Executive Board
President Jerry Wilson presented a list of recommendations on
behalf of the board. Included was a request that local churches
participate in the SBC's Planned Growth in Giving. This program

called for individuals and churches to gradually increase their contributions to the local church and to the Cooperative Program, and the Church Annuity Plan. The latter allowed the Convention to increase its annual contributions on behalf of "qualified ministerial staff." They also adopted a board recommendation to establish an Arkansas-Brazil partnership mission project, directed by former missionary Glendon Grober.

Before adjourning from Fort Smith, messengers reelected Stubblefield by acclamation, to be president for 1984–1985. Ferrell Morgan, director of Missions for Concord Association was elected President of the Executive Board.

By the mid-1980s the national economy began to recover, except for farm income, and the inflation rate dropped to more manageable levels. Ironically, the improved economic health of the nation was not reflected in the life of the ABSC. Growth in several critical areas including baptisms, gifts to the Cooperative Program, and enrollments in Sunday School and Church Training programs either declined in total numbers or by percentage increase when compared with previous years. Sunday School enrollment increased by only 364 new members, out of a total enrollment of 255,377 in 1,266 churches. Baptisms were down by over 700 since 1983. Even enrollment in Church Music programs declined. This marked the first time that department did not show an increase since becoming a part of the ABSC in the 1940s.

The apparent "leveling off" in ABSC growth came at a time when the Convention had added several new expenses. The 1983 decision to increase gifts to the Cooperative Program by three-fourths of 1 percent continued; the 1984 agreement to increase support to the Annuity Program for retired ministers added another $200,000 in costs; and Southern Baptist College's expanding to a four-year program increased ABSC cost by $102,000 in the first year.

These numbers may have tested the faith of many, but to Executive Director Moore they represented a challenge. He recognized that statistics for any given year did not necessarily reflect an overall trend, and he was determined not to be alarmed. Instead, in his visits among the churches, he chose to point out opportunities for growth. Using numbers compiled by Conway Sawyers and the State Missions' staff, showing more than one million Arkansans not affiliated with a church, Moore said that was almost half the state's population and represented "opportunity."

Addressing messengers to the 1985 Convention, the executive director called upon them to seek ways to "release God to greater activity." He cautioned his listeners about being "busy but lacking real influence in the world." To make the difference God wanted, Moore said Arkansas's Southern Baptist must show "greater obedience, effectual, persistent and believing prayer, actions of faith, and generosity and honesty in giving."

Messengers had agreed to hold their 1985 annual meeting on the campus of Ouachita Baptist University to join that institution for its Centennial Celebration. President Dan Grant welcomed the messengers to the campus, reviewed the highlights of the campus's first one hundred years, and pointed out two major projects then underway that would launch the second century. The first of these was a $2 million renovation and addition to Riley Library that included "electronic storage and retrieval systems." The second project, a new "Center for Christian Ministries" was designed for outreach. W. O. Vaught, who had accepted an academic position at OBU after retiring as pastor of Immanuel, Little Rock, served as coordinator of the new program designed to integrate the university's religion department with "field education and practical ministry experience for ministerial students."

There was also other good news to take messengers' minds off the gloomy statistical report. WMU director Julia Ketner reported that the ABSC members had set two records in giving to missions. Their contributions to the Lottie Moon foreign mission program exceeded $2.6 million and the total for all mission gifts was more than $3.2 million. That report was followed by a "stirring message" delivered by Nilson Fanini, a widely known Brazilian evangelist who highlighted the Arkansas-Brazil partnership. He said, "Together and togetherness are two words needed badly by the world today. We must work together," he said, "because God has just one family."

Fanini's words served as a rallying point for the messengers. A "steady stream of individuals and couples" responded when he gave an invitation to "express openness to God's call to missions." Director

Moore said, "I have been part of many great conventions, but this is the first time I have seen one turn into a revival meeting."

Messengers at the 1985 Convention elected Lawson Hatfield, pastor of First Church Fordyce, president for 1985–1986. Prior to his move to Fordyce, Hatfield had served as director of the State Sunday School Department for twenty-three years. He was thoroughly familiar with all phases of ABSC work.

Unfortunately, the revival spirit generated at the Convention did not extend into the state. Giving and baptisms continued to decline despite statewide, simultaneous revivals in March and April 1986. Executive Director Moore, while concerned about the numbers, noted that they "reflected a common trend throughout the country and were not unique to Arkansas."

Still, two consecutive years of decline required attention. Ferrell Morgan and some members of the Executive Board said they saw "a financial crisis in the making" and believed that "immediate measures were necessary to prevent potentially harmful effects" a short-fall in income would have on State Convention ministries. At its August meeting the board appointed a "Task Force of 100" pastors and laypeople and charged them to seek invitations from local churches in the coming year in order to promote ABSC and SBC mission programs.

The Executive Board also adopted a new budget formula to reflect the changes in contributions to the ABSC. The new formula continued the commitments to the Cooperative Program, Southern Baptist College, and the Annuity Board, as previously discussed. But in order to do that, the other agencies, institutions, and Executive Board programs had to be "slightly reduced."

News of that action did not dampen the spirit of messengers who met at Little Rock's Geyer Springs Church for the 1986 Convention. Host Pastor Paul Sanders welcomed the official representatives and their guests. Under rules used on an experimental basis the previous year, the Convention's business sessions were shortened. Under the new format, the Pastor's Conference was held on Monday and the Convention began on Tuesday and continued through Wednesday evening.

Messengers endorsed the new format, the new budget formula, the "Task Force of 100," and "Missions Advance 87–89," a two-year campaign to encourage churches to increase their contributions to world missions. The spirit of unity continued despite the dire financial picture. Some "hallway talk" suggested that circumstances may reflect unhappiness with the conservative-moderate division in the Southern Baptist Convention, but both ABSC President Lawson Hatfield and Executive Director Moore discounted that. Both men said the SBC problem was a "non-issue" among Arkansas's Southern Baptist. Instead, in his address to the Convention, Moore said if the messengers "did not like the reports," then "change the lives of individual Christians who make up the churches." Using Romans 12:2 as a text, he said "renewal of the mind will transform the individual . . . and with renewal comes the vibrant Christian life."

The Executive Director's words may have had a prophetic ring in light of the resolutions passed on the last day of the Convention. Of the eight proposals reported out of committee, six expressed opposition to gambling, alcohol, pornography, drugs, school-based health clinics, and media coverage of the same. Another resolution recognized the contributions farmers had made to the state and encouraged "prayer and ministry to farm families in the present crisis." The other resolution was appreciation for the host church.

Messengers were saddened to remember the deaths of Gene Devore, for twenty-three years resident manager of the Siloam Springs Assembly grounds, and L. L. Collins, former associate and interim executive director of the ABSC. The Executive Board voted to name the Baptist Building library in honor of Dr. Collins and former Executive Director Huber Drumwright.

The "spiritual news" on the home front may have been a bit discouraging. However, the Arkansas-Brazil partnership, now called the AMAR project, after the Portuguese word for love, continued to go well. Project Director Glendon Grober reported the number of churches in one northern province had doubled because of Arkansas teams working in the area. The partnership was scheduled to run through 1987.

Other good news came in a report on the Arkansas Foundation. According to President Harry Trulove, the foundation had exceeded $14 million—a fourteen-fold increase in just ten years. And, with the last quarter of the year still to go, the foundation had already earned seven times more than its operating budget for 1986.

After a slow beginning, the Arkansas Baptist Foundation began to experience significant growth in the 1970s. Taking almost twenty-five years to accumulate $1 million in assets; that figure has increased almost forty-fold in the last twenty-five years. Board Chairman David Ray (right) and Executive Director Harry Trulove (left) review the balance sheets.

Messengers reelected Lawson Hatfield president for 1986–1987. Ferrell Morgan was also chosen to continue as Executive Board President for the coming year. Keeping the same leadership team intact assured the ABSC continued in a spirit of harmony.

The new emphasis by the Task Force of 100 and the Missions Advance 87–89 began to produced results. Gifts increased in 1987, as did baptisms and enrollment in church programs generally. But much of that was relative. Executive Director Moore pointed out that Arkansas's Southern Baptists "at the end of the [Great] Depression" were giving a larger percentage of their church budgets to world missions "than is being given today." Part of the reason for that may have been due to the fact that most Arkansans, and Southern Baptist generally, were taking a different approach to missions in the 1980s. Increasingly, younger adults wanted a personal, hands-on program and were less inclined to send a representative to do a job.

Moore noted the changing emphasis in mission work in his address to the 1987 Convention meeting with First Church Fort Smith and host Pastor Ron Herrod. The Executive Director pointed out that "while more are volunteering for mission service, mission support is not comparably increasing." This was hurting the SBC's Bold Mission Thrust because "while Southern Baptist boast the largest mission force in the world, they stand near the bottom of the list in individual support, contributing barely $10 each to world missions." He went on to point out that SBC missionaries were serving every day with great personal sacrifice. But, "while they risk their lives," he said, "their brothers and sisters at home are looking for more ways to spend more money on themselves. When they repent of such hypocrisy and 'get right' on missions, God will begin to bless their other endeavors."

Stirred by those words, messengers voted to support "Church Arkansas," a plan put forward by the Missions Department to start twenty-five new churches in 1988, forty-five in 1989, and thirty in 1990. By comparison nineteen new churches were started in 1987. Messengers also agreed to participate in the 1990 SBC "simultaneous revivals" designed to "reach the nation for Christ."

Before adjourning at Fort Smith, messengers elected Cary Heard, pastor of North Little Rock's Park Hill Church, president for

1987–1988, Jere Mitchell, pastor of Fayetteville's First Church, was chosen president of the Executive Board.

The Church Arkansas campaign was a strong unifying theme in 1988. A month before the 1988 Convention convened at Park Hill in North Little Rock, Mitchell, reporting for the Executive Board, noted that twenty-one new churches had been started in the past ten months. He also said that three more planned to begin in October and three more before the end of the month was over. While technically this did not meet the goal of twenty-five new churches in the year it was a good start. However, Floyd Tidsworth, a specialist in "church planting," told the messengers, "at the pace we are going it will take 70 years to reach the unchurched population in Arkansas—assuming no additions were made to the existing population by birth or immigration."

Attendance at this Convention was unusually high with over 1,200 messengers registered. Rumors had circulated weeks in advance of the meeting of a "take-over" by the conservatives, but such did not materialize. Instead, President Cary Heard, pastor of the host church, was unanimously reelected president for 1988–1989. Those present also heard Associate Executive Director Jimmie Sheffield present the priority goals for 1988–1989 worked out by the Executive Board. These included beginning 200 new Sunday School units, beginning forty-five new churches, training 200 youth leaders to lead Youth Christian Life Seminars, and involving at least half the churches in a "Year of the Laity" emphasis. He also announced plans to began an Arkansas-Guatemala partnership for 1989–1992.

Messengers also honored Dr. Daniel Grant, who retired after eighteen years as President of Ouachita, and welcomed Dr. Ben Elrod, his successor. Ervin Keathley, who retired from the Church Music Department, was also recognized for his fifteen years of service.

Despite the challenging goals presented by the Executive Board and the ceremonial goodbyes to leaders with long records of service, messengers appeared to be most interested in the resolutions to be presented on Wednesday morning—particularly the one on "the priesthood of the believer" that had stirred controversy at the SBC's last Convention. However the proposal submitted by Randall Everett, chairman of the Resolutions Committee, "affirmed Baptists' emphasis on soul competency, religious freedom and the believer's priesthood."

An attempt to substitute language from the SBC resolution, which said in part that the priesthood doctrine "has been used to shield unbiblical beliefs and to undermine pastoral authority" failed to pass. The original resolution was then passed without incident.

The rumored "conflict" brewing before the 1988 Convention continued to haunt Arkansas's Southern Baptist in the last year of the decade. On two occasions in the course of the year, the secular press reported "meetings being held" to plan a "take-over" of the State Convention. Six weeks prior to the 1989 Convention meeting at First Church, Little Rock, a publication appeared in the Northwest portion of the state. The publisher was quoted as saying the paper was needed "to add to what news we receive from our state paper. Our difference is to write the news from a conservative viewpoint." Secret meetings and an alternative newspaper heightened the drama. As its history demonstrates, the ABSC was not immune to conflict and disagreement. However, Convention leaders had repeatedly expressed pride in the fact that Arkansas had not been caught up in the feuding engulfing the SBC—now it appeared that was no longer true.

Despite the tension, Executive Director Moore kept his focus on world missions as he addressed the messengers. Using Joshua 7 as his text and "Folly in the Family of God" as his theme, Moore told is listeners "[we] may be able to find some signs of progress that make us feel good, [but] the fact is we are not doing well." He pointed out that in the eleven years Bold Mission Thrust had been in operation there had been "an increase of only 1.1 person per church per year." Unless that trend was corrected, he said "Southern Baptist will show a statistical decline" by 1991. What disturbed the director about all this was "our resources and assets have never been better, but we have not been able to translate that into action. We are on the way down unless we experience revival."

Following the evening service Moore convened a "solemn assembly" to allow messengers to practice what they preached about revival." A large number of individuals remained until after 11:00 P.M. in prayer, giving testimonies, and in confession. Following the meeting Moore said he believed they had "turned a corner. . . . Something significant took place during the solemn assembly."

Electing a new president, which had been rumored to be the focus of the Convention, proved almost anticlimactic. Mike Huckabee, pastor of Texarkana's Beech Street Church, was elected by a two to one margin and used his time before the messengers to call for unity. While the ballots were being counted, Randall O'Brien, pastor of Little Rock's Calvary Church gave the annual sermon. Using a title "Your Devil Is Too Small," O'Brien said, "in recent years Satan has tempted us to be more concerned over who's boss and less concerned about who's lost." And, he said, "your devil is too small if you consign him to far away places in far away times." However, he concluded, "In Christ, but only in Christ, your Devil is too small to lick even one of God's children. Even one."

The disharmony issue all but overshadowed other significant action by the Convention. Messengers recommitted their support of the Guatemalan partnership, recommitted to a series of simultaneous revivals under the banner "Here's Hope," and adopted a Sunday School enlargement emphasis for the coming year. They also agreed to change the name of Southern Baptist College to the Williams College in honor of its founder, Dr. H. E. Williams, and changed the name of the Arkansas Baptist Family and Child Care Services to Arkansas Baptist Children's Homes and Family Ministries, making the name more descriptive of the agency's work.

The annual Convention was typically the highlight of the year for the ABSC. However, much of the day-to-day work was carried out by its departments and agencies. Their activities had a major impact on the scope and content of each annual meeting.

In that regard, the often overlooked Annuity Program began to make significant progress in the 1980s. Buoyed by high interest rates and an aging ministerial population, the voluntary retirement program began to be more attractive to a growing number of individuals. In the decade of the 1970s the number of new members and new employers increased almost 50 percent. By 1980 individual memberships exceeded 900. Nadine Bjorkman, who moved from an administrative assistant position in the executive secretary's office in 1976 to become Arkansas's representative to the Dallas based program, encouraged churches to support their pastor and staff to participate in the system.

Total assets managed by the Dallas office exceeded $1 billion in 1983 for the first time, and employees in Arkansas passed 1,000, also for the first time. With the Annuity Program on sound footing, Bjorkman decided to retire in 1983. She had spent a total of twenty-six years in service to the ABSC and was a perfect candidate for the program with which she had been working. Following her retirement, the Executive Board voted to combine the Annuity Office with the Stewardship Department and James Walker assumed responsibility for both programs. In 1987 the department introduced a new program "the Expanded Church Annuity Plan," which allowed, encouraged, individuals to increase participation up to 5 percent of their income and for churches to match that amount. This was the first change in the program in almost forty years and reflected the mounting problem of ministers retiring with so little income as to live in poverty.

In the 1980s the Assembly Program at Siloam Springs continued to be a essential part of the ABSC's evangelism and discipleship training efforts. Lawson Hatfield served as director, in addition to his Sunday School responsibilities, until his resignation in 1983. The newly added "sixth week" of camp proved to be one of the most popular, and total registrations reached a record 5,850 in 1980. Attendance declined slightly in 1981, but in that summer the Assembly staff installed "evaporative coolers" in the dormitories and other key buildings making "camping" more comfortable and improving mental outlook.

Freddie Pike replaced Lawson Hatfield in time for the 1983 Assembly season. The Executive Board voted to name the dining facility "Hatfield Hall" in recognition of his twenty-three years of service to the ABSC. The addition of a seventh week of activities in 1983 added over 700 new campers and broke the previous record set in 1980. Over 6,000 people attended at least one week of Assembly programs.

Changing lifestyles presented a constant challenge to Assembly personnel over dress codes and appropriate behavior. In 1984 the Executive Board approved a new dress code which stated "no attire that reaches more than six inches above the middle of the knee cap can be worn at the assembly." But this "strictness" did not effect attendance which continued on a record pace throughout the decade.

The *Arkansas Baptist Newsmagazine* began its first-year experiment of operating as an "agency" of the ABSC in 1980. The paper presented its "Articles of Incorporation" for Convention approval to that year's Convention. Under this agreement, the *Newsmagazine* was administered by a five-member board of directors and, in the event the "corporation" dissolved, its assets reverted to the ABSC. Editor J. Everett Sneed continued to promote the "every resident family" subscription plan, noting that the cost of the *Newsmagazine* under this option had only increased $1.84 since 1904. Betty Kennedy also continued to be recognized for her writing—winning seven awards in 1980.

By 1980, inflation had become the major issue facing the paper's future. Editor Sneed told messengers to the 1981 Convention that the publication's mailing costs had increased from $14,000 to $120,000 over the past ten years. If inflation continued at that rate he said the paper could not afford to be published.

As has been mentioned, the *Newsmagazine,* having successfully operated three years as "a separate agency" was made a permanent "agency" of the ABSC—no longer administered as a department in the Baptist Building. Messengers to the 1983 Convention approved the new arrangement including the "Board of Trustees" appointed to supervise the paper's operations.

The Baptist Student Union's "Third Century Campaign" exceeded the halfway point in 1980 and by 1982 reached its goal of $1 million. Director Tom Logue continued to promote the plan and call attention to the growing needs of international students. By 1980 more than 1,300 foreign students were studying at the state's colleges and universities. With Third Century funds now available the department was able to fund more activities for internationals and support more summer missionaries.

Tom Logue's retirement in 1987, after thirty-two years as state BSU director, left a major hole in the Baptist Building's institutional memory. Eight generations of college students had grown up under his leadership. He knew a large majority of them on a first-name basis. David James, BSU director at Oklahoma Baptist University, was named as Logue's replacement.

The state Brotherhood organization continued to search for "a strategy of mission involvement" during the 1980s. With director Neal Guthrie's leadership, the Disaster Relief Program initiated in the 1970s proved to be one of the more significant outreach and witnessing programs in the ABSC. After training a cadre of more than one hundred workers, volunteer leaders with this unit responded to numerous calls for help in the state and nation. Disaster Teams increased their activity almost every year of the decade. Baptist Men were also among the first groups to participate in the joint Arkansas-Brazil partnership previously discussed—constructing a building near San Luis for camp meetings.

In 1987, Neal Guthrie retired and was replaced by Glendon Grober. With the Arkansas-Brazil partnership coming to a close, and since Brotherhood groups had been such a integral part of that work, Grober made an easy transition.

The Royal Ambassador Program extended its outreach by sending teams to pioneer mission areas in neighboring states and to inner-city ministries. The State RA Congress also added a track meet to its annual meeting. Beginning in 1980, boys competed in various events according to the age bracket. In 1982, RAs constructed a "braille nature trail" in North Little Rock's Burns Park.

Camp Paron, under the leadership of Robert Ferguson, remained at the center of RA/GA summer programs and became the summer home for National Baptist youth after Hart of the Hills camp was closed in 1986. Planning for a new worship center began in 1981 and was completed in 1984. Almost all the work was done with volunteers from the Baptist Men and RA programs in the various churches.

The Christian Life Council (CLC), as the ABSC's second newest department, worked hard early in the decade to establish its identity among the churches. Director Robert A. Parker held numerous conferences with pastors and director of missions (DOM). The Council also hosted an annual Alcohol-Drug Prevention Seminar and coordinated its activities with the Arkansas Christian Civic Foundation as well as other similar agencies in the state. With council assistance, contributions for world hunger more than doubled in just three years (1979–1980).

The CLC continued to work closely with the Christian Civic Foundation, now headed by former ABSC President John Finn. Beginning in 1984 the two groups began sponsoring the "Freeway Program," a drug-education program for public and private schools.

As the decade progressed the CLC was forced to concentrate more of its attention on the various aspect of gambling. In 1984 progambling interest mounted a campaign to allow casino gambling in Hot Springs.

Another movement also initiated a petition to amend the state constitution to allow multiple types of gambling. Parker worked closely with Finn and related organizations in the state to counter both efforts. In both instances Parker and his colleagues were successful. In Hot Springs they utilized old-fashion political campaigning to deny Casino interest by a 70–30 percent margin. With the initiated petition, the group claimed the title was misleading and filed a lawsuit to prevent its appearing on the ballot. The state Supreme Court agreed with that argument and the so-called "lottery amendment" died with out voters having to act.

The Christian Life Department was discontinued in 1989. Its staff and resources were applied toward creating a new department known as the Church Leadership Support Department. This department related to the Church Administration Department of the Baptist Sunday School Board in Nashville, Tennessee. L. B. Jordon was employed as its first director.

The Church Music Department, under the direction of Secretary Ervin Keathley, continued to see enrollment grow faster than the Southern Baptist Convention average. In addition to the traditional age-grouped workshops, tournaments, festivals, camps, and concerts, the program extended its work to evangelism. In 1981, the department sponsored five music directors for crusades in Malawi, Africa, and sent twenty-five directors to assist the Nevada Convention in its pioneer mission work. The department organized a two-day workshop for "instrumental musicians," which proved quite popular. New types of music including "praise songs and choruses," as well as songs made popular by Christian artists, began to make their way into Sunday worship services.

Former director, Mrs. B. W. (Ruth) Nininger, was recognized by the SBC's annual Music Conference, for her years of outstanding service to the church music field and as the "first" state music secretary. Ervin Keathley retired in 1988 after fifteen years of service. He was replaced by Lester McCullough.

The Church Training Department, under the leadership of Robert Holley, emphasized leadership training in the early part of the decade. By 1980, enrollment in Church Training programs exceeded 75,000, and Arkansas ranked second among SBC churches in the percentage of its churches reporting CT programs.

The annual Associational Leadership Conference continued to be popular among the churches, as did the Pastor-Director Retreat, "M" Night, and the State Youth Convention. The decade also saw a growing interest in marriage-enrichment and family ministry conferences. To respond to the growing diversity both with in the ABSC, as well as the Southern Baptist Convention, Holley and his staff placed great deal of emphasis on individual spiritual growth and began a series of training conferences on "Equipping for Personal Growth." The MasterLife series was introduced in 1982. That same year the department organized the state's first Single Adult Conference, as well as a Conference on Senior Adults.

As the decade progressed the department put more emphasis on youth work. Beginning in 1982, Associate Director for Youth Bill Faulkner hosted a "Baptist Youth Day at Magic Springs," a theme park near Hot Springs. Over 7,000 youth and their leaders participated in what became an annual event. Faulkner and other members of the department used the opportunity to introduce a new program called "DiscipleLife" a curriculum series that placed a new emphasis on training youth for contemporary issues.

To assist the SBC's Bold Mission Thrust emphasis, the department also began offering a "Developing Believers" emphasis after 1983. But despite the persistent work, enrollment in discipleship training began to decline. By 1984 Director Holley reported that while 75 percent of the state's churches had training programs, the state had dropped to third among SBC states in the percentage of its churches having a CT program. The department continued to maintain that position throughout the decade.

In 1989 the Baptist Sunday School Board voted to change Church Training's name to "Discipleship Training." The change went into effect in October.

Cooperative Ministries with National Baptist, with Robert Ferguson as director, focused on training new leaders and providing in-service opportunities through its extension centers, clinics, and workshops. In 1980, Chaplain Lawrence Haley began working with young, black first offenders at Tucker Intermediate Reformatory.

The department also coordinated a joint meeting of the ABSC and two Conventions of National Baptist, the Regular Baptist Convention and the Consolidated Baptist Convention, as part of the ABSC's annual meeting in 1980. This was only the second time the three groups had held a united meeting—the other being in celebration of the nation's bicentennial in 1976. Following the 1980 Convention, representatives of the three groups continued to meet on an irregular basis. Beginning in 1982 the women's mission groups in the three Conventions also began holding joint meetings.

In 1986 the Executive Board sold the "Hart of the Hills" property, and the camp was closed following that summer's camping season. National Baptist Churches who had been using that facility for their children and youth summer programs were encouraged to use Camp Paron. Proceeds for the sale of the property were used to build a guest house at Camp Paron. Beginning with the 1987 camping season, the "Hart of the Hills" camp moved to Paron with its usual three-week schedule of activities.

Robert Ferguson retired in 1988 and was replaced by Jack Kwok.

The Evangelism Department, with Jesse S. Reed as director, introduced a new program called "Continued Witness Training" (CWT) in 1980. As with the established WIN (Witness Involvement Now), WOW (Win Our World), and TELL (Training Evangelistic Lay Leadership), CWT focused on personal evangelism. Youth evangelism continued through the annual "Joy Explo" conference. The WOW Program developed a "team strategy" to train junior and senior high school students in every school districts in the state as part of the Bold Mission effort begun in 1978.

Reed retired from the Evangelism Department in 1981, and Clarence Shell was named to replace him. Shell set "breaking the all-time baptismal record, set in 1950," as his goal for the coming year. To do that, he would have to increase the number by over 3,000 over the past year. Gaining that many baptisms would require extensive outreach and creativity in new areas of work.

Taking a creative approach to reach more people meant identifying new population bases. The growing number of retirees moving into the state was one such base, and Shell targeted that group with special efforts to get their attention. This included Golden Age Evangelism Conferences in the retirement settlements in the northern part of the state. As part of this special outreach the WIN Program was replaced with the Lay Evangelism School (LES), which was designed to promote "total evangelism."

James Lagrone joined the department in 1985 to work with youth. His addition allowed the office to increase its outreach activities. With giving to the Cooperative Program behind schedule, and enrollments in Sunday School, Church Training, and Church Music Programs also falling below the normal population growth, many felt that evangelism was the key to stimulating new growth. With encouragement and materials provided by the SBC, the department organized a Prayer for Spiritual Awakening Seminar at Camp Paron. The idea was to train associational representatives to lead similar seminars among their respective churches.

The Ministry of Crisis Support, the ABSC's newest office, began work in 1980 under the direction of Glen D. McGriff. Authorized by the 1979 Convention, the new program recognized the changing nature of Arkansas society. As conceived by the Executive Committee, the office was established "to assure that any hurting pastor or other church staff member will have confidential Christian counseling." Located in a private office away from the Baptist Building, the program also worked to be "a preventive resource to church staff members" before a crisis situation developed. Much of the office's activity went unreported; however, there was a steady increase in the number of counseling session as the decade progressed.

Perhaps symptomatic of the times, the number of people using crisis support services increased by more than 10 percent each year in the decade—even as response to other ABSC programs was either stable or in decline. A significant number of the new cases grew out of what church leaders called "forced termination" of church staff members. By the late 1980s poor relationships between professional staff and local church memberships had become a "near epidemic" throughout the Southern Baptist Convention. Admittedly, more churches had more staff members by the 1980s, and from time to time, historically, moral, and ethical problems were not new to staff-membership relations—at least in a limited way. Traditionally, too, the problem of "ministerial burn-out" was not uncommon.

But this new conflict typically did not so much involve moral and ethical issues. It was more about job expectations and communication.

The national and state culture, which became more and more focused on single issues, and the increasing "service mentality" that dominated individual lifestyle made its way into the church. While the individual situations were often complex, they nevertheless took a heavy mental toll on full-time Christian workers. Not only were the personal relationships stressful, but the matter of "job security" and being responsive to the "ministerial call" added weight to a difficult situation.

The ABSC was sensitive to this growing problem and initiated a series of activities to assist both individual and corporate concerns. Using materials developed by the SBC and working with the directors of Missions, the staff with the state Convention offered extensive training opportunities in Conflict Management/Resolution. The ABSC also began providing an "Orientation for New Pastors/Staff and their spouses at the Baptist Building and hosting a Pastor's Retreat at Camp Paron on an annual basis. Also, pastors and staff members terminated for other than moral or doctrinal reasons were offered limited financial assistance and free counseling service.

By the mid-1990s the forced termination issue had begun to subside a bit. But the matter was still a crucial one to the spiritual health of all levels of the ABSC's work in the state. By providing intervention, not only were many individuals and churches given timely assistance, but steps were also taken to gain a better understanding of the problem and provide some long-term solutions. In 1991 the Executive Board authorized that a new Church Leadership Support Department be created to maintain ongoing work in this area.

Johnny Biggs continued to serve as executive director of the Arkansas Baptist Family and Child Care Services through the 1980s. Work sites extended to seven associations and eight local churches. As with most departments in the Baptist Building, the decade of the eighties forced the agency to broaden its mission to meet the mounting needs of families under stress. Programs from infants through adults were in place, and in each section of the state, needs were greater than the program could meet. In 1986, the agency opened a new emergency receiving home in Paragould and had a client list of thirty-five referrals for battered mothers in the first four months of operation. New property in the form of a large, renovated, and redecorated house in El Dorado was deeded to the FCCM by Mr. and Mrs. Melvin Bell in 1987.

It was used as a "home for unwed mothers."

The state Missions Department expanded its outreach in the 1980s. Under the leadership of Conway Sawyers, the department received its first new opportunity of the decade when federal officials reopened Ft. Chaffee at Fort Smith to house some 19,000 Cuban refugees. The SBC's Home Mission Board employed Donosco Escobar, who had been director of the ABSC's Hispanic Ministry, to work with the Cubans. Ministry to migratory workers also expanded in the 1980s with Bible study programs at Hughes, Marion, and West Memphis.

The Chaplaincy Program under the direction of Leroy Sisk, extended its outreach to assist Escobar with the Cuban ministry at Ft. Chaffee. Traditional work continued at the state prison system, rehabilitation, and child/youth guidance centers, Baptist Hospital System, Camp Robinson, various units of the National Guard, and selected industrial sites. New work was begun at the Pulaski County jail. The department also assisted Ouachita Baptist University in developing a "student chaplain intern program" with the state Youth Services Division at Pine Bluff. In 1987 the program was extended to three Federal Job Corps sites at Cass, Ouachita, and Little Rock.

As the number of new immigrant groups increased in the decade, the Language Ministry also became more active. Programs for the deaf, Hispanics, and Indo-Chinese continued to be an important focus of the work.

Beginning in 1983 the department introduced its Christian Social Ministries Program. This initiative involved more intensive work with the migratory labor centers in the Southern and Eastern regions of the state. Increased efforts were also made to develop an "inter-faith witness training program" for reaching people in other denominations.

As has been mentioned in 1984, the Executive Board under Board President Jerry Wilson's leadership became particularly interested in new church growth. Responding to that directive, the Missions Department began an active program aimed at establishing new churches in the areas of the state showing the most rapid growth. According to department records, between 1970 and 1982 the ABSC had assisted had established 128 new congregations. However, 10 of those were reorganized and 63 were dropped, leaving a net gain of 74. Wilson and the board were concerned that the ABSC do its share in the

SBC's initiative under Bold Mission Thrust. To do that, the state must add at least 20 new churches in 1985 and average 30 new churches per year through the year 2000.

The new church emphasis presented the Missions Department with a bit of a dilemma. Church growth studies showed that membership increased more rapidly with new churches. However, as Conway Sawyers pointed out "over 70 percent of the churches in Arkansas are located in transitional communities." Transition was defined as change in lifestyle, population density, socioeconomic, racial, and or ethnic makeup. Therein was the paradox of the 1980s. With limited funds available, hard choices had to be made between sustaining "transition churches" and establishing new churches.

To assist the SBC with its emphasis on Bold Mission Thrust, the ABSC Executive Committee authorized a restructuring of the state's stewardship efforts in the 1980s. Under James A. Walker's leadership, the office mounted a statewide campaign to call attention to the SBC's mission outreach. Arkansas's Southern Baptist responded willingly to the call and by 1980 exceeded the SBC average in both total and per capita giving. The ABSC also ranked third, among SBC state conventions, in the percentage of its income shared with the SBC. Even so, the SBC needed an annual, 15 percent increase in giving through 1985 in order to reach its mission objectives. But Walker said, "the immediate challenge for Arkansas Baptists is to have all churches giving at least ten percent of their undesignated income to the Cooperative Program."

When giving to the Cooperative Program did not significantly increase over the next two years, the Executive Board asked the 1986 Convention to adopt a new budget formula. Placing a hold on the 50/50 plan, messengers approved a new "Unified Budget Formula," which tied "increases to the Cooperative Program directly to the amount of church gifts the ABSC received from the previous year." While not abandoning the 50/50 plan in concept, board members nevertheless recognized that basic needs of the ABSC's programs and agencies must be met before substantially increasing contributions to the SBC.

Following Collins's untimely death in May 1986, Jimmie Sheffield, a staff member with North Little Rock's Park Hill Church, was elected associate executive director and also assumed responsibility for Cooperative Program promotion.

The Sunday School Department under director Lawson Hatfield, entered the 1980s with a plan "to awaken and stimulate among the churches the greatest possible activity in evangelism, Christian education, and benevolent work." The program also placed new emphasis on children and preschool training, sponsoring a Weekday Early Education Workshop and a clinic for Regional Bus Children's Worship.

The added emphasis, plus the reemphasis on training workers mentioned below, allowed the department to have its best growth in Sunday School enrollment since the 1950s. However, Director Hatfield noted that if Arkansas did its share for the SBC's campaign of 8.5 million enrolled in Sunday School by 1985, the state would have to add almost 6,000 new members each year.

To enlist that many new members required a large core of trained volunteers in a coordinated effort. Associate Sunday School Director Freddie Pike alerted the churches and associations about a special promotion the SBC had for doing this. The plan was to utilize the Departments of Evangelism, Sunday School, and Church Training in a joint effort to train one million Sunday School teachers as personal witnesses. They were confident that prayer and personal witnessing would reverse the negative trends.

Hatfield resigned from the department in 1983 to return to the pastorate. Freddie Pike was named to replace him.

As with new church growth, Sunday School enrollment continued to be well below the average needed to reach national goals. Average growth per year was approximately five thousand through out the decade—well below the six thousand per year needed to meet national goals.

The ABSC's fourteenth decade became a plateau in its growth pattern. However, the growth pattern should be seen in context with cultural developments. The general disaffection with all forms of institutionalism that began in the 1960s continued through the 1970s and 1980s. Not only did churches of almost all denominations have trouble with numerical growth, but civic groups and national charitable groups did as well. Also, Arkansas's Southern Baptist became increasingly a part of regional and national culture. Traditionally, Baptist in the South had a "voice" that could be heard above the din. But as the decade wore on, the ABSC and Southern Baptist, in general, became only one "voice" in the proliferation of voices competing to for attention.

Discontent in the Southern Baptist Convention was also a factor. While the ABSC had been able to avoid becoming directly involved in the debate, as the controversy continued the general public became increasing aware of, if not the nature, at least the presence of trouble. As various opinion surveys indicated, the general public increasingly expressed negative attitudes toward Southern Baptist and became more resistant to the SBC/ABSC efforts at evangelism.

Given both external and internal hurdles to surmount, it is perhaps surprising that the ABSC was able to show any growth at all. But grow it did even in the face of the above mentioned problems. For example, the ABSC began the decade with a budget of $8.034 million—$2.99 million of which went to the Cooperative Program. By 1990 the budget was $13 million with $5.3 million going to the Cooperative Program. That its vital signs (i.e. baptism, enrollment, giving) were considerably stronger than national averages for "mainstream" denominations also gave evidence of both its personal and organizational leadership.

Developing strategies for keeping its message before the people of Arkansas remained the challenge for the Convention's fifteenth decade.

17

The 1990s

BY 1990 IT WAS EVIDENT THAT THE "REVOLUTIONARY eighties" had taken a toll on individuals and families. That decade had gotten caught up in the "ninety-nine lives" syndrome, defined by sociologists as "trying to do too much too fast." With two-income families making up almost half the work force, and single-parent households approaching 50 percent of all the family units, stress became one of the most common "illness" of the period. A generation of "latch-key kids" came home from school to empty homes, or homes with no adults present and added to the stress level for both themselves and their parent(s). These children were increasingly "entertained" by television and video tapes of almost every description. By the end of the decade, almost one-half of all new marriages were ending in divorce. And, an increasing number of new marriages included children from previous marriages. This practice was not new, but the scope and scale was, and it added another element of pressure on the family unit.

For many Americans, and Arkansans, the solution to the "busy life" was "streamlining." Also known as "buying back time," individuals became less enamored with things and schedules and opted for fewer choices in favor of "quality time" for self, family, and friends. Self reliance was again in vogue and a growing number of people began "cashing out," not "dropping out" as in the 1960s," but working at home, with flexible schedules, and/or moving to less-populated communities.

Most of these trends presented a challenge to the Arkansas Baptist State Convention. Developing strategies to minister to the new type of family unit and assisting churches to respond to a generation increasingly skeptical of "religion" shaped many of ABSC's programs in the new decade. Each of these issues was a major undertaking, and when added to the lingering problems of dissension, the ABSC leadership had its own form of stress.

Undeterred by the magnitude of the problems, the Executive Board, Director Don Moore, the staff in the Baptist Building, and new President Mike Huckabee laid plans for the new decade. Acting on the principle "healing self by healing others," ABSC leaders focused on "Building God's Family" as their theme for 1989–1990. New staff members joining the Baptist Building team to help carry out that theme included L. B. Jordon, director of the new Department of Church Leadership Support; Elias Pantoja, who joined the Language Missions section of the Missions Department, and J. Dawson Williams, enlisted by Jack Kwok in the Cooperative Ministries with National and Southern Baptist Department, to be director of the BSU work at the University of Arkansas at Pine Bluff.

The Guatemala Missions Partnership and the Here's Hope, Jesus Cares for You revivals, also helped ABSC leaders put the unpleasantness of the past year behind them. Glendon Grober, Brotherhood director and coordinator of the Guatemala Partnership, identified fifty-five projects to be completed during the three-year campaign. Seventeen of those were completed in the first six months by 200 individuals representing eighty-six churches and twenty-nine associations. These groups returning from the mission field and reporting on their activities helped to refocus priorities among the churches.

The Evangelism Department under the direction of Clarence Shell, spent more than $70,000 to promote the Here's Hope simultaneous revivals. Using television, radio, newspapers, and billboards, Shell's staff and others in the Baptist Building covered the state with information about the revivals. More than 850 churches participated in the campaign, and they reported more than 4,800 professions of faith. In addition to realizing the primary purpose of evangelizing, the widespread participation by local churches illustrated the nature of "Cooperative Baptist."

Campers at the Siloam Springs Assembly participated in an historic event in 1990 by worshiping for the last time in the Old Tabernacle—originally built in 1926. The Old Tabernacle had exhausted the possibilities of "adding on," and a generous gift from the Harvey and Bernice Jones Charitable Trust allowed for a new one to be built. Work on the new structure began at the close of the 1990 season and Assembly Director Freddie Pike announced the new facility was completed just days before the campers arrived for the 1991 season.

In preparing for the upcoming Convention, Director Moore and the Executive Board prepared a list of "priority projects" for 1991. Emphasizing missions, evangelism, and the Cooperative Program, the board decided to make the top priority a "One for All—A Cooperative Program Promotion Plan."

The 1990 Convention met at Immanuel, Little Rock with Dr. Rex Horne Jr. host pastor. If there was any tension lingering from the previous year's meeting, it was quickly dissipated by events during the opening session. Beginning with Esther Burrough's (consultant with the Home Mission Board) theme interpretation "Building God's Family; the Introduction of W. O. Taylor of Melbourne," the oldest minister in the Southern Baptist Convention, and a report by Glendon Grober on the Guatemala Partnership, the tone was set for cooperation. But, the other events were overshadowed in what the *Arkansas Baptist Newsmagazine* called "the most heralded message of the convention," President Mike Huckabee delivered his presidential address.

Calling his sermon "The Ten Commendations," he began by saying "we haven't communicated very well with each other. We've said a lot about each other, but not enough to each other." He then developed the commendations, built around forgiveness, Christian love, and toleration, in a forceful, insightful manner. In illustrating his seventh commendation "Thou shalt not lead by force," he said, "Jesus did not demonstrate his authority by taking a gavel in his hand, [but] by letting spikes be driven in his hand."

When President Huckabee finished his message, the *Arkansas Baptist* noted, "The messengers, who had filled every available seat and stair and were sitting in the aisles, rose for a prolonged and heart-felt standing ovation."

Many of Arkansas's Southern Baptists have held high political office in all three branches of government, at state and national levels. Two men have served as governor of the state and president of the ABSC—James Eagle and incumbent governor, the Honorable Mike Huckabee (pictured above). Governor Huckabee was ABSC President from 1990 to 1992.

The positive, upbeat tone continued for the rest of the meeting. Associate Executive Director Jimmie Sheffield explained the Witnessing-Giving Life Program—the Executive Board's top priority for the coming year. He said the plan was "a cooperative effort between the Stewardship and Evangelism" Departments, which emphasized a "call to commitment to witness and to give." A key part of the emphasis was built around a series of revivals planned for the fall of 1991.

In other matters Johnny Biggs, reporting for the Arkansas Baptist Children's Homes and Family Ministries, said the agency had recently received property for a "boys' ranch," and, that the home for unwed mothers at El Dorado was going well but needed more money to complete the remodeling. Harry Trulove reported that the Arkansas Baptist Foundation was continuing its strong financial performance and said the foundation could help in "Building God's Family" by helping with "careful estate planning." Williams Baptist College President Jack Nicholas noted in his report that the college was celebrating its fiftieth anniversary in 1990.

In one of the last actions of the Convention, messengers adopted thirteen resolutions. Six of those resolutions expressed opposition to the following: homosexuality (2), school based clinics, pornography, abortion, and tax subsidies for child care. Other resolutions denounced racism and segregation, affirmed support for the Cooperative Program, pledged to pray for and give to world hunger relief efforts, and support for the Child Care and Family Ministries' Home for Unwed Mothers at El Dorado.

Messengers also said goodbye to three department heads who were retiring. Robert Parker, the Christian Life Council, retired June 30 and the council was reorganized as the Church Leadership Support Department. John Finn stepped down from the Christian Civic Foundation. Although this was an interdenominational organization, Southern Baptist had contributed a major part of its budget and Finn a former President of the ABSC, made the foundation almost appear to be an ABSC agency. Conway Sawyers stepped down from the Missions Department after serving ten years. Huckabee and both vice-presidents, Dan Grant and H. E. Williams, were all reelected and the ABSC prepared to enter its 143rd year of service to the state.

Beginning in 1991, the Executive Board developed a five-year program (1991–1995) for "Building God's Family" that focused on "Hope for the Home," "Growing Churches," "Performing Ministry," "Reaching People," and "Living the Word." The first year of that program focused on "Hope for the Home." The board appointed a special task force to develop strategies for departments and agencies to use while implementing that theme. In addition to "all major meetings" in the year "highlighting the emphasis," the Discipleship Training, Sunday School, and Brotherhood Departments were given specific assignments to assist churches and associations in providing "Hope for the Home."

The Executive Board also appointed a task force to study "Conflict and Forced Termination" among pastors and church staff members. Calling the problem "an epidemic that has cut deeply into the witness of our churches and the vitality of their leadership," the board asked the task force to recommend measures that "will turn the trend around." Task force members worked closely with the newly created Church Leadership Support Department and its director L. B. Jordan. Among its duties, this department was assigned to maintain a confidential file of pastor/staff resumes. Many of those who had been terminated stopped by the office for consultation and counseling.

To assist with its missions programs the board elected Jimmy Barrentine to replace Conway Sawyers, who retired, as director of the Missions Department, and Paul Roaten was employed as director of the Hope Migrant Center. Barrentine came from the Texas Missions Department while Roaten, and his wife Betty had been missionaries to Peru when family illness forced them to return to the states.

The high inflation costs of the 1970s and early 1980s, coupled with the rapid increase in postage and publication costs caused a new financial crisis for the *Arkansas Baptist Newsmagazine*. The opportunity to operate as an independent agency, while a step for the tradition of freedom of the press, was more than offset by the economic burden of keeping subscription costs low in order to reach more people. At its August meeting the board asked the Program Sub-Committee to "study the possibility of placing the *Newsmagazine* back under the Executive Board. Until that study was completed, the board recommended changing the postage from second class to third class mail, reducing the number of issues from forty-eight to twenty-six per year, and that no new staff be added "at this time."

The 1991 Convention met with Little Rock's Geyer Springs Church and host pastor Paul Sanders. A key feature of the two-day event was the Church Music Department's celebration of "50 Years of Music." Church Music Department Director Lester McCullough coordinated the fifty-year history of the department with a medley of songs from each decade since 1940. Former department Director Ervin Keathley and Jean Pilcher, director of Arkansas Singing Women, served as narrators for the presentation. The presentation climaxed with songs from the third edition of the *Baptist Hymnal* and the combined choirs of Arkansas Master Singers and Singing Women performing a new anthem, "To God, All Praise and Glory," written for the occasion by native Arkansan Buryl Red.

President Mike Huckabee used his address to the messengers to give "Seven Warning Signals for Arkansas Baptist." Saying that he adapted his title from the American Cancer Society warnings about cancer, he identified Insignificance, Informationalism, Isolationism, Injustice, Idolatry, Institutionalism, and Intolerance. He particularly emphasized the latter two points saying about institutionalism, "There is something patently amiss when we forget who serves whom. A true Baptist believes that the local church is the highest level of ecclesiastical authority." On intolerance he said, "We need to be more tolerant of people who are a bit different, but we need to be intolerant of the godless and gutless way some people are being treated. Let us be mature enough to recognize that our most important fight is not with each other [it is] a battle to salvage our culture and our very civilization from a world view that thinks man is good and God is dead."

In other reports, Ouachita President Dr. Ben Elrod told the messengers that OBU had more students from the Soviet Union than any other college or university in America. He emphasized that Ouachita students had been active in witnessing to international students, both on campus and in their study-abroad programs. Newly elected President of Williams College Jimmy Millikin said he wanted his institution to be "perceived as a Bible college, but more, and as a preacher college, but also a full-fledged Christian liberal arts institution." He also said the college had just introduced its fourth baccalaureate degree. Johnny Biggs, in reporting for the Child Care and Family Ministries agency, emphasized the growing abuse and neglect among the nation's families. He noted that the recent completion of long overdue capital improvements had given the agency a "rebirth" and allowed it to expand its services.

Executive Director Don Moore told the messengers the Cooperative Program emphasis was beginning to pay off. "We are reaching our state budget," he said, "in times where other states are posting a 1 to 10 percent deficit, we are posting a 4 percent increase. He also said the gains were more than money. New church starts were up and in fact the ABSC had started 133 churches over the past seven years and only lost 35. That record had earned the Arkansas Convention an award from the SBC's Home Mission Board for having the highest number of church starts in relation to church membership in the SBC.

Moore also informed the messengers that the Executive Board had voted to adopt a Home Mission Board request for the ABSC to begin a partnership with the Iowa Southern Baptist Convention. With fifty-seven of that state's ninety-nine counties without a Southern Baptist church, the partnership promised to be a fertile field for mission work.

Clarence Shell in reporting for the Evangelism Department, reen-forced the executive director's report. He noted that the "Here's Hope, Jesus Cares for You," revivals led to a 15.8 percent increase in baptism over 1990. This growth gave Arkansas the second highest increase "in the old-line states" in the SBC.

Messengers also adopted fifteen resolutions. Nine of those opposed gambling, use and abuse of alcoholic beverages (2), pornography (2), school based clinics, abortion (2), and ordination of women as pastors. Six resolutions affirmed the Cooperative Program, the authority of the Scripture, the traditional family, members of the Armed Forces serving in "Operation Desert Storm," efforts to relieve world hunger, and the leadership of the ABSC officers for the past year.

Before adjourning, messengers elected William H. (Buddy) Sutton to be president for 1991–1992. An active member in Little Rock's Immanuel Church, he had also played a leading role in the Billy Graham Crusade's visit to Little Rock, and he had led a movement to defeat a 1990 attempt to again amend the state constitution to legalize gambling. He was the first layman chosen to lead the Convention since

G. W. Puryear was elected for three consecutive terms 1923–1925.

In developing its priorities for 1992, the Executive Board outlined four projects for special emphasis. Continuing the theme of Building God's Family, the board sponsored a statewide conference on "Moral Issues Confronting the Family." And, the board also scheduled special conferences on Senior Adult Convention, Single Adults, and a "Family Enrichment Emphasis for Ministers." The board also continued its task force on "Church Conflict and Forced Termination."

The Discipleship Training Department under the direction of Robert Holley took the lead in promoting the Hope for the Home emphasis. Using its Family Ministry section, the department trained twenty-eight individuals to be Associational Family Ministry Directors, conducted six Marriage Enrichment Conferences and a Patenting by Grace Workshop. Efforts in these areas seriously strained the limited personnel and resources of the department. However, even with their best effort, Holley and his associates had only reached about 60 percent of the associations. The cadre of workers prepared to pass the skills they had learned for strengthening families on to the associations and churches was extremely small.

Work in other areas for 1992 continued to go well for the ABSC. Freddie Pike reported that the Siloam Springs Assembly had a record number of campers, exceeding 7,000 in its six-week season. The Brotherhood, under Glendon Grober's leadership, completed the three-year Guatemala partnership with all goals met or exceeded, and Jimmie Sheffield noted that support for the Cooperative Program exceeded projections by more than 7 percent.

In its August meeting, the Executive Board reviewed the status of various "Hope for the Home" initiatives and outlined its emphasis for the new year on "Growing Churches." Part of the church growth initiative included a major emphasis on evangelism for 1994 and 1995. The board directed the staff to begin work on that project with associational and church leaders.

When messengers gathered for the 1992 Convention in Pine Bluff, Executive Director Moore challenged them to "move forward" on church growth. Using passages from Numbers and Joshua, he reminded his listeners of the wilderness wanderings of the nation of Israel that had brought them to the eastern bank of the Jordon River. Like Israel, he said that Arkansas's Southern Baptist were also confronted with a time of decision and had four choices: "to stay where they were and be content or go into new territories that had not been encountered," "to fight for, or with, each other," "to finish the task," and whether "to solve their problems or drive the wedge of separation deeper." He confided to the audience "I have no interest in us staying where we are. We have led out on this special emphasis on church growth because we are not willing to stay where we are."

To follow up on the executive director's message, Associate Director Sheffield presented messengers with the board's priority goals for 1993. These included plans to train individuals in how to witness from 300 churches each year, for the next three years; to equip at least 300 churches to develop personal and corporate prayer ministries; to provide growth assistance for 400 declining or plateaued churches, and to help churches involve 75,000 volunteers in projects that addressed ministry needs. With over 1,200 churches and almost 500,000 members, these goals seemed modest, but realistic. Messengers gave the priorities report, and the budget recommendations totaling $15.2 million their unanimous report.

Messengers observed a time of silence in memory of Dr. Everett Sneed, editor of the *Arkansas Baptist Newsmagazine*, who had died of a heart attack the previous June. Ironically, Dr. Sneed had told friends at the 1991 Convention that he planned to retire at the end of the year. Perhaps it was appropriate that the committee appointed to study the organizational status of the paper recommended that it be continued as a separate agency. The committee also suggested that the *ABN*'s board of directors be increased from 9 to 15 members and include at least one account. The Executive Board accepted the committee's report at its August meeting. The *Newsmagazine*'s board of directors employed Trennis Henderson, a native of Tennessee, graduate of School of the Ozarks, Point Lookout, Missouri, and Southern Seminary in Louisville, to be the new editor. Henderson was serving as managing editor of the Missouri Baptist newsjournal *Word and Way* at the time of his appointment.

Messengers also approved eight resolutions—four opposed gambling (including charitable bingo), consumption of alcoholic beverages, homosexual behavior, and "the humanistic safe sex message."

They affirmed the sanctity of human life and expressed support for "Christ-centered crisis pregnancy centers and the Promise House." Two resolutions also dealt with newly elected President Bill Clinton. In one, messengers pledged to pray for the President and Vice-President Al Gore. The other expressed opposition to President-elect Clinton's views on abortion, homosexual rights, and distribution of contraceptives in public schools.

With its emphasis on church growth, the ABSC entered 1993 with a variety of action plans. Priority projects included implementing the "Southern Baptist Church Growth Plan, which was designed to provide "balanced growth" in each ministry area; the Great Commission Breakthrough, another SBC program which addressed program changes needed for plateaued and declining churches; and Church Arkansas, an ABSC developed program, was designed to reach people in their own cultural and life settings. In addition to those projects, Tommy Goode and the Missions Department organized the Mississippi River Ministry to both evangelize and provide social services in the state's delta counties. The Iowa partnership, coordinated by Missions Director Jimmy Barrentine and assisted by Glendon Grober in the Brotherhood Department, continued in its second year.

Twenty-seven of the forty-one associations held church growth conferences in 1993. Freddie Pike and the associates in the Sunday School Department also trained twenty-eight individuals to be consultants in the Great Commission Breakthrough program. Jimmy Barrentine and the staff in the Missions Department assisted in organizing twenty new congregations. Eight of those were among caucasian, English-speaking, groups; nine were among ethnic groups for whom English was a second language; and three were among predominately African-American communities. Thirty-one churches, with 128 volunteers traveled to Iowa to assist with various partnership projects. Most opportunities came in the area of disaster relief for flood victims along the Mississippi River.

Changes in the ABSC during the year included Lester McCullough resigning to take a position with the Baptist Sunday School Board. He was replaced by Rob Hewell, a graduate of Southwestern Seminary and Minister of Music at New Orleans First Church when he was hired. Also, at its August meeting the Executive Board voted to change the name of the Discipleship Training Department to the Discipleship and Family Ministry Department. Subject to Convention approval, board members emphasized that commitment would still be with Discipleship Training. However, since the department had added responsibilities in the family ministries area, the new name would more clearly reflect that work.

The Guatemalan project ended in May. Glendon Grober noted that all projects had been met or exceeded—except for the evangelistic crusade planned for Guatemala City. Intended to climax the partnership, the crusade had to be canceled because the unstable political situation in the capital city. Even as the partnership was drawing to a close, plans were initiated to begin a partnership with the European Baptist Convention (EBC) beginning in 1994.

Messengers to the 1993 Convention met with North Little Rock's Park Hill Church and host pastor, Cary Heard. Spirits were dampened by the knowledge that Shirley Moore, wife of Executive Don Moore, was desperately ill with cancer. The messengers adopted a resolution "to pray for Shirley Moore" as the Convention came to an end.

Under second-term President Buddy Sutton's leadership, the messengers moved quickly through recommendations coming from the Executive Board. These included approval of the three-year partnership with European Baptists, accepting the name change of the Discipleship Training Department to drop "Training" and add "Family Ministry" to the title, approving a nine-member committee to plan the Convention's 150th anniversary, establishing a twenty-four-member Directions 2000 planning committee to recommend initiatives for the next five-year goals beginning in 1996, inviting the SBC's Foreign Mission Board to conduct a meeting and appointment service in the state for April 1997. Messengers also approved a rewording and editorial changes in the ABSC constitution. Betty Harp, who chaired the Constitution and By-Laws Committee, explained "there is no change in our doctrinal positions or in the procedures for appointments or elections." She also reminded the audience that previous Conventions had approved replacing Kerfoot's Parliamentary Law with Robert's Rules of Order, newly revised.

In agency reports to the Convention, Johnny Biggs told the messengers that the Children's Home and Family Ministries Department had cared for 500 children and youth over the past year and had processed another 1,600 referrals. Baptist Foundation Harry Trulove mentioned in his report that he planned to retire in 1994 before the next Convention. He told his listeners that when he came to the foundation in 1974, the agency was managing $1 million; in the past year that figure had increased to $38 million. And, Dr. Trulove said, "Every area of Baptist work (agencies, students, summer missionaries, retired pastors) is strengthened through the work of the Foundation."

Reporting for Williams Baptist College, new President Gary Huckabay told the messengers that Williams had been fully accredited in the past year and the college planned to offer several new baccalaureate degrees. President Ben Elrod noted that "all the vital signs are excellent" at Ouachita and reported that "the university has the largest transfer and freshman enrollment since 1973."

Associate Executive Director Jimmie Sheffield gave the theme interpretation, "Perform Ministry in Jesus' Name," for 1994. He challenged the messengers to "see ministry as an opportunity from God" and noted that the most dramatic illustration of that truth was the fact that Don Moore was unable to preach as scheduled because "he was ministering to his wife, Shirley, who is hospitalized with cancer." Sheffield also said "servanthood begins when we move beyond our own comfort to relieve the discomfort of others."

Before adjourning, messengers endorsed the ministry theme for the year; established a long-range planning committee for "Directions 2000" to plan the next five years, and adopted ten resolutions—including the one for Shirley Moore previously mentioned. Others included the traditional opposition to gambling, use of beverage alcohol, the humanistic safe-sex message, and same-sex marriages. They also called for a boycott of the television program *NYPD Blue* and affirmed the sanctity of human life and the True Love Waits campaign aimed at teenagers.

Messengers also elected Ronnie Rogers, pastor of Lakeside Church in Hot Springs, president for 1993–1994. A graduate of Criswell College in Dallas, with a master's degree in counseling from Henderson State University in Arkadelphia, Rogers was forty-one years old and had been in the ministry for thirteen years at the time of his election.

There was a great deal of sadness in 1994. Shirley Moore died within days after the 1993 Convention and Glendon and Marjorie

Grober were killed in an automobile accident in July. Still, the efforts to Perform Ministry in Jesus' Name went forward. The Iowa partnership increased in both numbers of projects and people involved. Work with European Baptist also got off to a good start. By Convention time, EBC churches had requested assistance with seventy-three projects. Doyne Plummer, who had been appointed to coordinate volunteers after the Grobers' deaths, tried to match requests with volunteers.

New staff members for the year included Milton Redeker, who replaced Freddie Pike when the latter returned to a church staff position. J. D. Stake took over the Ministry of Crisis Support after Glen McGriff retired March 1, 1994. James Hausler was named an associate in the Missions Department with responsibilities for language ministries. The Perform Ministry emphasis was particularly well received in the migrant labor camps at Hope and Hermitage. By 1994 there were twenty-eight ethnic congregations in the state. Eighteen were Hispanic; two, Laotian; five Korean congregations; two Vietnamese; and one Chinese.

The long-range planning committee for Directions 2000 met throughout the year. By Convention time they had developed an overall theme of "Arkansas Awakening," and five specific annual themes beginning in 1996. Within the general themes the committee targeted fourteen areas for specialized training. These ranged from the traditional focus on worship and leadership training, to more complex issues involving race relations, conflict resolution, and strategic planning.

Messengers returned to Little Rock's Immanuel Church for the 1994 meeting with Dr. Rex Horne as host pastor. For the year, enrollments in Sunday School, Discipleship Training, and Church Music were up by 1 to 2 percent. Gifts to the Cooperative Program remained essentially unchanged—a growth of only .02 percent. As has been mentioned, the Perform Ministry theme was particularly effective among migrant workers and new immigrants. But, interest among traditional groups was on the wan. There were also more subtle changes going on among the churches. Over 40 percent of the ABSC churches reported annual contributions under $40,000. But, seventeen churches had budgets of over $1 million. Differences in church makeup and areas of interest reminiscent of the decade following World War II were again working their way into the life of ABSC churches.

Executive Director Don Moore saw these changes coming and called upon his fellow Southern Baptist to revitalize their lives. "There is little consistent effort today to win the lost," he said, "because society teaches us not to acknowledge sin. We're on mission to build self-esteem, and there is little chance for old-fashioned repentance." Because of the lack of repentance he said, "There is an embarrassing impotence within the body of Christ, even the pagan world is appalled. . . . Easy compromise, unchanged lives, sham, show, sloughing off— these are the things that seem to bother the Lord."

Convention President Ronnie Rogers echoed Director Moore's message. Saying "the doctrine of self-love [self esteem] is from the garbage heap of hell," the ABSC president also said "the idea that scripture suggests that man's greatest need is more self-love is an assault on the truth."

In the agency reports to the messengers, Johnny Biggs noted that the Children's Homes and Family Ministries was one hundred years old in 1994. He also said, "Our founding fathers sought God's will to reach out and provide a home for orphaned children. It is the same truth that motivates us to minister today." David Moore, new director of the Arkansas Baptist Foundation, said, "I see the fruits of the seeds planted by Harry Trulove." He noted that the foundation "was alive and well with $45 million of assets in trust." Trennis Henderson reported that the *Newsmagazine* remained "debt-free and has a growing operating reserve fund."

Messengers adopted the Directions 2000 report on Arkansas Awakening, approved a record $16.6 million budget, and accepted the "priority projects" identified by the Executive Board for 1995. These included a statewide, simultaneous revival emphasis, coordinated revival efforts with the Iowa and European partnerships, and a goal of starting "200 new Sunday School units" on "Great Start Sunday, October 1, 1995." Messengers also agreed to change the name of the World Hunger Committee to the World Hunger Work Group to allow all ABSC programs that relate to hunger issues to be involved in the same emphasis.

Before adjourning, messengers also adopted eleven resolutions. Included were resolutions memorializing Shirley Moore, commemorating the work of Glendon and Marjorie Grober, and reaffirming the

Cooperative Program. Other resolutions opposed homosexuality, pornography, alcohol and illicit drugs, gambling, and upheld the sanctity of human life.

Messengers also reelected Ronnie Rogers for a second term as president for 1994–1995.

The state Evangelism and Sunday School Departments took the lead in implementing the "Reaching People" theme for 1995. Clarence Shell, director of the Evangelism, said the year saw "the most extensive evangelism process" in his twenty-six years of service. Milton Redeker, director of the Sunday School Department, reported that over 1200 workers, representing every association in the state, attended the annual Sunday School Convention. That attendance was the second highest in the Convention's history. But even so, Sunday School enrollment dropped by over 1,500.

More positive results were seen in the European and Iowa partnerships. Under Harry Black, who was appointed Brotherhood Director after Glendon Grober's death. Both partnerships had enthusiastic responses from ABSC volunteers. In Europe, Black was able to match forty-seven partners with seventy-seven different projects. In Iowa Southern Baptist work was extended into fifty-six of the state's ninety-nine counties, and the local churches were strong enough to form the Iowa State Baptist Convention. By mutual consent, work with both partnerships was extended beyond the original agreements—the European Partnership though 1997 and the Iowa agreement through 2001.

Messengers returned to First Church, Little Rock for the 1995 Convention. Dr. Bill Eliff was host pastor. This Convention concluded the five-year theme on Building God's Family. From a statistical point of view, the period remained stable. Total giving increased by some $3.25 million over the period, but the ABSC was not able to reach its goal of contributing one-half of its receipts to the Cooperative Program. Enrollments in Sunday School, Discipleship Training, and Church Music programs, baptisms, and new church starts, vital signs for the Convention's health, were irregular and did not keep pace with state population growth.

Executive Director Moore was perhaps thinking of this sluggish growth when he delivered his annual sermon to the Convention. He told the messengers, "We are at a time in history when it is apparent that something more must be done for this nation, our churches, our denomination. We have developed wonderful materials, great strategies, outstanding preachers, and extensive programs of trying to get the gospel to all the world. Yet we have not even succeeded in getting our churches alarmed about the situation in the kingdom and the situation in our nation and in our churches. The masses are still eaten up with social ills."

The overall tone of this Convention was subdued. President Ronnie Rogers had been forced to undergo heart surgery just days before the meeting and could not attend. Also, Don Moore had announced his intention to retire in February 1996. Love and loyalty to him, coupled with uncertainty over his successor, had an impact on the messengers. The ABSC Music Department, under the direction of Rob Hewell, tried to enliven the group with an outstanding musical presentation on the theme for next year, "Seeking His Face." Assisted by Jean Pilcher, minister of music at Little Rock's Parkway Place, and a number of other special groups, Hewell said he had chosen the music to help messengers "focus on those things which are important to bringing spiritual awakening to our state."

Testimonies from several individuals on the need for spiritual awakening also helped move the messengers beyond their immediate thoughts for Dr. Moore. And, the special recognition ABSC leaders extended to him helped revive the audience. Lieutenant Governor Mike Huckabee, and former president of the ABSC, expressed warm words of support for Moore's leadership, as did Associate ABSC Director Jimmie Sheffield and a number of others. Messengers gave him two standing ovations. In responding to the "gracious expressions of love," Moore said his one biggest regret was that the ABSC did not reach 1,500 in total churches. However, he was confident the Convention would do that "with in the next three years."

Agency directors, in making their reports to the Convention, addressed the Spiritual Awakening theme. David Perry, appointed director of the Children's Homes and Family Ministries when Johnny Biggs retired earlier in the year, said, "A spiritually awakened church can and will respond to the needs of children and youth served by the agencies ministries." David Moore, president of the Arkansas Baptist Foundation noted that 1994 had been a difficult year in the bond market, but 1995 had been "a wonderful year . . . our funds are up 18 to 25 percent. . . . It looks like long before our 50th anniversary in 1998, we will have $50 million in assets under management."

President Ben Elrod said "Never before has Ouachita Baptist University been in a position to have a bigger impact in Arkansas, around the nation and throughout our world than at this time." The reason for the president's optimism was because "there is more to Ouachita . . . than academics"; it was the "balance of academic excellence with spiritual excellence in every aspect of campus life" that gave the institution its distinction.

New President Jerol Swaim said that Williams College students "observed three days of spiritual awakening during the last week of September with four weeks of cottage prayer meetings preceding the renewal effort . . . more than 60 percent of the students living on campus attended the meetings." Swaim also reported that the Executive Board was recommending that WBC be given permission to begin a two-year fund-raising campaign among the churches for capital expenditures. Included in the recommendations was permission for a similar fund-raising effort for OBU to begin following the Williams campaign.

Before adjourning, messengers elected Dr. Rex Horne, pastor of Little Rock's Immanuel Church to be ABSC president for 1995–1996. They also approved ten resolutions including opposing to gambling, homosexuality, pornography, alcohol, and drug abuse; affirming the sanctity of human life; denouncing racism as "deplorable sin;" and calling for Arkansas Baptist "to become informed about the call for a constitutional convention." Messengers also approved an Executive Board recommendation that a "committee to study reorganization of the Executive Board" be established.

The 1996 theme for the five-year "Arkansas Awakening" campaign was "Live for the Word." To promote that emphasis, the Executive Board invited SBC staff member Henry Blackaby to lead a "prayer conference" the weekend after the Convention adjourned. Executive Director Moore believed the conference was necessary because as he told messengers at the Convention, "Great preaching is not going to bring revival to the church. It is not going to bring awakening to the communities. I can tell you that the ingenious structures in the SBC, the state or in the church is not going to bring revival. Is there anybody here so spiritually inept that you are counting on anything bringing revival besides God? Surely not." The prayer conference was well-attended and a good beginning for the new year.

In December, the suspense over who would become the new executive director was lifted when the board announced Dr. Emil Turner for that position. Turner, a native of Louisiana, had pastored in Arkansas for four years in the 1980s. He was a graduate of Louisiana State University and New Orleans Baptist Theological Seminary and had served as a director for Campus Crusade for Christ. He was pastor of First Baptist Church, Lake Charles, Louisiana, when the Executive Board selected him as its new director.

The Missions Department took the lead in Living the Word in 1996. Under the direction of Jimmy Barrentine, the department assisted in starting thirty new congregations. Included in the new starts was a congregation in the Caddo River Association, the first new church in seventeen years for that association. An Hispanic Youth Camp was added to the schedule at Camp Paron. The Hope Migrant Center also relocated to new facilities adjacent to a new rest stop along Interstate Highway 30. The Mississippi River Ministry continued to pay dividends, and the Iowa partnership maintained a strong attraction especially for men's groups. But, as Barrentine said, "We do not close our eyes to the fact that there are still more than 1,000,000 people in Arkansas with no church to call home."

A more comprehensive outreach was perhaps muted by a new controversy, rumors of which began to circulate in late summer. The issue concerned Ouachita Baptist University. When that institution received its initial charter in 1886, the language specified that its board of trustees "would be self-perpetuating and have absolute control of the college." In 1914, the trustees deferred authority to appoint new trustees to the ABSC. That procedure had not been a concern until divisiveness began showing up in the SBC after 1978. Typically, the ABSC Nominating Committee conferred with the various agencies, as a courtesy, not policy, to get recommendations for new trustees. In 1996, Ouachita had four vacancies on its board and recommend eight names to the ABSC Nominating Committee. None of the eight was selected when that Committee prepared its report to the Convention. Word of that action quickly leaked out and rumors quickly spread that the action was an attempt by "fundamentalists" to take control of the university.

Ouachita leaders, not wishing to take sides in the dispute, but concerned that the institution might get caught in the cross-currents, decided to reestablish the procedure for selecting trustees as spelled out in the original charter. In the words of OBU President Dr. Ben Elrod, they did so "to remove Ouachita from the line of fire of denominational dispute."

However, a number of ABSC members, and some on the Executive Board, took exception to OBU's action. The board's Executive Committee responded to the OBU action by escrowing the institution's funds being sent through the Cooperative Program. This amounted to about 10 percent of OBU's total budget. At the same time the board also appointed a "five-member reconciliation committee" to meet with Ouachita officials and hopefully resolve the matter. ABSC Executive Board Chairman Chuck McAllister chaired the joint meetings and the groups came to an agreement with only two meetings.

The "reconciliation plan" called for a joint committee made up of representatives from OBU's Board of Trustees and the ABSC Nominating Committee. This new committee would agree on nominees and recommend a slate to the annual Convention. This recommendation was proposed as an amendment to the ABSC By-Laws and required two-thirds affirmative votes by messengers at two consecutive annual Conventions. In urging messengers to approve the agreement, Chairman McAllister said, "Comparing the proposal to action in other state conventions, this is the strongest agreement in existence for the benefit of a state convention." He went on to say, "This is a time for restoration, to exhibit to a lost world that we are in fact a redemptive people." Opponents argued that such a agreement would "allow" the OBU trustees to "steal the University out from under Arkansas Baptists."

Following extended discussion the messengers voted by 63.7 percent to approve the reconciliation recommendation. Opponents of the agreement then made an effort to "defund" Ouachita in the 1997 ABSC budget. Convention President Rex Horne declared that motion failed in a "show of hands" vote.

The reconciliation issue was a proverbial "baptism by fire" for new Executive Director Emil Turner. In his first address to the Convention

Emil Turner (1996–present) the ABSC's seventeenth chief executive officer.

in his new role, Director Turner said Arkansas Baptists must "turn your attention . . . to your own relationship to Jesus Christ." Using the analogy of "heart disease," he noted that America/Arkansas was suffering from "a spiritual heart disease [that is] ravaging our churches—hardness of the heart." He pointed out that "those of us who are at high risk of hardness of the heart are the most religious among us—not the wicked and the worldly, but the worshippers."

The Ouachita issue garnered so much discussion, little notice was made of other actions growing out of the 1996 Convention. Messengers extended the European Partnership agreement and approved the Executive Board's priority projects of 1997. They also approved resolutions affirming Christian public school teachers and administrators, the opponents of legalized gambling, the sanctity of human life, and the need for racial reconciliation, while opposing homosexual behavior, anti-pornography, and consumption of beverage alcohol, and illicit drugs. Dr. Rex Horne was reelected president—to serve 1996–1997.

It was a bit ironic that the Ouachita controversy came up during Dr. Horne's presidency. Since Bill Clinton's election as president of the United States, Horne and Little Rock's Immanuel Church had been the target of numerous protests and the object of much criticism because of President Clinton's position on homosexuals, abortion, and other social issues. Horne's magnanimous personality and the even-handed manner in which he presided during the Convention was credited by many with keeping an emotional issue from becoming volatile.

The theme for the second year of Arkansas Awakening was Strengthening the Family. To assist in implementing that emphasis, the Executive Board and the Baptist Building planned an ambitious work among the associations and churches. Special attention was devoted to training children's workers and young people and the importance of the home environment in strengthening the family. Even the Missions and Evangelism Departments were involved the training process.

But the primary issue that most ABSC leaders were concerned about was the Ouachita-ABSC reconciliation plan. So large did it loom that when messengers returned to North Little Rock's Park Hill Church for the 1997 Convention, one of their first acts of business was to delay voting on the budget until after the reconciliation matter was resolved. Over 1,800 messengers registered—the largest ABSC meeting in history. A year had done little to change hearts on the matter. To the surprise of many, the motion failed to get the necessary two-thirds majority—by 1.3 percent.

Failure to pass the proposed by-law agreement raised a question about the future relationship between OBU and the Arkansas Baptist State Convention. Following Ouachita's decision in October 1996 to select its own board, the trustees filed a new charter with the Arkansas secretary of state. That document included a provision that reestablished the board's autonomy. Still, the OBU leadership, the ABSC leadership and 65.4 percent of Arkansas's Southern Baptist sought reconciliation and cooperation. To what extent that would happen continued into the ABSC's sesquicentennial year.

As in the previous year, the Ouachita issue so dominated Convention proceedings that other substantive decisions were all but overlooked. In addition to adopting a record $17.6 million budget, messengers approved seven priority projects recommend by the Executive Board for the Arkansas Awakening's 1998 theme of Build the Church.

Using awakening as the focus for his address to the Convention, Executive Director Emil Turner asked his listeners rhetorically, "will you experience an awakening?" Using Numbers 11 as his text, Turner warned his audience that "believers can be in the right, yet miss revival. Joshua is a man known for the Word. You can know Scripture and still miss the revival. Joshua was a man known for service. You can be a servant and still miss the revival. We many be in the early days of revival in our country but that doesn't mean every church and every member will experience it. . . . The question is, will you experience revival?"

The ABSC also began its 150th year with a new administrative organization. In 1995 the Executive Board appointed a "staff restructuring committee" and charged it with responsibility for developing a new organization model for the Convention doing its work in the twenty-first century. That thirteen-member committee, chaired by Tim Reddin, director of Missions for the Central Association, made its report to the messengers at the 1997 Convention. The recommendation called for a major restructuring of the "Baptist Building"—the most comprehensive reorganization since 1971.

Messengers approved the restructuring committee's report and the new organization was officially implemented in January 1998. It featured "seven ministry planning teams" including executive and administrative, evangelism and church growth, leadership and worship, mission ministries, missions support, collegiate ministry, and family ministry. This structure was put in place, according to the committee "to assist individual churches and associations to accomplish their biblical mission." The committee had also been asked to study the board structure of the ABSC's five statewide institutions "to position our agencies and institutions for the 21st century." However, when the Ouachita situation developed, the committee asked for, and was granted, a one year extension of its assignment.

Before adjourning, messengers adopted four resolutions. In addition to expressing appreciation to the host church, pastor, and ABSC leaders, they also endorsed the Baptist World Alliance and pledged to continue support for its ministries and, in light of "drastic changes," projected to develop from a new federal welfare system; messengers also agreed to provide greater assistance to the those individuals most adversely effected by the new policy. A fourth resolution was presented and adopted from the floor to oppose abortion. For the first time in the decade, there were no resolutions opposing gambling, pornography, alcohol, and/or drug abuse.

Messengers also elected Greg Kirksey, pastor of First Church, Benton as Convention president for 1997–1998.

Build the Church was an appropriate theme to begin the ABSC's 150th anniversary. In 1848, a small group of churches and local associations began seeking "some system or plan" to extend the influence of Christianity beyond their local congregations. As a product of church initiative, it was appropriate that the Arkansas Baptist State Convention commemorate that effort with its own initiative to build local churches. Now 1,389 churches and missions strong, with a program budget of $17,682,975, the ABSC had found a "System and Plan" to build churches and do Kingdom work.

Appendixes

A

Convention Charter

Section 1. Be it enacted by the General Assembly of the State of Arkansas, That T. B. Vanhorn, John H. Carlton, P. P. Siler, T. S. N. King, L. B. Fort, John Woods, Nat G. Smith, W. R. Trawick, M. Shelby Kennard, M. W. McCraw, J. J. Harris, E. M. Harris, A. Yates, D. C. Hall, James Woods, and R. M. Thrasher, and their successors in office, shall be, and the same are hereby created a corporation, under the name and styles of the Arkansas Baptist State Convention, and by that name and style shall have succession for 99 years, with power as a corporation, to sue and be sued, plead and be impleaded, acquire, hold and transfer, by deed or otherwise, real and personal property, contract and be contracted with for the use and benefit of the Arkansas Baptist State Convention, and shall have and use a common seal, and do other acts appertaining to a corporation, consistent with the constitution and laws of the State.

Section II. Be it further enacted, That the domicile of said corporation shall be Princeton, Ark., and all property, real and educational and charitable purposes, for the use and benefit and subject to the direction and control of said Arkansas Baptist State Convention.

Section III. Be it further enacted, That the trustees above named shall hold their office until the next annual meeting of said Convention, when their successor shall be elected; and the board of trustees shall be elected at every annual meeting of said Convention thereafter; and on failure of the Convention to hold any annual meetings the board of trustees shall hold over until the Convention does meet and elect their successors.

Section IV. Be it further enacted, That five of said trustees, shall constitute a quorum, for the transaction of all business; the board shall elect a president, secretary, and treasurer, annually; the secretary shall make an annual report of the proceedings of the board to the said Convention. The treasurer shall give bond with good security, in a sum to be fixed by the board of trustees, conditioned for the faithful performance of his duties, and that he will account for and pay over upon the orders of the board, or to his successors in office, all moneys, chosen in action, and other assets that may come to his hands as treasurer of the corporation; and the treasurer shall also make an annual report to said Convention of the state of his accounts and financial transactions of the board of trustees.

Section V. Be it further enacted, That the board of trustees shall have power to make by-laws for their own government, subject to the direction and control of said Convention.

Approved February 12th, 1859.

B

Historical Directory

Year	Place	President	Secretary	Preacher
1848	Brownsville, Dallas Co.	William H. Bayliss	Asbury Daniel	Edward Haynes
1849	El Dorado	Jesse Hartwell	Asbury Daniel	Jesse Hartwell
1850	Mt. Bethel, Clark Co.	W. H. Bayliss	S. Stevenson	Franklin Courtney
1851	Princeton	Jesse Hartwell	S. Stevenson	Jesse Hartwell
1852	Mine Creek, Hempstead Co.	E. Haynes	S. Stevenson	Allen M. Scott
1853	Camden	Jesse Hartwell	S. Stevenson	E. Haynes
1854	Tulip	Jesse Hartwell	S. Stevenson	S. Stevenson
1855	no report			R. M. Thrasher
1856	New Hope, Dallas Co.	Jesse Hartwell	R. J. Coleman	W. M. Lea
1857	Samaria, Dallas Co.	W. M. Lea	M. W. McCraw	W. M. Lea
1858	Charleston	W. M. Lea	R. M. Thrasher	W. M. Lea
1859	Little Rock	W. M. Lea	R. M. Thrasher	no sermon
1860	Pine Bluff	W. M. Lea	R. M. Thrasher	P. S. G. Watson
1861	Fort Smith	Lee Compere	E. L. Compere	H. F. Buckner
1862	Fort Smith	Willis Burns	E. L. Compere	no sermon
1863–6	inclusive (no meetings)	Willis Burns		
1867	Little Rock	W. M. Lea	W. H. Roberts	Peyton Smith
1868	Little Rock	W. M. Lea	W. H. Roberts	W. D. Mayfield
1869	Helena	W. D. Mayfield	J. B. Searcy	J. R. Graves
1870	Arkadelphia	Aaron Yates	J. B. Searcy	W. D. Mayfield
1871	Monticello	M. Y. Moran	J. B. Searcy	Moses Green
1872	Austin	M. Y. Moran	J. B. Searcy	J. M. Hart
1873	Little Rock	M. Y. Moran	J. B. Searcy	R. M. Thrasher
1874	Dardanelle	W. W. Crawford	J. B. Searcy	J. R. G. W. N. Adams
1875	Arkadelphia	H. H. Coleman	J. B. Searcy	J. B. Searcy
1876	Searcy	H. H. Coleman	J. B. Searcy	
1877	Forrest City	H. H. Coleman	T. P. Boone	W. A. Forbes
1878	Monticello	J. M. Hart	W. F. Mack	M. D. Early
1879	Hope	J. M. Hart	J. R. G. W. N. Adams	R. J. Coleman
1880	Russellville	J. P. Eagle	Benjamin Thomas	J. D. Jameson
1882	Lonoke	J. P. Eagle	J. B. Searcy	W. E. Paxton
1883	Fayetteville	J. P. Eagle	J. B. Searcy	W. D. Mayfield
1884	Pine Bluff	J. P. Eagle	J. H. Holland	A. J. Kincaid

Year	Place	President	Secretary	Preacher
1885	Hope	J. P. Eagle	J. H. Holland	A. J. Fawcett
1886	Forrest City	J. P. Eagle	J. H. Holland	A. B. Miller
1887	Morrilton	J. P. Eagle	J. H. Holland	A. S. Pettie
1888	Jonesboro	J. P. Eagle	Martin Ball	Enoch Winde
1889	Little Rock	W. E. Penn	J. G. B. Simms	J. R. Hughes
1890	Eureka Springs	J. P. Eagle	J. G. B. Simms	R. J. Coleman
1891	Arkadelphia	J. P. Eagle	J. G. B. Simms	W. T. Box
1892	Fort Smith	J. M. Hart	J. G. B. Simms	J. W. Lipsey
1893	Conway	W. P. Throgmorton	W. F. Blackwood	W. P. Throgmorton
1894	Lonoke	J. P. Eagle	W. F. Blackwood	J. H. Peay
1895	Monticello	J. P. Eagle	J. G. B. Simms	E. B. Miller
1896	Hot Springs	J. P. Eagle	J. G. B. Simms	A. H. Autry
1897	Pine Bluff	J. P. Eagle	J. G. B. Simms	O. L. Hailey
1898	Little Rock	J. P. Eagle	W. Theo Smith	W. H. Paslay
1899	Jonesboro	J. P. Eagle	W. Theo Smith	C. W. Daniel
1900	Hope	J. P. Eagle	W. Theo Smith	J. K. Pace
1901	Paragould	J. P. Eagle	W. Theo Smith	N. R. Pittman
1902	Conway	J. P. Eagle	Sam H. Campbell	O. J. Wade
1903	Little Rock	J. P. Eagle	Sam H. Campbell	A. J. Barton
1904	Pine Bluff	John Ayers	W. F. Doris	W. A. Freeman
1905	Fort Smith	John Ayers	W. F. Doris	Ben Cox
1906	Texarkana	W. E. Atkinson	Sam H. Campbell	F. F. Gibson
1907	Little Rock	W. E. Atkinson	John Jeter Hurt	H. L. Winburn
1908	Fayetteville	W. E. Atkinson	John Jeter Hurt	W. T. Amis
1909	Arkadelphia	H. T. Bradford	John Jeter Hurt	R. F. Treadway
1910	Fort Smith	H. T. Bradford	John Jeter Hurt	J. T. Christian
1911	Pine Bluff	H. T. Bradford	John Jeter Hurt	N. R. Townsend
1912	Hot Springs	P. C. Barton	E. P. J. Garrott	V. C. Neal
1913	Monticello	P. C. Barton	E. P. J. Garrott	N. M. Green
1914	Little Rock	P. C. Barton	E. P. J. Garrott	A. H. Autry
1915	Conway	P. C. Barton	E. P. J. Garrott	W. J. E. Cox
1916	Malvern	J. W. Conger	E. P. J. Garrott	T. D. Brown
1917	Jonesboro	J. W. Conger	E. P. J. Garrott	B. B. Bailey
1918	Little Rock	L. E. Barton	D. S. Campbell	C. D. Wood
1919	Little Rock	L. E. Barton	D. S. Campbell	R. V. Ferguson
1920	Fort Smith	A. H. Autry	B. L. Bridges	Austin Crouch
1921	Pine Bluff	A. H. Autry	B. L. Bridges	Calvin B. Waller
1922	Little Rock	A. H. Autry	B. L. Bridges	E. P. J. Garrott
1923	Arkadelphia	G. W. Puryear	B. L. Bridges	J. W. Hulsey
1924	Little Rock	G. W. Puryear	B. L. Bridges	W. W. Kyzar
1925	Conway	G. W. Puryear	S. R. Doyle	O. J. Wade
1926	Little Rock	H. L. Winburn	S. R. Doyle	L. M. Sipes
1927	Jonesboro	H. L. Winburn	S. R. Doyle	T. H. Jordan
1928	Texarkana	H. L. Winburn	S. R. Doyle	Ben L. Bridges
1929	Hot Springs	Otto Whitington	J. B. Luck	Otto Whitington
1930	Fort Smith	Otto Whitington	J. B. Luck	Perry F. Webb
1931	Batesville	E. P. J. Garrott	J. B. Luck	A. S. Harwell
1932	Little Rock	E. P. J. Garrott	J. B. Luck	C. V. Hickerson
1933	no meeting			
1934	El Dorado	O. J. Wade	J. B. Luck	L. M. Keeling
1935	Pine Bluff	O. J. Wade	J. B. Luck	J. G. Cothran
1936	Hot Springs	B. V. Ferguson	J. B. Luck	T. L. Harris
1937	Paragould (January)	B. V. Ferguson	J. B. Luck	C. W. Daniel
1937	Fort Smith (November)	L. M. Sipes	J. B. Luck	Thomas W. Croxton
1938	Arkadelphia	L. M. Sipes	J. B. Luck	Elmer J. Kirkbridge
1939	Camden	Calvin B. Waller	J. B. Luck	A. M. Herrington
1940	Monticello	Calvin B. Waller	J. B. Luck	O. L. Powers
1941	Jonesboro	J. S. Rogers	Taylor Stanfill	C. C. Warren

Year	Place	President	Secretary	Preacher
1942	Little Rock	J. S. Rogers	Taylor Stanfill	W. J. Hinsley
1943	Little Rock	T. L. Harris	Taylor Stanfill	W. R. Vestal
1944	Little Rock	T. L. Harris	Taylor Stanfill	J. F. F. Queen
1945	Little Rock	W. J. Hinsley	Taylor Stanfill	V. H. Coffman
1946	Texarkana	W. J. Hinsley	Taylor Stanfill	M. Ray McKay
1947	Little Rock	W. J. Hinsley	Taylor Stanfill	B. H. Duncan
1948	Little Rock	E. C. Brown	Taylor Stanfill	B. V. Ferguson
1949	Little Rock	E. C. Brown	W. Dawson King	J. A. Overton
1950	Little Rock	T. H. Jordan	W. Dawson King	H. A. Elledge
1951	Little Rock	T. H. Jordan	W. Dawson King	Lloyd A. Sparkman
1952	Little Rock	Lloyd A. Sparkman	W. Dawson King	W. M. Pratt
1953	Hot Springs	Lloyd A. Sparkman	W. Dawson King	W. O. Vaught
1954	Little Rock	W. O. Vaught	W. Dawson King	T. K. Rucker
1955	Little Rock	W. O. Vaught	W. Dawson King	C. Z. Holland
1956	Little Rock	Rel Gray	W. Dawson King	S. A. Whitlow
1957	Little Rock	Rel Gray	W. Dawson King	Hugh Cantrell
1958	Little Rock	T. K. Rucker	W. Dawson King	W. Harold Hicks
1959	Little Rock	T. K. Rucker	S. A. Whitlow	Don Hook
1960	Fayetteville	Bernes K. Selph	S. A. Whitlow	S. W. Eubanks
1961	Little Rock	Bernes K. Selph	S. A. Whitlow	Robert L. Smith
1962	Little Rock	C. Z. Holland	S. A. Whitlow	Minor E. Cole
1963	Little Rock	C. Z. Holland	S. A. Whitlow	Lloyd L. Hunnicutt
1964	El Dorado	Walter L. Yeldell	S. A. Whitlow	E. E. Griever
1965	Little Rock	Walter L. Yeldell	S. A. Whitlow	Lehman F. Webb
1966	Little Rock	Don Hook	S. A. Whitlow	Dale Cowling
1967	Little Rock	Don Hook	S. A. Whitlow	Thomas A. Hinson
1968	Hot Springs	Thomas A. Hinson	S. A. Whitlow	Andrew Hall
1969	Fort Smith	Thomas A. Hinson	Charles H. Ashcraft	Herbert Hodges
1970	Little Rock	Tal Bonham	Charles H. Ashcraft	William L. Bennett
1971	Little Rock	Tal Bonham	Charles H. Ashcraft	R. Wilbur Herring
1972	Hot Springs	Rheubin L. South	Charles H. Ashcraft	Bernes K. Selph
1973	Little Rock	Rheubin L. South	Charles H. Ashcraft	George T. Blackmon
1974	Little Rock	Don Moore	Charles H. Ashcraft	C. W. Caldwell
1975	Fort Smith	Don Moore	Charles H. Ashcraft	John McClanahan
1976	North Little Rock	R. Wilbur Herring	Charles H. Ashcraft	Lloyd Hunnicutt
1977	Little Rock	R. Wilbur Herring	Charles H. Ashcraft	Johnny Jackson Sr.
1978	Little Rock	Johnny Jackson Sr.	Charles H. Ashcraft	Kendall Black
1979	Little Rock	Johnny Jackson Sr.	Charles H. Ashcraft	Don Moore
1980	Little Rock	John Finn	Huber L. Drumwright	Ed Hinkson
1981	Fayetteville	John Finn	L. L. Collins Jr.	Jon Stubblefield
1982	North Little Rock (January)	Dillard Miller	L. L. Collins Jr.	
1982	North Little Rock (November)	Dillard Miller	Don Moore	Charles Chesser
1983	Pine Bluff	Dillard Miller	Don Moore	Joe Atchison
1984	Fort Smith	Jon Stubblefield	Don Moore	John Holston
1985	Ouachita	Jon Stubblefield	Don Moore	John Maddox
1986	Geyer Springs	Lawson Hatfield	Don Moore	R. H. Dorris
1987	Fort Smith	Lawson Hatfield	Don Moore	Trueman Moore
1988	North Little Rock	Cary Heard	Don Moore	Ron Herrod
1989	Little Rock	Cary Heard	Don Moore	Randall O'Brian
1990	Little Rock	Mike Huckabee	Don Moore	Paul Sanders
1991	Little Rock	Mike Huckabee	Don Moore	Rex Holt
1992	Pine Bluff	William H. Sutton	Don Moore	James McDaniel
1993	North Little Rock	William H. Sutton	Don Moore	Dale Thompson
1994	Little Rock	Ronnie Rogers	Don Moore	Cliff Palmer
1995	Little Rock	Ronnie Rogers	Don Moore	David Crouch
1996	Little Rock	Rex M. Horne Jr.	Emil Turner	Kerry Powell
1997	Little Rock	Rex M. Horne Jr.	Emil Turner	David Miller
1998	Arkadelphia	Greg Kirksey	Emil Turner	Rodney Reaves

C

Convention Structures

Arkansas Baptist State Convention, 1958

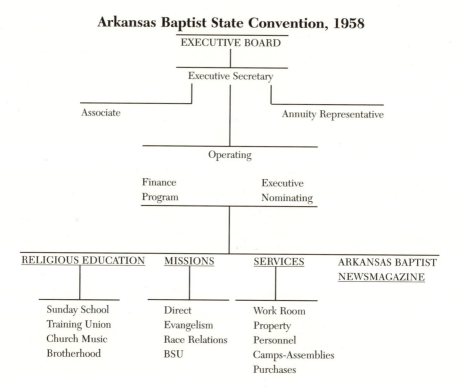

EXECUTIVE BOARD

Executive Secretary

Associate | Annuity Representative

Operating

Finance | Executive
Program | Nominating

RELIGIOUS EDUCATION | MISSIONS | SERVICES | ARKANSAS BAPTIST NEWSMAGAZINE

Sunday School | Direct | Work Room
Training Union | Evangelism | Property
Church Music | Race Relations | Personnel
Brotherhood | BSU | Camps-Assemblies
| | Purchases

Arkansas Baptist State Convention, 1971

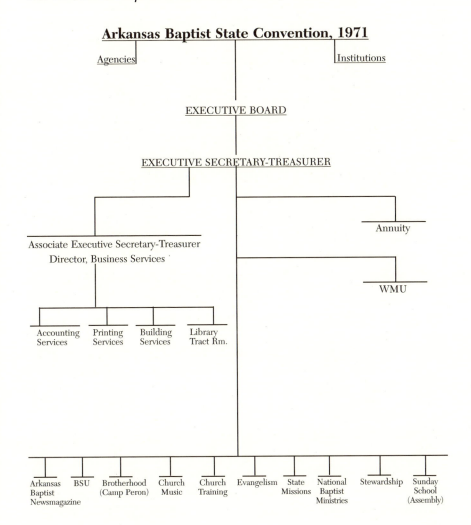

Arkansas Baptist State Convention, 1998

EXECUTIVE BOARD

MINISTRY PLANNING TEAM

Executive & Administrative Team
- Convention Management
- Office of Camps & Assemblies
- Office of Information & Communication
- Personnel Office
- Business Services
- International Partnerships
- Prayer Ministry
- Continuing Education
- Cooperative Program
- Promotions

Leadership and Worship Team
- Pastor & Staff
- Music and Worship
- Church Leadership
- Crisis Support
- Stewardship/Annuity & Capitol Fund Raising

Missions Support Team
- Women & Children
- Missions Education
- Promotion & Support

Collegiate Ministry Team
- BSU
- Resource Management
- Collegiate Church Involvement
- Student Missions

Missions Ministries Team
- World Mission Conferences/ Church Renewal
- Men & Boys Missions Education
- Missions Ministries
- Construction & Disaster Relief
- Cooperative Ministries

Family Ministry Team
- Single & St. Adult Ministries
- Marriage Enrichment
- Parenting
- Men's Ministries
- Women's Ministries

Evangelism & Church Growth Team
- Discipleship
- Bible Teaching
- Evangelism

Index

Page numbers in bold type indicate photo captions.

About the Authors

C. Fred Williams is professor of history at the University of Arkansas at Little Rock. He received his Ph.D. from the University of Oklahoma in 1970. A specialist in state and regional history, he has taught a course on Arkansas history for more than twenty-five years. He has published six books on the history of the state, including *Arkansas: An Illustrated History of the Land of Opportunity* (1986). He is a member of the deacon body of Calvary Baptist Church in Little Rock.

S. Ray Granade is professor of history and director of library services at Ouachita Baptist University. He received his Ph.D. from Florida State University in 1972. A specialist in social and intellectual history, Granade has written articles on aspects of education and a study of religion's portrayal in early American literature. He is a deacon and serves Arkadelphia Baptist Church as clerk and historian.

Kenneth M. Startup is academic dean and professor of history at Williams Baptist College. He received his Ph.D. from Louisiana State University in 1983. Startup is a specialist on the nineteenth-century American South and is the author of *The Root of All Evil: The Protestant Clergy and the Economic Mind of the Old South* (1977). He is a deacon at First Baptist Church Walnut Ridge, where he has taught an adult Bible class for the past fifteen years.